APICIUS

Biblioteca Apostolica Vaticana, Vrbinas Latinus 1146, fol. 2ᵛ; contents of Book I, recipes 19–28. (Reproduced with permission.)

APICIUS

A CRITICAL EDITION
WITH AN INTRODUCTION AND
AN ENGLISH TRANSLATION OF
THE LATIN RECIPE TEXT *APICIUS*

CHRISTOPHER GROCOCK and SALLY GRAINGER

with illustrations
by
Dan Shadrake

PROSPECT BOOKS
2006

First published in Great Britain in 2006 by Prospect Books, Allaleigh House, Blackawton, Totnes, Devon, TQ9 7DL.

ISBN 1-903018-13-7

Designed and typeset in Times Roman by Tom Jaine.
Printed and bound in Great Britain by The Cromwell Press, Trowbridge.

WINSTONI

FIDELISSIMO

COMITI ET IVDICI

PREFACE

Among the many enduring myths about ancient Rome is the view that much of the food consumed at high-status dinner-parties was overwhelmingly corrupt, rotten, over-seasoned and most definitely 'not to our taste'.[1] The simpler Hellenistic style of cooking, depicted in Archestratus and in some of the fragmentary plays cited in Athenaeus, has been thought of as the original Mediterranean cuisine.[2] By contrast, the recipes in *Apicius*[3] have been regarded as a corruption or adulteration of this 'ideal', standing for a 'silver' or even 'base metal' culinary tradition inferior to the 'golden age' which preceded it. Such a view might be supported by the grotesque tastes of emperors such as Vitellius or Heliogabalus, but we do not think it can be sustained from a careful reading of the *Apicius* recipes, and owes more to a Gibbon-esque idea that 'things got worse after the Republic'. It is true that, at first glance, the recipes in *Apicius* may appear all too complex and overpowering in their use of seasonings, and contrast with the

[1] Cf. Bober's comment that 'a perennial criticism from food writers is an alleged welter of ingredients of contrasting and self-defeating tastes' (P. P. Bober, *Art, Culture, and Cuisine. Ancient and Medieval Gastronomy* (Chicago, 1999), p. 156; and Wilkins and Hill, 'the predominant flavour we have found in ancient Greek food … is a rank, slightly rotting quality', J. Wilkins and S. Hill, *The Life of Luxury: Archestratus* (Totnes, 1994), p. 23; most recently Wilkins and Hill speak of 'the heavy spicing of Apicius' (*Food in the Ancient World*, Malden MA and Oxford, 2006, p. 29). The function of elaborate dining as a social ritual is explored by K. M. D. Dunbabin, *The Roman Banquet: Images of Conviviality* (Cambridge, 2003).

[2] Bober, op. cit., p. 146.

[3] Except in the *explicits* to each book, throughout this work we use 'Apicius' to refer to the individual of that name, and *Apicius* to refer to the eponymous recipe text. See pp. 35ff. below.

allegedly more palatable image portrayed in literature of the Greek cuisine which preceded the Roman. However, Greek and Roman food were largely indistinguishable in the imperial period, above a certain economic class, and *Apicius* shows that the essence of this international Mediterranean cuisine lay in the enhancing of natural flavours with complex compound sauces – a fashion which already existed in the Greek cuisine of Archestratus' day (the fourth century BC), for it is the origin of his protests.[1] Archestratus recommended serving foods simply, with the minimum of seasonings, and allowing the natural flavours of the food to shine through. This is an admirable style of cooking, but it does not satisfy an imaginative and experimental palate. As with literary tastes, surprise and complexity of expression came to dominate cuisine.

We fully accept that to turn the recipes in *Apicius* into successful dishes is a tricky business. Their very subtlety is easy to misinterpret, and the results of such misinterpretation would support a 'myth of corruption'; but with care, the flavours of the various ingredients can be balanced (*temperas* is a recurring instruction) and the results can be stunning. *Apicius* has often been defined as a high-status cookery book intended for the cooks of only a small élite in society but, in our opinion, it contains a more egalitarian selection of recipes reflecting the culinary expectations of a wider group in the Roman world who might be defined as financially secure, urban and cosmopolitan.[2]

This is *not* a book of recipes to use in a modern kitchen: if you are looking for adapted recipes, use those in *Cooking Apicius* or *The Classical Cookbook*.[3] Here, we have rather attempted to solve the major problems of the text that in the past made reconstructing the recipes so difficult, and also to illustrate the cooking techniques and procedures that are unique to this cuisine. We have assumed that the recipes were once perfectly understandable to the cooks who wrote and used them, and our aim has therefore been to translate the text into functional recipes, where at all possible, and to give suggestions where the Latin is obscure. We have tried to make the edition accessible to all who are interested in Roman food, whatever their background, by translating all references to ancient sources

[1] Archestratus, fragment 45 (Athenaeus 311a). See also below, p. 40.
[2] As Brandt recognized: E. Brandt, *Untersuchungen zum Römischen Kochbuche. Philologus*, Supplementband XIX, Heft III (Leipzig, 1927), p. 30; see also Wilkins & Hill, *Food in the Ancient World*, p. 208.
[3] Sally Grainger, *Cooking Apicius* (Totnes, 2006); A. Dalby and S. Grainger, *The Classical Cookbook* (London and Los Angeles, 1996).

(all translations are our own) and by keeping academic jargon in its place; all Greek terms have been transliterated. The translation of the text is expanded in parentheses where necessary, to make clear the sense of a text which is often very compacted, and which uses technical phraseology in an idiomatic way. Many of the technical terms are simply untranslatable: no single English word could possible convey the complexity of meaning found in terms unique to ancient cuisine. We have left these terms in italics, and recommend that the reader use the detailed glossary. We accept that some sections of our introduction (on the Latinity of *Apicius*, for example) may be of less interest to food historians than to others, but we have addressed these linguistic issues in order to inform and illuminate our arguments about the genre of culinary literature which the text represents.

Some have asked why it is necessary to have another edition and translation of *Apicius*. There are numerous works still available, which are discussed in the introduction. Previous editions have been edited and translated either by scholars whose understanding of the technology and processes of the kitchen was limited to varying degrees, or (in one instance) by a chef whose understanding of Latin was sometimes questionable. It would be rare indeed to find a single scholar who possessed the requisite skills in both areas. We trust that between us we have effectively brought our respective skills to bear on the problems posed by the *Apicius* text.

The text, translation and commentary contained in this volume are the result of studies and activities undertaken over the past 15 years in a broad range of fields, embracing philology, social history, and archaeology – the latter including practical experiments. Each of these has informed the other on a continuous basis in an iterative process which we believe has been well worth the effort involved. In particular, over a decade of experimental archaeology using replica equipment and trials of the cooking techniques using charcoal and wood has enabled us to understand the recipes to a much greater depth than we did at the start. We trust that our conclusions, which we do not claim to be the final word on *Apicius*, may prompt further research.

Finally, we have to confess that we are to some extent motivated by a concern for the long-dead individuals whose skills and talents have been too often overlooked or misunderstood. Previous editions and translations have concluded, following Brandt's work of 1927, that a late redactor was responsible for the Latin in the text and therefore to some extent for the recipes themselves. As this volume makes clear, we beg to differ. We conclude that *Apicius* originates not in any redactor or man of letters, but with cooks whose practical skills were perhaps better honed than their linguistic ones. Their care and thought for their trade, like the Faliscans who 'spent their life producing sumptuous dishes for pleasant living',[1] is infused in this legacy of the ancient world which they have left behind, though they themselves are unnamed in history and long forgotten. A key justification for the new edition is to raise their profile and return credit for the recipes to these ancient cooks.

We are deeply indebted for their generosity and assistance to Dr Andrew Dalby, Professor Alan Davison, Susan Weingarten, Larry G. Simpson, Miriam Mandelbaum and Arlene Shaner of the New York Academy of Medicine, and to Chris Lydamore of Harlow Museum. Particular gratitude is due to our publisher Tom Jaine for his limitless patience and unceasing encouragement, and to Dan Shadrake for the splendid illustrations. We would also like to express our thanks for their patience and professional support to the library staff of the Institute of Classical Studies, the Warburg Institute, the Biblioteca Apostolica Vaticana, the Bibliothèque Nationale in Paris, and the British Library. We beg any others whose assistance has gone unmentioned here to forgive us; we acknowledge our debt to numerous individuals with whom conversation and debate has borne fruit. Needless to say, we accept full responsibility for any errors or omissions which remain.

CHRISTOPHER GROCOCK
SALLY GRAINGER

[1] See Introduction, p. 67.

CONTENTS

ILLUSTRATIONS

INTRODUCTION

1. *APICIUS* AND ITS CONTEXT

What is Apicius?

The recipe text known as *Apicius* is the sole survivor of a process of collecting recipes which began long before it reached the form in which we know it, and which certainly continued for a long time afterwards. It is certainly not the work of one author, whether he be gourmet, cook or editor, but a rather haphazard collection assembled over many centuries. From the text as it survives, it is impossible to know who created the particular format, order and titles of *Apicius*, and when they did it. We can however be sure that the recipes were initially and primarily the work of cooks. The majority of the recipes are written in a style and with a vocabulary that belongs to cooks alone: *Apicius* is a 'special literature', and 'presupposes readers with a certain "technical" knowledge and appropriate skills'.[1] In order both to create and to understand the kind of recipes that survive in *Apicius*, hands-on culinary skills are a prerequisite. It is simply not possible to theorize a recipe without testing it, and this needs skill and experience.

---

[1] See N. Vasilieva, 'Semiological notes on the *De Arte Coquinaria* by Apicius', in *Latin Vulgaire, Latin Tardif: Actes du colloque internationale sur le latin vulgaire et tardif (Pécs, 2-5 Septembre 1985)* (Tübingen, 1987), 199-205, at p. 199.

The phenomenon of the amateur cook is a familiar one today: we all dabble in the kitchen and have a basic understanding of the science behind cooking, even if we have varying degrees of success with the outcome. But in the Roman world, the slave economy governed all areas of domestic labour. High-status cooking was very labour-intensive and simply not to be contemplated by the *gourmet* who was interested in food. Cicero defined all occupations that were involved with producing physical pleasure for others as disgraceful.[1] It is not impossible to imagine that a high-status gourmet might have broken through that barrier and learned how to cook for the sake of his interest, but it is not likely to have been thought socially acceptable and would have surely resulted in public condemnation. In *Satire* 2.4, Horace elevates culinary lore to a philosophical theory in order to ridicule gourmets, but this discussion of the *minutiae* of gastronomy nevertheless reflects precisely the kind of literary form we find and should expect from a gourmet genuinely interested in food.[2] The gourmet is interested in the theoretical, not practical, aspect of food before it reaches his table, and is more concerned with selecting produce, thinking up ways to enrich meat before slaughter, knowing where to get the best of everything, and eating the results.[3] The activity which takes place between selection and consumption, and which is carried out in the sooty, greasy kitchen, is simply not part of his world.

The majority of surviving (or reported) literature about food in the ancient world appears to be narrative-based: the various attributes of the foods are discussed in general and the recipes are interspersed. *Apicius* consists almost entirely of lists of recipes without a voice.[4] Such a narrative-free collection is much more suited to the use of cooks and cookery schools than to that of gourmets, and it is unlikely to have been 'published' in the way in which, say, histories were. Its literary merit is small, and such a collection is hardly likely to have satisfied trivia-hungry gourmets. It is perfectly possible, as we will argue,

[1] Cicero, *De officiis* 1.150.

[2] See the section 'Cooks and Ancient Cookery books', pp. 39ff., below. The passage is quoted in full in Appendix 4.

[3] This is precisely the kind of culinary knowledge that is firmly attributed to Marcus Gavius Apicius. See Pliny, *HN.* 8.209, 9.66, 10.133.

[4] There are two small indistinct voices in the recipes: at 1.13, ' you will be amazed at the flavour in your food' i.e. *laser*; and 4.2.12, ' no-one will know what they are eating'. Either of these remarks may have been directed to another cook or to a wider audience such as a gourmet selecting a menu.

that a collection of recipes without narrative could have been 'informally' copied and distributed for many years among cooks and cookery schools before possibly being appropriated by the literary establishment, either in part or in full, for use in general cookery books compiled and distributed by the literary élite. Recipes could have started their life in collections created and held by cooks and ended up as part of a named cookery book such as that written by Matius.[1]

An interesting question to ask at this point might be: whose recipes were they? Were recipes included in a literary work by a named author such as Matius regarded as his, or as belonging to others?[2] We would argue in any case that the recipes in *Apicius* are the cooks' recipes, and that the text as it has come down to us bears no evidence of shaping or tampering by a high-status compiler and/or collator.[3] To use an image from a later period, it is a text from 'below stairs'.

We know that other collections of recipes existed in the empire with the same title, as is demonstrated by the existence of the *Excerpta Vinidarii*, a small selection of recipes with a spice and ingredient list at the beginning. The identity of Vinidarius is obscure but, as his title indicates, he may have been a high-status functionary in the Roman regime of the late empire. While some of the recipes in the *Excerpta* are very similar to those in *Apicius*, others differ markedly in the terms they use and in the spices included. The Latin in the *Excerpta* is often of a considerably poorer quality than that of *Apicius*. The phonetic spelling and lack of case agreement suggest a 'Late Latin' text, in marked contrast to *Apicius* itself, which may have recipes in it of a much earlier period.[4]

Some of the recipes in *Apicius* probably date from at least the first century AD. At 1.16 and 7.1.1, we find reference to Cyrenaican *laser* which, according to Pliny the Elder, was extinct by *c.* AD 50.[5] At 1.10, the instruction to infuse pine nuts in *laser* may be an indication that the latter was in short supply. Parthian *laser* does not seem to have been particularly scarce in the later empire, though it was expensive. We find three recipes associated with Vitellius (*d.* AD 70), who

---

[1] See 'Cooks and ancient cookery books', p. 53, below.

[2] We find evidence that cooks could hold rights over their recipes as early as the fifth century BC. The Sybarites in the Gulf of Tarentum enacted a law allowing no one else but the cook-inventor to have sole use of his successful recipe for a year. See Athenaeus, 521d, A. Dalby, *Empire of Pleasure: Luxury and Indulgence in the Roman World* (London 2000), p. 68.

[3] Brandt identified a 'reviser' who put the collection together, but we disagree with this conclusion: see below, pp. 18ff.

[4] On Vinidarius, see p. 32.

[5] See Pliny, *HN.* 19.38-35, 22.100-6, and the Glossary, *silphium.*

was notorious for his appetite, and we can plausibly date them to his lifetime or soon after. Recipes attributed to Trajan (early second century AD) and Commodus (before *c.* AD 180) can be dated to that era.[1] We might also attribute the recipes given the title *Apiciana* to the various men known to have born that name, who all date to the first and second centuries AD.[2] It is perhaps unsurprising that the majority of the recipes have no evidence within them that could indicate a date of origin. However, given that a small but significant number seem to be early in date, there is no reason to suppose that many more recipes were not also of early date.

Some other recipes may hint at an early origin: *lucanicae* (2.4) were particular sausages that came from *Magna Graecia* and were introduced to Rome by the soldiers after the first conquests in the second century BC, though the name persists to this day. In addition, any recipe which survives may have had a long history; for example, the *patina* as a meal is attested in the mid-first century BC in Roman menus, and has its origins in a Greek term for a dish or vessel. A similar meal known as a *patella tyrotaricha* is also attested in the mid-first century BC.[3] *Apicius* also includes many recipes which are attributed to various apparently historical figures whose precise identity is obscure.[4] Dating these recipes with any precision is therefore impossible. We can only say that the names with which these recipes are associated may be linked with individuals identified in the historical record over a long period, spanning the second and third (and occasionally the fourth) centuries.

Because the collection seems to have been developed over a long period of time, the unclassical stylistic features and spellings preserved in the MSS cannot be used as evidence for dating the recipes as first devised, though they may indicate the period at which the recipe collection stopped growing. In any case, many of these unclassical Latin features are not definitely time-specific, and might be better considered the kind of vulgar Latin spoken and written by the lower classes throughout the Roman era.[5]

It might be more useful, therefore, to try to define the collection in terms of its origins. The recipes with a strong link to Apicius, the *Apiciana*, would seem

---

[1] See 8.7.16; 5.4.2.
[2] *Apiciana* recipes: 4.1.2, 4.2.14, 4.3.3, 5.4.2, 6.7, 7.4.2, 8.7.6.
[3] *Patina*: Macrobius 3.13.13; *Patella*: Cicero, *Ad fam.* 9.16.9.
[4] See Appendix 4 on these named recipes.
[5] See below, 'The language of *Apicius*', p. 95.

to be the most logical place to look. These recipes (there are only seven) may well have come from a single source. We know that a work 'On the luxury of Apicius', written in Greek in the first century AD by a man called Apion, existed, and it is possible that these recipes originated there.[1] An alternative view would be that all the *Apiciana* recipes are labelled thus because they are considered luxury or sophisticated and they have no direct link with the Apicius legend. The individual titles to the books in our text are in Greek; a great many of the recipes and their culinary concepts are also of Greek origin. It seems very likely that the order and chapter titles of *Apicius* were taken from an original Greek recipe book, given the prominence of that language, and that they were devised at an early stage in the evolution of the collection, though it is impossible to prove this.[2] However, the fact that Greek culinary tradition was predominant in the early empire makes it likely that many of the original recipes which formed the basis of the *Apicius* text were originally written in Greek. At that time there was no independent, truly Roman, culinary tradition in high-status Roman society: all available recipe books or general cookery books in the public domain in the late republic and early empire were Greek in origin, if not in language.[3] *Apicius* may be a Roman recipe book written (mainly) in Latin, but it was probably a Hellenistic collection of recipes at its inception, and continued to be one.

The Greek cuisine which arrived in Rome in the second century BC was not static; it was adapted to Roman tastes, disseminated and perfected (or not, according to your point of view) under the Roman empire. Thus, during the middle and late empire, the *Apicius* collection seems to have evolved, with the addition of many new recipes. Large sections in some books may have been added, particularly in Book 1, which contains some non-domestic recipes for preserving goods in bulk that we might not expect in the original recipe book. The version of *Apicius* from which the *Excerpta Vinidarii* was made also appears to have contained simple lists of supplies which a household should keep in stock. It is possible that recipe collections such as these were periodically

---

[1] See below, p. 37.

[2] See below, p. 47, on cooks and ancient cookery books.

[3] We are not suggesting that Greek and Roman food at every level was the same: there might be huge regional differences and specialities from one community to the next depending on local produce and tradition. However for the 'middle class' and above, and even at a domestic level, *patinae* and *minutalia* were cooked and served all over the empire; piglets were boned, stuffed and boiled, and fish served with rich fruity sauces.

rearranged when they were re-copied. In fact, recipe books throughout the ages rarely remain the same size. Early versions of the first French cookery book, from the fourteenth century, which is later known as the *Viandier of Taillevant*, are considerably smaller than the final versions.[1] A similar situation also occurs with the first Italian recipe book of the Renaissance: *The Art of Cooking composed by the eminent Maestro Martino of Como*. One of the three manuscripts has been greatly enlarged by a scribe or gourmet.[2]

As each new version of the collection was copied, new recipes could be added, written or dictated by cooks who were Greek or Roman, slave or freedman, imbued with the same 'classical' Greek cooking principles as their forebears. They continued to use the same Greek concepts and vocabulary, even though they did not necessarily recognize them as un-Roman; by this stage everything in the recipes could be termed 'Roman'.[3] One might equate this situation to that of the culinary climate of Europe 40 years ago: above a certain status, good food was based on the precepts of 'classical' French techniques. A chef in Britain created recipes that were basically French in style. Ancient Greece might usefully be compared to France in this scenario, while the rest of Europe including Rome maintains the same position in both eras. During this process the Latin used by the cooks may not have changed very much: they were skilled people and clearly not illiterate, but working men who wrote in a form of Latin that was spoken on the streets and among slaves and labourers, and was always considered inferior to literary Latin by their betters.

Brandt's extensive study published in 1927 concluded that the recipe collection was gathered into its current format at some time during the fourth century AD by a 'reviser' who took recipes from a number of different literary sources including some early Imperial culinary, dietetic and agricultural works.[4] Brandt's study is limited by his treatment of the recipes purely as text, and he gave no

---

[1] D.E. Scully, T. Scully, *Early French Cookery: Sources, History, Original Recipes and Modern Adaptations* (University of Michigan 1995), p. 9.

[2] Luigi Ballerini, *The Art of Cookery, the First Modern Cookery Book* (Berkeley CA, 2005).

[3] J. Herman, *Vulgar Latin* (trans. R. Wright, University Park PA, 2000) reflects that 'it is interesting to realize that the names of simple utensils and common dishes, were Latin, whereas more complicated utensils and less common but more luxurious dishes have Greek names; thus *puls* (porridge) and *farcimen* (sausage meat) are native Latin words, while *isicium* (a kind of rissole), *embamma* (a kind of strong sauce or acidic condiment), and others are taken from Greek' (p. 106).

[4] Brandt, *Untersuchungen*, pp. 30, 36, 130-3.

consideration to the practicalities of the food they reflect. Recipes are not like poems, fixed in their structure, but are far more likely to be fluid and constantly evolving. He took it for granted that all the recipes had a specific known literary source rather than being gathered in a random *ad hoc* fashion. Such a mechanical approach was bound to lead to false conclusions. Brandt wished to identify the original sources for the various recipes in the collection, and so he analyzed their form and content according to vocabulary, Greek terminology, and specifically by their use (or not) of precise quantities. The digestive remedies that occur in *Apicius* all contain precise quantites: this led Brandt to compare 1.13 with a recipe for a similar digestive remedy found in Marcellus Medicus 30.51. Though they are vaguely similar, it is not necessary to claim, as he did, that Marcellus was therefore the source of this recipe.[1] Brandt also attributed the other remedies in *Apicius* at 3.18.2 and 3 to Marcellus, using the principle that if one was derived from that work, they all must have been. He then concluded that recipes which use precise quantities must also be from a medical work, even though they give no other indication to support such an origin. Those recipes which use Greek terms were also attributed to a Greek dietetic cookbook.[2]

As we have already suggested, we think that the use of Greek terms denotes the primary and original source for the recipes, rather than late additions to an already-exisiting collection. The use of quantities in itself does not necessarily indicate medical recipes, and their inclusion seems to be more about the choice and habit of the cook, rather than an indication of a specific source.[3]

Brandt also suggested that recipes from Book 1 (and some in Book 3) came from agricultural manuals, which is a perfectly sound theory; the recipes in Book 1 clearly reflect a different strand of culinary writing. The Latin is more complex and polished, and the recipes themselves, he suggested, are more concerned with the cellarman than the cook, and seem out of place in a recipe book.[4] It is possible that a specific agricultural treatise was the source for those recipes

---

[1] Brandt, *Untersuchungen*, pp. 41-2.

[2] Brandt, *Untersuchungen*, pp. 38, 132-3.

[3] The recipes which Brandt links together here, 4.2.4/5/8/9/31/33/36, are *patinae* (see the Glossary). They all use precise quantities, while other recipes of a similar nature do not. They also use the Greek term *thermospodium* for 'hot ashes' in the cooking technique (see the Glossary). Such Greek words indicate a particular 'higher-status' culinary language: see above, p. 18 n. 3; Brandt, *Untersuchungen*, p. 38. See also 'Roman weights and measures', p. 83, below.

[4] Brandt, *Untersuchungen*, p. 37.

concerned with the preservation of a vegetable and fruit harvest, but the activities they describe are also the kind of techniques that individual cooks would need to know in order to preserve produce purchased in season from the market. These types of recipes are therefore not necessarily 'out of place' in a general cookery book and they also represent the kind of recipes which any rural or town household would hold. It is not possible to say that other books were used to provide these recipes, let alone suggest a single source.

Brandt compared numerous recipes in *Apicius* with others from works by Palladius, Apuleius, the *Geoponica*, Cato and Columella. When he found similarities of wording or structure he took them to be the original sources for the ones in *Apicius*, even though there is never any precise duplication. Thus a recipe for rose wine without roses at 1.4, when compared with Palladius 11.15, has a marked similarity of wording, which Brandt found to be proof that Palladius is its original source; we think it far more likely that Palladius, writing *c.* 350 AD, obtained the recipe from a collection already in existence, rather than that a 'reviser' used Palladius to fill out the *Apicius* collection. It is quite likely that a limited range of recipes circulated very widely,[1] and there is no reason why similar versions of the same recipes should not have been found in different books without the writers knowing or caring.

Brandt suggested that the wine recipes in Book 1 were also 'out of place' in a recipe book, and that their presence denoted a 'thoughtless reviser' choosing inappropriate recipes.[2] He identified anomalies, repetitions and inconsistencies in the order and selection of the recipes, which he suggested indicated the same reviser. We attribute these anomalies not to an inadequate guiding hand but to the complete absence of one. Brandt assumed that the 'misplaced recipes' had been consciously taken out of their correct place in the original source by the reviser. Thus, according to his theory, the recipe at 4.2.2, which is a sweet *patina* and is therefore placed in the *patinae* section of Book 4, must originally have been part of the section entitled *Dulcia et domestica et melcae* in Book 7 and was moved because of its title. However, this recipe is also repeated as 4.2.16; though the title of the recipe is different, the wording is similar, and concludes with an added instruction to turn the *patina* out on a dish. We think that this

---

[1] One can only speculate how many copies of a work of the genre of *Apicius* might have been existence at any one time, if every high-status household had a copy!

[2] Brandt, *Untersuchungen*, p. 47.

points to the separate existence of recipes, rather than that a controlling hand put it in two places unthinkingly.

Likewise, Brandt thought that 4.2.19, a recipe for a *patella* of horse-parsley, was originally placed before 4.2.7, because 4.2.19 ends 'You can make this dish with any herb you like', and 4.2.7 is entitled 'This is how you make a *patina* from wild herbs, black briony, mustard greens, or cucumber or spring greens'. However, the *patella* recipe at 4.2.19 involves cooking the greens and adding a sauce thickened with starch instead of using the eggs which are the standard setting agent for these *patinae/patellae*. Recipe 4.2.7 is for an egg *patina*, and its instruction *item facies* in fact refers to the previous *patina* recipe 4.2.6, which is made with asparagus that is not cooked, and is also set with eggs. The recipe has no rubric initial in either of the two early manuscripts, and is therefore associated with 4.2.6 in the manuscript tradition. Brandt assumed that the vegetables in the title of 4.2.7 would need cooking, and that the recipe could not therefore refer to 4.2.6, which does not cook the primary vegetable. Clearly, vegetables such as asparagus stalks can be pounded with water, without heat, to extract their flavour, while leaving all the material behind: the resulting 'custard' is smooth, but still flavoured with the vegetable.[1] There is no reason why such a treatment should not be undertaken with the vegetables in 4.2.7. The lack of eggs in 4.2.19 also indicates that it is not closely associated with either 4.2.6 or 4.2.7. We therefore conclude that these recipes are not 'out of place', but rather follow in a logical sequence, and have not been moved from an original position.[2]

Brandt identified a number of other 'out of place' recipes, seeing similarities between recipes as evidence for a conscious repetition by his reviser.[3] At 1.31, '*oenogarum* for truffles: pepper, lovage, coriander, rue, *liquamen*, honey, wine, and a little oil', is compared with 7.14.3, 'another truffle recipe: *oenogarum*: pepper, lovage, coriander, rue, *liquamen*, honey, wine, a little oil; warm it up'. While there is no doubt that these are in essence the same recipe, it does not necessarily follow that a reviser has placed one recipe in two separate books and created the titles to fit each book, and in the later case added an extra component, which is Brandt's conclusion.[4] We think that a natural repetition consistent with an evolving recipe collection is the simplest and most logical reason for this

---

[1] See *frigida aqua* in 'The Language of *Apicius*', p. 89 below.

[2] Brandt, *Untersuchungen*, p. 36.

[3] Brandt, *Untersuchungen*, pp. 36-7, 44-5.

[4] Brandt, *Untersuchungen*, p. 44.

similarity. There are marked similarities between 9.7 and 9.1.3, and in fact between these two recipes and 1.15.1. The word order is different in each case, and the titles are all different: 9.7 'Sauce for all kinds of shellfish'; 9.1.3 'Boiled spiny lobster with cumin sauce'; 1.15.1 'Cumin sauce for oysters and shellfish'. It is likely in our view that such duplication is the work of cooks rather than a collator or reviser; in this instance, the common factor is the particular taste for cumin sauce that the Romans seem to have had.

Duplication of recipes might perhaps indicate some kind of 'controlling hand' in the compilation of the text, but the existence of repeated recipes might equally be due to the widespread circulation of recipes in kitchens, all making use of a fairly limited range of ingredients. The insertion of similar recipes at different points in a collection would generate considerable natural duplication which a collator or scribe might not even notice when it was re-copied.[1] An apparent duplication occurs in Books 4 and 5: at 4.4 we find the title *Tisanam vel sucum*, with two recipes that are virtually duplicated in section 5.5 under the title *Tisanam et alicam*. The differences in the titles and small differences in the recipes themselves indicate a different source rather than a controlling mind putting the same recipe in two separate places.

A duplication between section 5.1.1 and 5.1.4 is of interest here, as we think it indicates that a disinterested scribe may be responsible for the final format. The recipes are the same in all but the titles: 5.1.1, 'Julian pottage is cooked like this'; 5.1.4, 'Pottage'. These are so close together in the book that it seems unlikely, as Brandt suggests, that a reviser consciously put the Julian recipe at the beginning and then forgot to delete it where it originally occured.[2] The titles themselves counter this. However, a disinterested scribe who was simply making a copy of all the recipes in the disparate collection that he had from scrolls or codexes (or even loose sheets of papyrus) so as to produce a single work would simply write out what was found, and would pass no judgment on the content. We find evidence of this disinterested approach in the diversity of Latin spelling, construction and grammar which the manuscripts contain. We might expect an interested reviser, or even an educated scribe, to feel compelled to correct some of the more heinous grammatical errors, and to have regularized the spelling, but the different forms and practices have all been copied quite faithfully for the most part.

[1] Brandt, *Untersuchungen*, p. 45.
[2] Brandt, *Untersuchungen*, p. 130.

For whom was Apicius *intended?*

The *Apicius* recipe book is often considered a 'high-status', luxury collection of recipes that only the very rich would have been able to afford. This is not surprising, given its namesake; however, the collection contains rather more then just 'rich recipes for the élite' and, as a whole, it might better be described as an 'urban and cosmopolitan' collection.[1] The original kernel of recipes may have been considered high-status, but as the collection developed it became a much more diverse. More than half of the recipes are well within the means of a large section of an urban population, if we take the prices recorded in Diocletian's edict as an indication of the *relative* costs of foods against the cost of labour.[2] It is true that the recipes which include large amounts of expensive meat, or whole beasts, and the more expensive spices and wines, would be way beyond the means of the majority if followed exactly. However, the basic principles of many of the dishes recorded in the text, such as those for *patina, minutal* and *isicia*, and many of the vegetable and pulse recipes, are made up of ingredients quite affordable to a successful craftsman, for instance.[3] Even the use of pepper, always deemed the height of luxury, was within the pocket of many, if its relative cost is measured against the earnings of a middle-income 'professional' such as a teacher.[4] Cumin, the most common of spices, used in a great many of the

---

[1] Brandt (*Untersuchungen*, p. 132) recognized this discrepancy between a supposed high-status recipe book and the numerous ordinary recipes we find in the book.

[2] Diocletian's Price Edict is difficult to use as evidence of the *actual* price of foods in AD 301 in Italy as the inscription is only found in the Eastern Empire. It may not have been enforced in Italy, though it was probably conceived as an empire-wide price control. It is also apparent that the inflation that necessitated the edict was so high in AD 301 that the prices recorded cannot be taken as current for very long; the price of foods may have been lower shortly before and a good deal higher shortly afterwards, as we know that inflation continued unabated. However, it is valuable as an indication or 'snapshot' of supposed contemporaneous like-for-like values. See S. Lauffer, *Diokletians Preisedikt* (Berlin, 1971); M. H. Crawford, 'Discovery, autopsy and progress: Diocletian's jigsaw puzzles', in T. P. Wiseman (ed.), *Classics in Progress: Essays on Ancient Greece and Rome* (Oxford, 2002), pp. 145-64.

[3] An architect received 100 *denarii* per month to teach one student, a teacher of grammar 200: Diocletian's Price Edict 7.74, 70 (Lauffer, p. 124.)

[4] A *pedagogus* received 50 *denarii* per month per child: Diocletian's Price Edict 7.65 (Lauffer, p. 124.) According to Pliny, *HN.*12.29, an Italian pound of black pepper cost 4 *denarii* and was duty-free in *c.* AD 70, while white pepper was 7 *denarii* and long pepper 15, both carrying duty. Even allowing for excessive inflation bringing the two figures much closer together, the income of the former would not preclude access to the latter, even if only on special occasions.

recipes, was also relatively cheap at 12 ½ *denarii* per pint in AD 301 (1 pt. = 10 oz., making an ounce of cumin 20 *asses*). It is also clear that ordinary working people in Rome could afford more meat than is often claimed: the edict gives the price of beef mince as 8 *asses* per oz.[1]

The term 'high-status' is in common use, but it needs some defining, as it can be a rather vague indication of wealth. At the top end of society stand the imperial family and the members of the court and their friends, senators and so on. Such fabulously wealthy people are said to have spent thousands of *sestertii* on such things as mullet because it had been caught in a special place or had just spawned. Contrast this with the price of freshwater fish with no special claims to fame at 8 *denarii* per Italian lb. in AD 301. A bath-house cloakroom attendant would have to look after just four people to buy this.[2] We believe that the members of this élite society did not eat different kinds of food from that found in *Apicius*, rather that they took pains to select their produce with the greatest care: everything they ate was individually selected, rather than simply taken from what was available in the market. At the next level we might find the equestrians, trading on a large scale and possessing substantial estates. On occasion they would dine with the group above them and also rank as 'high-status'.

We have to use terms like 'the middle classes' very carefully when talking of the ancient world, as the term carries with it such powerful connotations from more recent history.[3] Studies in the demographics of the ancient world focus on longevity and reproduction and mortality rates, and (perhaps wisely) make little attempt to quantify the different strata of Roman society apart from their legal status (citizen/freedman/slave).[4] However, a fair number of people appear

---

[1] Cattle were a source of motive power and of leather; the meat of older beasts may have been almost a by-product. Cf. Diocletian's Price Edict 4.14 (Lauffer, p. 104).

[2] Cf. Horace, *Satires* 2.8.44; Diocletian's Price Edict 5.4, 7.75.

[3] But cf. for example Garnsey's comment that 'a sizeable "middle class" existed in Rome whose members ate well in terms both of quantity and quality': P. Garnsey, *Cities, Peasants and Food in Classical Antiquity: Essays in Social and Economic History* (ed. with addenda by W. Scheidel: Cambridge, 1998), p. 245.

[4] Cf. for example P. Salmon, *Population et dépopulation dans l'Empire romain* (Brussels, 1974); T.G. Parkin, *Demography and Roman Society* (Baltimore MD, 1992); W. Scheidel (ed.), *Debating Roman Demography* (Leiden, 2001); W. Suder, *A Study of the Age and Sex Structure of Population in the Western Provinces of the Roman Empire* (Wroclaw, 1990); R. P. Duncan-Jones, 'City Population in Roman Africa', *Journal of Roman Studies* 53 (1963), pp. 85ff.

to have had an income which was both stable and sufficiently high to allow them to aspire to many of the recipes in *Apicius*. These people consisted of large- and small-scale traders and importers, builders, artists and so on, as well as farmers with small estates. Such people might still have a cook or slave to do the cooking who might have access to one of the many recipe collections that existed – particularly for special occasions. On occasion, even members of the lower strata of society might have access to some of the dishes described in the recipe collections, especially if they were members of a *collegium* or guild.

In addition, it is possible that some of the recipes recorded in *Apicius* reflect popular dishes which were served on the street from *popinae* and bakeries. The street bars known as *popinae* were frequently under strict regulation by the emperors: Nero, it seems, forced them to sell only vegetables and pulses, whereas, before, no kind of foodstuff was prohibited.[1] Under Claudius, we know that *popina* owners were charged with infringing these regulations, and we may therefore assume that they were serving something more elaborate, such as meat, sausages, *isicia* (meat balls) and *patinae*, as well as *lagana* (flat bread) with *moretaria* (relish), which would be suitable foods for sale in more respectable bars.[2]

The Apicius *text – an overview.*

In the description of *Apicius* which follows, we have highlighted those aspects which may indicate original sources and language. We also highlight those foods that might be seen as more commonplace and less high-status. Some anomalies and peculiarities of the text are also noted.

Apicius is divided into 10 books. In manuscript *E*, now located in the library of the New York Academy of Medicine, the titles of Books 6–10 are listed first in Greek, then in Latin. However the manuscript lacks its first page, which would have contained the Greek titles of Books 1–5 along with their Latin alternatives and also any main title the book would have had. The Vatican MS begins with the title *API CAE,* the sense of which is obscure.[3] It then starts straight in with

---

[1] Suetonius, *Nero* 16.2.

[2] Suetonius, *Claudius* 38.1. See also *Tiberius* 34.1, where even baked goods were prohibited from sale in *popinae.*

[3] See cover illustration and note ad loc. for further discussion.

Book 1, omitting the book titles found in *E*. In our text, we have restored the 'lost' titles using the Greek ones found at the start of each book in the body of the text, and have composed Latin equivalents for books 1–5, as follows:[1]

Book 1	*Epimeles*	*Condita*	Mise en place
Book 2	*Sarcoptes*	*Carnes*	Meat dishes
Book 3	*Ceperos*	*Olera*	Vegetables
Book 4	*Pandecter*	*Miscellanea*	Compound dishes
Book 5	*Ospreon*	*Fabae*	Pulses
Book 6	*Tropetes*	*Volatilia*	Fowl
Book 7	*Polyteles*	*Voluntaria*	Desirable dishes
Book 8	*Tetrapus*	*Quadrupedia*	Quadrupeds
Book 9	*Thalassa*	*Mare*	Seafood
Book10	*Halieus*	*Piscatura*	Fish

The majority of recipes in Book 1 are concerned with the preservation and storage of produce that might naturally come from an estate. There are 35 recipes for various kinds of wine, the preservation of fruit and vegetables, meat and fish. Brandt claimed that these recipes came from a work by Apuleius, and had parallels in an agricultural work by Palladius.[2] We acknowledge a similarity, but cannot attribute them to any author. The occasional recipe has reference to issues such as selling, which suggests the context of an estate or market garden but, as we have said above, a cook would still need to know how to preserve vegetables and fruit when they were plentiful.[3]

Towards the end of Book 1 there are a number of recipes for relishes and digestives such as *oxyporium* from the Greek *oxyporon* (32) and *mortaria* (35, a paste from a mortar), as well as a few sauces (29, 30). *Mortaria* may be linked with confidence to the kind of relish that was consumed by the most humble of farmers.[4] These particular recipes have parallels both in style and content to recipes in Columella.[5] It seems reasonable to suggest that the earliest collection

---

[1] At the beginning of Book 3, the Greek title *ceperos* is rendered as *de oleribus*. This may be a gloss, or an indication that the other books once had Latin titles in the body of the text too.

[2] Brandt, *Untersuchungen,* pp. 43-54.

[3] See above, p. 18, and 1.15.

[4] cf. *Moretum,* in the *Appendix Vergiliana.*

[5] Columella 12.49ff.

of luxury recipes under an Apician title would not at first have contained these basic 'estate' recipes, and that they were not added to the collection until the evolving book had lost its direct link with Apicius.

In this book and throughout the text there are a number of Greek terms that appear to be part of the normal Latin vocabulary of the kitchen, e.g. *oenogarum, oxygarum*: these are fixed culinary terms and form part of the technical vocabulary of the cook. Other terms in Book 1, such as *melizomum* (honey sauce, though used here as honey wine) are distinctly Greek with perfectly acceptable Latin alternatives, yet they remain untranslated.[1] The term *hypotrimma* (33) is derived from the verb 'to rub' or 'to grind' in Greek, and has a similar meaning to the Latin term *mor(e)taria,* a similar cheese and herb mixture.[2] A recipe for Roman absinthe (3) suggests that the original language was not Latin, or that the recipe was composed outside Rome.

Book 2 contains 24 recipes for *isicia* or forcemeat, sauces for forcemeat, and sausages. The origins of *isicia* are undoubtedly Greek.[3] We are told that the Emperor Heliogabalus was the first to have *isicia* made from fish, from oysters and also from *locusta, cammaris* and *scillis* (spiny lobster, crayfish and prawns).[4] It is noteworthy that recipes 2.1.1 and 2.1.3 are *isicia* made specifically from these ingredients, but we cannot assume that they therefore date specifically from AD 218–222. At 2.2.7 we have a suggestion that *isicia* were served *a balineo*; if this is rendered 'at the baths' it might imply that such foods were eaten by a wide range of people, though it might equally mean 'after bathing' in a private bath complex.[5] 2.2.8 refers to a *defrutum* made from dried figs 'which the Romans call colouring', indicating that the original was in Greek, though written down in the Roman era. Recipe 2.2.10 for *apothermum* (a dish that has gone cold?) seems to be a cold sweet pudding and probably should have been among the *dulcia* rather than with these sauces. Here, *apothermum* is perhaps conflated with *a balneis*, which perhaps might explain why the recipe has been placed here. The recipes in Book 2 do not have anything sufficiently distinctive about them

---

[1] *Melizomum* at 1.2 is in fact used for a spiced honey wine rather than as a *zomos* (sauce) for meat etc. See Aristophanes, *Knights* 279, *Clouds* 389, *Peace* 716. It may have its origins in *melizōron,* 'with honey'.

[2] Hippocrates, *Vict.* 2.56, 3.80, Galen 6.650 (ed. Kühn); cf. Aristophanes, *Assemblywomen* 292.

[3] See the Glossary, and Athenaeus 376d.

[61] *Scriptores Historiae Augustae, Hel.*18.4.19.

[5] See note ad loc.

to indicate a common origin, but their typical formulaic characteristics indicate that they were written by cooks. Brandt considered this whole book to be very disorganized, and thought many recipes were missing. He suggested that a larger selection of *isicia* recipes formed the basis for it, from which his 'reviser' made an ill-judged selection.[1]

Book 3 has 57 recipes for vegetables of all kinds. Many of the dishes are simple and straightforward, with few spices, and one would not be surprised to find Romans of modest means being able to prepare them. According to the Pliny the Elder, some wealthy Roman gourmets tended to reject some kinds of vegetables as they were seen as ordinary and the food of the common man.[2] The fact that they are found here in such quantity and variety suggests that although some high-status groups in society may have given second place to vegetables, other diners in the same social group or immediately below did not, and that at the time when these recipes were included in the collection, ordinary vegetables such as leek, cabbage, root vegetables and greens were an important feature of any meal.

In Section 3.2, recipes for *pulmentarium ad ventrem* (relish for the stomach) have a specific medicinal aim, and may not have been part of the vegetable section of an earlier high-status recipe book.[3] They need not have come from a specific medicinal or dietetic cookery book, as such recipes are regularly found in agricultural works, and each estate and household might possess its own selection of remedies.[4] Section 3.20 is titled *sfondili,* which can mean both 'vertebrae' and 'the fleshy part of shellfish'. It can also mean 'artichoke', and the compiler who is responsible for positioning this section clearly thought it meant 'artichoke' here, though it is fairly clear to any one with food experience that the recipes are for some kind of shellfish, in this case mussels. This misplaced section suggests that the person responsible for the final form of the book was without culinary experience and, as we suggested earlier, may have had no occupational interest in the content of the book.

---

[1] Brandt, *Untersuchungen,* p. 56.

[2] Apicius is said to have rejected *cymas* (young cabbage), even though it was the best kind of cabbage available: Pliny, *HN.*19.137.

[3] See also 3.18.2 for an *oxypor(i)um* for the digestion.

[4] See Dalby, *Food in the Ancient World*, pp. 116-7, 'Digestives', and also Dioscorides, *MM.* 3,51,3; Cato, *De agricultura* 151, 76, 77; Columella 12.59.4-5. Also see pp. 58-61 below.

The recipes in Book 4 are the most complex so far and are best described as 'compound' or 'composite' dishes. There are 55 recipes in five sections. The first is for salads; then comes a large quantity of *patina* recipes made with various kinds of meat, fish and vegetables bound with egg. Section 3 deals with *minutalia* (dishes cooked with a thick sauce), Section 4 covers *tisana* 'a soup or infusion' and 5 has a few hors d'oeuvre. Many of these *patinae* could be made cheaply and simply, and may represent an everyday lunch or snack meal potentially eaten by anyone – dishes which may have been available as street-food in cities. If the exotic spices and meats are replaced with ordinary items such as small fish, salt-fish or pork meat, then they cease to be high-status. A Greek dish called *tyrotarichus* (a salt-fish and cheese *patella*)[1] was a common Roman meal in Cicero's time.[2] Cicero makes it clear that this dish was an ordinary, unpretentious meal, in contrast to the luxury dinners he had begun to consume. There are other Greek terms in book 4, such as *patina zomoteganon* (lit. a fish *patina* with broth in a frying-pan), and the use of *thermospodium* meaning hot embers; their use reinforces the international nature of ancient culinary language.

An interesting anomaly in recipe 4.2.5 concerning the definition of *oenogarum* also reveals that some form of post-composition changes to this recipe have been introduced, either by an inexperienced scribe, or by a reader who could not understand the recipe as it stood: see under *oenogarum* in the Glossary. The recipes in Book 4 display many of the characteristics of the formulaic cooks' style; the ingredients and method of particular *patina* recipes are written identically, using precise word formulations. Other groups of *patinae* use different yet equally precise formulations. It might be possible, after detailed analysis (beyond the scope of the present book) to identify specific styles of recipe and to see behind them particular cooks or cookery schools (see below, section 2).

Book 5 has 31 recipes for many different kinds of beans and also for *puls* (pottage). *Puls* would normally be considered a low-status food for country folk, but the recipes in Section 1 are particularly luxurious, and far beyond the means of the average peasant: fine *alica* and pounded brains are made into a very rich soup. It seems as though the élite had appropriated the idea of *puls*, but could not bring themselves to eat it unadulterated.[3] One of the hybrid Greek/Latin terms

---

[1] 4.2.17. *Patella* and *patina* are synonyms.

[2] Cicero, *Ad fam.* 9.16.9.

[3] See Cato, *De agricultura* 85 for a similar luxurious porridge, *puls Punica*, which is made with *alica,* cheese, honey and eggs.

that we find in *Apicius, tractogalatae,* is found at 5.1.3. It is derived from *tracta* meaning 'dry pastry sheet' (see Glossary) and *gala,* the Greek for milk. The term *tracta* is an original Latin word, though similar kinds of pastry do seem to be part of Greek baking techniques. We find *tracta* in Cato's agricultural manual, in cakes that seem to be well established in Rome in the mid-second century BC, as they are used as sacrificial offerings.[1] 5.5.1, *alicam uel sucum tisanae,* is a virtual duplication of 4.4.1, *tisanam,* which suggests that only barley is used, whereas 5.5.1 may give a choice of barley or *alica* (wheat groats), though in Late Latin *uel* may be used in place of *et,* perhaps implying a mixture. There is an anomaly in these recipes: see the Glossary under *coloefium.*

Book 6 is titled *Tropetes,* and has 41 recipes for fowl and exotic birds. The titles at the beginning of the book indicate eight sections, but the text which follows contains only three titles and four sections, about ostrich, crane or duck, partridge, turtle-dove, dove, pigeon and various birds, goose (lacking its title) and then finally chicken. It seems possible that at some stage, an entire gathering of text has been left out. These pages would have had sections on thrush, figpecker, peacock and pheasant. These missing sections would be longer than one of the earlier books in the collection, though given the popularity of peacock, for example, it is not implausible, as the complete books which survive are very different in length. Previous editions have tried to readjust the section in order to fill the titles, causing some confusion; we have simply numbered all the recipes in Section 2 in order. There is no doubt that this book, and in fact the remaining books, are devoted to more expensive foods, beyond the means of most Romans on a day-to-day basis. This is the first book in *Apicius* that has high numbers of 'list' recipes for sauces, including little or no method. We believe they may represent the rapid transmission of recipes from cook to cook rather than from a cook to a wider audience.[2]

We find a repeat of the hybrid term *tractogalatus* at 6.8.13; here a sauce made with milk and *tracta* is used to bind chicken pieces. We also find *pullus oxyzomum* (chicken in a sour sauce) at 6.8.4.

Book 7 has 75 recipes for what are called 'luxury dishes'; these are perhaps the most extravagant found within the more general cookbook. It is particularly noteworthy that offal in all its forms is considered the most desirable of foods:

---

[1] Cato, *De agricultura* 75, and Chrysippus in Athenaeus 113d, where *tracta* is called *kapyria.*
[2] See below, pp. 70-71, 'Roman cooks and their recipes'.

we find recipes for womb, udder and testicles, tripe and lung, as well as liver, kidneys, trotters, ribs and crackling. A section called *ofellae* refers to particularly strongly flavoured meat from the belly of either pig or ox, marinaded and roasted whole, then broken up so that diners could eat individual pieces of meat with their fingers. A section on boiled meats and *copadia* (morsels) with sauces has a similar function. There is a very small section on *dulcia* (sweets), but no recipes for cakes, which is unfortunate but perhaps not surprising, given that cooks and bakers appear to have to performed separate functions in a Roman context.[1] We know of many different kinds of cakes from Athenaeus' account of food writing and we know of key texts on baking, particularly the works by Chrysippus and Gaius Matius. Either our compiler did not have access to these because they were no longer available, or he did not consider it necessary to find or take excerpts from them. It seems likely that books on pâtisserie were a completely separate genre. At the end of Book 7 we find a section on bulbs, in this case flower bulbs and particularly the grape hyacinth, and also mushrooms, truffles, taro, snails and eggs.

Book 8 has 64 recipes in nine sections, comprising wild boar, venison, wild goat, wild sheep, beef and veal, kid and lamb, piglet, hare and dormice. Many of the recipes are in a list-style that is common for sauces. There are a number of named recipes in this book which we can sometimes link to individual people or places: we find Tarpeian lamb or goat at 8.6.9, presumably named after the rock; piglet recipes are named after Vitellius, Flaccus, Fronto or Frontinus, Celsinus, and Trajan, and hare after Passienus. A full list of the 'named' recipes throughout the book with their possible (and admittedly very tentative) derivations is found in Appendix 4.

Book 9 is entitled 'The Sea', and Book 10 'The Fisherman'. The recipes they contain are predominantly 'list' recipes for fish and seafood sauces which are very simple and straightforward. The distinction between the two books is unclear; general sauces for fish are found in both. Book 9 has sections on shellfish and crustacea, followed by a general section on bonito, tuna and salted mullet. A strange recipe at 9.10.12, 'Another recipe for salt fish: for salt fish' is in fact a digestive remedy with no connection to its title or to fish. The two previous

---

[1] See below, pp. 53, 65 and n. 2, 68, 75. The dichotomy is well illustrated by a poem by one Vespa, the *Iudicium coci et pistoris iudice Vulcano* (Anthologia Latina, 199), French trans. and commentary by J-F. Lespect, in *Folia Electronica Classica* (Louvain-la-Neuve) 9, January-June 2005.

recipes are for a kind of pâté of nuts which is meant to be a substitute for salt fish. How such a disconnected recipe could end up placed here is difficult to understand: the title appears to have been added to make it fit in this section.

Book 10 has only three distinct sections, first, sauces for various fish, second, sauces for moray eel and last, sauces for common eel. The section on moray eel only contains 6 recipes for eel before it continues with recipes for various fish (which would be better grouped in the first section), and the common eel section contains only two recipes.

The Vinidarius collection.

The text entitled *Apici excerpta a Vinidario uiro inlustri* consists of 30 recipes excerpted from a separate collection which also apparently bore the *Apicius* title. We agree with Flower and Rosenbaum that 'Vinidarius' was an actual individual, not a *persona*;[1] his name is qualified with the rank of *uir illustris*, which means that he held one of a number of very senior positions in the imperial régime, such as prefect of the praetorian guard or *magister officiorum*;[2] he was a distinguished man indeed, and presumably one with more than a passing interest in food. His name indicates an Ostrogothic origin: the *Prosopography of the Later Roman Empire* vol. I refers to an Ostrogothic chieftain called 'Vinitharius' who succeeded his great-uncle Ermenaric and rebelled against Hunnic overlordship in the late fourth or early fifth centuries (that is, before Goths were settled in Rome). He seems to have been named after a Getic hero of that name.[3] A further reference to a 'mythic hero' of this name occurs in Cassiodorus' *Variae*, where heroes and their qualities are listed.[4] There are no other specific references to which we can attach our 'Vinidarius', but on the basis of his origins and of his qualifications we might possibly place him in the 460s, if we allow him a military role in Thrace,

---

[1] *FR*, p. 9.

[2] See *The Prosopography of the Later Roman Empire* (Vol. I, *AD 260–395*, ed. A.H.M. Jones, J.R. Martindale & J. Morris, Cambridge 1971), p. v, for a complete listing of posts which conferred this rank.

[3] Cf. Jordanes, *Getica* 79 (the list of heroes: *Vutuulf genuit Valarans; Valarans genuit Vinitharium; Vinitharius genuit Vandiliarium*), 246ff. (the chieftain). Cf. P. Heather, *Goths and Romans 332–489* (Oxford, 1991), p. 24.

[4] Cassiodorus *Variae* 11.1.19: *enituit enim Hamalus felicitate, Ostrogotha patientia, Athala mansue-tudine, Winitarius aequitate, Vnimundus forma, Thorismuth castitate, Walamer fide, Theudimer*

on the grounds that this is the earliest period in which a man of his background might have occupied an office which entitled him to style himself *uir illustris*.[1] Alternatively, if we assume an origin in Italy (and perhaps more opportunity, in a career combining military and civilian responsibilities, to develop an interest in culinary matters), then a date after 493, when Theodoric's kingdom in Italy became established, is much more likely.[2] Given that 'Vinidarius' must have been conversant in both the language as well as the social habits of Rome, then an even later date is probable for him: it was only in the early sixth century, as Moorhead puts it, 'the wealthy led the way' in fulfilling Theodoric's dictum that 'the poor Roman imitates the Goth, the well-to-do Goth the Roman'.[3]

We therefore assume that 'Vinidarius' was a gourmet, interested in food, and was of very high status given his title. The larger collection that he used to make his selection does not survive, but the excerpts from it show that it represents a different strand of recipes to that of our *Apicius*, as there is no exact duplication, although some recipes are very similar in structure and expression. This collection seems to throw up even more questions than it answers and there is much about the text that is perplexing.

The unique MS of the *Excerpta* starts with a numbered Section III before listing the seasonings which ought to be kept in the home. We have no idea what Sections I and II contained, or even if they were at all related to the text. Furthermore, the title *Apici excerpta a Vinidario uiro inlustri* is inserted half-way down the lists of seasonings, and this, coupled with the unusual numbering III for this first part of the *excerpta*, suggests that the list of seasonings might be a separate work, and that the heading should strictly refer to the *breuis ciborum*. The list of seasonings uses a Late Latin term, *pimentum*,[4] and the lists of unnamed items; 'seeds', 'dried herbs', 'liquids', 'nuts' and 'dried fruits' have many anomalies. Only half of the listed seasonings are actually used in the

---

pietate... 'for Hamalus was famed for his good fortune, Ostrogotha for endurance, Athala for gentleness, Winitharius for fairness, Vnimundus for good looks, Thorismuth for self-control, Walamer for good faith, Theudimer for devotion...'.

[1] Heather, *Goths and Romans*, p. 263, mentions for example a father and son, Arnegliscus and Anagastes, who were both *magristri utriusque militiae* in Thrace during the third quarter of the fifth century.

[2] J. Moorhead, *Theodoric in Italy* (Oxford, 1992), pp. 32ff.

[3] Moorhead, op. cit., pp. 101-2, citing the *Excerpta Valesiana* 12.61, *Romanus miser imitatur Gothum et utilis Gothus imitatur Romanum*.

[4] See note ad loc.

collection of recipes which follows, and there is a complete absence of any kind of fish sauce.[1] There is no possibility, therefore, that the list was created from the recipes.

The first section is untitled, but may be regarded as the more expensive seasonings. Among these is clove, which is absent from *Apicius*, and also *costus*, which was generally only used as a perfume and in wine rather than in food (along with cinnamon and spikenard) in references from the early imperial period. Their use in food is not noted by Pliny and they may be a late Roman culinary ingredient. In Anthimus (sixth century AD), clove and *costus* are used in a beef recipe.[2] There is also a unknown term *addena*, which if interpreted as a corruption of *addenda* may not refer to a spice at all, but to additional spices added later.

Using spices as a tentative indication of the dates of the recipes in *EV*, only 1, 1a and 2 seem to be from a much later period; the remainder could quite easily be contemporary with *Apicius*, which they resemble in a number of ways. A form of *patina* made in exactly the same way as the *patinae* in *Apicius* 4 is now called a *caccabina* (1). Later, *Excerpta* 19 is titled *patina solearum ex obis* (i.e. *ouis*: *patina* of sole with egg), indicating that the name was still applied to dishes of this nature. Terms of Greek origin are found in the *Excerpta* as they are also in *Apicius*. We find *porcello unococto* (i.e. *oenococto*) at *Excerpta* 21 and also at *Apicius* 8.7.11; these are very similar recipes, though distinct enough to indicate that they are from a separate strand. At *Excerpta* 24, *porcello exodiomum* (i.e. *ex oxyzomo*) is mirrored by *Apicius* 6.8 4, *pullum oxyzomum*, both featuring a 'sour

---

[1] The liquor *piperium* could quite reasonably contain fish sauce as a pepper mash seems to be a common component of a Roman sauce. It is possible that fish sauce did not need a separate mention: oil, wine, vinegar are also missing. Alternatively its absence may be linked with a decline in popularity of fish sauce as seen in Anthimus 9: 'we ban the use of fish sauce from every culinary role.'

[2] Cf. Pliny, *HN*. 12.30 where clove is noted for its scent. Anthimus 3 has a recipe that is perfumed with clove, *costus,* and spikenard, all of which are noted for their perfume and are not considered seasoning for food by Pliny: cf. *HN*. 12.41-2. Spikenard and *costus* are found in *Apicius* together as a food spice at 1.30.2 and 9.8.2, and they are particularly noted for their popularity in the Byzantine period, cf. A. Dalby, *Flavours of Byzantium* (Totnes, 2003). We believe the use of these perfumes (*costus,* spikenard, clove) in a recipe may indicate a late date. Cinnamon is not used in food at all until the Byzantine period, though *malabathrum* (cinnamon leaf) was used in food. See the Glossary, *malabathrum*, and also J. Miller, *The Spice Trade of the Roman Empire* (Oxford, 1969), pp. 42-51.

sauce'. *Excerpta* 13, *pisces zomotogono* (i.e. *zomotegcnon*), is virtually the same recipe as that found at 4.2.27 of *Apicius*. There are also linguistic differences between the *Excerpta* and *Apicius* which are noted below in section 5.

Apicius *in its context.*

The evidence for Apicius the man and *Apicius* the book is quite disparate and contradictory and is best divided into two parts and dealt with separately. The contemporary and personal material, as well as the references which we feel refer to the individual, will be dealt with below in the section titled 'Marcus Gavius Apicius – history and legend', while the more distant impersonal evidence, which we feel refers to the *Apicius* text and to other books about him, are dealt with here.

Writing at the beginning of the second century, Juvenal indicates that the name 'Apicius' had become synonymous with any gourmet regardless of his wealth and, as we shall see, the name continued to be used as an indication of a person excessively or obsessively interested in food.[1] It is also possible that any cook or gourmet who also collected recipes considered himself to be an 'Apicius' because of his skill or interest in food, and added recipes to a collection that ultimately formed part of the surviving *Apicius* text.[2] It is likely that the title itself may not have been used to indicate a person at all, but to reflect a general understanding at an early stage of the development of the text that 'Apicius' simply meant 'luxury food', and came to be a general term for 'good food' as it further evolved. We consider this to be the explanation for the title. We also find specific foods associated with Apicius: an amphora of fish sauce labelled *garum Apicianum* might be defined as luxury *garum* rather than a recipe associated with the man. The cakes named after Apicius mentioned by Athenaeus would be of a similar nature.[3] However, the recipes named *Apiciana* in the collection may have had more of an association with the original Apicius.

Late Roman writers were unaware that the book does not reflect one author, and continued to confuse the man Apicius with the wider connotations of

---

[1] Juvenal, 4.22-3.

[2] Tertullian, *Apol.* 3.6, mentions cooks or cookery schools named after Apicius.

[3] Athenaeus 7a, 647c; R. I. Curtis, *Garum and Salsamenta* (Leiden, 1991), Appendix II.

the name 'Apicius', and perhaps with the text *Apicius* too. The *Mythographi Vaticani*, tentatively dated to around the fifth century, records that 'Apicius was a very greedy fellow who wrote many recipes on seasonings'.[1] Extremely similar phraseology, suggesting that one is probably copied from the other, is also found in a tenth-century gloss added to the text of the *Querolus* (The Grumbler), an anonymous play likened to Plautus' *Aulularia*, written in Gaul with a dedication to Rutilius Namatianus that dates it after AD 410. The text itself makes a passing reference to the 'dishes of Apicius' and the gloss is as follows: 'Apicius, which is the proper name for a glutton, was the first to invent/make use of the kitchen and wrote many recipes on seasonings'.[2] The suggestion that he was first to make use of the kitchen is clearly confused and without merit but the reference to recipes needs consideration. A *scholia* on Juvenal, dated no more precisely than after the fourth century AD, also uses the same phrases: 'Apicius was the author of how to arrange dinners, who wrote about sauces: for he was the exemplar of a glutton.'[3] The similarity in the use of the term 'glutton' here and in the *Querolus* above implies a common source. The suggestion that Apicius wrote about arranging dinners is very interesting, as there is no reference to this aspect of dining in the *Apicius* recipe text. Are we to assume that these comments refer are to actual books known to the authors, or are they so confused and derivative as to be of no use in unravelling the origins of *Apicius*? We know that other collections of recipes were circulating in the late empire under the same title. The impression is given that there was quite a variety of recipe collections available, all with the *Apicius* title, and these obscure references cannot be associated securely with any of them.

Other later commentators believed that Marcus Gavius Apicius was responsible for or connected with some sort of book on food. The first of these is the *Scriptores Historiae Augustae*, which tells the histories of the later Emperors. Aelius Verus, who was made emperor-designate by Hadrian but never ruled, is said to have had 'things about Apicius reported by others', *Apicii ab aliis relata*, as well as Ovid's *Amores* and Martial's *Epigrams* by his bed.[4] This life is written

[1] *Mythographi Vaticani I et II,* II. <269> (Mai ed. 225), ed. P. Kulcsár (CSEL series, Turnhout, 1987). See Appendix 4 for the complete text of the *Mythographi Vaticani* reference.
[2] *Aulularia siue Querolus...* ed. R. Peiper (Leipzig, 1875); ed. F. Corsaro (Catania, 1964); ed. W. Emrich (Berlin, 1965); ed. C. Jacquenard-Le Saos (Budé, Paris, 1994), Act 2 Sc. 1 (§42 in the Budé edition). See Appendix 4 for detailed reference to these texts.
[3] Juvenal 4. 22-3 and *scholia* ad loc.; see below, p. 57.
[4] SHA *Aelius* 5.9, following Hohl's text (Leipzig, Teubner, 1971); see also Appendix 4.

by Aelius Spartianus and is addressed to Diocletian, giving a date after AD 285 and before AD 305 for its composition. The strange wording suggests that the name of the author was lost but that Spartianus knew that it was not Marcus Gavius Apicius. The wording also implies that an individual is the subject of the book rather than just gastronomy. Athenaeus reports that a book entitled *The Luxury of Apicius* was written by a grammarian called Apion, perhaps in the first century AD.[1] It was clearly a work of culinary theory, as the names of particular fish are discussed rather than any kind of cooking technique or recipe. There may be a reference to this book in the Aelius report, or it may refer to another unknown writer. It is not possible that the *Apicius* recipe text would stand comparison with Ovid or Martial as bedside reading matter: the recipe text is far too mundane to be entertaining. Anyone interested in food would want culinary theory, full of anecdotes and elaborate description of meals as well as details about where to get the best produce, so we must assume that the book which Aelius read was a work of culinary theory that may have had recipes but was mainly narrative.

St Jerome wrote in *c.* AD 370 that the works by Paxamus and Apicius were comparable and also 'always to hand' for people interested in food.[2] Paxamus is discussed in detail below; his written work on food seems to have been predominantly theoretical, though we know that it also contained recipes.[3] The context of this reference makes it clear that the audience for these books were educated and wealthy men who were concerned not with recipes, as such, but with the best locations, where the best fish could be obtained, with gastronomy. The Jerome reference may be to the same book which Aelius Verus had read, and suggests that the idea that someone other than Apicius had written it had been lost: this work of culinary theory linked to Apicius had become the 'work of Apicius'. It is also likely that the work referred to by the scholiast to Juvenal, which is defined as 'how to arrange dinners', is also this work of culinary theory, now lost.

We can only speculate whether this narrative book originally contained recipes and how they ended up in our recipe text. It seems that the work referred to in the scholiast on Juvenal and books of a similar nature (such as Paxamus' cookery book) did include recipes and therefore it seems highly likely that Apion's book did too. These recipes would have had a strong connection to Marcus Gavius

---

[1] Athenaeus 294f.
[2] Jerome, *Epistles* 3.33.
[3] See below on Greek culinary writing in the Roman period, p. 44.

Apicius and were quite likely to be his favourites (and therefore in the possession of his cook!) There are six recipes with the designation *Apiciana* in the collection and they may have a strong link with the man or men known as Apicius, which is why they survive in the *Apicius* text.[1] It is possible that the recipes in Apion's book were taken out of the body of the text by an innovative cook and put into a recipe collection which acquired the title *Apicius* at that time, because of those recipes. The book became an independent work, (and spawned others) that was controlled by cooks, under the name 'Apicius' which had become synonymous with 'good food' in the context of recipes, while still being associated with 'gluttony' and 'excess' from the point of view of the consumer.

In conclusion, it is not possible to say when or who was responsible for beginning the process of collecting recipes under the 'Apicius' banner. When a bare collection of recipes existed under the name 'Apicius' anyone, in theory, could add to the collection, and they clearly did. The collection of recipes made by Vinidarius still bears the name 'Apicius', as though every collection of recipes would automatically bear that name if the recipes were considered expensive, luxurious or even just good. Any personal reference to the man has been completely lost and is irrelevant. There are some references to 'Apicius' as an individual in the late empire, but in general the name was used as a generic term to refer to luxury or excessive eating.[2] For writers who wished to conjure up an image of indulgence and luxury, 'Apicius' was the perfect choice.

---

[1] *Apicius* 4.1.2; 4.2.14; 4.3.3; 5.4.2; 7.4.2; 8.7.6.

[2] See Appendix 4 for a complete list of the later references, and cf. M. Bode, *Apicius: Anmerkungen zum römischen Kochbuch* (St. Katharinen, 1999), p. 19.

2. COOKS AND ANCIENT COOKERY BOOKS[1]

It is worth emphasizing at the outset that only two recipe books have survived from the ancient world. Many other books have survived which *deal* with food, and as a result include recipes to a greater or lesser degree. There were many cookery books, according to Athenaeus, of which we only know the title, named author and an occasional fragment and, as we shall see, they appear to be of a similar nature to those that have survived in full: the fragments are discussions *about* food and its attributes rather than being simply a collection of recipes. The text of these books had narrative, and the writer had a 'voice'. The recipes they contain are interspersed in that narrative. Uniquely it seems, *Apicius* and *Vinidarius* are collections of recipes, bare of all narrative and without a voice. The process by which these two recipe collections happened to be made and survive is one of the purposes of this survey, which does not claim to be fully comprehensive but is simply an attempt to define the types and styles of culinary literature that existed in the Graeco-Roman world, and to fit *Apicius* into the genre.

The Greek tradition.

The origins of culinary literature as a separate genre can be traced to the fourth century BC. Sicily was the centre for the culinary arts at this time and the home of Philoxenus, a Greek *opsaphagos*, literally a 'relish-eater' rather than an eater of bread as staple, and as a result a gourmet: a Greek Apicius, you might say.[2] He was responsible for a poem called 'The Dinner' which described a lavish

[1] We are indebted to Andrew Dalby for his survey of Greek culinary literature in *Siren Feasts* (London, 1996), especially pp. 57-129. For a more literary approach, see J. Wilkins, *The Boastful Chef: The Discourse of Food in Ancient Greek Comedy* (Oxford, 2000) for example on p. 420: 'This is a book about "discourse" and only periodically about "reality".'
[2] The stories told of Philoxenus and of Apicius occur side by side in Athenaeus. The former is said by Chrysippus to have plunged his hands into hot water at the baths and drunk hot water in order to be able to consume hot food as it came from the kitchen. He is also said to have walked into houses during the time of dinner and seasoned the food to his taste before consuming it: Athenaeus 1.5d-f.

banquet probably held by the tyrant of Syracuse, Dionysius the Younger.[1] It was a popular work which everyone read even if they read nothing else, according to Aristotle.[2] As we will see when we come to consider the case of Marcus Gavius Apicius, these men were 'gourmands', that is, they were criticized for their love of luxury, not admired for it. Within Greek culture they were considered as moral degenerates on account of their lack of self control. An 'opsomaniac' was always defeated by his desires, powerless, impotent, and as a result unfit for office.[3]

The most famous early Greek food writer is Archestratus, also a Sicilian, whose gastronomic poem is dated to *c.* 350 BC.[4] He wrote an account of the produce of the Mediterranean, which was largely fish, almost as a guided tour. We find simple recipes within the fragments of the poem that survive in Athenaeus, though they are cast in a natural style rather then being formulaic and have no apparent link with the style of recipe that we find in later texts. The cooking style advocated by Archestratus is simple: he rejects the use of too many seasonings and wishes to let the natural flavours dominate. Archestratus is writing for a small sophisticated élite whose interest in a cuisine sets them apart and affirms their social superiority. He specifically rejects the style of cooking found in Sicily, where cookery schools were well known and where the consumption of good food was spreading to the other classes:

> When working on fish do not let any Syracusan or Italian (from Magna Graecia) come near you, for they do not understand how to prepare good fish. They ruin them in a horrible way by cheesing everything and sprinkling with a flow of vinegar and silphium brine.... They can bring clever ideas in a smart way to a banquet: little dishes which are cheap and sticky and based on nonsensical seasonings.[5]

Philoxenus, Archestratus and similar early food writers may simply have been knowledgeable consumers who gathered recipes from their cooks who, as

[1] A. Dalby, *Siren Feasts*, p. 115.
[2] Athenaeus 1.6d.
[3] Cf. J. Davidson, *Courtesans and Fishcakes* (London, 1997), p. 144.
[4] Cf. S. Douglas Olson, Alexander Sens, *Archestratos of Gela: Greek Culture and Cuisine in the Fourth Century BC: Text, Translation and Commentary* (Oxford, 2000); J. Wilkins, S. Hill, *Archestratus, the Life of Luxury*.
[5] Archestratus fr. 45 in Athenaeus 311a.

we shall see below, wrote their own cookery books, or they may have actually handled the food as well. The Archestratus recipes that survive appear written by a gourmet who displays some knowledge of cooking. Greeks were happy to display their empirical knowledge and were not inhibited by the association with slavery that such knowledge engendered in Roman times. Whether it be cooking, human and veterinary medicine or the sciences generally, the Greeks were dominant in these fields in the ancient world, and provided the main source of literary knowledge. Archestratus is known for his simple cooking style with the minimum of preparation or seasoning, and it is not at all unreasonable to imagine him actually involved in the cooking. However, in a high-status home, a slave or the household females would undoubtedly prepare food on a day-to-day basis.

The earliest Greek specialist cooks, *mageiroi*, 'were typically free men rather than slaves'.[1] The term denoted a minor priest who both sacrificed the animal for the feast and also cooked it along with other special items. Typically, professional, not sacerdotal, cooks were not of such elevated status.[2] These were available for hire from the market for special occasions such as weddings, coming of age, etc. Greek comedies of the fourth and third centuries BC, preserved in fragments in Athenaeus, are full of boastful and tedious cooks with delusions of grandeur who have invaded people's homes. A *mageiros*, on the other hand, had a certain minor status in Greek society and could have had financial independence. He would certainly have had the time and skill to write his own cookery books and have them published and read by his fellow cooks as well as gourmets. However, the *mageiros* cook was part of a different social stratum from cooks in general. The play *The Lawgiver* by Dionysius demonstrates these distinctions:

> We are able to garnish, to carve, to cook sauces, and to blow on the fire, anyone can chance to do that; someone like that is only a food processor (*opsopoios*): but the master chef (*mageiros*) is quite different. To have a grasp of location, occasion, host, yes and the dinner too! What fish and when he should buy it, that's not for anybody.[3]

---

[1] A. Dalby, *Food in the Ancient World from A to Z* (London, 2003), p. 102.
[2] Cf. Plato, *Gorgias* 518b, Athenaeus 325f.
[3] Athenaeus 405a.

It is likely that *opsopoioi* were in fact the household slaves who cooked, though it is also likely that many *mageiroi* owned slaves whom we might term *opsopoioi* too. A cook from the play *Foster-brothers* even admits that, 'I sit near by and watch, while others do the work; to them I explain the principles and the results'.[1] These master-chefs still had had to learn their trade, and we see that notable cooks could take on pupils. In the play *Behind the Veil* by Anaxippus, a cook names two pupils, Sophon of Acarnania and Domoxenus of Rhodes, who were being taught by Labdacus of Sicily.

> They removed from the books the old and commonplace seasonings and carried the mortar out from among us, ...but Sophon holds all Ionia now and he became my teacher, boss. And I am myself studying eagerly to leave behind new writings on the art.[2]

The cooks in Greek comedy are noted for their pompous and pretentious manner. They exemplify the term 'delusions of grandeur'. However, despite their exaggerated claims, they are depicted as quite naturally taking their profession seriously, and their training and expertise is wide-ranging. The cook in *The False Accuser* of Sosipater has received an elaborate education, including astrology, because 'all our fishes and foods virtually take on a flavour that is different at different times in the revolution of the universal system'. Training, too, in architecture, because one had to know how to design a kitchen with the correct draughts and light; and the natural world, for obvious reasons; and strategy, 'for to serve and then remove each course in order and to understand the proper time for them, when to lead them on more quickly, when slowly (and) how the guest feel towards the dinner ... all these points, you see, are carefully considered by military methods of study'.[3] There is obviously much exaggeration here, for comic effect; but behind this pretentiousness a degree of expertise and knowledge must have been claimed by such master-chefs in real life for the comedy to work at all. As we shall see below, this kind of culinary knowledge (apart perhaps from the architecture) is the preserve of the gourmet in the Roman period.

---

[1] Athenaeus 102f.
[2] Athenaeus 404b.
[3] Athenaeus 378c-379a. For the training of cooks in Rome, see below, p. 69.

That cooks were able to write their own cookery books is clear, but we seem to have a quotation from only one. Mithaikos was probably a *mageiros* from Sicily and was responsible for a work called *The Art of Cookery*. From Plato we hear that Socrates judged 'the author of the Sicilian recipe book the greatest benefactor of the human body' implying that it was familiar to Athenians at the end of the fifth century.[1] A recipe from it quoted in Athenaeus reveals a simple, terse style typical of what we find in ancient recipes from the fourth century BC right through to the *Apicius* text.[2] This direct, laconic style that cooks seem to have is parodied below in this rapid conversation:

In *Philotis* Antiphanes makes clear the wisdom of cooks, saying **A** Now then the small grey fish…I say you should poach it in salted water. **B** What about a small sea bass? **A** Bake it entire. **B** And a dog-fish? **A** It should be served in *hypotrimma*. **B** The little eel? **A** Salt, oregano, water. **B** A conger eel? **A** Same again. **B** The ray? **A** With green herbs. **B** Here's a slice of tuna. **A** Grill it. **B** What about pieces of kid? **A** Roast them. **B** And the other meat? **A** Just the reverse (i.e. boil it). **B** The spleen? **A** Stuff it. **B** Empty intestines? **A** This fellow is killing me![3]

Our next writers seem to span the period between Greece's decline and Rome's ascendancy in the culinary arts. Chrysippus of Tyana in Asia Minor cannot be dated, but is said to have written a work *On Bread Making* that has an international flavour. Andrew Dalby suggests he may have written in Rome, as he apparently wrote in a mixture of Latin and bad Greek.[4] The names of particular cakes from Chrysippus' book, which survive in quotes from Athenaeus, are also found in Cato's agricultural manual, which is dated to *c.* 150 BC.[5] We cannot know for certain that Chrysippus pre-dates Cato; it may be that Cato consulted other books containing such recipes. Chrysippus became a standard work on the

[1] Plato, *Gorgias* 518b; Olsen and Sens, *Archestratos of Gela*, p. xxxvi.
[2] Athenaeus 325f. See also Athenaeus 516c for a list of other Greek writers credited with 'Arts of Cookery'.
[3] Athenaeus 662b.
[4] Dalby, *Siren Feasts*, pp. 141,165.
[5] Cf. p. 39 n. 2 above, and especially Athenaeus 647d, Cato, *De agricultura* 77 'Spira', 78 'Scriblita'. Unfortunately, cake and bread recipes are not found in *Apicius* (see p. 30 n. 1 above), so we are unable to judge Chrysippus' influences on later Roman food.

subject of baking, and the apparent international flavour of his recipes represents the kind of culinary literature that we shall now find. The political centre of the ancient world may have shifted to Rome, but it seems that the vocabulary of the kitchen all round the Mediterranean was Greek.

Paxamus fits into the same category as Chrysippus, as he is likely to have written and been read in Rome. His works were available to Columella in the mid-first century AD, but that is as close to a date as we can get. Paxamus wrote a considerable body of work, none of which has survived. The cookery book he is said to have written is likely to be that mentioned by St Jerome, 'Paxamus et Apicius semper in manibus'.[1] This Greek cookery book remained current and worth reading well into the third century AD. For such a book to be worth reading it has to be a book *about* food rather than just a recipe collection, though that it also contained recipes is undoubted. Some may survive in *Apicius*. Two of his books on farming may also survive in fragments in the *Geoponica*.[2] Paxamus also wrote on dyeing and sexual postures! Such a mixture of topics suggests a dilettante without a speciality – certainly a gourmet and a relatively wealthy citizen, but not necessarily skilled in any one field or skilled in any practical sense. It is not likely that he would have had the time or inclination to learn how to cook. His work has been linked with that of Cato and Mago, technical writers who are knowledgeable but not craftsmen in their chosen subjects. They are collectors of other people's knowledge.[3]

Greek culinary writing in the Roman period.

One cannot fail to mention Athenaeus himself in this survey of Greek books on food. Without him the survey above would be very short. His unique and extensive work entitled *Deipnosophistōn* ('Sophists at dinner') records thousands of quotations from all forms of Greek literature from the fourth and third centuries BC which mention food, dining and related topics. He lived and worked in Rome in the early second century AD, yet rarely refers to his own time. He is the

[1] St Jerome, *Epistles* 33.3, though this 'Apician' work is unlikely to be our text: see above, page 37.
[2] A Paxamus recipe is attributed in the *Geoponica* at 18.21.
[3] Mago: a Carthaginian agricultural writer translated into Latin by order of the senate in the mid-first century BC.

ultimate dilettante, collecting obscure culinary references for the sake of their relationship to his chosen topic.

Two further key recipe sources in Greek need mentioning. First is the *Geoponica*, a tenth-century AD agricultural manual which contains material that may date back to the sixth century AD. It is attributed to a man called Bassus who is otherwise unknown. A recipe for *garum* is preserved in it, as well as typical agricultural recipes. The formulaic and repetitive style of recipes in *Apicius* is not found. Secondly, the Heidelberg papyrus is an undated fragment of a Greek recipe book from the Egyptian city of Oxyrhynchus.[1] It is fragmentary and as a consequence only five incomplete recipes can be identified. Their language, format and style are not so far removed from those found in *Apicius*. They are largely in list format with a cursory method, and display the distinct style we associate with cooks. The stew of salt meat contains pepper, cumin, coriander, thyme, anise and fennel as well as oil, wine, vinegar and honey. Such a sauce has all the hallmarks of *Apician* cuisine. There are no precise quantities for any of the ingredients, although most of the liquids are expressed as a direct ratio; two parts, four parts, etc.[2] There is a curious phenomenon in the 'ham' recipe: one of the Greek terms for ham is *colyphium*, but this recipe uses *pernon,* which is the Latin term for ham or bacon.[3] At the time of their composition it seems these recipes were using Latin loan words. We find that in the late empire Greek kitchen terminology has many Latin loan words. Diocletian's Price Edict, dated to AD 301, was written in Latin and in Greek, thus allowing us to have precise definitions of obscure words and identify which terms were then current. These include, for instance, the genitive forms *phabatos* for *fabae, alikos* for *alicae,* and *kondeitou* for *conditi.* These do not appear in Greek literature before the edict, and reveal the strength of Latin influence on cooking terminology in the later period.[4] Andrew Dalby goes further: 'to treat the phenomenon as one of borrowing from one foreign language is to oversimplify. Cultures were actually mingling and a technical term from one of the two languages might seem the only good way to denote a newly developed concept.[5]

[1] The text of the Oxyrhynchus papyrus is included in the edition of *Apicius* by Giarratano and Vollmer (Leipzig, 1922).

[2] The recipes in *Apicius* also convey liquid quantity this way. See the section on quantities, p. 83.

[3] Plautus, *Persa* 1.2.12-18.

[4] Diocletian's Price Edict 4.13, 14; 6.38; 1.25; 2.17. See *alica* and *isicia* in the Glossary for further discussion of their origin.

[5] Dalby, *Siren Feasts*, pp. 179-83, 'The culinary synthesis'.

Cookery books – the Roman tradition.

The process of the Hellenization of Roman eating habits is well documented. Livy records that soldiers returning from the war in Asia Minor in 187 BC brought back all manner of exotic booty such as marble sideboards, one-legged tables and 'lyre and flute girls and other entertainments for the feast…. the actual feasts also began to be prepared with greater care and expense'.[1]

Wealth, slaves (particularly Greek slave-cooks and their cookery books), new foods and dining habits infiltrated Roman culture over the late third and early second centuries BC. In the early second century BC Rome was not unfamiliar with the concept of the free Greek *mageiros,* whether from literary transmission or actual experience (or perhaps both). The plays of Plautus are translations and adaptations of fourth-century Greek comedies and as such they contain numerous outspoken cooks displaying all the characteristics of a *mageiros.*[2] It is possible that the Romans found these characters amusing simply because of the contrast between their own humble slave-cooks and the *mageiros* that they saw on stage but had little experience of. However, it seems that cooks from the Greek colonies in southern Italy might have willingly travelled to Rome to offer their services in the wake of the retreating army and its captives. A fragment of a speech by Cato implies that two men named Ocha and Dionysodorus, who appear to be cooks but free men (one has an obvious Greek name, while the other is harder to place), have had statues erected to them in the city (this is what enrages Cato).[3] If such people could circulate and offer their services and gain a reputation for cooking as these two appear to have done, then Greek *mageiroi* (and it must be assumed their cookery books) were circulating in high-status circles. It is not clear whose books were available at this time. It was probably a little early for the books of Paxamus, but Chrysippus' work is probably around and possibly those by Mithaikos and Sophon, the *mageiroi* and teachers of cooks.

---

[1] Livy 39.6.9ff.

[2] Cf. for example *Pseudolus* 810-25, discussed in detail below.

[3] Cato fr. 96, in *Oratorum Romanorum Fragmenta Liberae Rei Publicae* ed. H. Malcovati (3rd ed., Turin, 1953): *Catonem quoque in oratione aduersus Lepidum uerbum cantari solitum commemorasse, cum ait statuas positas Ochae atque Dionysodoro effeminatis, qui magiras facerent.*

If a Roman culinary tradition free of Greek influence did exist, it is not seen in the literature. It is difficult to define the cuisine that arrived in Rome at this time. There are some elaborate and fantastical dishes in Plautus which, as parodies, cannot be taken literally, but they may well nonetheless reflect what a Roman audience perceived that cooks (and, surely, *Greek* cooks) did with their food. Emily Gowers sees the use of food in Plautus as a metaphor for the 'identity crisis' felt in Rome as Greek culture spread: 'Food is also a focus for many of the Romans' anxieties about their whole culture: how to separate it from the Greeks.'[1] Plautus' Greek food is sophisticated and complex, in contrast to the primitive barbarian porridge and the profusion of pork and garlic consumed by the Romans.[2] According to Gowers, the Roman food in Plautus is bland and stupid, reflecting the Romans' anxiety that, though dominant militarily, they were culturally inferior. Food in Plautus has many layers of meaning, it is true, and attempts to build up a historical picture of social and culinary practice from them have been challenged. One particularly interesting passage deserves discussion:

> I don't season a dinner like other cooks, who serve up seasoned meadows in their *patinae*, who make the dinner guests cattle and pile on the greens and then go on and season those greens with other greens; they chuck on coriander, fennel, garlic, black cabbage, they put on sorrel, brassica, beet and orache, and they drench the lot with a pound of *laserpicium* and miscreant mustard is pounded up, stuff which makes the eyes of those who pound it run with tears before they have finished grinding it. When these fellows cook a dinner and season it, they don't season it with seasonings but with screech-owls which eat out the insides of the guests while they still live![3]

Analysis of this passage has been over-concerned with the ingredients, from the point of view of vegetarian-versus-meat, vegetables-versus-herbs, as well

---

[1] Emily Gowers, *The Loaded Table* (Oxford, 1993), p. 51.

[2] Gowers also suggests that the Romans eat stinking garlic, in contrast to the Greeks, but this is a class distinction not an ethnic one: all ancient farmers, soldiers and rowers knew the power of garlic. She also identifies pork as Roman rather than Greek, but even Old Comedy used pork products in its humour: see especially Athenaeus 655f., Aristophanes, *Acharnians* 719ff.; *Peace* 529-9.

[3] Plautus, *Pseudolus* 810-21.

as with the origin of the listed items: which might be Greek, which Roman. This last preoccupation has led to an assumption that the food being parodied is Roman. Gowers identifies the garlic, spinach and beet as part of a lumpen Roman diet, and even identifies the *silphium* with the garlic, as somehow only 'stinking' and therefore inferior: 'a crop grown by the uncultivated fisherman of Cyrene and a foul-smelling complement to their harsh lives'.[1] Against this view, it is clear that the use of silphium was prolific in ancient Greek food and it is surely the Greeks' use of this spice that is being highlighted in this parody. The consumption of garlic is a matter of status rather than one of national tastes: Greek soldiers and rowers were said to keep up their strength with garlic.[2] This passage can and should be taken more literally. What we have is a *patina* with too many and the wrong kinds of seasonings in it. The object of the parody is cooks and their masters who want dishes seasoned with too many things – the result a confused mess in every sense.

Given the date that Plautus was writing, *c.* 200 BC, *Roman* food as a cuisine was in its infancy, unformed and to some extent as yet 'uncorrupted' by the 'sophisticated Greeks'. One has to ask: whose cuisine is being parodied here, if it is not the cooking style and traditions of the Greeks? Either way, this passage suggests that Greek food had moved on quite considerably from Archestratus' simple style, and had already become more complex before it moved into the Roman sphere of influence.

Parody apart, evidence for the nature of Greek food at this time is sketchy. Most comes from Athenaeus, in the form of spoken recipes given by Greek cooks from Old and New comedy of the fifth and fourth centuries. The majority of recipes which survive in this format are simple and contain small numbers of spices in comparison with some of the instructions in *Apicius*. The majority are also for fish, which naturally require less intense seasonings. Recipes for more complex sauces, that might indicate continuity between the food then and in *Apicius*, would not naturally find a place in such a genre. Rarity, therefore, does not prove that Greek recipes of complexity did not exist. The ingredients

---

[1] Gowers, op. cit., p. 98.

[2] Silphium was not simply 'stinking', but a complex ingredient which, when used with skill, conveyed depth and complexity to food and was very common in Greek recipes: cf. Aristophanes, *Knights* 895-6; Dalby, *Food in the Ancient World*, pp. 303-4. The idea that greens such as cabbage, spinach and beet were somehow un-Greek is nonsense. See the Glossary, 'cabbage', and cf. Athenaeus 369a-372f. For garlic, see Dalby, op. cit., p. 155.

that go to make up a Greek or a Roman sauce are the same: oil, various wines, vinegar, fish sauce, honey. The same spices and herbs are used in different combinations. There may be more complexity in Roman recipes, but identical principles are followed.[1] There is one recipe which survives in Athenaeus which is both complex and highly seasoned, in the so-called *Apician* style. It is for meat and is pre-Roman, attributed to Epaenetus' *Art of Cookery*, dated to the Hellenistic period. The dish is a *myma*, a sacrificial meat-based stew made with the animal's blood and, in this case, with vinegar, cheese, *silphium,* cumin, thyme leaf, thyme seed, hyssop, coriander leaf, coriander seed, leek, onion, poppy seed, raisins or honey, and sour pomegranate seeds.[2] This would not be out of place in *Apicius*.

One of the earliest Latin works of literature had a popular culinary theme. It was a poem in imitation of Archestratus' *Life of Luxury* written by Quintus Ennius in *c.* 169 BC.[3] Ennius was from Apulia, one of the Hellenized parts of south-east Italy, collectively known as Magna Graecia. Ennius was befriended and mentored by Cato the Elder, whose agricultural manual contains our first Roman recipes. Cato, a senator, was best known for his public condemnation of the Hellenistic influences he saw about him, but he embraced Greek culture at home. His farming manual includes apparently traditional Roman recipes for sacrificial cakes that have hybrid Greek/Latin names. These names are also found in the Greek book *On Bread Making* by Chrysippus.[4] Such hybrid terms, neither purely Latin or Greek but a composite, are also very common in the *Apicius* recipe text. They reflect a merging of the two languages in the kitchen as an international 'Roman' cuisine develops, absorbing Greek practice and taste as happened in other aspects of social life.[5]

---

[1] See Athenaeus 1.5a-d: Philoxenus goes to other peoples' houses, seasoning their food to his taste with oil, wine, *garum*, vinegar and other relishes.

[2] Athenaeus 662d.

[3] Ennius, *Hedyphagetica* ('Delikatessen' or 'Sweetmeats'), in *Remains of Old Latin* I (Loeb series, ed. B. H. Warmington, Cambridge MA and London, revised ed. 1956).

[4] See above, p. 49 and n. 109; cf. Athenaeus 113c-d, 647 d-f for *placenta, spira, scriblita, spaerita.* The cake called *placenta* (Cato, *De agricultura* 75) is said to derive from the Greek *plakous.* This term is often used to mean a general flat cake in Athenaeus, but the term is also used specifically at Athenaeus 449c; this description corresponds precisely with the cake in Cato and suggests that the recipe as well as the name of the cake had travelled to Rome long enough before Cato for him to include it in a Roman agricultural manual.

[5] Dalby, *Siren Feasts,* pp. 179-183.

A typical recipe in Cato is very like those in Books 1 and 3 of *Apicius*. The bailiff's wife, rather than the cook, is expected to be responsible for the preservation of all the fruit harvest of the estate; for preparing medications for the slaves and animals (digestives and laxatives); and for making spiced wines and preparing thank-offerings to the gods. Also included are recipes for wine, simple porridges, and bread. As a food writer, Cato can be likened to Paxamus, whose general knowledge was quite good but whose practical skill was limited. Cato was skilled in gathering and sorting information provided by the craftsman. In his case Cato probably acquired some of his recipes from the bailiff's wife of his own estate, where simple written records would almost certainly be stored. It is also likely that the works of Paxamus and Mago were consulted and that some of their recipes are in Cato's book. For a linguistic comparison of these recipes with those found in *Apicius*, see pp. 99ff.

The nature of food preparation and consumption was transformed between Cato in around 150 BC and our next key writer in the early first century AD, but we are dependent on other forms of literature to inform us. There is a huge gap in the literary record available from the late Republic, when feasting in style became a necessity in the political climate of the time. The élite competed with more and more elaborate dinners, and sumptuary legislation followed not far behind. This new atmosphere was particularly conducive to an emerging group of gourmets: men competed over the size and variety of fish they could breed and over the size and number of dining-rooms they could use. Some who were unable to control their appetites were publicly condemned and often satirized, and they appeared in far greater numbers than before.[1]

We are given an insight into the nature of this increasing obsession with pleasure by Horace in his striking philosophical *Satire* 2.4, dated to around 30 BC. In it, Horace describes a meeting with a man who has just listened to a great philosopher lecture in a manner that would surpass Pythagoras, Plato and Socrates.[2] When the precepts are at last recounted, instead of moral or

---

[1] The first notorious fish breeder was C. Sergius Orata, who bred oysters at Baiae in 108 BC; Pliny, *HN*. 9.79, 170. For the general obsession with opulence and conspicuous consumption, cf. Plutarch, *Life of Lucullus* (106–56 BC).

[2] In *Satire* 2.4 the 'philosopher' is not named, though the man held under the sway of this philosopher is called Catius. Various suggestions have been offered for his identity, not least Marcus Gavius Apicius himself. He is unlikely to be Apicius, even as a very young man, as the date of *Satire* 2.4 is too early.

philosophical ideas, we hear a list of banal and unrelated culinary laws. The subject matter of each item roughly follows the order of a meal, so we hear that:

The cabbage which has grown in dry fields is sweeter than a town-grown one. *(l. 15)*

The giant Lucrine mussel is better than the murex from Baiae. *(l. 32)*

Oysters are best from Circeii, sea-urchins from Misenum. *(l. 33)*

The cunning man who mixes Surrentine wine with Falernian lees carefully collects up the sediment with a dove's egg, so that the yolk heads for the bottom, gathering up the impurities. *(ll. 55-7)*

This fatuous culinary trivia is all that the knowledgeable gourmet 'knows', according to Horace. It is the kind of 'knowledge' and skill that can easily be displayed while reclining at table with a captive audience. *Satire* 2.8 describes just such a scene. The host bores his guests with snippets of information about the dishes served: the lamprey 'was caught while she was pregnant; the flesh is inferior after spawning'. This host even recites a little speech giving a recipe for the *oenogarum* accompanying the lamprey. He claims to be responsible for innovative additions to the sauce, but we are left feeling that he would get lost looking for the kitchen in his own house. The statement in ll. 35-9 is very telling:

Nor should anyone claim for himself skill at organizing dinners without first working through the subtle science of flavours. Nor is it enough to have swept fishes from a pricey stall without knowing which are best served with sauce, which go best on the grill, to get the flagging guest back on his elbow.

The skill claimed by the host is in organizing the skills of others. We are not being told here that the host understands the subtle science of flavours from a practical point of view. Such scenes are not to be taken literally – we are dealing with satire – but the impression given in *Satires* 2.4 and 2.8 is that in Rome in the late first century BC wealthy men took pains to show off their culinary knowledge to their guests. This much at least is necessary for the satire to function effectively.

However, in the 'real' Roman world, away from the artificial atmosphere of satire, we find the situation not all that different. When Cicero was at a loose end politically in 46 BC, he took up this 'art' of dining, and wrote to Papirius Paetus, an Epicurean, to warn him that he was no longer satisfied with leftovers: 'I may well have Hirtius and Dolabella as students of rhetoric, but when it comes to dining they teach me. I imagine you have heard, they give speeches at my place and I eat dinners at theirs.'[1] Shortly after this, another letter to the same man gives us more detail: 'So get yourself ready: you are matched with a man with an appetite and one who already knows a thing or too; but you know how arrogant late-learning pedants are. You will have to unlearn your leftovers and flat bread. I am so well versed that I quite often dare to invite your friends Verrius and Camillus. Look how cheeky I am: I even gave a dinner to Hirtius, but without a peacock; in that dinner my cook was able to copy everything except his hot sauce.'[2] Cicero enjoyed himself eating other people's peacock, but he was also poking fun at his friends and their 'art' just as was Horace in his *Satires*. The 'art' was entirely theoretical, trivial even, and had little to do with what went on in the kitchen. It is interesting to note that, despite the fact that Cicero is noted for his humanity towards his slaves (albeit the ones who are educated) he did not bother to name his cook or think him worthy of consultation on this subject.

There are echoes of the *mageiros* in the nature of this knowledge and this art. Contrast Athenaeus 404f: 'Which fish is in the market and when, that is not for everyone', with Horace *Satire* 2.4.39, 'Nor is it enough to have swept fish from a pricey stall'. In the context of the Roman world there was a huge gulf between the physical act of cooking, which was always considered disgraceful, and the art of knowing what you are consuming, which was elevated to a philosophy. This 'literary food' is respectable and 'clean', free from the taint of kitchen dirt and smells. In Greece, the concept of physical labour was less demeaning and so cooking as an art, and understanding food in all its facets, were combined in the person of the *mageiros*. In Rome the cook was always seen as an inferior being without a name or a voice.[3]

---

[1] Cicero, *Ad fam.* 9.16.7.
[2] Cicero, *Ad fam.* 9.20.2.
[3] The topic of cooks and their status is dealt with below at p. 63.

Gaius Matius is the name of one of three food writers given by Columella: 'Marcus Ambivus, Maenas Licinius and Gaius Matius'. All three apparently wrote on the general topics of 'the baker, the cook and the cellarman'. Columella later says that Matius wrote three separate books entitled *Coci, et Cetarii, et Salgamarii* ('The Cook', 'The Fishmonger' and 'The Pickle Maker').[1] Matius' books do not survive, though we may assume that recipes were included in them. When Columella refers to these writers, he only makes specific reference to their comments on the nature and personal habits of a cook. We know nothing about the first two writers he mentioned, but we do have a lot of information about someone called Gaius Matius. He was a close friend of Caesar and remained loyal to his memory, even after his assassination. He was one of two men who celebrated the games in honour of Caesar's funeral on behalf of Octavian, the future Emperor Augustus. He wrote to Cicero in late 44 BC suggesting he was in the 'evening of his life' and ready to retire.[2] The other correspondence with Cicero does not suggest a particular interest in food. A further reference to a Gaius Matius by Pliny the Elder, in the mid-70s AD, suggests that he invented new techniques in apple pruning 'within the last 80 years' and that he was a friend of Augustus.[3] The implication is that a son of Caesar's friend was our gourmet. He was of patrician family and very wealthy, one assumes, certainly not a freedman or potential cook. He seems to fall into the same group we have seen before: the amateur literary gourmet and dilettante, collecting other people's knowledge.

It is at this point that Marcus Gavius Apicius enters the stage. His life and possible contribution to culinary lore will be dealt with below, in order to explore the connections (or lack of them) between the historical Apicius and the *Apicius* text. However, before that is undertaken, a brief note shall be made of other Roman writers who contribute recipes to the body of food literature. Columella's agricultural manual, *De re rustica*, is dated to *c.* AD 65. The recipes he records are similar to those in Cato, and also to those in Book 1 of *Apicius*, with the preservation of the estate's produce as the main theme. Columella is unusual in that he had considerable experience in running his own estates as opposed

---

[1] See Columella 12.4.2 and 12.46.1 for the confused reference to the titles of the books.
[2] Cicero, *Ad fam.* 11.28, and especially section 8, where Matius says he will retire to Rhodes if allowed.
[3] Cf. Pliny, *HN.* 12.13.4 and 15.49 for particular fruit named after him. See *Apicius* 4.3.4 for *Minutal Matianum*, named for or after this man or his apples.

to using estate managers. This practical experience is reflected in the quality of his work on agriculture. He includes a few interesting recipes that have a particular resonance in *Apicius*: at 12.59 he includes a number on spreads and sauces similar to the *mortaria* and *oxyporium* found in *Apicius* Book 1. There is no duplication, but the language and grammatical forms are particularly similar, and the distinctive *aliter* between recipes suggests a more definite link in style and therefore a common background.[1]

There are a number of later Latin authors who contribute recipes to our collection. Pliny the Elder's *Natural History* details (among much else) food products, their cultivation and medical properties. As a result, the occasional simple recipe can be extracted from the narrative. These recipes differ quite a lot in style from those we find in the agricultural manuals, being more like the culinary advice and theory that consumers might share and that we might expect to find in a general book about food rather than in a recipe book. Some of the key references to 'Apician lore' survive in Pliny.[2] Other agricultural writers followed the same format as Cato and Columella but do not add anything new to the body of recipes that survives.[3]

Marcus Gavius Apicius – history and legend.

Marcus Gavius Apicius seems to represent the archetypical 'gourmand', so reviled by his contemporaries that one almost feels he was too bad to be true. The biographical material, free of overt personal criticism, is brief. The tradition is that he was best known during the reign of Tiberius, when he is said to have influenced Drusus Caesar, Tiberius' son, to reject *cymas* – young cabbage – as too common a food.[4] Drusus died in AD 23, aged 36. We cannot know how old he was when this all-too-familiar rejection took place, though it is likely to have been in his youth, which places the beginning of Apicius' influence in the very early years of the first century AD when Augustus was in power. A Martial epigram records a dinner at which Apicius and Maecenas, Augustus'

---

[1] See pp. 99ff. for a linguistic comparison between Columella's recipes and *Apicius*.
[2] See below, p. 58.
[2] Varro, first century BC; Gargilius Martialis, third century AD; Palladius, fourth century AD.
[2] Pliny, *HN.* 19.137.

friend and literary patron to the new régime, dined together.[1] Apicius was also linked with Sejanus in his youth and almost certainly moved in imperial circles. A rarely-acknowledged reference to banquets held at Apicius' house is found in two fragments of letters by Claudius Aelianus, writing *c.* AD 200.[2] The tone is condemnatory: the banquets are wasteful, licentious, drunken orgies and Apicius an altogether bad fellow. Claudius Aelianus records that two consuls were present and names them: Junius Blaesus and Lucius Antistius Vetus. These men are known to have been consuls in AD 28. The key question here is not whether the event took place, but rather, how did Claudius know? Such anecdotes as these suggest the existence of a literary work containing stories about Apicius rather than recipes.

Athenaeus tells us that in the time of Tiberius a rich voluptuary called Apicius, after whom many cakes were named, lived in Minturnae in Campania. It is from here that he made his famous trip to Africa for prawns.[3] Athenaeus also gives us the only unambiguous reference to a literary work connected to this man. The work known as *The Luxury of Apicius* by the grammarian Apion is quoted in Athenaeus in a debate about the names of particular kinds of dogfish, suggesting that general culinary theory was the subject of the book. It is possible that stories about Apicius and his banquets were contained in it too.[4] Though lost, it is particularly noteworthy that this work, on the most notorious gourmand Rome ever had, was written in Greek: the concepts, ideas, and (one must assume) recipes which it contained epitomized luxury dining in Rome in the first century AD, yet these concepts were preserved in Greek not Latin. We have suggested that it was still widely read in the third century AD and that it represents the only book genuinely associated with Marcus Gavius Apicius. It needs to be stressed that not one of his contemporaries suggested that Marcus Gavius Apicius ever wrote a cookery book or recipes. Columella and Athenaeus recount numerous names of food writers who are otherwise unknown, but Apicius is ignored as a writer in his own time. He seems to have been entirely devoted to his stomach and is clearly defined by his near-contemporaries as the worst of all gourmands,

---

[1] Martial 10.73.1-4.

[2] Claudius Aelianus, *De natura animalium, epistularum fragmenta* 110, 111, ed. R. Hercher (Leipzig, 1866, repr. Graz, 1971); nos. 113, 114 in the ed. of D. Domingo-Forasté (Stuttgart/ Leipzig, 1994); see also Bode, *Apicius,* p. 12 n. 49.

[3] Athenaeus 7a, 647c.

[4] Athenaeus 294f.

who kept bad company (including Sejanus, who, Tacitus says, increased his income in his youth as a result of associating with Apicius as a rent-boy!)[1]

The notorious stories of M. Gavius Apicius' exploits and bizarre death deserve a brief retelling.[2] The anecdotes recorded cover a much longer period than fits the lifetime of a single man, and tend to outrageousness, building up the 'myth of profligacy' associated with his name. This suits Seneca, who lived at the time of Nero and is known for his excessive moralizing. On one occasion Tiberius came across a mullet of majestic proportions in the market, and is reported to have said to himself, 'if neither Apicius or Publius Octavius buys that mullet, I'm a monkey's uncle!' He then instigated a furious round of bidding, which Octavius won.[3] Other stories, preserved by Athenaeus, have Apicius undertaking a fruitless voyage 'in the days of Tiberius' from Minturna in Italy to Libya in search of giant prawns, and sending oysters to Trajan when the latter was miles inland in Parthia.[4] Athenaeus names another character from 100 BC 'Apicius' because of his prodigality, but it is not clear whether this name was given retrospectively.[5]

The condemnation of pleasure is found in a passage from Seneca discussing Apicius and fellow-gourmet Nomentanus: 'See these very men looking down from their lofty rose garlands on their cook-shops (*popinae*)'. Is it being suggested that Apicius owned a low-status bar? We think not. Seneca is talking of the household of the gourmand and suggesting that his kitchen is a vulgar *popina*. Apicius is dismissed in like manner in other references:

> Their whole body is excited with soft and gentle caresses and, if they didn't stop inhaling from time to time, the very place in which pleasures are born would be killed by the different aromas. You would say they were in ecstasy, but it will do them no good, for they take no pleasure in the good.[6]

> May the gods and goddesses ruin those whose greed crosses even the boundaries of our invidious empire! They wish produce to be caught

---

[1] Tacitus, *Annals* 4. 1.
[2] See also Appendix 3, 'Sources on Apicius', below.
[3] Seneca, *Epistles* 95.42.
[4] Athenaeus 6a-b, 6d.
[5] Athenaeus 168e.
[6] Seneca, *Vita* 11.4.

beyond the Phasis to equip their pretentious cook-shops (*popinae*)....
Apicius, whom we remember well – he who proclaimed the science of
the cook-shop (*popina*) and afflicted a generation with his doctrine in
the city from which philosophers were once ordered to leave, as though
the corruptors of youth. It is worth the trouble to know about his death.
When he had squandered thousands of sesterces in his kitchen, when he
had sucked dry numerous gifts of money from the imperial court and a
massive income by throwing various parties, overwhelmed by debt he
was compelled to examine his accounts for the first time: he calculated
that only hundreds of sesterces would be left to him and, as if living on a
budget of hundreds of sesterces would be like dying of utter starvation,
he ended his life with poison.[1]

The episode is also mentioned by Martial, who adds a touch of detail: it was
with his final draught of wine that the poison was consumed.[2]

Intriguing as these stories about Apicius are, they do not really help us
understand the work that bears his name. There are some oblique references to
an 'Apicius' as a figure of mythic status in Martial and Juvenal, who refers to
him ironically. Describing the excesses of his own day, he wrote, 'we see many
things which that poor miser Apicius did not do'. The *scholia* on these verses,
which is undated but probably late, reads, 'Apicius was the author of how to
arrange dinners, who wrote about sauces: for he was the exemplar of a glutton'.
Later, Juvenal makes the point that 'the common people find nothing funnier
than a poor Apicius'.[3]

As we have seen, Seneca preserves a tradition that Apicius was the origin
of teaching, a *disciplina*, though he makes no mention of a book. The phrase
'Apicius who proclaimed the science of the *popina* and inflicted a generation
with his doctrine' is obscure, but we have a good idea what kind of teaching
Apicius would have given from our survey of earlier cookery books. The culinary
theory recorded in Pliny and satirized by Horace would, we think, illustrate it
well, and it is not difficult to imagine Apicius lecturing on his favourite topic.
He was allegedly able to influence the eating habits of the imperial family, and

---

[1] Seneca, *Ad Helviam* 10.8-9.
[2] Martial 3.22.
[3] Juvenal 4.22-3, and *Scholia* ad loc.; 11.2-3; Martial 2.29.3, 2.89.5, 10.73.1-4.

this suggests that he may have spoken publicly. Certainly, at his own banquets, guests would have been very well informed about what they were eating. A number of references in Pliny suggest that Apicius was interested in exactly the same kind of theory as the Philosopher and the Host in Horace's *Satires* 2.4 and 2.8. 'Marcus Apicius, who was born to conjure up every kind of luxury, thought it exceptionally good for mullet to be killed in a garum of their own kind' (*HN.* 9.66). 'Apicius, the deepest abyss of all the prodigals, taught that flamingo's tongue has superb flavour' (*HN.* 10.133). 'Soda retains their (cabbages') green-ness even during cooking, as in the Apician method of cooking them, where they are marinaded in oil and salt before being cooked' (*HN.* 19.143). 'We should also mention the treatment of sows' livers as if they were goose livers discovered by Marcus Gavius' (*HN.* 8.209). Apicius was long dead when Pliny was writing, and it is therefore likely that he obtained these ideas from secondary sources, perhaps the grammarian Apion or another unknown writer. We cannot assume that only one book containing Apician ideas was written.

Greek and Roman medical writing.

As a genre, medical writing resembles the culinary theory espoused by the gourmet, in that the technical medical knowledge of remedies was held in the hands of slaves and freedmen, while the theory of dietetics was a more respectable form of study. Medical writing may also be compared with culinary writing in that the store of knowledge was largely Greek, and there were no entirely Latin works of repute. Food was central to medical theory, and a doctor was expected to understand all about food and its effects on the body from a practical as well as a theoretical standpoint. Galen, the foremost medical writer, said, 'I do not consider it right for doctors to be completely ignorant of the art of cooking, because whatever tastes good is easier to digest'.[1] He implied that some doctors knew very little about cooking and did not necessarily understand how to make their prescriptions at all or make them palatable. The doctor, like the *mageiros,* was respectable in the Greek East, but in Rome his role was frequently taken by freedmen or slaves, and a free doctor rarely rose to prominence. Galen rose to eminence as a Greek doctor, but he was the exception. Physicians often worked

[1] See M. Grant, *Galen on Food and Diet* (London, 2000), p. 131.

as surgeons too, and were to some extent tainted with the slur of physical labour. A doctor who was a slave or freedman may well have had practical experience of preparing remedies and cures himself, as well as administering them. Doctors of higher standing would have had slaves to prepare the remedies for them and, as we shall see, the same was true of veterinarians.

In the ancient world, treatments involved a strict diet of particular foods prescribed by physicians who understood the body in terms of the four humours and the four qualities.[1] The majority of dietetic writing describes foods in terms of their particular qualities and therefore their effect on the humours and on the body. Food is only really recognized for its ability to loosen or bind the bowels, promote or restrict urination and whether it warms, cools, moistens or dries the body. That it gives pleasure is of no consequence.

The key authority is Galen, a Greek writing in Rome in the mid-second century AD. He had some status and respect within his field but would still have been viewed as 'inferior' because of his trade. In his work *On the Properties of Food*, each item of produce is described in detail; if a recipe can be extracted, it is in the simplest of terms with a very few ingredients. Food eaten as a cure required that the items administered should be unadorned and even eaten separately. There is little possibility that elaborate or composite dishes, similar to those found in *Apicius*, might be included in these books. Galen made it quite clear that he had no time for cooks: 'The common habit of cooks is to use unsuitable seasonings in large quantities'. He also thought cooks caused indigestion and that they made *tisana* – the barley soup which served as a ubiquitous cure-all – very badly.[2]

The straightforward recipes, such as those in the vegetable section (Book 3) of *Apicius*, have the language and laconic style of a cook, not a doctor: doctors seem prone to write three lines when one word from a cook would do. There are, however, a number of recipes in *Apicius* that have been attributed to a dietetic or medical recipe book because of specific reference to the health benefits of the finished dish and the inclusion of quantities. 1.27 lists *sales conditos ad multa*, 'multi-purpose salt preparations' that prevent disease, plague and all chills; 1.32 describes *oxyporum*, a fast-acting digestive; 1.34 *oxygarum digestibilem*, 3.2.1-5

[1] These were 'blood, phlegm, black bile, and yellow bile', 'and hot, cold wet and dry': Grant, op. cit., pp. 15-36, 68-78.

[2] Grant, op. cit., pp. 44, 87, 180. The lack of a clear link between the *Apicius* text and dietetic cookery books does not preclude the possibility of cooks from working with doctors, which they surely did.

pulmentarium ad uentrem, (easily-digested relishes); 3.18.2 gives the recipe for another *oxyporum*. Similar recipes are found in medical literature, such as Galen or Oribasius, but we also find parallels in agricultural manuals, offering guidance on practical home medicine to practise on slaves and farm hands as well as on animals.[1] There is no other evidence, apart from the recipes themselves, that these remedies came from a specific dietetic or medical book. They are few in number and starkly different from the majority of recipes in *Apicius*, which are at least meant to be indulgent and, as a result, unhealthy in the eyes of the doctor. These quasi-medical recipes may have been added at a late date in the evolution of the *Apicius* book when its high-status, luxury image had changed.

Reference should also be made to Anthimus, whose work 'On the observance of food' was written in the sixth century AD in Gaul and is quite rightly referred to by Grant as the first French cookery book.[2] As a doctor he wrote to inform Theuderic the king of the Franks what was best to eat to stay healthy. It contains a few recipes of interest which may be defined as early medieval rather then Roman, though there are similarities to some recipes in the *Excerpta Vinidarii*.[3]

The late imperial Greek writer Oribasius collected medical texts, including Galen, and has among his writings a simple recipe for cabbage which is attributed to Mnesitheus of Cyzicus, a fourth-century BC medical writer from Athens.[4] The recipe proposes serving cabbage with coriander, rue, honey, vinegar and *silphium*. It is reproduced almost ingredient-for-ingredient in Cato (but with salt and no *silphium*). A third version is recorded by Pliny the Elder, where mint and the *silphium* root are added.[5] Pliny recommends it for particular ailments such as headache and dimness of the eyes, and for the spleen and stomach. It is clear this dietetic prescription has been passed from writer to writer down the ages, first appearing in the fourth century BC, when it may have originated under the teachings of Pythagoras, and surviving into the fourth century AD. This unique example shows how recipes could be copied and re-copied by each generation without giving any credit to the original source. It is reasonable to expect a

---

[1] See Dalby, *Food in the Ancient World*, pp. 116-7, 'Digestives', and also Dioscorides, *MM*. 3.51.3; Cato, *De agricultura* 151,76, 77; Columella 12.59.4-5.

[2] Grant, op. cit., back cover.

[3] See above, p. 32.

[4] Oribasius 4.4.1, writing *c.* AD 350. See M. Grant, *Dieting For An Emperor* (Leiden, 1997), pp. 300-3.

[5] Cato, *De agricultura* 157.7, Pliny, *HN.* 20.80.

similar pattern to occur in non-medical cookery books. However, although there are numerous cabbage recipes in *Apicius*, none corresponds exactly to that ascribed to Mnesitheus. Coriander and rue are deployed, but with the addition of *liquamen,* oil, wine and cumin. (It should be noted that the combination of coriander, rue and the *oxymel* is outstandingly good and it is not surprising the recipe survived so well.)

Veterinary texts.

A number of Greek (and, subsequently, Roman) writers concerned themselves with the properties of food, their medicinal and digestive benefits for veterinary medicine as well as human. The veterinary texts that survive have much in common with culinary recipe books: remedies for treating horses and cattle are recorded in a very similar style, with the same basic preparation techniques. The recipes may be written out in full with a title, indication of condition treated, list of ingredients and method. Recipes that survive as simple lists with no other detail are also common and mirror those found in *Apicius*. A major difference between culinary recipes and veterinary remedies is the presence of precise quantities and also the presence of a narrative in the veterinary texts that survive. The remedies are worthless without the accompanying detail about application, and precise quantities are essential for the remedies to be effective. However, the veterinary texts themselves were copied and preserved in the same informal way as the recipe books: remedies were added or taken away at the whim of the collector/copier. There is no reason why a collection of remedies under one man's name should be preserved intact or that other remedies could not have been added. The collection evolved over many years and no 'original' selection of recipes can be identified. We can also see that the Latin authors of the veterinary works that have come down to us were dependent for much of their scientific knowledge on Greek originals which do not survive. These authors were also high-status and, like the gourmet, they lacked any real or substantial empirical knowledge of their subject.

The veterinary writers whose works survive largely date to the late fourth century AD. There are three key Latin writers: Pelagonius, Vegetius and the author of *Mulomedicina Chironis*. We can gain little from the latter as its MSS are corrupt and the writer unknown. Vegetius' text is largely made up of material taken from the other two. A stud owner, he was of the same social class as his clients, the race-horse owners who consulted him. He made a point of searching the material available to find suitable treatments for his friends because the so-called professional *ueterinarii* were apparently untrustworthy slaves who were also scarce and poorly trained.[1] Vegetius was also asked by his friends to look through the literature for remedies for oxen to be passed on to the herdsman by the estate owner.[2]

Pelagonius was of the same class as Vegetius and set himself up as a kind of consultant in imitation of his source, the Greek veterinary writer Apsyrtus, who was a horse-doctor of some repute. Apsyrtus was consulted by letter and the replies, imitated by Pelagonius, constitute the format of his work: a letter, often addressed to a named person, offering advice and a remedy. Adams has pointed out that Pelagonius' skill is limited: he is ignorant of the internal organs of a horse and also displays a vagueness about anatomy generally. 'He is the sort of literary layman who might have found remedies in earlier handbooks while not necessarily performing treatments himself.'[3] Vets were largely of low status and were looked upon with scorn. The majority were freedmen or slaves, and many worked in the imperial cavalry.[4] Vegetius asserts that the profession is short on dignity and that honest good intelligent men will not take up the job as it is base and vile.[5] The private horse-owner, as we have seen above, did not trust the *mulomedici* and sought information from the texts themselves.

Evidence for the process by which remedies were collected and stored by individuals is a little better illustrated in the veterinary literature than it is for culinary texts. Pliny recounts that Cato recommended that the *uilicus* or 'estate manager' should hold copies of remedies to treat the whole household, that is, both slaves and animals.[6] One imagines these remedies writen on papyrus or even wooden sheets not unlike the Vindolanda tablets. One can also imagine

---

[1] For the status of vets, see J. N. Adams, *Pelagonius and Latin Veterinary Terminology in the Roman Empire* (Leiden, 1995), pp. 1-65 and Chapter 9 (epilogue), pp. 662-71. Subsequent footnotes in this section will amply demonstrate our indebtedness to Dr Adams' penetrating study.

[2] Vegetius 1. prol. 2.

[3] Adams, *Pelagonius*, p. 663.

[4] Inscriptions suggest that freedmen and public slaves worked for the army as *ueterinarii*: *CIL* v 2183, iii 11215.

[5] Vegetius 1. prol. 2.

[6] Pliny, *HN*. 2.9.15. Varro also recommends that the head herdsman should keep written records, *RR*. 2.7.16

the collection of remedies being kept and stored side by side with the other essential recipes for an estate, such as the cakes, relishes and other food items. The distinction between recipe as 'remedy' and recipe as 'food' was very narrow, as was the distinction between veterinary and human remedies.

Roman cooks and their recipes.

Cooks in Roman society were very different characters from the Greek *mageiroi*. They were slaves or freedmen, and as a result far less able to determine their life choices. We have a very limited picture of their existence as they rarely speak to us directly: they are seen through the eyes of poets and prose writers who are the observers of Roman dining habits. The cook is the butt of jokes, and is often a whipping boy, but never, it seems, the source of any of the culinary knowledge flaunted in Roman dining-rooms, for which the *mageiros* was famous. Perhaps the cook was never consulted, or even seen as possessing the kind of knowledge that gourmets wanted. In Roman society the cook was destined never to achieve the same literary success as his Greek counterpart. We have no names of fame or notoriety, and at no time do we hear that cookery books or recipe collections existed in a particular Roman cook's name.[1] Writing works of note or quality required time, economic security and (if the work was to sell) a reputation, all of which even a successful cook who was a freedman would find difficult to achieve. It was the slave culture in Rome which kept cooks hidden and silent. The process of training produced skilled *opsopoioi*, 'food processors'. They might have no inclination to write themselves, even if literate, beyond the crucial recording of recipes. Nor would they know or care where the fish was caught, how rare it was or whether the apples were picked under a full moon! Such things are largely irrelevant so long as the produce is fresh. It seems that the Roman gourmet (and Apicius has to be included) is the true inheritor of this aspect of the *mageiros*' skill.

Cicero puts cooks firmly in their place when he says: 'Now we have by and large been taught these points about which trades and occupations are to be thought decent and which ones are disgraceful: those trades are to be thought

---

[1] But see above, p. 46 n. 3, for the named Greek cooks Ocha and Dionysodorus, allegedly commemorated with statues by Lepidus.

least proper which are the servants of physical pleasure: fishmongers, butchers, cooks, poultry-men, fishermen, … add to these if you like perfume-sellers, dancers, and the whole entertainment industry.'[1] There is a conflict between the slavish nature of a cook's actual work and the luxurious results. Kitchens were dirty, sooty places. The cook would smell badly of smoke and grease most of the time, while the physical work was strenuous, dangerous and, if full-scale banquets were expected each night, exhausting. Yet the slave-cook was expected to play a part in a theatre of a most elaborate kind, producing impressive dishes that were expected to taste as good as they looked.[2] Martial's Saturnalia gifts included a cook, and his comments suggested he recognized this dichotomy:

> *A cook*
> Mere skill is not sufficient for a cook. I do not want to be a slave to his palate: a cook ought to have his master's taste.[3]

The comedies of Plautus use a mixture of Greek and Roman ideas, as we have seen.[4] Plautus purposely mixes up the character of a *mageiros* and a Roman slave-cook to enhance the humour. The dominant feature of a *mageiros* is his independence and arrogance, features not normally associated with slavery. Lowe has identified the characteristics that are Roman rather than Greek in these Plautine cooks; they appear to have a propensity to violence, especially associated with the knife they always carry, which is rarely or never seen in the Greek models, and they have a reputation for stealing, which may be associated with household slaves in general.[5] At this time the Roman cook was, as we have seen, a slave who happened to cook rather than one with great skill or repute. Livy tells us that cooks were 'for the men of old the cheapest slave to purchase by valuation and in practice'. The change came in the early second century when a new interest in cooking overtook Rome after the army (and Romans in general) were affected by the influx of wealth and luxury from the East. Cooks 'became

---

[1] Cicero, *De off.* 1.150.

[2] A story is told that Cicero and Pompey invited themselves to Lucullus' villa in order to see what he ate when he did not expect guests. A secret code allowed him to tell the slaves in the kitchen that in a few hours he expected a meal worth 200,000 *sestertii*: Plutarch, *Lucullus* 41.4-7.

[3] Martial 14.220.

[4] See above, pp. 47-48.

[5] J. C. B. Lowe, 'Cooks in Plautus', *Classical Antiquity* 4 (1985), pp. 72-102.

an expensive commodity and what had been a slavish occupation began to be thought of as a skilled one'.[1]

A Roman household needed a certain number of domestic slaves to function well and to be seen as socially acceptable. Cicero shows us in what contempt Romans who failed to provide the correct standard were held: 'In his house (L. Calpurnius Piso) nothing is praiseworthy, elegant or refined: to his credit, nothing there cost very much – apart from his appetites! … grubby slaves wait at table, some of them even elderly; one man is both cook and doorkeeper; no domestic baker, no cellarman, but bread from the barrow and wine from the barrel.'[2] Juvenal, writing some 150 years later, suggests that having a baker, a head cook and no doubt various under-cooks, as well as specially trained carvers to present the food, were essential requirements. Their master whipped them regularly and they spread rumours about him to avenge this treatment.[3] Cooks, as slaves, were often liable to be whipped and abused by their owner. In the *Satyricon* by Petronius, the cook is involved with a mock whipping as it seems he has not gutted the boar before cooking. In fact it was full of sausages, but we are left with the distinct impression that such a whipping was normal. Martial also highlights this phenomenon:

I seem savage to you, Rusticus, and far too gluttonous because I beat the cook on account of the dinner. If that seems like trivial grounds for whipping to you, on what grounds do you want the cook to be whipped?

You say the hare's not cooked and demand the whip. Rufus, you'd rather cleave the cook than the hare.[4]

---

[1] Livy 39.6.7-9.

[2] Cicero, *In Pisonem* 67.

[3] Juvenal 9.107-19. Even Cicero has spare cooks about him to send to Tiro, his soon-to-be-manumitted slave: Cicero, *Ad fam.* 16.15.2. Pliny raises a debate (*HN.* 18.107-8) concerning the origin of the bakers in Roman households. We are told that early bakers were in fact millers, and that women made bread in poor households while the cook would do it in the rich ones. The bakers who sold bread to city-dwellers without the facilities to make their own came into being in the early second century BC.

[4] Martial 8.23, 3.9.

It is possible that the gourmet entered the kitchen and flaunted his knowledge to the cook. It is equally likely that the gourmet's cook had a pretty difficult time. In Ausonius' poem which follows, the barrier between cook and master is obvious, even in the rather gentle and playful relationship that is depicted:

> *The time for giving the cook his instructions*
> Sosia, lunch must be served. The sun is already warming all the fourth hour, and the shadow is bent to the fifth mark. Are the seasoned relishes nice and juicy? Do they taste piquant? They have a habit of fooling you! Check them. Try them out. Twirl your hand and stir the seething pots, quickly dip your finger in the hot sauce, which your salivating tongue darts out to lick, trembling.[1]

For Martial, culinary activity is more distant – and sordid:

> Whose present do you want to become, little book? Hurry up and get yourself a claimant, or swiftly snatched off into a dirty kitchen you'll wrap up baby tuna with your sodden papyrus, or you'll be a bag for incense or pepper.[2]

The price of cooks was a controversial subject for some Romans, serving as a marker to indicate just how decadent things had become. Pliny the Elder reflects that the price of a mullet 'makes the mind wander to thinking of those men who, in sounding off about excess, used to complain that individual cooks were being bought for more money than horses; but now cooks are got ready (for sale) at a price of three of these (horses), and a fish for the price of three cooks, and practically no man alive is valued at a higher price than one who can with the utmost skill plunge his master's account into the red.'[3] A cook who was also a freedman was able to hire himself to the historian Sallust at a cost of 100,000 *sestertii*. This is presumably a yearly fee for his services and it is not clear whether he took the whole fee or if, in the normal way, his patron – the man who freed him – took the bulk of it.[4]

---

[1] Ausonius, *Ephemeris* 6.
[2] Martial 3.2.-5.
[3] Pliny, *HN.* 9.31.
[4] Porphyrion, *scholiast* on Horace, *Satires* 1.1.101. The cook was called Damam.

Lowe has raised some doubt whether cooks were available for hire in Rome at all. He believes that when Pliny says Romans 'did not have cooks as slaves either and used to hire them in the meat market' he was basing this entirely on this scenario in Plautus' plays.[1] Lowe believes that, because the cooks were not free *mageiroi*, they could not hire themselves or be hired out when and if they were needed. Pliny meant 'skilled cooks' here, but even so we are less inclined to accept Lowe's interpretation and see a more fluid and spontaneous situation arising in Rome which incorporated elements of the Greek system. If the demand for skilled cooks was high from the mid-150s BC, and it appears to have been, then hiring out trusted slaves seems perfectly feasible.

In Athenaeus the whole question of slave versus free cooks is discussed at some length, and the issue of whether a slave-cook could be free to come and go is raised in a play written by Posidippus, who happened to be the first playwright to introduce slave-cooks in 289 BC. In the play, a cook is challenged over his status as he was out of doors, and he replies that he works for another cook who hires him out from the market.[2] Lowe's objection revolves around the perceived freedom of a *mageiros* contrasted with the lack of freedom of a slave, but the latter seems able to work in a hired capacity at his owner's bidding, without supervision, and still be a slave. This scenario is feasible for Rome. An inscription from Falerii, just north of Rome and dated probably to the second century BC, refers to some Faliscan cooks who displayed considerable pride in their work and an independence of spirit which is not generally seen or expected from slaves:

A guild which is welcome for spending its life (in the production of) sumptuous dishes for pleasant living and festal days, who with their delicious skills and with the help of Vulcan enhance banquets and games again and again; the cooks have given this to their highest commanders, so that they may willingly give them the good aid they desire.[3]

The 'highest commanders' (*summis imperatoribus*) seem to be the deities Jupiter, Juno and Minerva, to whom the tablet is dedicated on its reverse, though

---

[1] Lowe, 'Cooks in Plautus', p. 79; Pliny, *HN.* 18.107-8.
[2] Athenaeus 659d.
[3] *CIL* 1.2.364; *Remains of Old Latin* I.151.

this has been questioned.[1] Alternatively it might refer to the cooks' potential clients, who as high-status men were connected to the army as a matter of course and so might be termed 'commanders'. One assumes that at this time the cooks were probably slaves, but they do seem to have had many different opportunities to 'enhance banquets and games' and this in turn suggests that they were either able to take their skills to different places or that numerous holders of banquets came to them. A plausible scenario for both free and slave occupation here would be that the controllers of this guild were freedmen, while the majority of cooks were slaves. We imagine a temple and arena combined, akin to a modern leisure centre, for such a guild to ply its trade. Another inscription concerning cooks is a *collegium* of slave-cooks from Praenesti who define themselves as *coques atrienses*, 'cooks of the *atria* or hall'. This is almost certainly a temple precinct.[2] The Romans traditionally dined in their *atria*, which we term 'curial dining halls'. The feasts they held there were meant to be frugal, to represent a simple and uncorrupted past, but these inscriptions suggest more elaborate food.[3]

The process of hiring cooks would most likely have taken place in the market place, as described by Plautus, though the reference to a *forum coquinum* might be a literary conceit, or just the place where all kinds of labour were hired.[4] We also find an indication of the existence of hired catering staff in the following from Juvenal: 'no matter what size the house, someone will come to arrange the dishes properly and someone will come who seasons the delicacies'.[5] Lowe gives little credence to these lines, and suggests that Juvenal is referring to either a long-term hire or to a slave purchase.[6] A far more easy-going attitude to slave-cooks is found in Apuleius' *Metamorphoses*, written *c.* AD 160. In this tale, a Roman master who travels the country on business takes with him his slave-cook and baker; they are brothers and share lodgings near where their master is housed. Their kitchen is portable: their equipment and some form of cooking platform is carried on the donkey (the hero of the story) and they prepare

---

[1] Lowe, 'Cooks in Plautus', p. 82 and n. 75.

[2] *Remains of Old Latin* I.145.

[3] Servius on *Aen.* 1.726; Livy 39.44.7; Dionysius of Halicarnassus 11.23

[4] See Plautus, *Pseudolus* 790 for the *forum coquinum* that is contrasted with a *furinum forum* or 'market for thieves', in order to accentuate the untrustworthy nature of cooks at Rome.

[5] Juvenal 7.184.

[6] Lowe, 'Cooks in Plautus', p. 80.

their master's dinner each night before retiring to their own separate lodgings to consume all the leftovers. Not a bad life![1]

The system of training for cooks that we found in the third century BC in Greece appears to have been a kind of apprenticeship. A *mageiros* would take fees for training relatively small numbers of cooks. As mentioned above, Posidippus' evidence indicates that in the third century BC, slave-cooks began to be used in Greece more often: the Macedonians are said to have begun the practice.[2] *Mageiroi* owned their own slaves, Posidippus confirms, and it is likely that they were continuously training slaves for re-sale. Young boys were taught on the job as kitchen hands and under-cooks until they were skilled, at which time they might be sold on. Cato encouraged his own household slaves to purchase boys in order to train them and sell them on. Their particular skills are not mentioned, and were more likely to be general household duties, but the principle was well established.[3] The frugal Atticus, Cicero's regular correspondent, had a similar attitude to his slaves, who had all been trained within his own household.[4] There is no evidence of larger schools of a more permanent nature in the Republican period and it is impossible to prove beyond doubt that they existed in the empire, though the existence of slave schools for *some* types of catering services at the height of the craze for elegant dining is clear. Juvenal recounts the elaborate system in place in the 70s AD for the training of *carptores*, 'carvers', those who have to present the meat to the guests. The teacher is named as Trypherus, and his disciples learn to carve various kinds of cooked meat such as antelope, flamingo, gazelle and wild boar, albeit with blunt knives and with elm-wood models which must have come apart like a three-dimensional jigsaw.[5] Much later, in *c.* AD 200, Tertullian suggested that a cookery school existed named after the great man himself, though it is possible that Tertullian was speaking generally of the whole idea of good food being named after Apicius, rather than of a specific school at Rome.[6] There were certainly *collegia* of schools in Rome: one inscription makes specific reference to the *collegium cocorum Caesaris* and names one Titus Aelius Mitiuus, a freedman and *archimagirus* (head chef).[7]

---

[1] Apuleius, *Metamorphoses* 10.13-14. Another cook in the story has a wife and child with him as he works, but is so in fear of his master that he attempts to take his own life when the dinner is stolen by a dog.

[2] See above, pp. 67-68.

[3] Plutarch, *Cato* 21.

[4] Nepos, *Atticus* 13.4.

[5] Juvenal 11. 136.

[6] Tertullian, *Apologia* 3.6; see Appendix 4.

[7] *CIL* VI.2 no. 8750.

If cookery schools existed, it is likely that they developed recipes as well as made collections of useful materials. The guilds mentioned above might also be sources of original recipes. It is in such places that private collections, on papyrus or wooden leaves, could have been gathered together for the first time into a book. We think that some of the recipes in *Apicius* may have been developed in such schools. The language of cooks speaking to cooks via their recipes can be difficult to decipher if you are not 'in the know'. Aspects of techniques that would be familiar to a Roman cook are simply left out, as it is assumed that the reader knows what to do. There would have been no need to be precise about quantity or method, as cooks would understand what level of a particular ingredient to use in relation to another. We therefore believe that those recipes in the format of a plain list are more likely to be cook-to-cook recipes, that Roman cooks shared recipes in this format, and that this is the origin of the list-recipes throughout *Apicius*. Those others that have detailed methods and precise quantities in them may well have begun life as simple lists but, in order for the recipe to be included in a cookery book that might be read by a more general readership, they have been extended. On the other hand, they may simply represent a different strand of recipe-writing, in which more complex detail and instruction were the norm.

We lack precise information on the process by which ancient cookbooks were formed, but it is worth pausing to look at how recipe collections could have been made and how they were added to the general cookbooks that the dilettante was able to write. At the earliest stage, as with agricultural recipes, a temporary record may have been made on sheets of papyrus, or perhaps on thin slivers of wood. Once a dish had been accepted and deemed successful, a good copy might be made and stored among the other recipes held by the cook. These would be a mixture of his own ideas and those of his friends and colleagues, as well as long-standing recipes from books that the cook or the household might own. If the recipes were written on separate sheets, the new ones could have been inserted 'approximately' in the right place – and may easily have been misplaced after use or lending. If added to a scroll, they may have been attached as extra leaves, and subsequent copying would have led to their incorporation – possibly not in the 'ideal' place.

We can imagine Cicero's cook going to the house of Hirtius to speak to his cook in order to discover what dishes he was expected to copy at his master's dinner.[1] The recipe collection of a cook with a great reputation for his food would have been desirable knowledge, though a slave-cook, no matter how great his reputation in the household, would not have the status to be able to publish a cookery book. Writers such as Gaius Matius, who had the leisure to write and the status to publish, might well have sought out the collections of well-known cooks to add to their literary excurses on gastronomy. It is also possible that recipe collections could have been published (in the sense that they were made available to a wider audience) by the cookery schools themselves. Given the number of households in Rome itself (let alone in Italy and in the provinces), there may have been a large number of recipe collections in existence, each with its own peculiarities and with numerous individual additions and repetitions; it is more than likely that *Apicius* represents a single strand of this very diverse and organic tradition.

Conclusion.

In the pre-Roman period we have identified three types of Greek food writer in whose work recipes could be found: the gourmet poet such as Archestratus, the gourmet dilettante such as Paxamus, and the skilled cook such as Sophon. Some form of recipes can appear in all three types of book, though it is likely that the cook was ultimately responsible for most if not all of the recipes that we find. In this period we saw that the *mageiroi* had some status and respect in Greek society. They were responsible for the actual cooking and they also possessed the knowledge of how to eat well: 'To have a grasp of location, occasion, host, yes and the dinner too! What fish and when he should buy it, that's not for anybody'.[2] They published general cookery books in their own right and displayed a confidence and self-assurance in their field.

The gourmet in Greek society also wrote cookery books, alongside and no doubt in conjunction with cooks. It was possible for a rich gourmet and writer of poetry or prose to wield the *teganon* – frying-pan – without incurring particular sanction and to develop recipes as a result, but the main source of recipes was the person who makes the food. The culinary knowledge in the form of recipes was devised by the producer – the cook – but he was also able to take credit for

[1] See above, p. 52 n. 2.
[2] Athenaeus 405a.

and publish that knowledge in his own right. Empirical scientific knowledge of all kinds, whether culinary, medicinal or veterinarian, was recognized for its intrinsic worth. Those that possessed it were accorded respect and status.

In the Roman period, the nature of slavery governed all aspects of the work economy, and domestic activity that involved physical effort was deemed unworthy, no matter how valuable. The source of knowledge associated with technical and scientific skills continued to be Greek and was divided into 'acceptable' and 'unacceptable' forms. High-status writers could collect, disseminate and even advise in veterinary and human medicine, but the production and application of the remedies were not acceptable, and were left in the hands of slaves and freedmen. This separation of knowledge into the practical and theoretical in a veterinary context led to an inadequate and inferior service for the animal owner. In relation to cookery, it resulted in a division of the skills of the *mageiros*. The practical remained with the slave-cook, who was no more than an *opsopoios* or 'food processor'. His appreciation of the art of dining with the associated culinary theory was taken up by the wealthy gourmet. This knowledge was controlled and disseminated by the wealthy in the form of books about food rather than recipe books. At the end of the Roman empire, the large body of literature written about food by dilettante culinary theorists did not survive, but a recipe book written by slave-cooks did, and one can only speculate that ultimately their practical skills may have been recognized as the more valuable.

3. COOKING TECHNIQUES IN THE ANCIENT WORLD

Our knowledge of high-status Roman kitchens is largely dependent on the extensive remains at Pompeii and Herculaneum. The kitchen could be a room within the house, as we find in the House of the Vettii, or constructed as an open-sided lean-to against an inner courtyard wall. This type of structure seems to have been the most common, but it was also the most readily destroyed as the walls and roof were less durable. A semi-outdoor kitchen was also essential if you were going to make use of the more energy-efficient heat from wood in ovens and under large *dolia*: the smoke would be able to drift up and away from the living quarters and the rest of the house. We hear from a Greek cook as early as the fourth century BC that kitchens needed designing with precision:

> To lay out the kitchen correctly, to have it receive all the light it should, to understand where the draught of air comes from, have great importance in promoting the business. Whether the smoke is carried this way or the other is apt to make some difference to the dishes.[1]

The kitchen in the House of the Vettii is very small, and is surrounded by other private rooms which are decorated with scenes of a sexual nature. There is little evidence of an efficient draught system and it is unlikely that a wood fire was used in so enclosed an environment. Charcoal would have been less obviously polluting, though fumes could build up and cause considerably more health problems than wood smoke. This particular kitchen may have only been used to re-heat food and wine. Snacks and light meals may have been brought in, as the kitchen itself is too small for elaborate cooking.

The cooking area proper was a large platform of masonry built against a wall and sometimes stretching from one side of the room to the other. The surface of the hearth was not just for cooking; food could be prepared there and equipment stored. In one kitchen in Herculaneum an integral oven is fixed at the corner of an L-shaped platform (fig. 1).[2] Below the cooking shelf, the masonry is formed

---

[1] Athenaeus 378d.

[2] The kitchen in the 'House of the two Atria' of Moderatus and Sabinus. (VI 28,29): see V. Catalano, *Case Abitanti e Culti Di Ercolano* (Bardi Editore, Roma, 2002), plate 25.

Figure 1. An artist's reconstruction of the kitchen in the 'House of the Two Atria' of Modestus and Sabinus (VI.28,29), Herculaneum.

into an arch, which was used for storing wood and/or charcoal. At no time was this space ever used as an oven. Apart from an oven on the platform itself, the cook might have access to other ovens – large enough even to take whole animals – built into the wall of the house. The literature suggests that whole roast boar was a fashionable component of an elaborate meal, but such a beast would need a very large oven or spit-roasting facilities, perhaps located outside in the kitchen garden. A wealthy household would also need separate bread ovens for the baker and pastry cook. A Roman tomb relief from Frascati depicts a large, free-standing circular masonry stand that would support a large pot (*dolium*); a fire would be raised beneath and continually stoked from below so that whole animals could be boiled.[1] Such a variety of permanent structures suggests a large kitchen area in high-status homes.

[1] Dalby and Grainger, *The Classical Cook Book*, p. 137.

It is now clear that various forms of portable hearths were available. In the artefact stores in Pompeii there are some very coarse ceramic hearths constructed of a flat base about 5-7 cm. thick and about 2 m. by 1 m., with raised sides to hold the coals or wood inside a 'box'.[1] At the rear of the structure are two or three brazier supports that are integral to the structure, with semi-circular wall supports allowing access to the space where the fire is raised. Bronze or ceramic pots sat on lugs at an ideal distance from the fire, while the box at the front is a small but adequate area to allow more delicate and intricate cooking with embers from a mature fire. Although these hearths are theoretically portable, it would not be easy to move them while in use and it is likely that they were used in a fixed position, raised off the floor on bricks. They would be suitable for a modest home, or even in the *insula* flats above the main buildings of a town. Similar fireboxes made of riveted and beaten steel stood on 15 cm. legs and had the same brazier structure at the rear of the box, so that sauces and stews could be cooked or re-heated over the fire. At the front, these boxes are quite deep, in contrast to the ceramic hearths, and are unsuitable for charcoal cooking or for the techniques using *cineres calidi* (hot embers). They may have been better designed for outdoor cooking in garden dining-rooms. These boxes were found during the earliest excavations of Pompeii, so that contextual evidence is absent.[2] They may not have been used for domestic cooking at all but for the more elaborate catering demanded by organizations such as trade guilds. 'Restaurants' of this nature (or at least extensive dining areas) are clearly to be seen in Ostia, where the *schola* of the guild of builders contains a central garden and fountain with a row of five separate dining-rooms, each with masonry *triclinia*, down one side.[3] The food on offer in these places would probably not be the usual *popina* menu – sausages with *puls* or meat and vegetable pasties – but dishes closer to those described in *Apicius*.

---

[1] See fig. 2 for an artist's impression; we have not yet been able to examine these items in detail.

[2] The firebox is illustrated in fig. 3. One of the boxes is in the National Museum of Naples, 121321; field M. 26145. Seneca, *Ep.* 78.23-24 describes a process of cooking at table which resembles modern *guéridon* service.

[3] R. Meiggs, *Roman Ostia* (Oxford, 1960), p. 324.

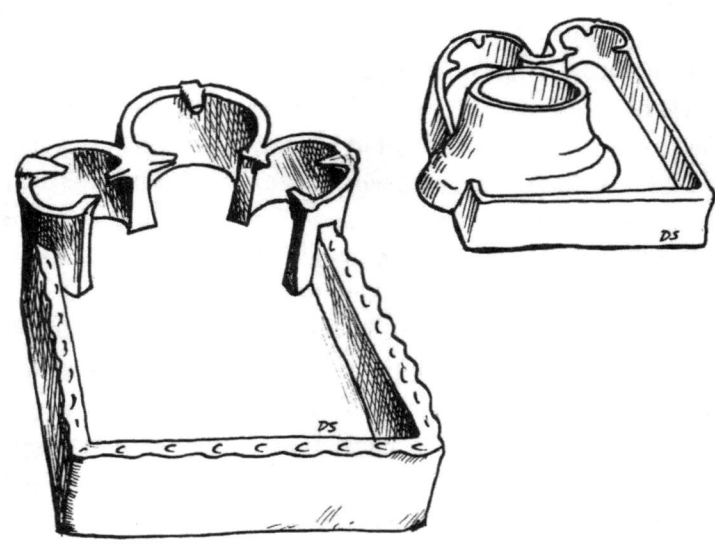

Figure 2 (above). An artist's impression of ceramic hearths from Pompeii.

Figure 3 (below). An artist's impression of a metal fire box from Pompeii.

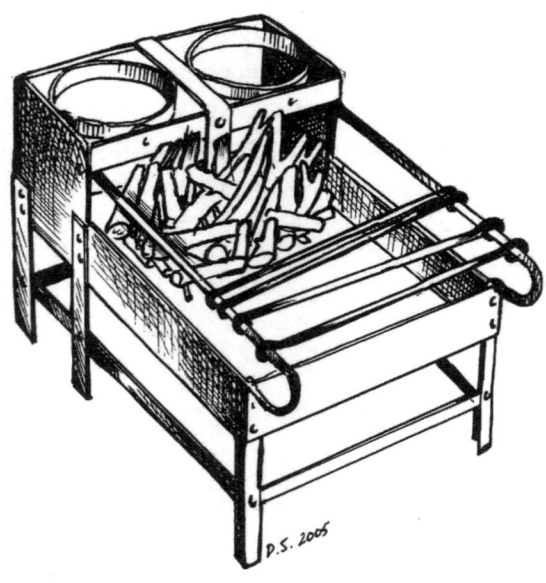

Wood or charcoal.

There are subtle differences in the quality of heat from a wood or charcoal fire, and therefore the kinds of dishes that can be cooked on them. Charcoal has the advantage of being light and easily transported into cities, but the heat it generates limits the kind of food that can be prepared. If you want to boil relatively large amounts of fluid rapidly (as in any recipes in *Apicius* Book 5 for pulses or the meat in Books 6 and 8), then a mature wood fire is essential.[1] This might be placed on the platform next to a charcoal fire (though the smoke would be hard to cope with indoors) or, in the case of a whole beast, raised under large *dolia*. Charcoal can be used to heat sauces gently and to cook delicate *patinae*. It will also hold food at a simmer after it has been brought to the boil on a wood fire. Charcoal can be used to grill or barbecue meat, and it could also fire the small portable ovens known as *testa* or *clibani* which are discussed later. There are numerous qualities and degrees of heat obtainable from a particular fire, and it takes considerable experience to 'read' the fire so that it provides the right amount of heat to cook the dish at the desired time. In a large household, where nine people (the traditional number accommodated in a *triclinium)* might dine in style every night, the cook would need much skill and judgment to cook and serve the hot dishes.

The recipes in *Apicius* have surprisingly few instructions for or descriptions of fires to help us to understand the cooking techniques required. The *conditum paradoxum* (spiced wine) in Book 1 uses a 'gentle fire of dry wood' to boil the cordial. A sauce is heated *lento igni* (on a gentle, lit. 'slow', fire) at 2.2.8 and a delicate *patina* is cooked likewise. A simple sauce for fish has the instruction *igni mollissimo calefacies* (bring it to heat on the gentlest of fires).

The heat from a fire is sometimes termed *uapor ignis*, which has been interpreted as steam by other commentators but should, in our opinion, rather be defined as the 'vapour' or indirect heat further or higher up from the fire bed. The difference between this kind of heat and a gentle fire is subtle and its occasional use may indicate particular styles of language or terminology used by regional schools of cookery rather than a distinct technique. The cooking liquor or *court*

---

[1] On different types of fire, cf. the detailed discussion in W. Rubel, *The Magic of Fire* (Berkeley CA, 2002*),* pp. 254-68.

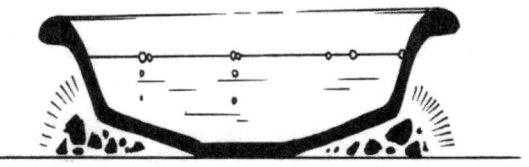

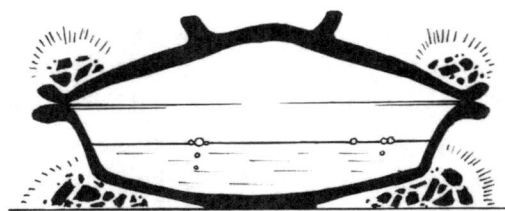

Figure 4 (top). A patina *buried in the hot embers. Drawing based on form 191.3 in Hayes, 1972.*

Figure 5 (middle). A patina *with hot embers on the top of the lid as well as below. Drawing based on the North African ware form 465 and 766 in Riley, 1979.*

Figure 6 (bottom). A patina *used on a trivet above the fire with a lid that functions as a* testum. *The flange keeps the coals high on the lid so that they generate heat into the air space. Drawing based on form 465 in Riley, 1979 and form 22.II.20 in S.L.Dyson, 'Cosa – The utilitarian pottery',* Memoirs of the American Academy at Rome *(1976), p. xxxiii.*

bouillon used to poach *isicia* (forcemeat) is placed *ad uaporem ignis* and a recipe for a fish *patina* also uses this term.[1]

Most cooking procedures involve cooking over a fire using a trivet or gridiron. The former is a support for a single pot, while the latter can hold more than one. Gridirons can have short legs, suitable for charcoal, or longer legs to fit over a wood fire at ground level. A *craticula* seems to be a particular kind of barbecue grid designed for grilling: liver, kidneys and lamb pieces are roasted on a *craticula*.[2] This device will also be used to finish cooking and to give colour to various meat items that have been pre-cooked. Many recipes use the term *subassare*, meaning 'grill or roast a little' and it would be on such a *craticula* that they would be cooked.[3]

Certain recipes in Book 4 of *Apicius* suggest that vessels were placed directly in the embers of a mature wood fire already used for other purposes. These could be the embers left over after heating a separate bread oven, or the remnants of a charcoal fire mixed with other embers. This technique requires that the fire has matured and the heat generated used to cook other dishes. The embers no longer produce flame – which would crack a ceramic vessel – but still put out considerable warmth. Embers in this state can also be used to bury a round-bellied pot full of liquid in a more primitive form of hearth cooking. The technique occurs at 4.2.4 for a horse-parsley *patina* cooked in a vessel of the same name. From the recipes, we can reliably infer that these vessels were shallow, low-sided ceramic or metal dishes that we can equate with oven-to-table ware. Archaeological finds suggest they had a curved wall with a relatively small base, allowing the dish to be pushed down into a bed of embers. Some of these vessels are found among the imported African red slip fabrics and their typical shape corresponds with form 191.3 in Hayes 1972 and in the local African form 469 in Riley 1979.[4] The fabric is a rough, coarse unslipped orange clay with natural or added lime, quartz and mica giving the vessel a granular texture. This additional material in the clay allows the vessel to take the thermal shock of

---

[1] *Isicia* 2.2.2; *patina* 4.2.12; see below for a detailed discussion, p. 93.

[2] 7.3.2; 7.8; 8.6.4.

[3] See below under *subassare*, p. 92.

[4] J. W. Hayes, *Late Roman Pottery* (British School at Rome, 1972); A. Riley, 'The Coarse Pottery', in J. A. Lloyd (ed.), *Excavations at Sidi Khrebish, Benghazi (Eerenice)* (Tripoli, 1979), vol. 2, pp. 91-467.

Figure 7 (above). A testum *with a loaf of bread inside. Experiments have resulted in temperatures of at least 400°F inside during the initial stages. Drawing based on form 2.6 in A.L. Cubberley et al.,* 'Testa *and* clibani: *The Baking Covers of Classical Italy', in* Papers of the British School at Rome *61 (1988), 98-119, at p. 105.*

Figure 8 (below). A testum *being used as an oven to cook meat. Form based on fig. 7.*

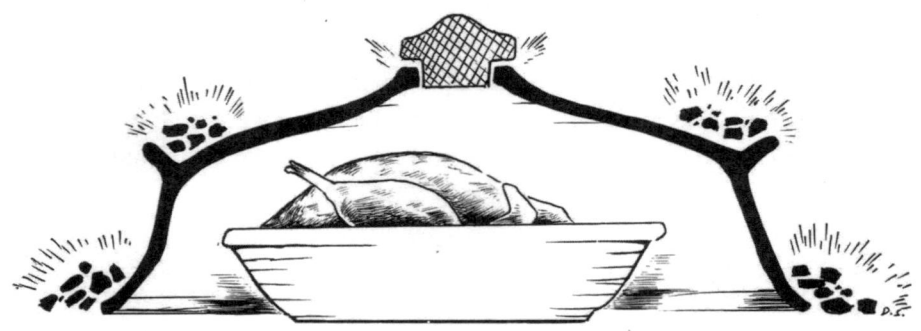

contact with the fire without breaking.[1] The shape is a standard late-Hellenistic form made and exported throughout the empire from the second century BC through to the second century AD.

In Book 4.2.33, a *patina* is cooked according to the instruction *in thermospodio pones, ac subtus supra thermospodium habeat* (put in the hot embers, let it have hot embers above and below).[2] We have ascertained that 'embers below' is a possible procedure with these *patina* vessels, but how would the embers be above as well? Form 191 in Hayes has a 'flat recessed band on the inside at the junction of the rim and wall to receive a lid'.[3] Lids occur in a similar fabric designed to fit these vessels in equal numbers and are form 192 in Hayes. They have a low domed shape with a plain rim and a large inverted foot which acts as a lifting knob (see figs. 4 and 5). The inside of this inverted foot is the ideal surface to place hot ashes, as is the rim. Some lids from local African ware even have a pronounced turned-up edge to the lid, preventing the ash from falling into the dish as it is lifted off.[4]

A recipe at 5.3.2 of *Apicius* has a dish called *pisam farsilem* (stuffed peas) which we translate as 'pease mould'. It is a form of terrine, in which mushy peas are interlayered with various kinds of meat and vegetables. It seems to be made in a vessel similar to but deeper than a *patina*. The finished article should be turned out. It is easier to turn it out of a dish with straight sides, allowing the cook

---

[1] This fabric is also fired at a relatively low temperature (estimated at 900°F rather than 1000°F+). This is indicated by its soft, easily-scratched surface. This soft fabric is less inclined to break in a fire as the clay particles are not fixed, as in harder fabrics, and are able to move as they are heated.

[2] Previous commentators have believed that the 'thermospodium' was a separate piece of equipment of some sort such as a hearth box, or a distinct kind of cooking oven. See A.L. Cubberley et al., '*Testa* and *clibani*: The Baking Covers of Classical Italy', in *Papers of the British School at Rome* 61 (1988), 98-119; A. Cubberley, 'Bread-baking in Ancient Italy: *clibanus* and *sub testu* in the Roman World', in *Food in Antiquity*, ed. J. Wilkins, D. Harvey, M. Dobson (Exeter, 1995), 55-68; J. Frayn, 'Home baking in Roman Italy', *Antiquity* 52 (1978), 57-157. *In thermospodio* is used interchangeably with *cineri calido*, 'hot embers,' in recipe 4.2.9; they are simply synonyms.

[3] Hayes, op. cit., p. 205.

[4] Lid with turned-up edge: D766 in Riley, 'The Coarse Pottery', 1979; many of these vessels and lids are discoloured grey or black on the outer surfaces and this is defined as damage caused by inadequate firing in the kiln. Replica vessels used to cook varicus *patinae* turn grey/black after being used in a distinctive manner that may indicate that the genuine vessels have been used in hot embers.

to start the process by loosening the cooked food with a knife-blade. Hence the cooking dish here is specified as *angularis*. To cook, it is either put in the oven or over a slow fire so that it sets *ad se deorsum* (from the top down). This term has been misunderstood by previous editors. In his French translation, André reversed the meaning and suggested that the pease mould would cook from the bottom up. The entire phrase was left out of their English translation by Flower and Rosenbaum. It is now clear that embers were placed on the lid so that the pease mould would cook downwards as well as by the heat rising from the fire beneath. In this case the *angularem* was placed on a trivet over a fire rather than in the embers (see fig. 6). This technique continued to be used in medieval and Renaissance cookery, for example to set and give colour to egg-based tarts that resembled *quiche*.[1]

Similar techniques were employed with the portable ovens known as *testa* and *clibani*. We understand these to be dome-shaped ceramic lids that functioned as ovens when hot coals or embers were placed on top.[2] Some forms of these ovens had a central hole which aids temperature control; this is confirmed in the literary evidence.[3] The *testum* was an oven for cooking individual loaves of bread or cakes. We see it in action in Cato's agricultural manual, where we are told that it is first heated on the hearth, the raw cake is placed on the hearth then covered with the *testum*, and hot charcoal is arranged on top and round the sides (see fig. 7).[4] In this recipe we are advised to lift the *testum* off to look at the cake two or three times, so we must assume that a hole is not always present. In *Apicius*, small items of meat are cooked in ovens called *clibani* and we assume these to be a similar kind of oven (see fig 8). Cubberley *et al.* have concluded that the difference between a *testum* and a *clibanus* is minimal: the terms are synonyms for portable dome-shaped ovens. The interchange of Greek and Latin in *Apicius* would seem to confirm this. There seem, however, to be different shapes and styles, and there is still controversy among archaeologists as to identification. Many finds that we would recognize as ovens are drawn upside

---

[1] Ballerini, *Art of Cooking*, p. 80.

[2] Cubberley *et al.*, '*Testa* and *clibani*'. See also Barbara Santich, '*Testo, Tegamo, Tiella, Tian*: The Mediterranean Camp Oven', in *The Cooking Pot: Proceedings of the Oxford Symposium on Food and Cookery 1998*, p. 139.

[3] Dioscorides, *De materia medica* 11.81;96.

[4] Cato, *De agricultura* 76.

down and identified as casseroles or, when drawn the right way up, as lids for which there is no companion vessel.[1]

As part of the background research for the present volume, we have replicated all the techniques described above using specially-commissioned vessels.[2]

4. ROMAN WEIGHTS AND MEASURES

We have always found the subject of ancient weights and measures perplexing, and suspect many readers of the various English translations of *Apicius* have felt the same.[3] In this section we therefore intend to try to work through the terminology to achieve some clarification. Many of the recipes appear to use quantities as precise terms, but there is no consistency and their meaning can be unpredictable. The ratio of one ingredient to another is more important than precise quantity when transmitting a recipe, particularly with liquids, and we find that this is often what the cook was trying to convey even when he used terms for specific quantities. Our policy has been to translate those terms that are both familar and precise such as the *sextarius* and the *hemina,* which we have rendered as 1 pint and ½ pint. Words such as *calix, acetabulum* and *cyathus* are often used to indicate a ratio rather than precise quantity and in this case they have been rendered as 'cup'. When they appear to refer to their specific quantity they have been left in Latin and the reader should refer to the table below.

The standard interpretation of the terminology used in the text is as follows:

---

[1] We identify form 196 in Hayes, op. cit., as a *testum/clibanus.* We also agree with Cubberley that form 23b in Hayes is another style of these ovens (Cubberley, op. cit., p. 114).

[2] For a more detailed analysis of the vocabulary of cooking techniques see below, p. 102.

[3] For a basic introduction to the topic, which addresses some (but not all) of the issues discussed here, see W.F. Richardson, *Numbering and Measuring in the Classical World: An Introductory Handbook* (Auckland, NZ, and Bristol, 1985; 2nd revised ed. Bristol, 2004).

Libra	12 ounces	323 grams[1]	
Vncia	1 ounce	27 grams	
Semuncia	½ ounce	13.5 grams	
Drachma	⅛ ounce	3.37 grams	
Scripulus	1/24 ounce	1.12 grams	
Amphora	48 sextarii	48 pints	25.9 litres
Sextarius	1 pint	0.539 litres	
Hemina	½ pint	0.269 litres	(12 fluid *uncia* = *libra*)
Quartarius		¼ pint	0.134 litres
Acetabulus*		⅛ pint	0.067 litres
Cyathus*	1/12 pint	0.045 litres	
Calix*	wine cup	unknown quantity	

The last three terms are those that interested us the most. An *acetabulum* is a Latin term for a cup or vessel originally used for vinegar, and as a result can mean any kind of cup-shaped vessel. It is also a precise measure of roughly 2 ½ fl. oz. It is used in both a precise and imprecise way in the recipes. At 2.2.5 a sauce called *hydrogarum* has a ratio of 1 part *liquamen* to 7 parts water using an *acetabulum* as a simple cup measure of no particular quantity. At 2.2.4 the unique reference to a *calix* is used in a similar way to make the same kind of sauce. A *calix* is a general term for a wine cup or goblet without any precise quantity. At 8.7.12 an *oenogarum simplex* of pepper, *liquamen* and wine is blended in an *acetabulus*, meaning simply a vessel. The term is used with more complexity at 6.8.4, where the recipe contrasts an *acetabulus maior* of oil with an *acetabulus minor* of *liquamen* and an *acetabulus perquam minor* (somewhat smaller) of vinegar. The *acetabuli* here cannot refer to a fixed measure and appear to be contrasting sized 'cups'.[2] Recipe 16 of the *Excerpta Vinidarii* uses *acetabulus* as a ½ cup measure and a ⅓ of a cup rather than the precise quantity: *vini acetabulum, liquaminis dimidium, mellis tertiam partem*. Other references to *acetabulum* seem to be used in a more precise way, especially as they often occur with quantities such as *hemina* and *sextarius*.[3]

---

[1] According to R. Duncan-Jones, *The Economy of the Roman Empire: Quantitative Studies* (Cambridge, 2nd ed. 1982), pp. 369-71, the average weight of a *libra* fluctuated between 321 and 325 gms. It seems the Romans found it difficult to be consistently accurate.

[2] A similar formulation using *acetabulum maius* and *minus* occurs at 8.7.17, though it also has precise terms such as *hemina* as well.

[4] 7.5.4; 8.6.5; 8.6.7.

The *cyathus* is a Greek term from *kyathos*, a small ladle used to serve wine from the crater to the drinking cup. As a precise measure in Rome it was ¹⁄₁₂ of a *sextarius* or just over 1½ fl. oz. The term as an accurate measure occurs most often in the *patina* section of Book 2, where small, precise quantities of liquids such as wine, *liquamen, passum* etc. are required so that the eggs as setting agent are not over-diluted.[1] At 7.4.4 it is ambiguous whether the cook means 'cup' or precisely 1½ fl. oz. If it is a sauce, then a cup is intended, but if the mixture is to 'fry or seeth' the *ofellae* in, then a precise measure must be meant.[2] At 6.8.11 *cyathus* is used as a cup measure for pine nuts and therefore has been used in the same way as the imprecise *acetabulum*. It is interesting to note that *cyathus* and *acetabulus* do not ever occur together in a recipe. Their liquid value is very similar and it is therefore quite probable that individual cooks would use one or the other, depending on their particular training.

The *sextarius* and *hemina* are clearly used with precision. At 7.11.7 a *tyropatina* or milk pudding is described thus: 'put 5 eggs into a *sextarius*, and if you have a *hemina*, put in 3 eggs'. Even today, the traditional ratio of 4 or 5 eggs to 1 pint milk is used to make a *crème caramel*. The *hemina* was also divided into 12 *uncia* (the origin of our fluid ounces), and this measure by analogy was also called a *libra* when it was used for measuring oil, though it may have been used for other liquids.[3] We find this usage in recipe 3 of the *Excerpta Vinidarii*: *adicies liquamen libra 1, olei similiter.* We translate this as a *hemina*, i.e. ½ pint. The previous recipe to this has wine, *liquamen* and honey, all apparently weighed using *pondo* (lb.), while the milk in the recipe is measured in *sextarii* (pt.). It may be the case that the *pondo* in this recipe is the equivalent of a *libra*, and should be understood as a *hemina* (i.e. ½ pt.), though we retain the literal sense of the word in our translation.[4]

Brandt's suggestion that precise quantities in a recipe represent a medical or dietetic source for that recipe is unfounded.[5] Some of the *patinae* recipes in book 4 do use quantities in a precise way, but there is no other indication that a medical book was used to provide these recipes. For the argument to be sound,

[1] *Cyathus* occurs at 4.2.4,5,8,9,31,33,36.

[2] See below, pp. 90-91, on the terminology of frying and boiling.

[3] Cf. Richardson, *Numbering and Measuring* (1985 ed.), §92.

[4] Recipe 23 of the *excerpta* mixes *pondo* and *heminae*, which may be a further variant of equivalent terms or simply indicate utter confusion!

[5] Brandt, op. cit., pp. 25-6; Bode, op. cit., p. 26.

one might expect some kind of indication of health benefits to be gained from the *patina* in question.[1] Exact quantities can be found in other recipes in Latin texts, and the mere use of quantities is therefore not a sufficient criterion to determine origin. [2]

5. THE LANGUAGE OF *APICIUS*

The vocabulary of cooking techniques.

The idiosyncratic and diverse language used by cooks in the recipes is indicative of the numerous 'schools' of cookery or different traditions of teaching cooking which would naturally occur in such a trade. Many contracted phrases are unique to the language of cooks and as they convey intricate cooking processes that are lost to the modern practitioner, they can be hard to interpret. Many terms have proved difficult to translate because the process or concept they describe has no meaning in a modern kitchen and can only be understood through an exploration of the processes involved in ancient cooking techniques, arrived at through a combination of study of the texts and experimental archaeology.

Many of the recipes in *Apicius* involve the production of sauces and stuffings in a *mortarium*. The language used to convey the simple stages in this process is quite diverse. The production of sauces follows a set procedure: various seeds, always including pepper, are put in the mortar and ground. Only a few recipes call for the spices to be roasted before being ground. For centuries, the normal procedure with seeds has been to dry-roast them to release the flavour and aid the grinding process; we therefore assume that all seeds are roasted despite the rarity of the instruction. The most common verb used for this initial instruction is *teres*, though often the instruction to grind is omitted and *adicies* or *mittes* is found.

[1] The recipes with precise quantities: 4.2.4, 5, 8, 9, 31, 33, 36.
[2] Numerous examples illustrate the point: see for example Cato, *De agricultura* 74-82, 84-8, 104, 112; Columella 12.59.1-5.

The list of ingredients always starts with pepper and seeds, then the herbs. A number of liquids (always including *liquamen*) are then added, and occasionally the instruction *fricabis* (rub, or grind) occurs, with the inference of 'again' if used after the *liquamen* is mentioned, suggesting that the liquid helps to turn the mixture into a mash. In fact a 'pepper mash' is a common concept: cf. 2.2.8. *Fricabis* can also be the only term used for 'grind' or 'pound' and sometimes no verb meaning 'grind' is used, though the action is always necessary. *Tundes* is used just once to convey the action of grinding, at 3.18.2, where cumin is infused with vinegar and dried beforehand. *Contero* is also used to convey the general idea of 'reducing to a fine consistency' by rubbing and is used in the context of spices and green leaves.[1] Various nuts or fruits may be added at this stage so that they may be ground into a paste before the other sweet and sour liquids are added, indicated by compounds of *–fundere*: *suffundes*, *perfundes*, *infundes*, *defundes*, and *superfundes*. Occasionally a simple *mittes* or *addes* is used.[2] These terms are used indiscriminately to convey the addition of liquids or finished sauces.

In previous English editions the verb *temperare*, used extensively in *Apicius*, is translated as 'blend' or 'mix', and is always used in relation to individual liquids such as the various forms of wine, *liquamen,* vinegar etc. However the word has a far more complex meaning than its physical function alone. *Lewis and Short* defines *tempero* as 'to divide' or 'proportion duly', 'to mingle in due proportion', 'to combine' or 'compound properly', 'to qualify', 'to temper' etc.

When *temperare* is used in *Apicius*, it can sometimes just refer to a physical act of blending ingredients which have already been specified, as at 7.11.7 where milk and honey are blended together. In these cases we have translated the term as 'blend'. In the vast number of cases however *temperare* has the more complex meaning of 'balance' or 'temper' the dish by adding additional flavourings in the form of liquids which may be mentioned but which are sometimes left to the discretion of the cook. On these occasions we have for the most part translated this word as 'flavour', and when no liquid is suggested we

---

[1] *Conterare*: 'to grind, bruise or pound' of just pepper 2.2.4; of a composite sauce 4.1.2; of greens 4.2.4.

[2] *Infundere* also has the meaning of 'infuse' or 'soak in', but can be used as a general term for 'pour in or on': cf. 4.2.13 where pine nuts are soaked. Cf. also *defundes* at 9.10.11 with the sense 'pour in'.

have translated it as 'balance the flavour', implying the added sense of 'taste and adjust accordingly'.

This means that in our text *temperare* has been translated in three separate ways, depending on the context. The normal term for 'flavour' is *condire*, but as a general rule this verb refers to the act of adding a composite spice mix or a finished sauce rather than to the addition of individual liquids.[1] At 6.8.14 the ingredients of a chicken stuffing are 'blended' together to make them smooth, *ut unum corpus efficias*, and then this action is followed up with the instruction *liquamine temperas*; this phrase clearly refers to flavouring with *liquamen* and not to the purely physical act of blending the ingredients. *Temperare* is often used to indicate that sauces should be 'tempered' with wine (or its derivates such as *caroenum, defrutum* and *passum*). It is often found without any seasonings, for example at 5.4.5, where in a *conchicla* of peas, eggs are added to a mortar that has spices and *ius de suo sibi* 'cooking liquor' already in it, and is then 'tempered'. In this recipe the sauce has no *liquamen* in it and we interpret the term *temperas* here with the added meaning of 'adjust the balance of flavours', which could quite easily mean 'add *liquamen*'.

At 7.9.3 a similar omission is found: a *piperatum* or 'pepper sauce' that is usually made with *liquamen* has only pepper, *passum*, rue and wine; it is prepared for a boiled ham and then 'tempered'. Even allowing for the saltiness of the ham, the lack of *liquamen* is striking. We think that on this occasion the term *temperas* means 'balance the flavour with fish sauce if it is needed'. We might say 'bring the sauce to completion'. *Excerpta Vinidarii* 2 has the most precise use of this word: a *caccabina* (late type of *patina)* is seasoned with an *oenogarum* which *gustata item permixta et temperatam mittes in patinam* (you taste, mix again and balance the flavours, then put in the dish).

A finished sauce or mixture intended for a stuffing or purée can be beaten in a specific way using the phrase *tutunclabis ut in mortario teres* (pound it (with a stick?) as you would grind (it) in a mortar), suggesting that the *mortarium* has a more general purpose as a mixing bowl.[2] At this point the sauce can be decanted

---

[1] *Condire* can mean 'preserve', as in 1.19 for quinces in honey. For its use as 'flavour' for cabbage cf. 3.9.5, for bulbs 4.5.2, of a finished sauce 5.1.1, 2, of salt 5.3.4, of a sauce 5.3.5; of a listed sauce 5.3.7; 8.8.8, 12, 13; of 'flavour as you like' 9.4.3. In the *Excerpta Vinidarii* 1, *condire* is used of liquids, *liquamine et oleo*.

[2] 5.2.2. *tutunclabis* is the clear reading of both MSS at 5.2.2 and 5.3.6, and we follow André in retaining it. It appears to be a cognate form with *tudicula*, 'a small olive-press' (found in

into an all-purpose *caccabus* and cooked. This simple process can be expressed in numerous idiosyncratic ways suggesting that different cooks had their own preferred forms of expression.[1] This basic method of sauce production seems the most common and simple, but there is another which involves pounding all the dry and moist ingredients into a paste, then formed into a ball, a *globus*. This is then stirred into a *ius simplex* of wine, *liquamen,* etc.[2] This only occurs twice in the recipes, but it should be remembered that many of the recipes with similar lists of ingredients have no method specified and that the technique may have been more common than the text suggests. This pre-ground 'wet' spice-mix has obvious parallels with Indian curry pastes today.[3]

There is considerable confusion in the meaning of the term *frigida* as used in the recipes. The term always means 'cold water' but sometimes the reference is to chilling already-cooked food, and on other occasions to cold water into which food is placed so that it can be cooked. Occasionally, we cannot determine whether cooking is actually required or not. At 4.1.1 we are told to place the salad *super frigidam* (water assumed), yet if we interpret the *sala cattabia* as a salad then the vessel must be 'in' rather than 'over' the cold water in order to chill it.[4] At 4.5.3 the gourd is put in cold (water assumed) and later it is described as half-cooked, suggesting that the water was only cold at the beginning. At 4.5.4

Columella 12.52.7) and *tudes*, 'a hammer'. *Tutuclabis* is found in the *Mulomedicina Chironis* 409, while *tudiculare* 'to grind, crush' is noted by A. F. Buccini as the origin of the term *ratatouille* ('Western Mediterranean Vegetable Stews and the Integration of Culinary Exotica', in *Authenticity: Proceedings of the Oxford Food Conference 2005*, Totnes, 2006). Other suggestions have been *tudiclabis* (Humelberg, followed by Milham), and *turundabis* (Schuch). Whatever the original word or phrase was, it survives as *stusar* in Reggio, Modena, Parma, Mantua and elsewhere in northern Italy, as *tozar* in Aragonese, and as *tuduculus*, 'stirring-stick', in French dialects, all derived from a putative *tuditiare* (see Meyer-Lübke, *Romanisches etymologisches Wörterbuch* (Heidelberg, 1935), nos. 8971, 8972). We are indebted to Dr Andrew Dalby for this reference.

[1] *Facies ut fereat,* 'bring it to heat'*; in caccabum mittes ut calefiat,* 'put in a pan so that it warms through'; *sic bulliat,* 'so boil it'; *mittes ut ferveant,* 'place it so that it may come to heat'; *illic ferveant,* 'let it come to heat there'; *pones ut coquatur,* 'set it to cook'; *facies ut bulliat,* 'bring it to the boil'; *calefacies,* 'warm it up'; *fervefactum,* 'make it simmer'. The most common formulation seems to be *facies ut ferveat, cum ferbuerit,* 'bring it to heat; when it is simmering…'

[2] 8.1.5; 8.8.4.

[3] See also the dry pre-mixed spices found in a London warehouse, p. 341 n. 2 in the Glossary.

[4] Cooks appear to use *super* in the sense 'in' as well as 'on': cf. 8.6.11, where *super* is used for the sausages that are put back 'in' the cavity of the goat to represent intestines.

under-ripe and hard apricots have subsequently to be cooked in the cold water they are placed in; at 9.4.3 a similar instruction appears regarding cuttlefish, and we assume that they too are cooked. At 5.3.4 cooked peas are simply chilled *in frigidam* and we find this simple chilling process in the *Excerpta Vinidarii* 23, where a whole piglet is chilled after boiling. The key recipe that gives us pause is 4.2.33, where sorb apples are apparently pounded and sieved without being cooked at all. The title *patina de sorbis calida et frigida* may contain a hidden or confused instruction to 'cook from cold'. However, the sorb apples may be sufficiently ripe that they need not be cooked at the beginning of the recipe, but only with the eggs at the end.

There is a similar problem with recipes 4.2.5 and 6. The *patina de asparagis frigida* is translated as 'cold patina', but the asparagus is apparently only trimmed and pounded in a mortar with the addition of a little water before being strained and mixed with a sauce and cooked with eggs. The second of these recipes involves using the hard woody ends of the spears of asparagus that would normally be thrown away, and they are treated in the same way without heat until they are cooked with eggs. However the construction of recipe 4.2.36 suggests that we have translated these recipes correctly: here, the nettles in a 'hot or cold' *patina* are washed, strained and dried before being cooked in *liquamen* and oil. The *frigida* in the title must refer to a way of serving the dish. In the case of the two asparagus recipes, it seems strange to attempt to extract flavour from these vegetables in their raw state, but it is very successful in practice.

The word *frigere* is translated in *Lewis and Short* as 'to roast, parch or fry'. It seems to be a dry form of cooking, despite the association with frying, in contrast to *bullire,* 'to boil'. However, the original Greek terminology made a distinction between 'dry cooking' (*optân*) variously meaning 'bake' or 'roast', and the wet form of cooking (*hépsein*) which is both 'boiling' and 'frying' depending on the context.[1] This has caused confusion when the concepts are transferred to Latin. Recipes 2 and 3 in the *Excerpta Vinidarii* use the verb *frigis* to refer to meat pieces being fiercely boiled in a shallow amount of liquid that may contain oil but which is technically a sauce.

A number of recipes are constructed with particularly odd and badly worded phrases which would be meaningless if rendered literally. It is possible that the confusion we find has been introduced by scribal error and was not present at the

---

[1] Dalby, *Siren Feasts,* p. 113 and n. 1.

time of the recipes' creation. However, it is possible that some of these anomalies may indicate that some recipes were dictated and that some of the cooks giving the instructions were less than coherent and struggled to express themselves. We also acknowledge that the confusion could be entirely of our own making, given that we do not have a full picture of Roman cooking techniques and have to reconstruct them. A simple mistake such as omitting to put instructions in the right order and adding them at the end is a possible indication of oral transmission. This occurs at 6.8.14, where we are told that the chicken needs boning right at the end of the recipe. The *patina Apiciana* at 4.2.14 lists an egg and oil mixture that should have gone into the sauce before the *patina* was constructed but is forgotten until the end. At 7.1.6 a recipe for roasted womb is worded *in cantabro involve et postea in muriam mitte et sic coques.* The recipe is repeated using stomach at 7.7.2 with the omission of the *et.* As it stands the recipe requires you to roll the womb in bran and then wash it off with the brine. This is totally illogical. We think that the *muria* is brine rather than fish sauce and is used to clean the womb before it is rolled in bran to form a crust in the oven. The phrase is worded in such a brief and contracted form that its meaning is obscure. The *postea* clause must mean 'after you have put it in the *muria*', not 'after this, put it...'. We have translated the sentence as 'roll the womb in bran after you have put it in brine and cook it like this'.

A similar kind of contraction and reversal of words appears at 3.18.2 in the instructions for an *oxyporium*, a 'digestive' made up of a spice mix with a large amount of cumin. We read *tundes cuminum et postea infundes in aceto. cum siccauerit postea melle omnia conprehendes,* literally 'pound the cumin and afterwards steep it in vinegar. When it has dried afterwards mix all the ingredients with the honey'. The same *oxyporium* is described at 1.32, but the order of action is recorded correctly: soak whole cumin seeds, dry them, pound them and then mix with the honey.[1]

The recipe for *patina Apiciana* at 4.2.14 has a very odd sentence in the middle: a sauce with various meats is ladled *ita ut per singula coria substernas diploidem in laganum similiter* ('in such a way that, with each layer, you spread out a double layer like a *laganum*'). The sentence seem to be twisted around in its meaning in a similar way to the recipe for womb above. The *laganum* should

---

[1] The recipes are very similar with regard to ingredients and method but 3.18.2 is by far the more comprehensive even though it does not record the method correctly. They appear to have survived quite separately within the body of available recipes.

be like a double-layered cloak (a *diplois*) rather than the reverse, and a more logical word-order would have been *in laganum diploidem similiter*. We see the confusion in terms of a verbal misunderstanding rather than a written one.

The phrase *ab ossibus tanges* occurs at 8.7.8 and 9 and has the meaning of 'smother (the sauce) down to the bone', referring to a whole, sometimes boned, cooked animal. This seems to be a specific cooks' term for 'covered it in sauce very well'. There is no suggestion that the joint or whole animal is cut down to the bone so that the sauce can seep through; it rather reflects an exaggerated term for a simple process. At 8.8.7 we find a similar expression, *a dorso tanges* meaning touch or smother the sauce 'down its back'.

The term *subassare* occurs ten times in the text, and is normally translated as 'grill' or 'roast'. However, this instruction is usually conveyed by *assas*. The prefix *sub-* came to mean 'under' or 'beneath' in Late Latin contexts, but in *Apicius* it has a further meaning of 'a little', and frequently occurs when the meat in question has already been pre-cooked. The word thus has the added meaning of 'finish' the cooking by roasting over charcoal. At 2.5.3 we find *subassas* used of sausages which have been boiled. We also see it clearly at 7.5.3 and 8.2.3 where meat pieces are boiled and then *subassatam*.[1]

The verb *exbromare* is found only twice in *Apicius*, *exbromas* at 2.2.9 and *exbromari possint* at 6.2.3 and once, *exbromabis*, in *Excerpta Vinidarii* 4. One instance is also found in Anthimus 3. Previous translators have either taken the verb to mean peeling (*FR*) or have linked it with the removal of bad smells or *humores*.[2] André notes the great obscurity of the verb, and at 2.2.9 Humelberg proposed the reading *expromas*, 'bone the chicken', which, as André notes, is so obvious as to be otiose. At 2.2.9, *exbromas* indicates that something is done to the chicken to produce a liquid that becomes the basis of a sauce, so the term has to involve cooking or boiling of some kind (and possibly for some time). Despite the rarity of this verb, it evidently meant something specific to the writers of these recipes and it seems illogical to translate it differently in different places. We suggest that *exbromare* is linked to the Greek *ekbroma* ('that

---

[1] The development of the meaning of the preposition *sub-* from 'up, upwards' to 'below' or 'on the underside' is traced by B. García-Hernández, 'La reinterpretacíon de *sub* (-), prefijo y preposición en latín tardío', *Latin Vulgaire – latin tardif. Actes du Vᵉ Colloque international sur le latin vulgaire et tardif, Heidelberg, 5-8 septembre 1997* (Heidelberg, 1999), 222-33.

[2] Flower and Rosenbaum, ad loc.; M. Grant, *Anthimus de obseruatione ciborum* (Totnes, 1996), p. 87 n. 3.

which is eaten away or thrown out') and/or *ekbrasis* ('boiling'or 'foaming') and *ekbrasma* ('that which is thrown up by boiling,' that is, 'scum'). *Exbromare* would then mean something like 'boil so something can be removed'. It would seem that the normal procedure of 'skimming' is adequately dealt with by the term *despumare* as used in the pea recipes of Book 5.3. We asked ourselves, what process could be severally applied to a turnip, a joint of pork and chicken bones? The one which appears to fit all the contexts is that the first water is brought to the boil in order to clean the item and then discarded. In 6.2.3, the turnip is then washed, diced and added to the dish to finish cooking with duck. At 2.2.9, the same process occurs with chicken bones prepared for a stock, but here it is the bones which are discarded, not the water. Finally, the *ofellae* in *Excerpta Vinidarii* 4 would be treated much like gammon, which is traditionally boiled in one lot of water that is thrown away, and then cooked in fresh water. One might even interpret the *ofellae* as salted belly pork in these circumstances. This procedure of boiling and throwing the water away (*pace* Grant) also seems to be that envisaged by Anthimus.[1]

The phrase *(ad) uaporem ignis* has been interpreted in the past as 'steam', from *uaporare* (to emit steam or vapour). However, *uapor* has the more general meaning of 'heat or warmth from a fire' rather than 'steam from water'. This particular phrase appears in *Apicius* on three occasions and we believe it always refers to a gentle fire, the rising vapours of charcoal rather than water. It is a peculiar way to express this kind of heat and may reflect the expression of a particular cook or cooks. At 2.2.2 *isicia* are warmed and served in *hydrogarum*. They are placed in the pan with the sauce, not over it, before being put *ad uaporem ignis*. Even if water was available and steam generated, it simply would not affect the sauce or the *isicia* through the *caccabus*. The *isicia* must have been pre-cooked as we are only told to warm them through using this method. Recipe 2.2.5 specifically instructs us to cook *isicia* in a *hydrogarum*. However most *isicia* are grilled or roasted. Steaming is an extremely inefficient way to cook *isicia*, or any other kind of meat for that matter (see below).

The phrase in question appears without *ignis* at 4.2.12, where the instruction *inpones ad uaporem* refers to a *patina de apua sine apua*. The internal logic of the recipe means that steam could not possibly be the intended cooking medium.

[1] The relevant passage in Anthimus 3 is 'beef flesh can be used baked and cooked in a *sodinga* (vessel of some sort) and also in a sauce, provided that, having been *exbromare* 'boiled' in one lot of water, it is cooked in as much fresh water as suits the size of the meat'.

The sea-urchins placed on top of the egg mixture are expected to dry out and so a steamy moist atmosphere would not be suitable. At 9.10.1 a stuffed bonito is wrapped in papyrus and placed in a covered pan and then *sic supra uaporem ignis*. What would be the point of extra water producing steam at this point? The fish is in fact steamed, but in its own juices, not any other water source. A simple vessel suspended over simmering water may have been used to heat sauces gently and even cook dishes such as the *patinae* of Book 4. At 4.2.1 an 'everyday *patina*', using brains with various seasonings, eggs and milk is 'cooked on a gentle fire or over hot water' (*ad ignem lenem uel aquam calidam coques*). This has been interpreted as a simple bain-marie.

There is one clear reference to steaming in all the surviving ancient recipe texts, at Anthimus 34. An egg sponge called *afrutum,* made from whisked egg-white, is held in a *gauata* – an unknown vessel but we suspect one with small holes at various points – and *sic uapore ipsius iuscelli coquatur.* We think that this method warrants such precise instructions because it is so unusual. The *afrutum* is well suited to steaming as it needs gentle cooking. The sauce is in fact a *hydrogarum* similar to those that the *isicia* are cooked in in *Apicius* Book 2, but this should not fool us into thinking that the *isicia* in Apicius are cooked in steam.

Anthimus also uses the term *uaporata* in relation to meat cooking. It has been translated as 'steaming' by Grant, though he does acknowledge there is some doubt.[1] It is implausible that joints of meat big enough to be spit roasted could be enclosed in one kind of vessel, then suspended over another vessel of water. It would take days rather than hours to steam the meat unless it was under pressure, and it would be a complete waste of fuel. The contrast in Anthimus is between spit roasting, which is a direct dry heat, and the *uaporata* heat which is moist and indirect. We think that when Anthimus says *uaporata* he means 'baked'. He hardly mentions oven-baked meat at all, which is in itself strange, yet when he does, the term he uses for the heat of the oven is *vapore*. Anthimus appears a little confused with the terminology of the kitchen at this point.[2]

---

[1] Grant, *Anthimus,* p. 88 n. 4.
[2] See above, p. 93 n. 1 for a translation of one of the relevant passages concerning *vaporata* in Anthimus 3.

The style and grammar of Apicius.

The Latinity of *Apicius*, as preserved in the two principal manuscripts, is extremely varied. Some of the recipes incorporate grammar and syntax which, for all its simplicity, is classical in style; others are redolent of Vulgar Latin. While we use the term 'vulgar' to describe these features, this should not be taken as indication of a later date for particular recipes, since in both syntax and spelling they mirror the language found in inscriptions from relatively early periods in the empire, and even the late republic. They conform, therefore, to Roger Wright's definition: '"Vulgar Latin"… is just a collective label, available for us to use to refer to all those features of the Latin language that are known to have existed, from textual attestations and incontrovertible reconstructions, but that were not recommended by the grammarians'.[1] The quality of the Latinity of any given recipe might be an indication of date, but it might equally reflect the writer's ability to write or spell since, as will be detailed in the notes which follow, many of the departures from what might be termed 'normative' Latin of the classical and imperial periods co-existed with more learned registers. The presence of 'vulgarisms' does not argue against our conclusions about the extended time-span during which the collection was assembled. Similar conclusions have been reached about Latin veterinary texts, which include technical expressions and recipes very similar to those in *Apicius*.[2]

By its very nature, the text is couched in simple terms, and its Latinity rarely reaches great sophistication. *Apicius* as a whole is made up of 459 separate texts, many of which are no more than lists of ingredients. Even where instructions are included, the need for grammatical subordination is limited if those instructions are laid out in a logical sequence (which is not always the case). As we have seen, the texts themselves seem to be gathered from a range of sources and may have been composed over a lengthy period. Some were probably composed originally in Greek, subsequently translated into Latin. It is remarkable – and fortunate, given its evidence that such a variety of styles could co-exist – that neither the final compiler of *Apicius* nor the subsequent transcribers saw fit to emend or

---

[1] In the foreword to J. Herman, *Vulgar Latin* (trans. R. Wright, University Park PA, 2000).

[2] Adams, *Pelagonius*, p. 640; as we remarked earlier, we are indebted to Dr Adams' penetrating study for much of the thought behind our conclusions. Our work on *Apicius* leads us to disagree with those who consider that Roman cooks are unlikely to have been literate (cf. J. Wilkins and S. Hill, *Food in the Ancient World*, pp. 2, 245).

correct the varieties of expression, to produce a homogenized version. The nature of the text – a series of practical instructions – may mean that it incorporates idioms from the spoken rather than the written language and, as Roger Wright noted in a recent collection of studies, it might well be the case 'that spoken Imperial Latin was ... more like the Romance languages than we usually give it credit for'.[1]

In addition, as we have argued elsewhere,[2] the intended readers and users of these texts were expected to have the wherewithal to supply whatever might be needed to complete the sense of what was intended by the recipe from their own mental resources, the training they had received, and their hands-on practical experience. Thus they needed not only a certain degree of fluency in Latin, but also culinary skills to make sense of the text. Moreover, their language may have had quirks and peculiarities not found in other applications of Latin, similar to the Greek style of Mithaikos' *Opsartytikon* noted by Dalby, where a 'fourteen word quotation ... contains one otherwise unknown verb ... one intransitive verb elsewhere always transitive ... and one unique cognate accusative phrase: ... "Sicilian cookery" had, on this evidence, already developed a technical vocabulary and a laconic style.'[3]

This point provides an explanation of the simplest of the recipe-texts in *Apicius* from a stylistic point of view. Of the grand total of 459 recipes spread over the ten books (excluding the *Excerpta Vinidarii*), 76 (17 per cent of the total) are simple lists of ingredients, with little or no grammatical joining, and no verbal instruction. This 'list' feature occurs in a further 94 recipes, in combination with more elaborate expression. Its use is hardly surprising, considering the nature of the material with which we are dealing, and had antecedents in Greek recipe texts.[4] The subject-specific vocabulary incorporated in *Apicius* also poses problems; some nouns, not a few verbs, and other phrases such as *de suo sibi* may be part of an idiosyncratic cooks' language which is not attested elsewhere.[5]

---

[1] R. Wright, *Latin and the Romance Languages in the Early Middle Ages* (University Park PA, 1996), p. 2.

[2] See above, p. 70.

[3] Dalby, *Siren Feasts*, p. 110.

[4] See above, and cf. Athenaeus 309f, 662 d-e. Adams, *Pelagonius*, p. 490, comments that 'the processes involved in preparing and cooking ingredients are limited and banal.'

[5] This in itself poses a problem for the editor, in that there is little by way of similar texts to compare *Apicius* with: cf. A.G. Rigg's comment that 'the only successful enterprises in the description of Medieval Latin grammar are studies of the usage of specific authors or in limited collections of

Writing of the fourth century, Jósef Herman posits a divergence between the stylistic Latin of the *docti*, men such as Jerome or Augustine, who were not only familiar with the classical language but were also faced with the task of communicating with men whom they regarded as *indocti*: 'a man like Jerome knows very well that the usage of the *imperitum uulgus* does have a vocabulary which is to a certain extent specific, with elements which normally do not occur at the level of the texts, not even those which adhere to the stylistic ideal of simplicity'.[1]

For the purposes of stylistic analysis, we have attempted to classify the recipe-texts in *Apicius* into four broad categories:

1. List only – there is no verbal instruction, just a list of ingredients;

1a. List-element – used to indicate the presence of a list-feature in recipes which also contain verbal instruction, some being syntactically complex in the remainder of the text;[2]

2. Simple – verbal instructions are straightforward and there is no grammatical subordination;

3. Semi-complex – there is a single element of subordination, or subordination is confined to temporal clauses (e.g. *when/while you have done/are doing this, do this*);

4. Complex – reserved for recipe-texts in which there is more grammatical subordination, including for example gerund/gerundive constructions, ablative absolutes, purpose clauses. Even in these, the bulk of the text may be 'simple' in construction.

---

documents or texts from a particular period or region', A. G. Rigg, *Medieval Latin. An Introduction and Bibliographical Guide* (Washington DC, 1996), pp. 91-92, cited in the review article by R. Hexter, *Journal of Medieval Latin* 10 (2000), 307-37, at p. 311.

[1] J. Herman, 'Spoken and written Latin in the last centuries of the Roman Empire. A contribution to the linguistic history of the western provinces', in R. Wright (ed.), *Latin and the Romance Languages*, 29-43, at p. 30.

[2] N. Vasilieva, 'Semiological notes in the *De Arte Coquinaria* by Apicius', in *Latin Vulgaire – latin tardif* (Tübingen, 1987), 199-205, notes that whereas modern recipes tend to separate the list of ingredients and then describe the method, a 'characteristic of the *De Re Coquinaria* is that the list is integrated into the steps' (p. 200).

CATEGORIZATION OF RECIPE-TEXTS IN *APICIUS*.

Book	Total recipes	Lists only	List-element	Simple	Semi-complex	Complex
I	35	4	8	11	6	11
II	24	5	3	11	6	6
III	57	12	20	36	3	6
IIII	54	6	10	21	12	20
V	31	2	8	10	7	9
VI	41	10	17	11	7	12
VII	77	10	29	40	12	13
VIII	69	12	30	37	13	5
VIIII	36	8	14	25	3	0
X	35	7	31	28	0	0
Sub-total	*459*	*76*	*170*	*230*	*69*	*82*
Vinidarius	32	0	6	17	14	1
Total	**491**	**76**	**176**	**247**	**83**	**83**
Cato	25	0	2	14	0	2
Columella	14	1	2	8	4	1
Anthimus	3	0	0	0	0	3

The table shows the distribution of texts in the ten books of *Apicius* and in the *Excerpta Vinidarii* according to these categories, with a number of similar texts from Cato, Columella and Anthimus included for comparison.[1]

Half of the recipes in the collection are classified as 'simple'. These may include only a single verbal instruction, such as *inferes* at the conclusion, or may be made up of a string of simple commands which may take a variety of forms:[2]

[1] The recipes used in this and the table opposite are to be found in Cato, *De agricultura*, 74-82, 84-88, 116-23, 125-6, 162; Columella 12. ii. 70, v, viii.1-3, xvi. 3, xix.1, xxi, xxvii, xxxv, lix.1, 2a, 2b, 3-4a, 4b,5; Anthimus 3, 34, 35.
[2] Cf. Adams, *Pelagonius*, pp. 460ff.

1. the imperative;

2. the so-called 'future' imperative;

3. the present indicative of the verb – usually 2nd person singular active, but occasionally 3rd person singular or plural in the passive;

4. the present subjunctive – again, usually 2nd person singular active, but occasionally 3rd person singular or plural in the passive;

5. the 2nd person singular future tense.

Given the nature of a recipe text, the imperative form of the verb might be expected to be found most frequently, but this is far from the truth. The frequency of different means of conveying instruction may help to illustrate the possible origins of recipes from earlier collections, and perhaps their relative dates. The frequency of each type of command per book is shown in the following table.

TYPES OF VERBAL INSTRUCTION USED IN *APICIUS*.

Book	Total recipes	Imperative	'Future' imperative	Present indicative	Present subjunctive	Future indicative	Use of passive
I	35	14	4	18	4	21	3
II	24	0	0	20	3	21	3
III	57	2	1	12	5	34	3
IIII	54	3	0	34	10	52	0
V	31	0	0	29	4	26	5
VI	41	5	0	28	3	31	0
VII	77	4	0	47	1	44	1
VIII	69	2	1	42	9	49	7
VIIII	36	1	1	12	1	22	2
X	35	0	0	6	0	25	0
Total	*459*	*31*	*7*	*248*	*40*	*325*	*24*
Vinidarius	32	6	0	24	7	30	2
Cato	25	1	24	1	11	13	0
Columella	14	1	6	8	8	9	1
Anthimus	3	0	1	3	3	1	2

NB. The number of recipes in each book which use each type are indicated – not the **total** occurrences of each type. The present subjunctive is only noted when used in **jussive** sense, not in purpose clauses, etc.

The so-called 'future imperative' is of an archaic nature[1] and is found in legal and religious texts, as well as in the recipes contained in Cato, *De Agricultura*, where one recipe-text (76) contains no fewer than 42 of this type of imperative, together with 5 verbs in the future tense and 6 present subjunctives. The use of imperatives is similar to that found in some of the Greek recipes preserved in Athenaeus, where both present and aorist imperatives are regularly found.

Use of the present indicative, either in 2nd person singular active or in the passive, might be used as 'descriptive' rather than in an imperative sense. It is found used in this way in a number of recipes found in Columella (cf. in particular 12.16.3, 12.21), and in Anthimus, but only rarely in Cato – only one instance in the recipes studied, in *De Agricultura* 125. The present indicative is only found in one of the recipes studied from Athenaeus, at 113c, where 6 of the seven present indicative verbs are in the passive; this type of construction is found only rarely in *Apicius*, but cf. 8.7.14 (9 passives out of 11 verbs) and 9.10.1 (7 passives out of 8).

The present subjunctive usage is, according to Woodcock, 'regularly used even in classical Latin, in addressing an *indefinite* second person, i.e. in giving general instructions or precepts'.[2] It is also found in the recipes from Cato and Columella which were examined for purposes of comparison (see the tables above.)

One Archestratus recipe, in Athenaeus 320b, includes a 3rd person singular passive subjunctive.

Most unusual is the use of the future indicative in giving instruction. As the table shows, however, the future tense is by no means normative in the *Apicius* collection.[3] Many of the recipes use both present and future 2nd person singular to give instructions, and occasionally recipes are found in which only the present is used (e.g. 7 4.3, 7 9.3, 9.10.1: 8 verbs, 7 of them passive). However, no fewer than 111 of the 459 *Apicius* recipes have direct instruction using this form (i.e. the present subjunctive may also be found in some of these following *ut*). Many of these are categorized as 'simple', with the one command *inferes* at the end.

Rather than being a 'survival of the ancient modal force' of the future tense,[4] found (along with other means of instruction) in 13 of the 25 recipes selected for

---

[1] L. R. Palmer, *The Latin Language* (London, 1954, 1961), p. 276; E. C. Woodcock, *A New Latin Syntax* (London, 1959), §126; Adams, *Pelagonius*, p. 460.   [2] Woodcock, op. cit., §126.
[3] The issue is complicated by the confusion in the MSS of *e* and *i*; see below, p. 101.
[4] Woodcock, *Latin Syntax*, p. 307.

comparison from Cato (though in 3 of these, they are used with *si* or *ubi*), it is now clear that 'forms such as *mittis* and *mittes* had the same pronunciation once *ē* and *ĭ* had merged, and scribes must have had difficulty distinguishing between them. The frequency of such second-person forms in relation to the ordinary imperative must reflect the fading from colloquial use of the imperative'.[1] It does not appear to conform to any *classical* Latin usage, though it does occasionally crop up in Greek texts (though only in one of the recipes selected from Athenaeus for purposes of comparison, at 320b).[2] Curiously, it occurs more commonly in verbs of the third and fourth conjugations, and particularly in the case of the term *inferes*, which (along with other specific word-usages) might be regarded in *Apicius* as a kind of 'jargon' or 'cook's Latin'. There are four instances of this exclusively future-tense pattern of recipes in the *Excerpta Vinidarii,* including one example of a false form, *inferebis*, at the very end of *EV* 13.

Some specific usages of forms of common verbs in *Apicius* may be noted:

inferes This is the unique active form of the verb *infero* in *Apicius*; a false form *inferebis* is found at *EV* 13. The forms *infer/inferte, infers, infert, infertur, inferas* are not found. Paradoxically, the future passives *inferetur/inferentur* are not used, though there are 10 instances of present indicative *inferuntur* (cf. 3.11.2) and the subjunctive passive *inferantur* occurs once, in *EV* 5.

facies This future indicative form occurs on a total of 112 occasions, 34 times in the recurring phrase *facies ut ferueat*, of which 22 are part of the longer technical term *facies ut ferueat; cum feruuerit*.[3] The compound form *calefacies* is found 17 times in *Apicius*, but not in *EV.* The imperative *fac* occurs only once in *Apicius*, at 6.8.14, and once also in *EV* 2; *facis* is also found only once in *Apicius*, at 2.2, and once at *EV* 13. The subjunctive form *facias* is found a total of 15 times, 12 with *ut*, and only three times with a jussive force (twice in the phrase *feruere facias*).

coque This form, including the compound form *percoque*, is found three times in *Apicius* and twice in *EV.*[4] *coquis* occurs twice in *Apicius* and once in *EV.* As with *inferes*, the future *coques* is the most frequently occurring form, being found 80 times, with *praecoques* twice and *incoques* once, and *decoques* three

---

[1] Adams, *Pelagonius* p. 461, citing in support V. Väänänen, *Introduction au latin vulgaire* (Paris, 1981), p. 143. See also the comment by J. Herman, p. 113 n. 2, below.

[2] Abbott & Mansfield, *A Primer of Greek Grammar* (London, repr. 1977), *Syntax* §74.

[3] See Adams, *Pelagonius*, p. 468.

[4] This summary does not take acount of the variant spellings *quoquere* etc. for *coquere.*

times. *coques* is found three times in *EV.* The subjunctive *coquas* is found seven times with *si*, and four times in a jussive sense, *decoquas*. The phrase *dum coquitur/praecoquitur* etc. is found 12 times in *Apicius* and twice in *EV. cum coquitur* is found twice in *Apicius* and once in *EV. sic coquitur* is found twice in *Apicius*. The passive subjunctive *coquatur* is found slightly more frequently: there are 13 occurrences in *Apicius*, 10 with *ut*, 2 with *antequam*, and one each with *si* and *quousque*. It is not found in a jussive sense. It occurs once with *ut* in *EV.* The plural passive *coquantur* and compounds occur 8 times with *ut* in Apicius, and once in a jussive sense, at 4.3.3; there are a further 11 examples, including *habeatur, uideatur, impleatur, obligetur*. Adams regards the present passive subjunctive as a mark of an 'epistolary' style, more literary than the other imperatival constructions. Consecutive *ne*, with the sense *ut non*, is found 17 times, while the more classical *ut non* is found just twice.[1]

The three verbs referred to above are all third conjugation; as a comparison, we may note the ways in which two common first-conjugation verbs, *elixare*, 'to boil', and *obligare*, 'to thicken', are used. The present indicative form *elixas* occurs 28 times in *Apicius* and twice in *EV*; the future *elixabis* 9 times in *Apicius* only. *elixatur* occurs twice, and *elixantur* once in *Apicius*. Subjunctive forms are not found. *obligas* is found 55 times in *Apicius* and twice in *EV*, with 18 instances of *obligabis* in *Apicius* and 5 in *EV. obligatur* is found once in *Apicius*, and *obligetur* once with *ut*. Plural forms are not used. There is, evidently, an overall preference for using present forms of first-conjugation verbs, whereas future forms are preferred with common verbs of the third conjugation.

Some peculiarities of usage may be noted: there are just three examples of an imperatival gerundive,[2] at 1.2 *adiciendum*, 4.2.24 *addendum acetum*, and 8.8.1 *coquendus*. The present participle is not used in a substantival sense,[3] though it is used in a descriptive mode on 10 occasions. There are some particular uses of adverbs found in *Apicius*, including *diligenter* (19 occurrences) and *bene* (28 occurrences). As Adams points out, these are 'empty' words, adding little more than intensity to the instructions.[4] A number of adverbs in *–atim* are found: *tenuatim, frustratim, decusatim, particulatim* and *uariatim* once each, *tessellatim* twice, and *minutatim* a total of 19 times. In Pelagonius, Adams regards them

[1] See Adams, *Pelagonius*, pp. 480ff.
[2] Adams, *Pelagonius*, p. 197f.
[3] Adams, *Pelagonius*, pp. 153ff.
[4] Adams, *Pelagonius*, pp. 191-2.

as 'all belonging to the sphere of surgery or, more particularly, cautery'.[1] The reflexive *sibi* is found particularly in the phrase *ius de suo sibi* (26 times), *cum sua sibi tegilla* at 4.3.4, and *ut combibant sibi* at *Excerpta Vinidarii* 30. These are regarded by Adams as 'interchangeable with the possessive adjective rather than a genitive' in Pelagonius.[2] The phrase *ita ut*, frequent in Pelagonius, is also found frequently (22 times) in *Apicius*,[3] and there are 23 instances of *simul* (19 in *Apicius*, and four in the *Excerpta Vinidarii*), frequently in a local sense rather than a temporal one.[4] The word *globulus*, found at 8.8 4, is an interesting usage in that it is found 'from Pelagonius onwards'.[5]

Two prepositional uses may be noted. First, *de* marking provenance is found in a number of places; in some instances this has a locative force, as at 1.4 *post septem dies rosam de uino tollis,* 1.17 *accipies uuas de uite inlaesas,* and 1.27 *oliuas de arbore sublatas*. This usage is extended into the equivalent of a partitive genitive and an instrumental equivalent, such as at 1.1 *intercedente prius suffisione uini de suo modo ac numero,* 1.14 *dulcia de melle,* 2.1.1 *esicia fiunt marina de cammaris ...,* among numerous examples found throughout these books. This usage is also found in the technical writings of the Latin veterinarians and as Adams points out 'the expression cannot be classified as vulgar. Comparable expressions are found even in Republican writers.'[6] In a similar extended manner, *ex* is used in phrases such as 1.6 *uinum ex atro candidum facies: lomentum ex faba factum* it implies 'made from' with a separative force; it is also used in a specific way in frequently-found phrases such as 2.3.1 *sic coquuntur ex aqua oleo liquamine fasciculo porrorum et anetho* and 3.4.2 *cucurbitas coques ex aqua* in what Adams calls a 'sort of recipe-shorthand ... it is doubtful whether speakers by the fourth century would have been aware of any separative force in *ex* in expressions such as *coquo ex*.'[7] The usage is illustrated

---

[1] Adams, *Pelagonius*, p. 541.

[2] Adams, *Pelagonius*, p. 456. See the comment on the 'odd reflexive phrases; such as *et sic plecaremus nos ad montem* in the *Peregrinatio* of Egeria' by John N. Green, 'The collapse and replacement of verbal inflection in Late Latin/Early Romance: how would one know?', in R. Wright (ed.), *Latin and the Romance Languages*, 83-99, at pp. 93-4.

[3] Adams, *Pelagonius*, p. 483f.

[4] Adams, *Pelagonius*, pp. 620ff.

[5] Adams, *Pelagonius*, p. 556.

[6] Adams, *Pelagonius*, pp. 430-8, at 430-1 and citing V. Väänänen, *Recherches et récréations latino-romaines* (Naples, 1981), pp. 80-119.

[7] Adams, *Pelagonius*, pp. 440ff.

by comparing 4.2.5 *patina de asparagis* with 4.2.7 *patina ex rusticis siue tamnis siue sinapi*, and 1.12 *uas ab aceto aut ex aceto uasculum picatum laba*, which must mean something like '(take a) vinegar-jar or wash a little pitched jar with some vinegar...' It is found juxtaposed with a plain instrumental ablative, with which it is interchangeable, as for example at 3.4.4 *aliter cucurbitas elixatas: ex liquamine oleo mero* and 3.4.5 *aliter cucurbitas frictas: oenogaro simplici et pipere*. As in the veterinary texts studied by Adams, 'the complement had become an almost fossilised instrumental-equivalent (i.e. sociative instrumental) in the language of recipes, in association particularly with certain verbs.'[1]

The periphrastic future perfect passive, formed from the past participle passive with *erit/erint*, is entirely absent from *Apicius*. In its place is the participle with *fuerit* (32 times) or with *fuerint* (9 times). Adams notes that this form of the future perfect is found once in the *Anonymus Valesianus II*, but that it occurs 12 times in the Ravenna papyri. Woodcock notes that this construction is 'loosely used' from Livy onwards.[2] The future tense *erit* is found twice in Book 1, at 1.2 *si uas erit* and 1.6 *alia die erit*. It is also found in the phrase *quod satis erit* at 4.2.24, 8.4.2, and 9.4.2. The future perfect *fuerit* is also found in similar phrases, *si opus fuerit* at 1.34, 1.35, 5.2.3 and 8.8.4, and *cum necesse fuerit* at 1.4, 1.33 and 3.18.2. The classically-formed future tense is found throughout *Apicius*, particularly as a form of command; but there are also two instances of the periphrastic future formed from the future participle active + *esse*, at 1.4 *facturus es*, and 3.10.4 *manducaturus es*.[3] Alongside these may be noted the frequent occurrence of *coctura* (24 instances, plus one in the *Excerpta Vinidarii*), a noun-type described as denoting abstractions which develop a concrete meaning with collective value.[4] Cf. also 7.4.3, *sunt conditura*.

Quantities are in the vast majority of cases found with the genitive, following classical usage. There are some exceptions: a mixture of both genitive and accusative is found in 1.27 (9 genitives and 6 accusatives – cf. 1.27, where only

---

[1] Adams, *Pelagonius*, pp. 440-1.

[2] J. N. Adams, *The Text and Language of a Vulgar Latin Chronicle (Anonymus Valesianus II)* (Institute of Classical Studies, London, Bulletin Supplement No. 36, 1976), pp. 66-7; Woodcock, op. cit., p. 80.

[3] Adams, *Anonymus Valesianus II*, p. 68.

[4] E. Espinilla Buisán, 'Les mots en *-tio*, *-tura*, *-tus* dans la prose technique de S. I. Frontin: *De Aquaeductu Vrbis Romae*', in *Latin Vulgaire, Latin Tardif* IV (Hildesheim, Zurich, New York 1998), 643-54, at pp. 648-9.

the genitive is found) and 4.2.4. *gengiber* seems to be treated as an indeclinable, as *piper* often seems to be, in 1.27 and 4.2.29, though it is declined classically elsewhere. *asareos* is found with a qualifying noun indicating quantity at 7.5.4 and 8.6.5; it appears to be a Greek third-declension genitive from an otherwise unattested *asarus* or *asaris*.[1]

The *-o* ending is found indicating the second declension masculine singular accusative (see for example 4.1.2, and frequently in the *Excerpta Vinidarii*). Third declension adjectives may have a neuter accusative in *–em*, as at 3.20.4 *coriandrum uiridem* (unless this is an otherwise unattested masculine form *coriandrus*). Adjectives and nouns of the third declension may have ablatives in *–i* for *–e* (cf. 7.6.13), or *–e* for *–i* (for example, 9.10.9). This *i/e* confusion may be a further example of the identical pronunciation of these vowels noted above where they occur in 2nd person singular verb endings.[2]

There are several instances of non-classical case usages with prepositions: *cum* is found with both the ablative and the accusative;[3] a number of instances are to be found in section 4.2, and there are other instances at 3.19, 3.20.6, 8.7.9, 9.8.4, and 9.10.7. There are also instances of *in* taking either the ablative or the accusative (for example, at 8.1.10);[4] *pro* is also found with the accusative at 7.11.6. Other confusion of the these two cases may be noted at (for example) 7.1.6. At 4.2.10 we have rejected Hummelberg's emendation *de curcurbitis* for *de cucurbitas* found in *VE*: *de* is found with the accusative in the reconstructed text of a recently-found Romano-British lead tablet from Radcliffe-on-Soar tentatively dated to the fourth century, *annoto de duas ocrias*, and was used in the sixth century by Theodosius, *monasterium . . . de castas*, so the usage is not without attestation, however unclassical it may be.[5] We have also retained *VE*'s reading *de fumum* at 2.1.4; here *de* has a sense of motion from noted by Adams, though its use with the accusative appears unparalleled.[6]

---

[1] The forms attested for this rare noun are *asarum, -i* n. in *Lewis and Short*, and *asaron* in *Liddell and Scott*.

[2] See p. 101.

[3] cf. also Adams, *Anonymus Valesianus II*, pp. 54-5, and J. Herman, 'Spoken and written Latin', p. 40: in inscriptions of the fourth century, 'the ablative-accusative opposition did not work any more'.

[4] cf. Adams, *Anonymus Valesianus II*, pp. 53-4.

[5] R. S. O. Tomlin and M. W. C. Hassall, 'Inscriptions', *Britannia* XXXV (2004), pp. 336-7; Theodosius, *De situ terrae sanctae*, 11, cited by Herman, *Vulgar Latin*, p. 60.

[6] Adams, *Anonymus Valesianus II*, p. 56.

The MSS readings show quite clearly that a number of commonly-used nouns were acceptable in different genders: for example, *pisa -ae* f. and *pisum –i* n. are interchangeable in 5.3.1–5, and *ouam* is found at 7.13.6; *sub cute suo* is read for *sub cute sua* at 8.7.12. At 7.6 both MSS read *petrosilenem* for *petrosilenum*, while there is an apparent first declension form *petrosilene* at 7.5.2. Both *piper* and *laser* are sometimes treated as indeclinable nouns. Neuter plural nouns in *-a* become feminine nouns of the first declension – for example, *intubae* at 3.18.1, and *ouam* at 7.13.6.[1] Conversely, *uulua steriles* is the MSS reading at the start of Book 7, but we regard this as scribal error. At 4.5.2 a neuter plural noun is found in the MSS with a singular verb, in Greek manner, but we accept the plural reading offered by the Renaissance MSS.

'Vulgar' vocabulary:

manducare is used instead of *esse* at 2.1.4 and 6.2.2, and in the forms *manducet* (4.2.12), *manducatur* (7.2.2) and *manducaturus es* (3.10.4). Regular verb conjugations were easier to use than irregular ones, and longer words were less likely to be confused with other homonymic words than short ones.[2] *foris* is found in place of *extra* at 6.2.3, 7.11.1, and 8.6.8.[3] *postea* is used in a classical sense in 24 of the 26 times it appears in *Apicius*, indicating that an action just described is followed by what comes next: 'do *"A"*, *postea* do *"B"*.' Three instances of this are also found in the *Excerpta Vinidarii*. However, at 3.18.2 the obvious sense of the recipe demands that it must stand for *postquam*, in the sense 'after', i.e. 'do *"A" postea* you do (or, have done) *"B"*.'[4]

It is noteworthy that compound terms such as *facere habeo* and *facere debeo* are not found in *Apicius*.

Peculiarities of spelling found in the MSS of *Apicius* and the *Excerpta Vinidarii* are discussed in section 6, below.

[1] Cf. for similar instances of this phenomenon Adams, *Anonymus Valesianus II*, pp. 54, 90.
[2] Herman, *Vulgar Latin*, pp. 100-1.
[3] Adams, *Anomymus Valesianus II*, p. 85.
[4] cf. Adams, *Anomymus Valesianus II*, p. 120; see above, p. 91.

6. EDITORIAL PRINCIPLES AND METHODS

Apicius presents a challenge to an editor in that the two principal manuscripts very largely agree in preserving a text written in a technical rather than literary style which, as we have argued earlier, is the result of a drawn-out process of gathering and collating recipes. These are – so far as one can tell – left in an 'original' state, with little obvious attempt at editing them into a homogeneous style. Behind the text there thus lies a multiplicity of authors rather than a single mind, and there can be no question of emending the text to try to restore the 'author's intention' as might be the case with a classical literary work. Moreover, it is impossible to define in what region of the Roman world this collection was assembled – it may even have been eclectic, gathered from different provinces, with some material definitely demonstrating a Greek rather than Roman origin, and assembled over not decades but centuries. This might account for the variety of linguistic practice found throughout the text, to say nothing of some of the 'late' spellings contained in much of *E* and *V* which are discussed below.

However, it is fair to assume with Milham[1] that the two principal manuscripts, which are described below, are copies of a single source – an archetype in a stemmatic, but not authorial sense, referred to as α in the stemma below, which had survived the ravages of change and lay accessible in a Carolingian monastery (or monasteries, if it were loaned or transferred), possibly at Tours.

It is interesting to speculate why these two copies of *Apicius* should have been made, even if such speculation remains just that. In the case of *E*, it is possible that it is the product of a routine copying exercise, 'updating' a monastic library's holdings. The presence of several hands – one very erratic in places – might also suggest that it was suitable work for a novice, using non-sensational material, working alongside a more experienced scribe, though there would have been no shortage of more edifying textual matter available for such purposes! This is hardly the case with *V*, the Tours manuscript whose highly decorated opening pages mark it out as a special product, quite possibly destined to be

---

[1] M. E. Milham, 'Toward a Stemma and Fortuna of Apicius', *Italia Medioevale e Umanistica* X (1967), 259-320, at pp. 259-65.

a gift for Charles the Bald.[1] What interest *he* had in culinary matters remains lost in obscurity. By the time of its copying (and to judge by the quality of its presentation) we can hardly assume that it was intended for practical use in the royal kitchens. Perhaps it was more of a kind of literary conceit, a text on matters of interest to the royal household prepared in a manner fit for a king.

A further question arises on which one can only speculate: what was the source of *V* and *E* like? Where was it written, and why? One might imagine a copy of *Apicius* being made in order to preserve a text which might otherwise be lost, for its own sake, at the end of the Roman imperial period, during the years of turmoil in the sixth century. The source of this might well have been a 'working copy', and was almost certainly a codex, for we find in our current copies that in Book 6 what seems like an entire gathering of it appears to have been lost at some late stage in the transmission (certainly after the process of collecting recipes had ended). Perhaps it was chanced upon in some great household, and its preservation was felt to be key to the survival of a culture under threat. Then this putative sixth-century volume, or a copy of it, may have made its way into a monastic house, and then – perhaps *pari passu* with the spread of Benedictine monasticism – arrived at last in the Merovingian kingdoms.

All this is, as we have said, speculation (and of a rather romantic kind); but the text was preserved *somehow* and, however it may have happened, it ended up in Merovingian Gaul, where it was destined for preservation during a crucial stage of the transmission of texts when so many other works, arguably of greater value and importance, were lost.

The presentation of the Latin text of *Apicius* itself presents a dilemma to any prospective editor. It may be argued that, given the fluid nature of the text's composition, and the likelihood that a number of redactors have successively shaped the collection, the only safe course of action is to print the readings of *VE* for *Apicius* and of *A* for the *Excerpta Vinidarii*. Such an argument would satisfy those who would contend that the MSS texts are all that we have, and that it is impossible to penetrate beyond them. This argument is further strengthened by the orthography and syntax of *Apicius* as they are documented in the two principal manuscripts, which make little effort to smooth out or 'regularize' a remarkable variety of spellings; it is likely that the oddities found in the text accurately reflect the style of the late-Imperial formulation of *Apicius*, and

---

[1] For a detailed description of this manuscript, see pp. 118-119 below.

improbable that they are the product of a later copying process. In this respect, they are akin to the text of *Anonymus Valesianus II* as preserved in one of its principal manuscripts, *B*. Adams comments on its practice, 'although copyists habitually introduce orthographic vulgarisms (involving usually the change of single letters), it would be another matter to accept that the scribe introduced syntactic and lexical vulgarisms (involving the changes of words, phrases and whole constructions) on an extensive scale'.[1] Given the putative dates and locations of our principal MSS, it is therefore unlikely that any of the 'vulgar' orthography has been introduced by their scribes, and must go back to an earlier period.

If the non-classical spellings are thought to be the work of a late compiler, it seems odd that changes were not made to the text as a whole. Though it is a truth that scribes are never consistent, the evidence from the two *Apicius* MSS would require on almost every page that their scribes were inconsistent on a consistent basis; the inconsistencies must therefore be attributed to some other cause. It is possible (and in our view probable) that the inconsistent orthographical practice of *VE* is due either to the varied dates of composition of the recipes, or to the abilities and predilections of their composers. The resulting anomalies do not seem to have bothered any transcriber enough for them to have been 'ironed out'. They should not be taken as indicative of a *place* of production, either: Varvaro notes that relations between 'norms' and 'variations' were homogeneous throughout the Roman world, and in his view only ceased with 'the collapse of the empire', wherever that occurred in the sense that central control failed.[2]

Of previous editors, only André has made any efforts at reflecting the Late Latin orthography of *V* and *E*; however, given the nature of the text as a whole, this seems to be the correct course to pursue, to do it justice not only as a source of information for food history, but as a linguistic document in its own right. Other editions of *Apicius* and studies of the text have either regularized the spelling completely, or have tended to alter it to correspond to Latin morphology and syntax found elsewhere.[3] Now it is true that *Apicius* is a compilation of earlier material – according to internal criteria, there are no grounds for dating the vast majority of the recipes to later than *c.* AD 250–300 – and, as noted in section 5

---

[1] Adams, *Anonymus Valesianus II*, p. 13.

[2] A. Varvaro, 'Latin and Romance: fragmentation or restructuring?', in R. Wright (ed.), *Latin and the Romance Languages*, 44-51, at pp. 48-9.

[3] André's edition in the Budé series is the notable exception to this rule.

above, it incorporates different levels of syntax, some recipes approximating more to classical 'norms' than others. However, it seems quite possible that even among cooks a number of different registers of expression may have co-existed, and it is clear from the lack of editorial interference in the recipes that in the form in which they survive, complex recipes are allowed to co-exist with others whose expression is clumsy, obscure, and lacking in any linguistic depth or accuracy by classical standards.

It is possible that some of the more clumsy specimens are also early, but reflect the work of a cook who was *indoctior* than others: Varvaro notes that 'from the chronological point of view this "vulgar" documentation is spread over a period of several centuries, from archaic Latin right through to the High Middle Ages. From the social point of view it is towards the "low" end of the scale, but the stratification is complex'.[1] Thus although a number of the recipes included in *Apicius* can be dated to an early Imperial or even late Republican period,[2] there seems no justification for 'normalizing' all spellings in the Latin text, but rather every justification for regarding the text in its own right as evidence of actual practice, even when there are no other instances of a usage it presents, for example in treating *coriandrum* as a masculine (3.20.4). Literary Latin may be a woefully insufficient guide to Latin as spoken and written by non-literary groups, as is shown by the examples of words such as *coxale* (belt) used by St Jerome in his Vulgate translation, noted by Herman.[3] Thus our practice is closer to that of André than to that of Giarratano-Vollmer or Milham in this respect, but where we have italicized Latin terms in the translation, we retain the classical forms of words which are used in any Latin dictionary so that readers unfamiliar with later spellings can more easily carry out word-searches of their own.

The principle we have therefore adopted in presenting a text of *Apicius* is to retain the readings of the two ninth-century manuscripts as far as possible. Beyond the evidence they present, we have no way of knowing what was the orthographical practice of whoever finally copied, assembled, or revised the exemplar – or the codex from which the exemplar derived – from which *VE* are descended. Moreover, as we have stated earlier, we have no way of knowing what level of Latinity each or any of the recipe authors may have possessed, except in so far as it may be preserved by *VE*. Theirs is the only authority to

[1] Varvaro, op. cit., at p. 46.
[2] See pp. 15-16.
[3] Herman, 'Spoken and Written Latin', at pp. 32-4.

which we can refer. That said, the lack of 'normalization' in them, and the extraordinary variety of treatment of the same word, even on a single page, which is sometimes found, may be an indication of careful copying – and the fact that both often reproduce identical *variations* in spelling may indicate that they are copies of the same exemplar. However, in the case of each manuscript, multiple scribes have been identified and, given their putative dating, it remains a clear possibility that a certain amount of 'normalization' may have taken place. Where *VE* agree, we print their spelling; variations in spelling the same word, even on the same pages, are very often reproduced identically by both MSS. Where the MSS disagree, we have adopted the practices set out below, based on the assumption that differences between the two MSS reflect occasions where one or other of them has 'normalized', and the other has preserved a more 'vulgar' spelling, which we prefer; this is often *V*, as Brandt pointed out,[1] although there are occasions when the less classical orthography is preserved in *E*.

In the case of the *Excepta Vinidarii*, the spellings preserved in *A* are much more indicative of proto-Romance than is the case in *V* and *E*, but even in *A* there is a divergence in practice, with many instances of 'phonetic' spelling.

In cases where the recipes as transmitted make no obvious sense, and we have as a consequence adopted emendations, we employ an orthography which mirrors the most common practice of *VE* elsewhere. We correct readings which we think may be due to scribal errors caused by phonetic spelling or to evident misreading of letter-forms in the original copy with which the scribes of *VE* may have been unfamiliar. Thus we print *aquam* for *adquam*, *tracta* for *fracta*, *coriandrum* for *coliandrum*, *ligusticum* for *libusticum*, *cnechi* for *enechi,* and *obligas* for *oblizas*, but retain phonetic vulgar forms such as *maziana* for *matiana*, and forms attested elsewhere, such as *frustra* for *frusta*.[2] Where the MSS readings present *hapax legomena*, as for example at 7.7.1 *aqualicum* (otherwise untraced), we have cautiously followed Hummelberg's emendation *aqualicium*, but we have to accept that the reading preserved may well be evidence of the existence of a variant form of the noun.[3] All rejected readings are recorded in the apparatus, which is as a consequence more detailed than might be expected in a critical text.

---

[1] Brandt, *Untersuchungen*, p. 20.

[2] Adams, *Anonymus Valesianus II*, p. 30.

[3] We accept that we may be too cautious in this respect: cf. the example of *coxale* in Jerome, p. 110 n. 3 above.

DIVERGENT READING	WE PRINT THE FOLLOWING (AND REPORT THE REJECTED READING IN THE LEMMA)
ciatus/cyatus	*ciatus*
i/y in words of Greek origin	*i*
ciatus/ciathus	*ciatus* (i.e. assumes medial '*h*' is added by the scribe)
citrium/cytrium etc.	where *VE* agree we print their reading; where they vary, we prefer the non-classical spelling, e.g. *ciatus*, but *cytrium*
com-/con-/cō-[1]	where *com*- is found in both *VE*, we print it; *con*- preferred over both *com*- and cō-, which are both reported in the apparatus; where both MSS read cō- we expand to *con*-
cū	*cum*
b/u confusion, e.g. *sauanus/ sabanus, bulbula/uuluula*	*sauanus, uuluula*[2]
BUT *obligaueris/-beris* and *ouum/obum*	*obligaberis, obum* etc. preferred where either or both of *VE* have it
ferbuerit/feruuerit	*ferbuerit* is preferred where either or both *VE* read it
initial *h-* (e.g. *holus/olus*)	*h* omitted (*olus*) except where both have it, and where it is 'incorrect' e.g. *hostrea*[3]

[1] Herman, *Vulgar Latin* p. 39, notes that the dental nasal [n] replaced the bilabial nasal [m] found in classical Latin. *con*- is found on numerous occasions written out in full, though this was not the practice (for example) of the Venerable Bede, who insists on an ·*m*· in such verbs as *comburo, comparo, compono, complaceo, comprehendo*: see his *De Orthographia*, ad. loc. As elsewhere in this work, Bede's protest may reflect a dislike of commonplace orthographical practice in his day, or familiarity with Late Latin spellings in some of the MSS available to him in Wearmouth/ Jarrow.

[2] Herman, *Vulgar Latin* p. 45, comments on the intervocalic conconant [-b-] that forms such as *siui* for *sibi* or *uiba* for *uiua* 'are common all over the (Latin-speaking) area from the first century AD', and that *u*, representing the semivowel [w], was confused with *b*, 'which represented the normal voiced bilabial plosive [β]' (p. 39).

[3] Herman, *Vulgar Latin* p. 38: 'we can mention a change that happened in the Republican period, that is, even before the Empire: the laryngeal aspirate /h/ was dropped in all positions in a word'. Cf. Adams, *Anonymus Valesiana II*, p. 48; *Apicius* 4.2.13.

DIVERGENT READING	WE PRINT THE FOLLOWING (AND REPORT THE REJECTED READING IN THE LEMMA)
medial *–h (ch-/c-, th-/t-)*	*h* omitted
inp-/imp-	*inp-* at start
ī	*in*
isicia/ esicia	*esicia*
ispisso/spisso, etc.	*ispisso*, etc.[1]
mittis/mittes	*mittes* is preferred[2]
p/b confusion (e.g. *apua, abua*)	*abua* is preferred
g/b confusion	*g* is preferred

We print forms of *quoquere* in preference to *coquere*, etc., wherever they are found, and note variants in the lemma. Where both MSS read *coquere*, etc., we print it.

Where the two MSS differ in their treatment of *cauliculi* in its various guises, we print *V* and report *E*. Likewise where they diverge in the spelling on *petrosilenum* and its variations, we print *V* and report *E*.

In the case of diphthongs, we think that on balance is it fair to assume that by the ninth century, scribes were more likely to abbreviate diphthongs than to expand them (despite the Venerable Bede's comments in his *De Orthographia*, where he identifies some words as specifically requiring a diphthong – implying that they were not always so written).[3] Thus on any occasion we adopt the 'fullest' clear reading found in either of the MSS, and report other readings such as æ/ę/e in the lemma. However, we do *not* report other abbreviations, such as *p* with the macron, frequently found in *V*. In this case, we print the expanded version found in the other MS, or, where both MSS use *p* with the macron, we expand to *pre-*.

---

[1] Herman, *Vulgar Latin*, p. 35: the prothetic vowel 'turns up all over Romance, but particularly in the West'.

[2] Herman, *Vulgar Latin*, p. 34: 'most of the Romance regions have /e/ in an unstressed final syllable coming from all of Latin long /e:/. short /e/, and short /i/. Thus in fifth-century epitaphs we are as likely to find written *iacit* as *iacet* (which is the correct form, "lies"), and *requiescet* as *requiescit*'. See also the detailed treatment in Adams, *Anonymus Valesianus II*, pp. 40-42.

[3] Bede, *De Orthographia*: among several examples, *celo celas . . . per simplicem ·e· scribendum; caelo caelas . . per dipthongon ·ae·*.

Herman comments that 'the diphthongs also developed ... *ae* and *oe* ... became monophthongs at an early date ... these changes are attested by countless spelling mistakes'.[1] All forms of ae/æ/ę/e are found in *VE*, whereas Adams notes that in the *Anonymous Valesianus II*, 'there are only 7 examples of <ae> ... compared with 79 of <e>'.[2] Given the variety of practice found in the two MSS on even a single page, it seems more than likely that they reproduce the exemplar from which they are copied with some fidelity.

We write numbers as words when either MSS does so, and report any abbreviations in the lemma; where both MSS use numerals, we print numbers as e.g. I, III. The *incipits* and *explicits* of each book are spelled out in full, and use of numerals is noted in the apparatus.

Where the text of *Apicius* seems to us to be utterly garbled or incoherent, we have attempted to make some sense of it by emendation, and where we have declined to make use of earlier editors' suggestions, we have recorded their suggestions in the apparatus. As the reader will note, the text as preserved has from time to time proved indecipherable, and emendation has been our only recourse without resorting to the presentation of a diplomatic transcription of one or other (or both) manuscripts. At any event, we have tried to keep emendations to a minimum. We are aware that in doing this, we may be doing one or other of the sources of *Apicius* an injustice, since it is perfectly possible that an ancient cook was quite clear what he meant by a form of words, possibly mispronounced and then written down as accurately as his level of literacy would allow, but still clear to him, but whose meaning completely eludes us.

For the purposes of establishing the text, we first collated *V*, *E* and (for the *Excerpta Vinidarii*) *A*, both through the use of microfilms and examination of the manuscripts at first hand. We then compared their readings with the texts of Milham, André, Marsili, Giarratano and Vollmer, and Schuch. We accept Milham's contention that the later MSS are all derived from *VE* and are strictly speaking *codices eliminandi*.[3] However we have verified this in some small part by collating those manuscripts which were readily available to us during the course of our other research: N (Rome, Vaticanus latinus 6337); J (Rome, Vaticanus latinus 6803); T (Rome, Vaticanus Vrbinas latinus 1145); Q (Rome,

---

[1] Herman, *Vulgar Latin*, p. 31.

[2] Adams, *Anonymus Valesianus II*, p. 43.

[3] Milham, 'Stemma and Fortuna', p. 263: 'Thus V, through ζ, was the ultimate source of every extant humanistic copy of Apicius'.

Vaticanus Vrbinas latinus 8086); P (Paris, Bibiliothèque Nationale 8209 (λ in Milham); D (Oxford, Bodleianus Canonicianus class. lat. 168) and B (Oxford, Bodleianus Add. B 110). In addition we had access to the various sixteenth-century printed texts located in libraries in London and Oxford.

In the case of the *Excerpta Vinidarii*, we print the readings of the sole MS, following the practice established by André. Its spellings may seem peculiar to readers unfamiliar with the practices of Vulgar Latin, but the text seems to be an accurate representation of the language one would expect in a sixth-century compilation, a date for which we have offered arguments elsewhere.[1] In particular, lists of nouns with endings in *–um* are spelled without either final *–m* or with the macron *ū*. This appears to be common practice at a late date: the pronunciation of the final *–m* may well have been omitted by the early empire, while Wright comments that 'we can deduce, for example, from the phrasing of the orthographical instructions that Cassiodorus gave to his monks in sixth-century Italy, that the addition of a final *–m* to a noun was seen as a matter of written correctness alone.'[2] A similar practice may be found in *Anonymous Valesianus II*: 'it is worth mentioning that some of the accusatives without <m> in *B* occur in strings of accusatives … the author apparently felt it sufficient to mark the case in the classical manner just once; in the rest of the series he would employ a spelling which better represented his pronunciation. The inconsistency is thus due on the one hand to his desire to use a classical form with which he would only have been familiar in writings; and on the other hand to his uneasiness about the artificiality of a string of terminations no longer in everyday use.'[3] This phenomenon is particularly frequent in the *Excerpta Vinidarii*, where other apparent case-confusion is also evident.

---

[1] See above, pp. 32ff.

[2] Cf. Herman, *Vulgar Latin,* p. 39; R. Wright, *A Sociological Study of Late Latin* (Turnhout, 2002), p. 9.

[3] Adams, *Anonymus Valesianus II*, p. 52.

7. DESCRIPTION OF THE MANUSCRIPTS AND STEMMA

The fact that the text of *Apicius* can confidently be based only on the two early manuscripts which have come down to us, *E* and *V*, both benefits and hampers the prospective editor of the text.[1] The benefits lie in the relatively straightforward and simple nature of the two manuscripts, their clarity, legibility, and the close relationship which they portray; accepting the authority of their shared readings, we can be confident that they faithfully represent whatever lost source they derive from. On the other hand, the editor is hampered by their limited scope and range, and by their obvious shortcomings: *E* has at least one leaf missing at the start, and is thus defective, while *V* begins with a conundrum of a title page which has defied any convincing explanation.[2]

The stemma set out below is a simplified version of that proposed by Milham[3] and is intended to highlight the relations of these two manuscripts as deriving from a lost common parent α, which ultimately derives from the complex process of gathering recipes which is described elsewhere in this edition.[4] Also deriving from this process, we believe, was another collection of recipes which evidently carried the name *Apicius* and from which excerpts were made by one Vinidarius, *uir inlustris*, an unknown but historical figure of senior senatorial status. As Milham demonstrated, all the late manuscripts are derived from *V* and are considered strictly as *codices eliminandi*, though some of their scribes attempted to make sense of the more perplexing passages which lay in front of them; *E* entered this tradition through Politian's acquaintance with it, though not in time to be included in the text of the *editio princeps* (Rot[1], Rot[2]).

---

[1] The case was first put by F. Vollmer, in his *Studien zu dem römischen Kochbuche von Apicius*, "Sb. Bayer. A. W.", Abhandlungen 6, Munich, 1920, and incorporated in the Teubner edition of 1922 on which he and Giarratano collaborated; it was fully and convincingly explored by Milham in 'Stemma and Fortuna', at pp. 259-65. See also L. D. Reynolds, 'Apicius', in L. D. Reynolds (ed.). *Texts and Transmission: A Survey of the Latin Classics*, (Oxford, 1983), pp. 13-14.

[2] See below, *ad loc.*

[3] 'Stemma and Fortuna', p. 279, and in M. E. Milham, *Apicii Decem Libri...* (Teubner, Leipzig 1969). p. IX. Both these attempt to identify the derivations and relationships of the many fifteenth-century manuscripts, which lie outside our present interests.

[4] See p. 70 above.

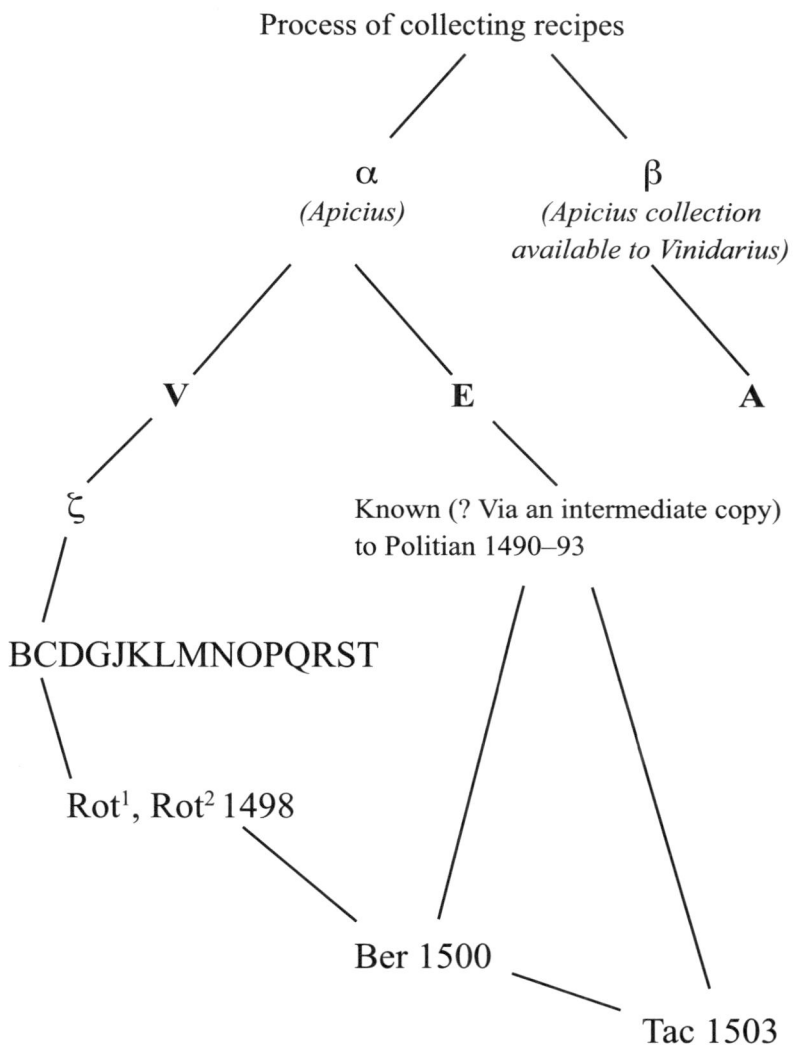

Process of collecting recipes

α
(Apicius)

β
*(Apicius collection
available to Vinidarius)*

V

E

A

ζ

Known (? Via an intermediate copy)
to Politian 1490–93

BCDGJKLMNOPQRST

Rot¹, Rot² 1498

Ber 1500

Tac 1503

Apicius is found in two early (ninth-century) manuscripts, as follows:

E New York Academy of Medicine 1 (formerly Phillipps 275, Cheltenham) – dated to 825–840. Parchment (calfskin), 173 x 223mm., 20 lines per side.[1] The MS was joined to Geneva Bodmeriana 84, which contains the text of the *Pseudo-Hippocrates*. The first leaf (at least), with the incipit/title and the Latin and Greek titles of books I–VI, is missing. The manuscript is written in a large number of distinct hands: ff. 2–6v (top 7 lines), 23r–24v (23r is very untidy in places, and may be a different hand to that of ff. 1–6) and 27v–34v are written in Caroline script; the remainder are in insular hands.[2] Visual inspection of the manuscript suggested that Books 1–6 and 7–10 were written by different groups of scribes, for almost an entire blank side follows the end of Book 6, whereas the text is written continuously up to this point, fresh books beginning at any point on the page. In addition, this gathering is made up of five sheets of parchment, with a single additional leaf (35) added to incorporate the last words of Book 6, written by one of the insular hands, in contrast to 27v–34v, which is written by one of the Caroline hands.[3] In addition, the manner of rubrication (largely carried out by the insular hands) in Books 7–10 differs markedly from that found in 1–6. There are a number of careful corrections to the text, some of which are identifiable as the work of one of the Caroline hands (e.g. 25r, l. 14). First readings and corrections are noted as E1 and E2 in the apparatus, no matter which hand they may be made in.

V Vatican City, Biblioteca Apostolica Vaticana Vrbinas latinus 1146. Parchment, 195 x 235mm., written at Tours either in the second quarter or the final quarter of the ninth century.[4] This is a luxury text, with lavish decoration

[1] See B. Bischoff, *Katalog der festländischen Handscriften des neunten Jahrhunderts (mit Ausnahme der Wisigotischen) Teil II, Laon-Paderborn* (Wiesbaden 2004), p. 314, entry no. 3596.

[2] According to E. Löwe, there are four Caroline and two insular hands *(Berliner philologische Wochenscrift* 40 (1920), cols. 1174-76; Dr H. Spilling has identified five Caroline hands ('Die frühe Phase Karolingischer Minuskel in Fulda', in G. Schrimpf (ed.) *Kloster Fulda in der Welt der Karolingier und Ottonen* (Frankfurt, 1996), pp. 249-84, at p. 266. We are indebted to Prof. David Ganz for his assistance in pointing us to these sources.

[3] Gatherings in *E* are formed as follows: 4 sheets; 4 sheets; 4 sheets; 5 sheets + 1; 4 sheets; 4 sheets; 3 sheets + 1. Each of gatherings III–VII carries original numbering at the foot of its last page.

[4] The most recent description is by P. S. F. Martini, '12. Apicio *De Re Coquinaria*', in *Vedere i classici: l'illustrazione libraria dei testi antichi dall'età romana al tardo medioevo*, ed. M. Buonocore (Rome, 1998); see also E. K. Rand, *A Survey of the Manuscripts of Tours* (Cambridge, Mass.: Medieval Academy of America, 1929), p. 144 n. 90, table CXII, 1-2.

on the opening pages,[1] and it is possible that like other MSS written in this region and at this time it was produced as a gift for Charles the Bald, though it cannot be identified from the surviving inventories of MSS which were in Charles's possession. That he was a bibliophile is without question: among books definitely presented to him are copies of the *De Arithmetica* of Boethius, the *Epitoma* of Vegetius, the 'Vivian Bible' from Tours, the 'Sao Paulo Bible' from Rheims, and the so-called 'Second Bible' from St Amand. McKitterick comments that 'the court and the king, and the possibility of his patronage, were becoming the focus of intellectual and artistic activity'.[2]

Fifteenth-century manuscripts

(NB: all these derive from VE and are therefore *codices eliminandi* apart from the useful suggestions and emendations which their copyists frequently made.)

L	Florence, Laurentianus 73, 20 (*c.* 1458).[3]
M	Munich, clm 756 (*c.* 1495).[4]
N	Rome, Vaticanus latinus 6337 (1494, acc. to Milham).
Q	Rome, Vaticanus latinus 6803 (*c.* 1483, acc. to Milham).
O	St. Petersburg, Instituta Istorii Akademii Nauk 627/2.[5]
Pol	St. Petersburg, Instituta Istorii Akademii Nauk 627/1 (1490–93).
T	Rome, Vaticanus Vrbinas latinus 1145.
J	Rome, Vaticanus Vrbinas latinus 6803.
Q	Rome, Vaticanus Vrbinas latinus 8086 (*c.* 1483).
C	Florence, Riccardianus 141.

[1] The initial highly-illuminated pages (1r – 3v) are a separate gathering of three sheets, the outer one of which is much finer parchment than the rest. The subsequent gatherings are made up of 3, 5, 3, 4, 4, 4, 4, and 3 sheets respectively. The parchment of the last gathering is thicker than that used in the preceding ones.

[2] See R. McKitterick, 'The Palace School of Charles the Bald', in M. Gibson and J. Nelson, with the assistance of D. Ganz (edd.), *Charles the Bald: Court and Kingdom: Papers based on a Colloquium held in London in April 1979* (BAR International Series 101, 1981), pp. 385-400, at pp. 385-6; R. McKitterick, 'Charles the Bald (823–877) and his library: the patronage of learning', *English Historical Review* XCV no. CCCLXXIV (January 1980), pp. 28-47, at pp. 31-2.

[4] Dates are those given by Milham in 'Stemma and Fortuna' and in her Teubner edition.

[4] A copy of *Pol*, according to Milham.

[5] In 'Stemma and Fortuna', Milham regards this MS as fifteenth century; in the stemma in her Teubner edition she refers to it as O1, i.e. first hand in this MS, later collated with N etc., ?after 1565.

R	Florence, Riccardianus 662 (1464).
P	Paris, Bibiliothèque Nationale 8209 (λ in Milham).
S	Florence, Laurentianus Strozzi 67.
D	Oxford, Bodleianus Canonicianus class. lat. 168 (1490).
G	Cesena, Malatestianus 167, 154.
K	Copenhagen, Gl. kgl. Sammlung 3553 (1479).
B	Oxford, Bodleianus Add. B 110.

8. PREVIOUS EDITIONS AND STUDIES

The *Editio Princeps* was printed at Milan, *per magistrum Guilermum Signerre Rothmagensem*, in 1498; this appeared in two guises with slightly different title-pages in the same year.[1] It was rapidly followed by two editions printed in Venice, the first *per Bernardinum Venetum,* n.d. (dated to 1500 in Milham's stemma in 'Stemma and Fortuna'), and the second *per Iohannem de Cereto de Tridino alias Tacuinum* 1503. Some forty years later, two thoughtful Renaissance editions appeared, by A. Torinus (Basle, 1541), and G. Hummelberg (Zurich, 1542). Both these editors are the source of a number of conjectures which are still valuable.

It was a century and a half before any further work was done on *Apicius*. Lister's Amsterdam edition of 1709 was a slight improvement on its predecessors, and then a further century and half passed before Schuch's edition appeared (C. T. Schuch, Heidelberg, Winter, 1874, 2nd ed.). This edition in many ways constituted a retrograde step, because Schuch conflated the texts of *Apicius* and the *Excerpta Vinidarii* with unfortunate results, and tried to incorporate further changes which do injury to the text as it survives. A separate nineteenth-century work which must be mentioned is Ihm's edition of the *Excerpta Vinidarii* (*Archiv für lateinische Lexicographie und Grammatik* XV (1908), 63-73).

Larger events of history – namely, the First World War – led to two important scholars, Giarratano and Vollmer, working independently on *Apicius* before

---

[1] Milham, 'Stemma and Fortuna', p. 289.

peacetime brought them together. During the war, Giarratano produced an edition based solely on *V*, while Vollmer's researches on the text culminated in his important study of 1920.[1] Following the cessation of hostilities, the two scholars collaborated on what was to become the accepted, authoritative text of *Apicius* in the *Bibliotheca Teubneriana* series.[2] The resulting text is very much a product of its age, and shows a preference for correcting what was considered 'barbarous' in the two principal manuscripts rather than accepting the validity of some of the readings where they do not conform to 'classical' norms.

Further studies on the text and its meaning followed, notably by E. Brandt,[3] who prepared an edition of his own which sadly never saw the light of day, but is held in the archives of the *Thesaurus Latinae Linguae* in Munich. Other work was carried out in the 1930s by Svennung.[4] The edition of A. Marsili (Pisa, Colombo Cursi, 1957) kept interest in *Apicius* alive while adding little to our understanding of the text; in fact it reproduces even the typographical errors of the Giarratano-Vollmer edition of over 30 years previously. Finally, there is an unpublished edition by M. B. Wilson in the archives of the New York Academy of Medicine which also dates from this period.

Jacques André edited the text for the *Collection Guillaume Budé* series, with facing translation in French, (J. André, *Apicius, L'art culinaire*, Paris, 1965) and revised it in 1974 following publication of Milham's edition. André reversed the tendency of Giarratano and Vollmer to emend the spellings preserved in *EV*, and offered a very conservative text, as indeed we do. His translation is largely accurate, and contains some valuable points, but is occasionally too influenced in our opinion by classical French culinary tradition, especially where he deals with sauces.

Apart from André's revision, the most recent critical edition prior to the present work was prepared by Mary Ella Milham, based on her very detailed earlier studies of the manuscript tradition.[5] Milham's work concentrated on textual matters, and offered no translation or indications of how the text might

---

[1] F. Vollmer *Studien zu dem römischen Kochbuche von Apicius*, "Sb. Bayer. A. W.", Abhandlungen 6, (Munich, 1920).

[2] ed. C. Giarratano, F. Vollmer (Leipzig, 1922).

[3] Brandt, *Untersuchungen*.

[4] J. Svennung, *Untersuchungen zu Palladius und zur lateinischen Fach- und Volkssprache* (Uppsala, 1935); 'De locis nonnullis Apicianis', *Eranos* XXXIV (1936), pp. 14-24.

[5] M. E. Milham, 'Stemma and Fortuna'; *Apicii Decem Libri...* (Teubner, Leipzig 1969).

be interpreted. While not so conservative in her text as André, she incorporated some forty of his suggestions in her own edition, as André himself points out.[1]

The limitations of earlier translations, and the shortcomings they exhibit in explaining the nature of Roman cookery as exemplified in *Apicius*, are dealt with where they arise in the notes. There are a number of translations in other languages,[2] but three translations which are well known to readers of English are worthy of particular mention.

Vehling may have been an excellent chef but his understanding of ancient cooking was defective in many ways and – despite the effusive testimonial to his ability which prefaces his work – his Latin was, to say the least, extremely limited.[3] Vehling's interpretation is hampered by a complete misunderstanding as to the nature of *garum* and *liquamen*. He assumed that *garum* was a thick anchovy paste, while *liquamen* was a basic stock – liquor. He was also entirely imbued with classical French cooking and attempted to understand the recipes by relating them to dishes familiar to him from French cooking. This of course led him up a great many false avenues of conjecture. His work was based on an eclectic text drawn at random from Torinus, Lister and Giarratano-Vollmer, with little or no critical judgement in evidence. Nevertheless, at some points of difficulty he often came closer to what the text means than others who have followed in his footsteps, simply because he was a chef and had a chef's instinctive knowledge of the nature of food, while the most erudite and scholarly Latinists tend to have a limited knowledge of the kitchen and in that respect they mirror the Roman gourmet!

Most familiar to English-speaking readers is the edition by B. Flower and E. Rosenbaum (London, 1958). They used Giarratano-Vollmer's text with a few minor changes and made no attempt to deal with the more perplexing aspects. The translation is sound but limited by the fact that they were researching and writing in a British post-war context: there is no concept of the Mediterranean

---

[1] J. André, *Apicius, L'art culinaire* (Paris 1965), p. xviii.

[2] In French, B. Guégan *Les dix livres d'Apicius* (Paris, 1933); in Italian, G. Baseggio (Venice, 1852), P. Buzzi (Milan, 1930), of Book 10 only, A. A. Del Re, *De Re Coquinaria Libro X: Il Libro del Pesce* (Milan, 1998); in German, R. Gollmer (Breslau-Leipzig, 1909; 2nd revised edition, Rostock, 1928), E. Danneil (Leipzig, 1911); in Flemish, N. Van Der Auwera, *Apicius De Re Coquinaria: De Romeinse Kookkunst* (Brussels, 2001).

[3] As Flower and Rosenbaum point out, p. 16, 'his text is so full of mistakes that it becomes almost useless as a translation' – a view with which we fully concur!

cuisine that was to burst on the scene in the UK in the early 1960s under the influence of Elizabeth David. Flower and Rosenbaum were also somewhat in awe of Brandt and accepted his theories on the origin and date of the text without question.

John Edward's translation was based largely on the text of Milham (J. Edwards, *The Roman Cookery of Apicius,* New York, 1984), with some readings from André and Giarratano-Vollmer via Flower and Rosenbaum. He understood *garum* in the same way as Vehling and consequently made the same fundamental mistakes. He gives a 'fish pickle' recipe which is so far from the true nature of *liquamen* to be within the realms of fantasy. He was unable, in the early 1980s in the USA, to obtain many of the more obscure spices and herbs in *Apicius* and in consequence he recommended many bizarre and entirely unsuitable substitutes. Many people have used the book with success and told us that they like his recipes but unfortunately they barely have a passing resemblance to Roman food.

Other works on Roman food that translate *Apicius* in part or in full include E. Salza Prina Ricotti, *L'arte del convito nella Roma antica* (Rome, 1983); I. G. Giacosa, *A Taste of Ancient Rome* (Chicago, 1992); P. Fass, *Around the Roman Table,* (Basingstoke and Oxford, 1994); Attilio A. Del Re, *Marco Gavio Apicio De Re Coquinaria: Libro X, il libro del pesce* (Milan, 1998). A number of *Apicius* recipes devised for a modern kitchen were included in *The Classical Cookbook* (A. Dalby and S. Grainger, London and Los Angeles, 1996), and a wider selection is now available in *Cooking Apicius* (S. Grainger, Totnes, 2006).

APICIUS

LATIN TEXT

&

ENGLISH TRANSLATION

SIGLA

Ninth-century MSS

E   New York Academy of Medicine 1.

V   Vatican City, Biblioteca Apostolica Vaticana, Vrbinas latinus 1146.

Note: first readings and corrections in either MS are noted as E1/E2, V1/V2, no matter which hand seems to have made the correction.

Fifteenth-century MSS

(NB: all these derive from VE and are therefore *codices eliminandi* apart from the useful suggestions and emendations which their copyists frequently made.)

L   Florence, Laurentianus 73, 20 (*c.* 1458).

M   Munich, clm 756 (*c.* 1495).

N   Rome, Vaticanus latinus 6337 (1494, acc. to Milham).

J   Rome, Vaticanus latinus 6803 (*c.* 1483, acc. to Milham).

O   St. Petersburg, Instituta Istorii Akademii Nauk 627/2.

Pol St. Petersburg, Instituta Istorii Akademii Nauk 627/1 (1490-93).

T   Rome, Vaticanus Vrbinas latinus 1145.

Q   Rome, Vaticanus Vrbinas latinus 8086 (*c.* 1483).

C   Florence, Riccardianus 141.

R   Florence, Riccardianus 662 (1464).

P   Paris, Bibiliothèque Nationale 8209 (λ in Milham).

S   Florence, Laurentianus Strozzi 67.

D   Oxford, Bodleianus Canonicianus class. lat. 168 (1490).

G   Cesena, Malatestianus 167, 154.

K   Copenhagen, Gl. kgl. Sammlung 3553 (1479).

B   Oxford, Bodleianus Add. B 110.

Other sigla used in the apparatus

σ used by Milham in her stemma as lost copy at one remove of L.

ζ used by Milham, following Vollmer, as the lost parent (at several removes?) of TLSC. C plus γ are regarded as parents of BJP. André used MSS TCP as these were the only three MSS he seems to have collated in detail from this group.

λ used by Milham in her apparatus to denote the parent of BOJPQ, *Pol* etc.

π used by Milham to denote the hypothetical source of D and Rot[1].

Abbreviations for previous editions and studies

Rot¹	Milan, *per magistrum Guilermum Signerre Rothmagensem* (sic), 1498.
Rot²	Milan, *per magistrum Guilermum Signerre Rothmagensem* (sic), 1498.
Ber	Venice, *per Bernardinum Venetum*, n.d. (1500 in Milham's stemma).
Tac	Venice, *per Iohannem de Cereto de Tridino alias Tacuinum* 1503.
Tor	A. Torinus, Basle, 1541.
Hum	G. Hummelberg, Zürich, 1542.
Lis	Lister, Amsterdam, 1709.
Sch	C. T. Schuch, Heidelberg, Winter, 1874 (2nd ed.).
GiVo	C. Giarratano, F. Vollmer, Leipzig, Teubner, 1922.
Bra1	additions to *GiVo* made by Brandt (so Milham).
Bra2	E. Brandt, *Untersuchungen zum römischen Kochbuche, Philologus* Supplementband XIX., Heft III, Leipzig 1927.
Bra3	E. Brandt, unpublished edition in the archives of TLL, Munich.
Mars	A. Marsili, Pisa, Colombo Cursi, 1957.
Wilson	Unpublished edition by M. B. Wilson in the archives of the New York Academy of Medicine.
FR	B. Flower, E. Rosenbaum, London 1958.
Milham	M. E. Milham, Leipzig, Teubner, 1969.
André	J. André, Paris, 1965 (1st ed.), 1974 (2nd ed.).
CGSG	C. Grocock, S. Grainger (the present edition).

.	letter missing or illegible
/	end of line in MS text
< . . .>	conjectural supplement.
[. . .]	conjectural deletion.
†. . . †	seat of corruption.

INCIPIT

BOOK ONE

INCIPIT †APICAE†

	<I	EPIMELES	condita
	II	SARCOPTES	carnes
	III	CEPVROS	olera
5	IIII	PANDECTER	miscellanea
	V	OSPREON	fabae
	VI	TROPETES	uolatilia>
	VII	POLITELES	uoluntaria
	VIII	TETRAPVS	quadripedia
10	VIIII	THALASSA	mare
	X	HALIEVS	piscatura

APICII EPIMELES LIBER PRIMVS

I. conditum paradoxum. II. conditum melizomum. III. absinthium Romanum.
IIII. rosatum et uiolacium. V. oleum Liburnicum sic facies. VI. uinum ex atro
candidum facies. VII. de liquamine <emendando>. VIII. ut carnes sine sale [sine]
quouis tempore recentes sint. VIIII. callum porcinum uel bubulum et ungelle
cocte ut diu durent. X. ut carnem salsam dulcem facias. XI. pisces fricti ut diu
durent. XII. ostrea ut diu durent. XIII. ut uncia laseris toto tempore uti possis.

1. *Title*: INCIPIT API CAE *V*: *no incipit in E, whose first page is missing*: API<CI. CAE<NA>
Milham: API<CII ARTIS MAGIRIC>AE <LIBRI X> *Vo*: *interpreted as* Apicii Caelii *in the
Renaissance MSS represented by* ζ*(Caelii S, B in explicit*: Caeli *CJ in explicit*: Celii *DGLOT*:
Coelii *R). The only general attribution used anywhere else in the text of VE, in the incipits and
explicits to each book, is* Apici(i)   2-11. *Book titles: the Greek of* I–VI *is taken from the
body of the text itself. Previous editors have only included Greek terms, but since* VII–X *in E
are given in both Greek and Latin, we have included our own suggestions for the Latin of* I–VI
7. uolatilia] uoluntaria uolatilia *E, both words placed against* politiles   12. APICII *om. V*
LIBER I *V*   14. Liburnicum *CGSG, cf. 1.5 below*: liburnium *VE*   15. emendando
add.CGSG from internal chapter heading below | sine sale quouis *CGSG*: sine sale sine quouis
VE: cf. 1.8 below   16. bulum *V*   18. uncia λ: unicia *VE*

APICIUS BEGINS

1. *Mise en place*[1]
2. Meat dishes
3. Greens
4. Compound dishes
5. Pulses
6. Fowl
7. Luxury dishes
8. Quadrupeds
9. Seafood
10. Fish

BOOK ONE OF *APICIUS, MISE EN PLACE*

1. Spiced wine surprise. 2. Honeyed wine. 3. Roman absinthe. 4. Rose wine and violet wine. 5. How to make Liburnican oil. 6. How to make cloudy wine clear. 7. On restoring *liquamen*. 8. How to keep meat fresh whenever you like without salt. 9. How to preserve cooked pork or beef rind and trotters. 10. How to make salted meat sweet. 11. How to preserve fried fish. 12. How to preserve oysters. 13. How to make an ounce of *laser* last for ever. 14. How to preserve sweets

---

[1] *Epimeles* means 'careful' or attentive', hence *FR*'s 'The careful housekeeper'. Such care is understood as preparations done in advance and is very aptly rendered by the standard French culinary term *mise en place*, which fits well with the actions prescribed in Book 1.

XIIII. ut dulcia de melle diu durent. XV. ut mel malum bonum facias. XVI. mel corruptum ut probes. XVII. uuae ut diu seruentur. XVIII. ut mala et mala granata diu durent. XVIIII. ut mala Cidonia diu seruentur. XX. ficum recentem mala pruna pira cerasia ut diu serues. XXI. citria ut diu durent. XXII. mora ut diu durent. XXIII. olera ut diu seruentur. XXIIII. rapae ut diu seruentur. XXV. tubera ut diu seruentur. XXVI. duracina Persica ut diu seruentur. XXVII. sales conditos ad multa. XXVIII. oliuas uirides seruare ut quouis tempore oleum facias. XXVIIII. ciminatum in ostrea et concilia. XXX. laseratum. XXXI. oenogarum in tubera. XXXII. oxyporium. XXXIII. hypotrimma. XXXIV oxygarum digestibile. XXXV. mortaria.

EXPLICIVNT CAPITVLA

I. CONDITVM PARADOXVM. conditi paradoxi conpositio: mellis pondo XV in eneum uas mittuntur, praemissis uini sextariis duobus, ut in cocturam mellis uinum dequoquas. quod igni lento et aridis lignis calefactum, commotum ferola dum quoquitur. si efferuere coeperit, uini rore conpescitur, praeter quod subtracto igni in se redit. cum perfrixerit rursus accenditur. hoc secundo ac tertio fiet, ac tum demum remotum a foco postridie despumatur, tum <mittes> piperis uncias quattuor iam triti, masticis scripulos III, folii et croci dragme singulae, dactilorum ossibus torridis quinque, isdemque dactilis uino mollitis, intercedente prius suffusionem uini de suo modo ac numero, ut tritura lenis habeatur. his omnibus paratis supermittis uini lenis sextaria XVIII; carbones perfecto aderunt †duo milia†.

---

4. diu serues *om. E* | mora utq. *E1*, q *erased*   5. rapæ *E*   6. Persica ut diu seruent *E*   7. amulta *V1*   8. concilia *CGSG from internal chapter heading below*: conciliis *VE* | lasseratum *E*   9. XXXII] XXXI *E*   11. EX PLICIVNT CAPI TVLA *V: not in E*   12. INCIPIT CONDITVM PARADOXVM *V, on a page to itself* | compositio *V* | pondo *Sch*: per *VE*   13. praemissi *V* | cocturam *V, E1*: coctura *E2*   14. decoquas *E*   15. ferula *E* | coquitur *E* | ceperit *V*   16. perfrixerit *σ*: perfixerit *VE*   17. postridie *E*: post pridie *V* | tum *Gi*: cum *VE* | <mittes> *Gi* iiii *E*   18. iamtristis *V1*: iamtri ti *V2* | mastices *E1* | dragme singulę *E*: dragmas singulas *GiVo* 19. toridis *E1* | uine *V*   20. suffusione *Milham, L*   22. duo milia *del. Sven*

made with honey. 15. How to make tainted honey good. 16. How to find out if honey is tainted. 17. How to keep grapes for a long time. 18. How to preserve apples and pomegranates. 19. How to keep quinces for a long time. 20. How to keep fresh figs, apples, plums, pears and cherries for a long time. 21. How to preserve citron. 22. How to preserve blackberries. 23. How to keep greens for a long time. 24. How to keep turnips for a long time. 25. How to keep truffles for a long time. 26. How to keep unripe peaches for a long time. 27. Multi-purpose salt preparations. 28. How to preserve fresh olives so that you may make oil whenever you like. 29. Cumin sauce for oysters and shellfish. 30. *Laser* sauce. 31. *Oenogarum* for truffles. 32. *Oxyporium.* 33. *Hypotrimma.* 34. *Oxygarum* for the digestion. 35. *Mortaria.*

HERE END THE TITLES.

1.1. Spiced wine surprise: how to make spiced wine surprise:
15 lb. of honey by weight is put into a bronze pan containing 2 pints of wine so that the wine and the honey cook together. Warm the pan on a gentle fire of dry wood and stir with a stick as it cooks. If it begins to boil it is settled with a sprinkling of wine, besides which it will subside when it is removed from the fire. When it has cooled down, it is heated again. This will be done a second and a third time, and then at last it is removed from the hearth, and it is skimmed the day after. Then you put in 4 oz. of ground pepper; 3 scruples of mastic; one *dragma* each of *folium*[1] and saffron; 5 roasted date stones and the dates themselves softened in wine of the same kind and quality, added in beforehand so that a smooth paste is produced. When all these are ready you pour on 18 pints of smooth wine. Charcoal is put in when it is finished (to avert the sour taste).[2]

---

[1] *folium*: an aromatic leaf of some sort, though it is unlikely to be bay leaf, which appears quite often in the proceeding text in an unambiguous form i.e. *folium lauri.* See the Glossary for a detailed discussion.

[2] See 1.3, 'Roman absinthe', which suggests that the natural bitterness of the wormwood does not require the addition of extra charcoal. Whether the charcoal is left in place for any time, or the wine is strained through it, is not clear. Brandt, *Untersuchungen*, p. 25, makes the ingenious suggestion that the meaningless *duo milia* at the end is a misreading during the translation process from Greek, mistaking the sigma of *duschulō* (ill-flavoured, sour: cf. Xenocrates 12) for an omega, and producing the false reading *duō chilia* (two thousand).

II. CONDITVM MELIZOMVM VIATORIVM: conditum melizomum perpetuum, quod subministratur per uiam peregrinanti: piper tritum cum melle despumato in cupellam mittis conditi loco, et ad momentum quantum sit bibendum, tantum aut mellis proferas aut uinum misceas sed, si uas erit, nonnihil uini melizomo mittas, adiciendum propter mellis exitum solutiorem.

III. ABSINTIVM ROMANVM: **absintium Romanum sic facies**: conditi Camerini praeceptis utique pro absintio cessante, in cuius uicem absenti Pontici purgati terendique unciam, Tebaicam dabis, masticis, folii <scripulos> III, costi iscripulos senos, croci iscripulos III, uini eiusmodi sextarios decem et octo. carbones amaritudo non exigit.

IIII. ROSATUM SIC FACIES: folias rosarum albo sublato lino inseris ut sutilis facias et uino quam plurimas infundes ut septem diebus in uino sint. post septem dies rosam de uino tollis et alias sutules recentes similiter mittis ut per dies septem in uino requiescant et rosam eximis. similiter et tertio facies et rosam eximis, et uinum colas et cum ad bibendum uoles uti addito melle rosatum conficies. sane custodito ut rosam a rore siccam et obtimam mittas. similiter ut supra et de <uiolis> uiolacium facies et eodem modo melle temperabis.

rosatum sine rosa sic facies: folia citri uiridia in sportella palmea in dolium musti mittes antequam ferueat et post quadraginta dies exime: cum necesse fuerit mel addes et pro rosato utere.

V. OLEVM LIBVRNICVM SIC FACIES: in oleo Spano mittes ellenium et cyperi et folia lauri non uetusta. tunsa omnia et criuellata, ad lebissimum

---

1. MILIZONVM *E*   2. sumministratur *E*   4. uini misceas *E* | si uas erit *André*: suaserit *VE*   5. solitiorem *V*   6. ABSINTHIVM *E* | absinthium *E2*   7. absintio *V, E1*: absinthio *E2*   8. uncias singulas et unam Thebaicam *Vo* | <scripulos> *add. Hum*   9. scripulos *E (both occasions)* | XVIII *V*   11. ROSATVM SIC FACIES *VE*: <ROSATVM ET VIOLACIUM> rosatum sic facies *Hum; see chapter headings* | folia rosarum *E*   12. et uino *Hum*: ut uino *VE*   13. sutules *E*: sutulas *V1*: sutulæs *V2* | mitis *E1*   16. optimam *V*   17. <uiolis> *CGSG*: <uiola> *O*   18. rosatum …facies *is not a heading in the MSS but we think it should be treated as such*   21. Spano *VE*: Hispano *GiVo* | mittis *E*   22. cypery *V* | et *om. E* | cribellata *E* | alleuissimum *E*

1.2. Traveller's honeyed wine:[1] a long-lasting honeyed wine, which is served to travellers on the road: you put ground pepper with skimmed honey in a small cask instead of spiced wine and, as required, you pour out as much honey and mix with it as much wine as is to be drunk; but if you use a (thin-necked) vessel, you put a little wine in the honey mixture. Add enough for the honey to pour freely.

1.3. Roman absinthe: you make Roman absinthe like this: follow the instructions for Camerinian spiced wine, particularly when the absinthe is running out,[2] and add in its place an ounce of cleaned Pontic absinthe which should be ground up, a Theban date,[3] 3 scruples of mastic and *folium*, 6 scruples of *costum*, 3 scruples of saffron and 18 pints of the same type of wine. Its bitterness does not require charcoal.[4]

1.4. You make rose wine like this: string rose petals, with the white parts removed, on a thread so that you make a garland and steep as many as you can in wine so that they are in the wine for seven days. After seven days remove the petals from the wine and put in other fresh garlands in the same way so that they remain for a further seven days, then remove them. Do the same again for a third time and take the roses out and strain the wine. When you wish to use it for drinking, add honey to make up the *rosatum*. Obviously you should take care to use the best rose petals, not those wet with dew. In the same way as above you may make violet wine from violets, mixing it with honey in the same manner.

You may make rose wine without roses like this: you put fresh green citron leaves in a little palm-leaf basket into a vat of must before fermentation begins and after 40 days you take it out. When you want to use it add honey and use it instead of rose wine.

1.5. How to make Liburnican oil:[5] you put elecampane, some sweet rush[6] and fresh bay leaves into Spanish oil: grind all these and sieve them so that you

---

[1] *uiatorium* is not part of the title in the MSS here or at the start of Book I, but given the additional information given in the description of this item in the recipe, we think that it should be treated as such.

[2] The text is rather confused here.

[3] *Thebaica*: the palm date. Cf. Pliny, *HN*. 23.4.51, 97

[4] See p. 133 n. 2 above.

[5] Liburnica in Illyricum (modern Croatia).

[6] *Cyperus:* the root of a sweet sedge similar to iris in appearance, *cyperus esculentus*, the little rhizomes of which are known as *amande de terre* in French. Papyrus is of the same genus. See Grieve, *Modern Herbal*, p. 730.

puluerem redacta, et sales frictos et tritos et per triduum uel plus permisce diligenter. post haec aliquanto tempore patere requiescere et Liburnicum omnes putabunt.

VI. VINUM EX ATRO CANDIDVM FACIES: lomentum ex faba factum

5 uel ouorum trium aluorem in lagonam mittis et diutissime agitas. alia die erit candidum. et cineres uitis albae idem faciunt.

VII. DE LIQVAMINE EMENDANDO: liquamen si odorem malum fecerit, uas inane inuersum fumiga lauro et cupresso, et in hoc liquamen infunde ante uentilatum. si salsum fuerit, mellis sextarium mittis et moues. picas et emendasti.

10 sed et mustum recens idem prestat.

VIII. VT CARNES SINE SALE QUOVIS TEMPORE RECENTES SINT: carnes recentes quales uolueris melle tegantur, sed uas pendeat et, quando uolueris, utere. hoc hieme melius fit; aestate paucis diebus durauit. et in carne cocta itidem facies.

15 **VIIII. CALLVM PORCINVM VEL BVBVLVM ET VNGELLA ET COCTA VT DIV DVRENT**: in senapi ex aceto sale melle facta mittis ut tegantur, et quando uolueris utere miraueris.

X. VT CARNEM SALSAM DVLCEM FACIAS: carnem salsam dulcem facies si prius in lacte coquas et postea in aquam.

20 **XI. VT PISCES FRICTI DIV DVRENT**: eodem momento quo friguntur et lebantur ab aceto calido perfunduntur.

XII. OSTREA VT DIV DVRENT: uas ab aceto aut ex aceto uasculum picitum laba, et ostrea conpone.

XIII. VT VNCIAM LASERIS TOTO TEMPORE VTARIS: laser in spatiosum

25 doliolum uitreum mittis et nucleos pineos ut puta uiginti, cumque utendum fuerit lasere, nucleos conteres, et in cibis mirabiris in sapores; et tantum numero nucleorum doliolo reserentur.

1. permisce *M*: promisce *VE*   3. putabuntur *V*   5. in *om. E1* | mittis *om. E1* | agita sali adierit *V*   6. cinerem *V* | alba eidem *V*   8. inuersum *om. E1* | cupresso *V, E1*: cypresso *E2* | infunde *GiVo*: fenunde *VE*   9. mittes *Milham* | moues picas *V*: moue spicas *E*: moue spica *Hum*   13. æstate *E* | durabit *E*   15. VNGELLAE *E* | ET COCTA *VE*: COCTAE (*om.* ET) *Hum*: NB ET *is not in the contents list at the start of this Book*   17. miraberis *Milham*: miscebis *Hum*   19. aqua *Hum*   20. piscem *E1*   22. uas *VE*: lauas *Vo* 23. laua *E* | con pone *V*: compone *E*   24. VNCIA *GiVo*   25. XX *V*   26. fuit *E1* | et in cibis *CGSG*: ex incibis *VE*: et cibis *Hum* | miraberis *E* | in *del. Tor* | saporis *V1* | numerum *E* 27. reserentur *E, V2*: resererentur *V1*: referentur *Ber*

have a very fine powder and mix this carefully with rubbed and ground salt crystals and leave for three days or more. After this allow to stand for a while and everyone will think it is Liburnican oil.

1.6. How to make cloudy wine clear: you put a paste made of beans or the white of three eggs into a large flask and stir for a long time. The next day it will be clear. The ashes of white vines do the same.[1]

1.7. On restoring *liquamen*: if the *liquamen* has produced a bad smell,[2] fumigate an empty upturned pot with bay and cypress, and pour the *liquamen*, having whisked it, into the pot. If it is too salty you put in a pint of honey and stir it.[3] You seal it with pitch and you have restored it. Fresh must also has the same effect.

1.8. How to keep meat fresh whenever you like without salt: any meat you want to keep fresh should be covered with honey, so long as the vessel is hung up; you can use it when you like. This is better done in winter; in summer it will only last a few days. You may do the same with cooked meat.

1.9. How to preserve pork or beef rind and trotters when cooked: you put them in a mustard made with some vinegar, salt and honey so that they are covered up. When you want to use them you will be amazed.[4]

1.10. How to make salted meat sweet: you may make salted meat sweet if you cook it first in milk and afterwards in water.

1.11. How to preserve fried fish: as soon as they are fried and lifted out, they are drenched in hot vinegar.[5]

1.12. How to preserve oysters: (take) a vinegar-jar; or wash a small pitched jar with some vinegar and pack the oysters in.

1.13. How to make an ounce of *laser* last for ever: you put the *laser* and roughly 20 pine nuts in a wide little glass vessel and when you need to use some *laser* you grind the nuts, and you will be amazed at the flavour in your food. The same number of nuts is replaced in the vessel.[6]

---

[1] It is possible that the 'dark' wine here is actually 'cloudy' and 'white' refers to 'clear' wine.

[2] i.e. the vessel was not airtight: liquamen oxidizes when exposed to the air.

[3] *Liquamen* is always salty to some extent as it is the means by which salt is added to Roman food.

[4] We take *utere* to be the rare active infinitive of *uto* (see *LS*); alternatively it may be read as the imperative of the more common form *utor*: 'use them when you like: you will be amazed.'

[5] We might expect 'plunged' but would then perhaps want *in* + accusative.

[6] Reading the MSS *reserentur*; the replacement nuts are literally 're-sown'.

XIIII. VT DVLCIA DE MELLE DIV DVRENT: accipies quod Greci dicunt nechon et facies farinam; et admisces cum melle eo tempore quo dulcia facturus es.

XV. VT MEL MALVM BONVM FACIAS: mel malum bonum facies ad uendendum unam partem mali et duas boni si simul miscueris.

XVI. MEL CORRVPTVM VT PROBES: inlunium infundes in melle et incende. si incorruptum est, lucet.

XVII. VVAE VT DIV SERVENTVR: accipies uuas de uite inlesas et aquam pluuialem ad tertias dequoques, et mittis in uas in quo et uuas mittis. uas picari et gipsari facies et in locum frigidum ubi sol accessum non habet reponi facies, et quando uolueris uuas uirides inuenies. et ipsam aquam pro idromelli aegris dabis. et si in ordeo obruas, inlesas inuenies.

XVIII. VT MALA ET MALA GRANATA DIV DVRENT: in calidam feruentem merge et statim leua et suspende.

XVIIII. VT MALA CIDONIA DIV SERVENTVR: eligis mala sine uitio cum ramolis et foliis et condies in uas, et suffundes mel et defritum, et diu seruabis.

XX. FICVM RECENTEM MALA PRVNA PIRA CERASIA VT DIV SERVES: omnia cum petiolis diligenter legito et in melle ponito ne se contingant.

XXI. CITRIA VT DIV DVRENT: in uas citrium mitte; gipsa; suspendet.

XXII. MORA VT DIV DVRENT: ex moribus sucum facito et cum sapa misce et in uitrio uaso cum moram mitte; custodies multo tempore.

---

1. DE MELLE *CGSG from index*: MELLE *VE*   2. nechon *VE*: cnecon *Vo* | cum *om. E1* | eo *π*: et *VE*   3. es *BS*: est *VE*   5. unam] uam *E1* | bonis simul *V*   6. VT MEL *E* | in lunium *E*   8. accipies *V*   9. fluuialem *V* | dequoquas *V1*: dequoquæs *V2*: decoques *E* | picari *π*: picem *VE*   10. gypsari *E* | habere poni *V*   11. idromeli *E* | aegrui *V*   16. mel *om. E1* | defritum diu (*om.* et) *E*   17. regentem *E1* 20. citrium *ξ*: citrum *VE* | gypsa *E* | suspende *ζ*   21. MORA VT DIV DVRENT *Lis, from headings at start of Book 1*: E *puts this recipe after XXIII, numbering it XXIIII, and reads* sucum facito et cum sapa misce ex moribus et in uitrio | MORA *om. VE* | derent *E1* | moribus *VE*: moris *ζ*   22. uase *E* | mora *E*

1.14. How to preserve sweets made with honey: you take what the Greeks call *cnecon* (safflower) and you make a fine powder,[1] and you mix it with honey at the time you are going to make the sweets.

1.15. How to make tainted honey good: you will make tainted honey good for sale if you mix one part of tainted honey with two parts of good honey.

1.16. How to find out if honey is tainted: you put a wick in the honey and light it. It burns if it is good.

1.17. How to keep grapes for a long time: you take unblemished grapes from the vine, and (then) reduce rainwater to one third of its volume and put it in a vessel in which you also put the grapes. You will seal the vessel with pitch and plaster,[2] and have it placed in a cool spot where the sun does not reach. And when you want them you will find the grapes fresh. You can also give the water itself to the sick instead of honey water. You will also find they keep undamaged if you bury them in barley.

1.18. How to preserve apples and pomegranates: plunge them in boiling hot water, lift them out straightaway and hang them up.

1.19. How to keep quinces for a long time: you pick unblemished quinces with their stalks and leaves, and put them in a vessel, and pour on honey and *defrutum*, and you will preserve them for a long time.

1.20. How to keep fresh figs, apples, plums, pears and cherries for a long time: pick them all carefully with their stalks and put them in honey so that they do not touch.

1.21. How to preserve citron: put the citron in a vessel, seal it with plaster; it should hang up.

1.22. How to preserve blackberries:[3] make a purée from some blackberries and mix it with syrup and put it in a glass vessel with (some more) blackberries. You will keep them for a long time.[4]

---

[1] There is some ambiguity here. Safflower is an alternative to saffron in producing yellow colour. Flour is often an ingredient in *dulcia* so we assume the safflower is added to the flour before it is combined with honey in the various recipes. See 7.11. However, the safflower may be made into a fine powder i.e. a flour which is then simply added to the honey. Safflower seed is a common ingredient in the dyeing industry today in India: it may be that the seed rather than the petals are referred to here.

[2] A double layer of sealant. See Columella 12.39.2, where pine-resin and plaster are used to seal a vessel.

[3] Or possibly mulberries.

[4] The only reference to *sapa* (an unflavoured, grape-juice syrup, boiled down to a third of its volume).

XXIII. OLERA VT DIV SERVENTVR: olera electa non satis matura in uas picitum repone.

XXIIII. RAPE VT DIV SERVENTVR: ante accuratas et compositas perfundes mirte bacis cum melle et aceto. aliter senapi tempera melle aceto sale et super compositas rapes infundes.

XXV. TVBERA VT DIV SERVENTVR: tubera quae aquae non uexauerint conponis in uas alternis; alternis scobem siccam mittis, cooperis et gipsas, et loco frigido pones.

XXVI. DVRACINA PERSICA VT DIV DVRENT: eligito obtima et mitte in muriam; postera die exime et isfongiabis diligenter et collocabis in uas. fundes salem acetum satureiam.

XXVII. SALES CONDITOS AD MULTA: sales conditos ad digestionem ad uentrem mouendum; et omnes moruos et pestilentiam et omnia frigora prohibent generari. sunt autem et suauissimi ultra quam speras: sales communes frictos libra I; sales ammonicos frictos libras II; piperis alui uncias III; gengiber uncias II; ammeos uncias I semis; timi uncias I semis; apii seminis uncias I semis (si apii semen mittere nolueris, petrosileni mittis uncias III); origani uncias III; erucæ semen uncias I semis; piperis nigri uncias III; cheochi unciam I; ysopi cretici uncias II; folium uncias II; petrosilenum uncias II; aneti uncias II.

XXVIII: OLIVAS VIRIDES SERVARE VT QVOVIS TEMPORE OLEVM FACIAS: oliuas de arbore sublatas in illud mittis et erunt tales quouis tempore quasi mox de arbore demptae; de quibus si uolueris oleum uiridem facies.

XXVIIII. CYMINATVM IN OSTREA ET CONCILIA: piper ligusticum petrosilenum mentam siccam folium malabatrum cuminum plusculum mel acetum et liquamen.

aliter: piper ligusticum petrosilenum mentam siccam cuminum plusculum mel acetum liquamen.

1. XXII *E*   3. XXIII *E* | perfundes *Bra3*: perdes *VE*: asperges *Gi*   4. myrte *E* | sinapi *E*
5. rapes *VE*: rapas *ζ*   6. ?tuberæ *E* | quæ *E* | aquae *V1*: aqua *V2,E*   7. componis *E*
| mittis cooperis et *Vo*: mittis ris et *VE*: mittis et *André*   9. optima *V*   10. et is
fongiabis *VE*: et spongiabis *Hum* | conlocabis *E*   11 sature iam *V*   12. SALIS *E*
13. morbos *E* | pestilentiae *E*   15. ammoniacos *Hum* | albi *E* | gingiber *E*
17. eruce *V*   18. cheochi *VE*: croci *ζ*| vsopi *V1*   22. arbore demtę *E*: arbore
redemptae *V*   26. mentem *V*

1.23. How to keep greens for a long time: select young greens and put them in a pitched vessel.

1.24. How to keep turnips for a long time: prepare and arrange the turnips and pour on a <mixture of> myrtle-berries, honey, and vinegar. Alternatively blend mustard with honey, vinegar and salt and pour this over the prepared turnips.

1.25. How to keep truffles for a long time: you put truffles which moisture has not damaged into a vessel in layers, putting dry sawdust between the layers; cover it and seal it with plaster and put it in a cool place.

1.26. How to keep unripe peaches for a long time: choose the best ones and put them in brine;[1] take them out the following day, and sponge them carefully and store them in a vessel. You pour on salt, vinegar and savory.

1.27. Multi-purpose salt preparations: salt preparations for the digestion, to ease the stomach;[2] they also prevent all diseases and plague and all chills from developing. Moreover, they are very sweet, more than you can hope for: 1 lb. ordinary salt, ground; 2 lb. ground sal ammoniac;[3] 3 oz. white pepper; 2 oz. ginger; 1½ oz. ajwain;[4] 1½ oz. thyme; 1½ oz. celery seed (if you don't want to put in celery seed, put in 3 oz. of parsley); 3 oz. oregano; 1½ oz. rocket seed; 3 oz. black pepper; 1 oz. saffron; 2 oz. Cretan hyssop; 2 oz. *folium*; 2 oz. parsley; 2 oz. dill.

1.28. How to preserve green olives so that you may make oil whenever you like: you put olives taken from the tree into it (oil) and at any time they will be as though just taken down from the tree; you can make green oil from them if you want to.[5]

1.29. Cumin sauce for oysters and shellfish: pepper, lovage, parsley, dried mint, *folium, malabathrum,*[6] plenty of cumin, honey, vinegar and *liquamen*.

Another cumin sauce: pepper, lovage, parsley, dried mint, plenty of cumin, honey, vinegar, *liquamen*.

---

[1] *muria* here must mean 'clean' brine and not brine from salted fish.

[2] Here and elsewhere, this may refer to an indigestion remedy or a laxative.

[3] A resin or gum from a plant native to Persia, *dorema ammoniacum;* presumably ground and mixed with salt.

[4] A different kind of cumin, also known as 'Ethiopian cumin' in ancient times and 'ajwain' today: see Pliny, *HN.* 20.20.58.

[5] Cf. Dalby, *Empire of Pleasures*, p. 60 n. 108; Cato, *De agricultura* 65. 'Green' oil was a luxury product.

[6] *malabathrum* is believed to be the leaf of cinnamon. Current thinking is that the term *folium*, when it occurs on its own, also means *malabathrum*; but see the Glossary.

XXX. LASERATVM: laser Cyrenaicum uel Partitum tepida dissoluis cum aceto liquamine temperatum, uel piper petrosilenum mentam siccam laseris radicem mel acetum liquamen.

    aliter: piper careum anetum petrosilenum mentam siccam silfi folium malabatrum ispicam Indicam costum modicum mel acetum liquamen.

XXXI. OENOGARVM IN TVBERA: piper ligusticum coriandrum rutam liquamen mel <uinum> et oleum modice.

    aliter: timum satureiam piper ligusticum mel <uinum> liquamen et oleum.

XXXII. OXYPORIVM: cumini uncias II; zingiberis unciam I; rutae uiridis unciam I; nitri iscripulos VI; dactilorum pinguium iscripulos XII; piperis unciam I; mellis uncias VIIII; cuminum uel Ethiopicum aut Siriacum aut Libicum aceto infundes, sicca, et sic tundes. postea melle conprehendis. cum necesse fuerit oxygaro uteris.

XXXIII. YPOTRIMA: piper ligusticum mentam aridam nucleos pineos uuam passam cariotam caseum dulcem mel acetum liquamen oleum uinum defritum aut caroenum.

XXXIIII. OXYGARVM DIGESTIBILEM: piperis simunciam; silis Gallici iscripulos III; cardamomi iscripulos VI; cumini iscripulos VI; folii iscripulum uno; menta sicca iscripulos VI. tunsa cribrataque melle colligis. cum opus fuerit liquamen et acetum addis.

    aliter: piperis unciam I, petrosileni carei ligustici uncias singulas melle colliguntur. cum opus fuerit liquamen et acetum addes.

XXXV. MORTARIA: mentam rutam coriandrum feniculum, omnia uiridia; ligusticum piper mel liquamen. si opus fuerit acetum addes.

EXPLICIT LIBER APICI EPIMELES

1. Parthicum ζ | aceto <et> *GiVo*   2. mentem *V*   4. mentem *V*   5. accetum *E* 7, 8. <uinum> *Bra3*   10. OXYPORIVM: *so list of chapters at start of VE: here both have* OXYPORVM | cummuni *V* | rutæ *E*   12. ethiopicum *E*: hiopicum *V*   13. cōprehendis *V* | neccesse *V*   14. oxygaro uteris *written as header for XXXIII, E*   16. oleum uinum *V2,E*: uinum oleum *V1*   17. caroenum *Hum*: cariotam *VE*   18. DIGESTIBILE *GiVo* | silis *Hum*: silfi *VE* | gallicii *E*   19. scripulos III cardamomii scripulos VI *E* | iscripulo *V*   20. uno] I *E* | cribataque *E*   23. colliguntur *Sch*: colligunt ut cum *VE* 24. MORTARIA *V*: MORETARIA *E, but* mortaria *in list at start of Book I* | uiria *V* 25. ligusticum ζ: libusticum *E*: libuticum *V*   26. APICII *E*

1.30. *Laser* **sauce**: you dissolve Cyrenaican or Parthian *laser* in warm water blended with vinegar and *liquamen*. Or use pepper, parsley, dried mint, *laser* root, honey, vinegar, *liquamen*.

Another *laser* **sauce**: pepper, caraway, dill, parsley, dried mint, *silphium, folium, malabathrum*, spikenard, a little *costum*, honey, vinegar, *liquamen*.[1]

1.31. *Oenogarum* **for truffles**: pepper, lovage, coriander, rue, *liquamen,* honey wine, and a little oil.

Another: thyme, savory, pepper, lovage, honey, wine,[2] *liquamen,* and oil.

1.32. *Oxyporium*: 2 oz. cumin, 1 oz. ginger, 1 oz. fresh rue, 6 scruples soda, 12 scruples date flesh, 1 oz. pepper, 9 oz. honey. Soak Ethiopian or Syrian or Libyan cumin in vinegar, dry it and grind it.[3] Afterwards you mix everything with the honey. When necessary you use it with *oxygarum*.[4]

1.33. *Hypotrimma*:[5] pepper, lovage, dried mint, pine nuts, raisins, dates, sweet cheese, honey, vinegar, liquamen, oil,wine, *defrutum* or *caroenum*.

1.34. *Oxygarum* **for the digestion**: ½ oz. pepper, 3 scruples Gallic sesely,[6] 6 scruples of cardamom, 6 scruples of cumin, 1 scruple of *folium*, 6 scruples dried mint. Pound and sieve, and bind with honey. Add *liquamen* and vinegar as required.

Alternatively: 1 oz. pepper and 1 oz. each parsley, caraway, and lovage are bound with honey. Add *liquamen* and vinegar as required.

1.35. *Mortaria*:[7] mint, rue, coriander, fennel, all fresh; lovage, pepper, honey, *liquamen*. Add vinegar if required.

HERE ENDS APICIUS' BOOK, *MISE EN PLACE*

[1] See the Glossary for a discussion of *laser* and its various forms.

[2] The omission of wine in these two recipes is interesting. It is rare to find ingredients so taken for granted that they are left out; we have therefore restored them. See the Glossary for *oenogarum*.

[3] The vinegar is presumably only for the cumin, but all the other dry ingredients are pounded and then bound with the honey for subsequent dilution. See 3.18.2 for a similar recipe where the method is confused.

[4] *garum* and vinegar balanced together and probably cooked together: this is a typical digestive known as *oxyporon* in Greek: cf. Dioscorides, *MM.* 3.51.3.

[5] Meaning 'something ground up', a paste as in a *mortarium*.

[6] The MSS read *silfi Gallici(i)* which seems highly unlikely.

[7] The Latin equivalent of *hypotrimma:* that which is mixed in a *mortarium*, a paste.

BOOK TWO

< INCIPIT EIVSDEM SARCOPTES LIBER SECVNDVS>

I. isicia. II. hidrogarum et apotermu et amolatu. III. uuluule botelli. IIII. lucanicae. V. farcimina.

5　**I. ISICIA.**
[2.1.1] isicia fiunt marina de cammaris et astacis de lolligine de sepia de lucusta. esicium condies pipere ligustico cumino laseris radice.

[2.1.2] **esicia de lolligine**: sublatis crinibus in fulmento tundes sicuti adsolet. pulpa et in mortario et in liquamine diligenter frigatur et exinde esicia plassantur.

10　[2.1.3] **esicia de iscillis uel de cammaris amplis**: cammari uel iscille de testa sua eximuntur et in mortario teruntur cum pipere et liquamine optimo. pulpe esicia plassantur.

[2.1.4] **omentata ita fiunt**: assas iecur porcinum et eum eneruas. ante tamen teres piper rutam liquamen; et sic super inmittis iecur et teres et misces sicut pulpa
15　omentata, et singula inuoluuntur folia lauri et ad fumum suspenduntur quamdiu uoles. cum manducare uolueris tolles de fumum et denuo assas.

[2.1.5] **esicium**: adicies in mortarium piper ligusticum origanum; fricabis; subfundes liquamen; adicies cerebella cocta; teres diligenter ne astulas habeat; adicies oua quinque et dissolues diligenter ut unum corpus efficias. liquamine
20　temperas et in patella aenea exinanies. quoques. cum coctum fuerit, uersas in tabula munda, tessellas concides. adicies in mortarium piper ligusticum origanum; fricabis; <liquamen et uinum addes>; in se conmisces in caccabum;

---

1. < INCIPIT EIVSDEM SARCOPTES LIBER SECVNDVS > *from subsequent incipits CGSG: no incipit VE*: <SARCOPTES> *Milham, from explicit to Book II*　　3. lucaniae *V*　　6. de lusta *E1*　　7. esicum *E* | ligustico *VE*: liquamine *Bra2*　　8. criminibus *V* | pulpa *Sch*: pulma *VE*　　9. frigatur *VE* : fricatur *ζ*: friatur *Sch*　　10. scillis *E* | scille *E*　　11. piper *V* | pulpa *Sch*　　13. iecor *E* | eum *VE*: id eum *P*: tum *Lis*: *del. GiVo*　　14. super immittis *V*: superimmittis *Milham* | iecor *E* | sicut *VE*: suitur *Gi* | misces <isicia plassantur et omento teguntur> sicut *Bra2*　　16. fumo *Sch*　　17. esicium *André*: et sicium *VE*: aliter isicium *GiVo*: isicium *Milham*　　18. suffundes *E*　　20. coques *E* | fuerat *V1*　　21. tesselas *E*　　22. <liquamen et uinum addes> *add. CGSG* | commisces, <mittes> in *GiVo*: commisces, <suffundes liquamen uino et passo temperabis mittes> in *Bra2* | in accubum *V*

BOOK TWO OF THE SAME, 'MEAT DISHES', BEGINS

1. Forcemeat. 2. (Forcemeat served with) *hydrogarum*, a cold sauce or a thick sauce. 3. Womb and blood sausage. 4. *Lucanica*. 5. Sausages.

2.1 FORCEMEAT.[1]

2.1.1. Seafood forcemeat is made from prawns and lobster, from squid, cuttlefish, and spiny lobster. You will season the forcemeat with pepper, lovage, cumin, and *laser* root.

2.1.2. Forcemeat from squid: with its hair[2] removed, beat the squid on a board in the normal way. The flesh is carefully pounded in a mortar with *liquamen,* and the forcemeat balls are formed from it.

2.1.3. Forcemeat from prawns or large crayfish: the crayfish and prawns are shelled[3] and ground in a mortar with pepper and best *liquamen*. The flesh is formed into forcemeat balls.

2.1.4. Faggots are made this way: you roast pork liver and remove the sinews. Beforehand you grind pepper, rue, and *liquamen,* pour this over the liver, grind it and prepare it like meat faggots.[4] Individual bay leaves are wrapped around the faggots and they are hung in the smoke as long as you like. When you want to eat them take from the smoke and roast them again.

2.1.5. Another forcemeat recipe: put in a mortar pepper, lovage, oregano; grind it. Pour on *liquamen*, add cooked brains, pound carefully so it has no lumps, add 5 eggs, mix in carefully to make a smooth emulsion. Flavour with *liquamen* and pour into a bronze pan. Cook it. When it is cooked, turn it out on to a clean board. Cut into squares. Put in a mortar pepper, lovage, oregano; grind them together. Add *liquamen* and wine. Put all together in a pan. Bring to the boil.

---

[1] This general term for chopped or minced meat is found in the price edict of Diocletian but can have a more specific meaning, as in 'forcemeat balls' or pâté. *Isicia* seems to be a flavoured meat mixture, that may be formless or shaped and with or without a skin or wrapping. The items known as *omentata* are wrapped in caul fat, and as a consequence are translated as faggots; the *farcimina* are stuffed in *intestinum* and must therefore be a form of sausage. See the Glossary.

[2] Probably the longer tentacles on a squid are meant.

[3] Lit. 'are removed from their heads'.

[4] Lit. 'mix it like meat faggots', i.e. wrap them in caul fat first.

facies ut ferueat. cum ferbuerit tracta confringes, obligas; coagitabis et exinanies in uoletari. piper asperges et appones.

[2.1.6] **esicia ex fondilis**: elixatos fondilos contere et neruos eorum eximes; deinde cum eis alicam elixatam, oua conteres, <piper, liquamen; isicia ex his

5 facies cum nucleis et > pipere. in omento assabis. oenogaro perfundes et pro esiciis inferes.

[2.1.7] **esicia omentata**: pulpam concisam teres cum medulla siliginei in uino infusa; piper, liquamen; si uelis, et bacam mirta extenteratam simul conteres. pusilla esicia formabis intus nucleis et pipere positis; inuoluta omento subassabis

10 cum caroeno.

II. HIDROGARVM ET APOTERMVM ET AMVLATVM.

[2.2.1] **esicia plena**: accipies adipes fasiani recentes, preduras et facis ex eo tessellas. cum pipere liquamine caroeno in esicio includes; et idrogaro quoques et inferes.

15 [2.2.2] **idrogarata esicia sic facies**: teres piper ligusticum piretrum minimum, suffundes liquamen, temperas aquam cisterninam. dum inducet exinanies in caccabo, et cum esicia ad uaporem ignis pones et caleat et sic sorbendum inferes.

---

1. feruuerit *V* | tracta *CGSG*: tractu *VE*: tractam *Bra3*   3. conteres *Hum*   4-5. <piper …nucleis et> *Bra3, from 3.20.7 below, where this recipe is repeated*   5. in omento *Hum*: momento *VE* | oenagaro *E* | perfundes *Hum*: profundes *VE*   7. siliginei *Bra2* : siligine *VE* 8. infusa *Helmreich*: infusi *VE* | myrtae *Sch*   9. emento *E1*   10. careno *E* 11. HYDROGARATVM *Hum* | APTHERMVM *E*   13. tessalas *E* | carono *V1*: careno *E* ex hydrogaro *Sch* | coques *E*   16. cisternam *E*   17. pones ut *Bra3*

When it has boiled, crumble *tracta*,[1] stir it so that it thickens,[2] pour out on to the serving dish.[3] Sprinkle with pepper and set it forth.

2.1.6. **Faggots from mussels**: cook the mussels, beard them and pound them.[4] Next you pound with them cooked *alica* and eggs, pepper and *liquamen*. Make the forcemeat with this and with pine nuts and pepper. Roast them wrapped in caul fat. Sprinkle them with *oenogarum*. Serve them as you would forcemeat (faggots).

2.1.7. **Forcemeat faggots**: you pound chopped meat with fresh white bread-crumbs soaked in wine, with pepper and *liquamen*; if you wish, you pound crushed myrtle berries with them.[5] You shape the faggots with pine nuts and pepper placed inside. Wrap them in caul fat and roast[6] them with *caroenum*.

2.2 (FORCEMEAT SERVED WITH) *HYDROGARUM*,[7] (WITH) A COLD SAUCE AND A THICK SAUCE.

2.2.1. **Stuffed forcemeat**: you take fresh pheasant fat, fry it until crisp and cut it into cubes. Place it inside a forcemeat ball made with pepper, *liquamen,* and *caroenum,* and cook in *hydrogarum* and serve.

2.2.2. **You make forcemeat with *hydrogarum* this way**: pound pepper, lovage, a pinch of Spanish camomile, pour on *liquamen* and blend with well-water. Empty this into a pan while it infuses and place it with the forcemeat balls over the heat of the fire and let it warm through. Serve like this for immediate consumption.[8]

---

[1] *tracta* is a form of dried pastry made from semolina or *alica*; see the Glossary.

[2] Lit. 'thicken, stir', but the mixture would have to be stirred for the *tracta* to work.

[3] i.e. in which you have put the forcemeat.

[4] Lit. 'boil', but one would not want to do this to a mussel! The next instructions are reversed in the Latin: the mussels must be bearded first.

[5] *extenteratam* is a term found both in *Apicius* and in veterinary texts, where it seems to mean something like 'open up the cavity'. The berries are opened up, but not necessarily de-seeded, for the flavour to be released.

[6] Elsewhere, *subassas* has the meaning 'grilling/roasting a little' to finish cooking. See below, 2.5.3 and 4 of this book where sausages are pre-cooked by boiling and then *subassata*.

[7] These sauces are far more complex than just a mixture of water and fish sauce. See the Glossary.

[8] Literally 'serve to be supped' and so eaten while hot. It is our belief that the term *ad uaporem ignis* is not a reference to steam, though other translations disagree. See the Introduction, p. 93, for discussion.

[2.2.3] **in esiciato pullo**: olei floris libram I, liquaminis quartarium, piperis semuncia.

[2.2.4] **aliter de pullo**: piperis grana XXX conteres, mittis liquaminis optimi calicem, careni tantundem, aquae undecim mittes et ad uaporem ignis pones.

5 [2.2.5] **esicium simplex**: ad unum liquaminis acetabulum aquae septem mittes, modicum apii uiridis, triti piperis cocleare. esiciola inquoques et si ad uentrem soluendum dabis, idrogaro feces conditi addes.

[2.2.6] **esicia** de pauo primum locum habent ita si fricta fuerint ut callum uincant. item secundum locum habent de fasianis; item tertium locum habent de cuniculis; 10 item quartum locum habent de pullis; item quintum locum habent de porcello tenero.

[2.2.7] **esicia amulata a balineo sic facies**: teres piper ligusticum origanum modicum silfi gingiber minimum mellis modicum; liquamine temperabis; misces adicies super esicia; facies ut ferueat. cum bene bulliuerit amulo obligas ispisso 15 et soruendum inferes.

[2.2.8] **amulatum aliter**: piper teres pridie infusu cui subinde liquamen suffundes ita ut bene tritum ac lutulentum facias piperatum; cui defritum admisces quod fit de coctomiis quod sole torrente in mellis substantiam cogitur. quod si non fuerit uel caricarum defritum mittes quod Romani colorem uocant, ac deinceps 20 amulum infusum adicies uel orize sucum et lento igni feruere facias.

1. in esiciato pullo *André*: in isiciato pullo *Mar*: in isicia de pullo *Ven*: in esiciat opullo *E*: is esicia topullo *V*: esicia de pullo *written as a gloss in B*: *del. GiVo* | oleo *V1*   2. semunciam *MO*
3. XXX *CGSG*: XXXI *VE*   4. mittis *V*   6. colcleare *V* | si *CGSG*: sic *VE*
7. feces *V*: facies *E*   8. fuerit *V*   9. niculis *E1*   12. amulata *Hum.*: multa *VE* | a balineo *Milham*: ab alieno *VE*: ab aheno *Sch*: a balneo *André* | terres *V*
14. bulliuerit *Milham*: boluerit *V*: oluerit *E*: bullierit *GiVo*: bulliuerit *Hum*   15. soruendum *E*: suruendum *V* | inferes *Sch*: feres *VE*   16. amulatum *Hum*: amulum *VE*: *both MSS start this recipe with* aliter piper | infusu *V*: infasu *E*   17. facies *E*   18. coctomiis *V*: coctomus *E*
19. caricarum *Hum*: camcarum *V,E2*: carum *E1* | ac deinceps *λ*: accede inceps *VE*   20. igni *ξ*: igniti *VE*

2.2.3. Sauce for a forcemeat of chicken: 1 lb. finest quality olive oil, a quart of *liquamen,* ½ oz. of pepper.

2.2.4. Another sauce for chicken forcemeat: pound 30 grains of pepper;[1] add a cup of best quality *liquamen,* the same amount of *caroenum* and 11 cups[2] of water and put it over the heat of the fire.

2.2.5. A simple forcemeat (sauce): you put 7 small cups of water to 1 of *liquamen,* a little celery leaf, a spoonful of ground pepper. Cook small forcemeat balls in this, and if you give this for easing the stomach, add the dregs of spiced wine to the *hydrogarum.*

2.2.6. Peacock faggots rank in the first place, provided that they are fried until they burst their skins. Pheasant faggots rank in the second place, then rabbit third, then chicken fourth and tender young pork ones are fifth.

2.2.7. A thick forcemeat sauce served after bathing:[3] pound pepper, lovage, a moderate amount of oregano, a minimum amount of *silphium* and ginger and a moderate amount of honey;[4] flavour[5] with *liquamen,* stir together and pour it over the forcemeat balls; bring to the boil; when it is boiling well, thicken with starch and serve for immediate consumption.

2.2.8. Another thick sauce for forcemeat: soak pepper overnight, grind it and immediately pour on *liquamen* so that you make a finely ground pepper mash. Stir in *defrutum* made from quinces that has been left in full sun until it is as thick as honey. If you don't have any of this add a *defrutum* which has been made from dried figs, which the Romans call 'colouring'; and then add a starch emulsion or the liquor from (cooked) rice,[6] and bring to heat over a slow fire.

---

[1] The MSS read *xxxi* grains of pepper, but it is unusual to have such an odd number, and is probably a scribal misreading of *xxx*[a].

[2] See the Introduction, p. 84, for *calix,* here interpreted as 'a cup.'

[3] Previous editions print *ab aheno* , meaning 'served from a bronze pan', but the text probably refers to a bath. The phrase also occurs at 9.4.3, where cuttlefish is served in a sauce. The Romans often snacked at the baths and it is not unreasonable to expect recipes for such a context. Archaeological remains from such locations reveal such items as lamb chops, chicken wings, oysters and shellfish generally. Meatballs fall neatly into the category of 'small finger-food' ideal to eat as a snack.

[4] We have taken *modicum* and *minimum* with the nouns which precede them, as this appears to be the customary practice elsewhere in *Apicius.*

[5] See the Introduction, p. 87, on the complexity of the instruction *temperabis.*

[6] See Pliny, *HN.*18.76. for *amylum,* which is simply wheat starch, in this case in an emulsion. The 'rice juice' will come from a starchy rice which is boiled in order to extract the cooking liquor as thickener. See the recipe below, where the cooked rice is retained and pounded.

[2.2.9] **amulatum aliter**: ossucla de pullis exbromas, deinde mittis in caccabum porros anetum salem. cum cocta fuerit, addes piper, apii semen; deinde oridiam infusam teres, addes liquamen et passum uel defritum, omnia misces et cum esiciis inferes.

5   [2.2.10] **apotermum sic facies**: alicam elixa cum nucleis et amindalis depilatis et in aqua infusis et lotis ex creta argentaria ut ad candorem pariter perducantur; cui iam miscebis uuam passam carenum uel passum; desuper <piper> confractum asparges et in uolitari inferes.

III. VVLVVLE BOTELLI.

10   [2.3.1] **bulbule esiciatae et sic fiunt**: piper tritum et cuminum capita porrorum breuia duo ad molle purgata rutam liquamen. admiscentur pulpæ bene tunsae et fricatæ denuo ipso subtrito ita ut commisceri possit. mittas piperis grana et nucleos et calcabis in materia bene lota, et sic quocuntur ex aqua oleo liquamine fasciculo porrorum et aneto.

15   [2.3.2] **botellum sic facies**: ex ouis uitellis coctis nucleis pineis concisis cepam porrum concisum ius crudum misces; piper minutum <addes> et sic intestinum farcies; adicies liquamen et uinum et sic quoques.

IV. LVCANICAE. lucanicas similiter ut supra scriptum est. [lucanicarum confectio]: teritur piper cuminum satureia ruta petrosilenu condimentum bacæ
20   lauri liquamen et admiscetur pulpa bene tunsa ita ut denuo bene cum ipso

---

2. oridiam *VE*: oryzam *Milham*   5. apotermu. *V, in large letters*: apotermu *E, in large letters* | elixa cum nucleis *Sch*: elixatam nucleis *E*: elixam nucleis *V*   6-7. cui iam miscebis *CGSG*: cum iam miscebis *E*: cum iamiam missebis *V1*: cum iam iammiscebis *V2*: cui ammiscebis *Vo*   7. <piper> *add. Gi*   8. et *om. V1* | in boletari *ζ* 10. esiciatae *CGSG*: esiciata *VE*: isiciatae *GiVo*   11. pulpę *V* | tunse *E*   12. fricate *E* | denuo *E1*: denuo denuo *V,E2* | commisceari *V* | mittas *Ven*: mittat *VE*: mittantur *Milham* 13. nucleos *Tor*: nuclei *VE* | materia bene lota *VE*: matrice bene lota *Lis*: mortario bene loto *Hum* 15. sic *om. E1* | ex ouis *CGSG*: exeo uis *V*: exoui *E*: sex *Sch, edd*   16. ius *Hum*: tus *VE* | <addes> *FR*: <asparges> *Gi*   17. farcies *D*: facies *VE* | coques *E*   18. lucanice *E* | lucanicarum confectio *del. Sch*   19. petroselinu *E* | bace *V*

2.2.9. **Another thick sauce for forcemeat**: boil and strain chicken bones to make a stock,[1] then put in the pot leeks, dill, and salt. When they are cooked, add (pounded) pepper and celery seed; then make a paste of boiled rice; add *liquamen, passum* or *defrutum*, mix all in together and serve with forcemeat.

2.2.10. **You make a cold dessert like this**:[2] boil *alica* with pine nuts and almonds which have been soaked in water and skinned[3] and washed in some 'silver' chalk so that they are all equally white. Add to this raisins, *caroenum* or *passum*. Sprinkle ground pepper over the top and serve in a dish.

2.3 WOMB AND BLACK PUDDING.

2.3.1. **Forcemeat stuffing for womb is made like this**: ground pepper and cumin and two small leeks[4] peeled down to the tender parts, rue and *liquamen*. These are mixed with pieces of meat which have been thoroughly beaten and pounded so that they can then be blended with the spice mix. Add peppercorns and pine nuts, stuff (the mixture) into a well-washed womb;[5] they are cooked like this in water, oil and *liquamen*, with a bundle of leek and dill.

2.3.2. **Blood sausages are made like this**: you mix blood with chopped leeks and onion, with the some yolks of hard-boiled eggs and chopped pine nuts. Add ground pepper and stuff into a sausage skin. Put *liquamen* and wine (in a pan) and so cook them.

2.4 *LUCANICAE.* *Lucanicae* are made in a similar way to that written above.[6]

Pound pepper, cumin, savory, rue, parsley, bay berry spice[7] and *liquamen*. Add meat which has been thoroughly pounded so that it can then be blended well with

---

[1] In fact you make a stock and the chicken bones are removed. See the Introduction, p. 92, for a full discussion of the term *exbromas*.

[2] This is seemingly a dessert of some kind and as such out of place in this chapter, an example of the random order in which some of the recipes have been placed. *Apothermum* may have an equivalent sense to *a balineo* and refer not to the dish but to the occasion when it is served.

[3] The nuts would be soaked to allow the skins to be removed; the Latin text reverses the practical order of instructions.

[4] *Capita porrorum*: a kind of leek from the Middle East with a bulb or head (*A. currat*). See the Glossary.

[5] The wombs (presumably indicated by *materia)* must also be tied or sewn up before cooking.

[6] The gloss *lucanicarum confectio* means 'the making of *lucanicae*'.

[7] Bay berries contain a large pale brown seed, which when roasted and ground adds a distinct bay flavour, while the leaves add flavour but cannot be eaten.

subtrito fricetur; cum liquamine admixto pipere integro et abundanti pinguedine et nucleis inicies in intestinum perquam tenuatim productum et sic ad fumum suspenditur.

V. FARCIMINA.

[2.5.1] oua et cerebella teres; nucleos pineos piper liquamen laser modicum, et his intestinum implebis. elixas, postea assas et inferes.

[2.5.2] **aliter**: coctam alicam et tritam cum pulpa concisa et trita una cum piper et liquamine et nucleis. farcies intestinum et elixabis, deinde cum sale assabis et cum senapi inferes, uel sic concisum in disco.

[2.5.3] **aliter**: alicam purgas et cum liquamine intestini et albamine porri concisi minutatim simul elixas. elixa tolles, pinguedinem concides, et copadia pulpe in se omnia conmisces. teres piper ligusticum oua tria; haec omnia in mortario permisces cum nucleis et piper integro. liquamen suffundes, intestina imples, elixas et subassas, uel elixa tantum appones.

[2.5.4] **aliter circellos esiciatos**: reples intestinum inpensam esicii et circellum facies rotundum. fumas. cum miniauerit subassas, exornas; oenogaro fasiani perfundes sed cuminum addes.

EXPLICIT LIBER SECVNDVS APICI

SARCOPTES

1. integre *V* | pinguidine *E*   2. productum *Hum*: perductum *VE*   5. crebella *V*
7. tritam cum *ξ*: trita cum *VE* | *?*pipere *V2*   8. farcie sint testinum *V*   10. abamine *V* |
porro *V*   11. elixa tolles *ξ*: elixato tolles *V*: elixa to tolles *E* | pinguedinem *V1*: pinguidinem
V2,E | 5. conpadia *V*   12. hæc *E*   13. inples *E*   14. uel elixa *Milham*: uel
elixam *VE*   15. isicii *E*   17. perfundes *Sch*: profundes *VE* | cuminum addes *Hum*:
cuminumates *E*: cum inumates *V*   18. II *VE* | APICII *E*

the spice-mix. Stir in *liquamen*, whole peppercorns, plenty of fat and pine nuts. Put the meat in the skins, draw them quite thinly and hang them in the smoke.

2.5 SAUSAGES.

2.5.1. Pound eggs and brains; (add) pine nuts, pepper, *liquamen* and a little *laser*. Stuff into a sausage skin, boil and afterwards roast and serve.

2.5.2. **Alternatively**: take cooked *alica* and pound it with chopped meat and grind with pepper, *liquamen*, and pine nuts.[1] Stuff into sausage skins and boil. Then roast them with salt and serve them with mustard or cut them up on a round dish like this.[2]

2.5.3. **Alternatively**: soak *alica* and boil it together with blood *liquamen*[3] and finely chopped white of leek. Strain the boiled mixture. Chop fat and mix small pieces of meat thoroughly with all this. Pound pepper, lovage, 3 eggs; you mix all these things in a mortar with pine nuts and whole peppercorns. Pour on *liquamen* and fill the sausage skin. Boil and then lightly roast, or serve them simply boiled.[4]

2.5.4. **Alternatively, sausage ring**: you fill a sausage skin with a forcemeat recipe and shape it into a ring. Smoke. When it has gone dark red, roast it lightly and arrange it; pour on *oenogarum* used for pheasant, but add cumin.

HERE ENDS BOOK TWO OF APICIUS, 'MEAT DISHES'

---

[1] The *alica* here would be a coarse variety not dissimilar to modern cracked wheat.

[2] *sic concisum* might possibly refer to an illustration now lost (cf. 4.2.14.) The *discus* is a dish to serve the sausage in. Alternatively the sausages themselves are cut into discs.

[3] In this case, we think that a fish sauce made with the addition of blood and intestines from other fish may have been indicated; see the Glossary on *liquamen*.

[4] This and the next recipe have *subassas* after the sausages are pre-cooked, the former by boiling, the latter by smoking. In this context, roasting or grilling a little is very apt.

BOOK THREE

INCIPIT EIVSDEM CEPVROS DE OLERIBVS LIBER TERTIVS

I. ut omne olus smaragdinum fiat. II. pulmentarium ad uentrem. III. asparagos. IIII. cucurbitas. V. cidrium. VI. cucumeres. VII. pepones melones. VIII. maluas. VIIII. cimas et culiclos. X. porros. XI. betas. XII. olisera. XIII. rapas siue napos. XIV. rafanos. XV. olus molle. XVI. erbe rusticæ. XVII urticæ. XVIII. intibæ et lactucæ. XIX. cardui. XX. funduli siue spondili. XXI. caroetae.

I. DE OLERIBVS: **ut omne olus smaragdinum fiat**: omne olus smaragdinum fiat si cum nitro coquatur.

II. [3.2.1] PVLMENTARIVM AD VENTREM. betas minutas et porros requietos elixabis; in patina conpones. teres piper cuminum, suffundes liquamen passum ut quaedam dulcedo sit. facias ut ferueat; cum ferbuerit, inferes. similiter polipodium in tepidam mittes. ubi mollierit rades et minutum cum pipere et cuminum tritum in patenam feruentem mittes et uteris.

[3.2.2] **aliter ad uentrem**: facies betaciorum fasces; deterge, ne laues; in eorum medium nitrum asparges et alligas singulos fasces. mittes in aquam. cum coxeris condies patinam cum eadem passum uel caroenum, et cuminum et piper asparges et oleum modicum. ubi ferbuerit, polypodium et frustra nucum cum liquamine teres, feruentem patenam fundes, cooperies. statim depones ut uteris.

2. III *V*   3. smaragdinum II fiat pulmentarium *V*   4. pemones *V*
5. culiclos *CGSG*: culiclus *V*: auliclos *E*: coloclos *André*: cauliculos *Milham* | bitas *V*
6. molle *TC*: molles *VE* | herbe *E* | rustice *V* | urtice *V* | intibe *V*: intuba *ζ*   7. lactuce
V | funduli siue *del. André* | siue spondili *del. GiVo* | caroetæ *E*: careotae *V*   9. fit si
E | nitroquatur *V*   10. bitas *V* | minitas *E*   12. quædam *E* | cumfer.uerit *V*
14. cumino trito *ζ*| patena *V*: patinam *ζ*   15. fasces *Hum*: facies *VE* | deterge, ne *GiVo*:
detergi ne *V*: detergine *E*   16. nitrum *Hum*: nigrum *VE* | adligas *E*   17. caroenum
ζ: caroenim *VE* | piper *Hum*: super *VE*: piper <super> *André*   18. feruuerit *V* | frusta *SC*
19 <in> feruentem *GiVo* | quo operies *E* | ut *VE*: et *Hum*

BOOK THREE OF THE SAME, 'VEGETABLE DISHES', BEGINS

1. How to make all kinds of leaf vegetables emerald green. 2. Easily digested relish. 3. Asparagus. 4. Gourd. 5. Citron melon. 6. Cooking 'cucumbers'. 7. Long and round sweet melons. 8. Mallows. 9. Young greens and cabbage sprouts. 10. Leeks. 11. Beets. 12. Alexanders. 13. Turnips and swede. 14. Radish. 15. Vegetable mash. 16. Rustic herbs. 17. Nettles. 18. Endives and lettuce. 19. Cardoon. 20. Mussels.[1] 21. Carrots

3.1. ON LEAF VEGETABLES: how to make all kinds of leaf vegetables emerald green: Every kind of leaf vegetable may become emerald green if it is cooked in soda.

3.2. EASILY DIGESTED RELISH. [2]

3.2.1. You boil chopped beets and stored leeks, and arrange them in a dish. Pound pepper and cumin and pour on *liquamen* and *passum* so that there is a certain sweetness. Bring to the boil, and when it has boiled, serve it.

In the same way you put polypody[3] into warm water (to cook). When it has gone soft, peel it and put it, cut up, into a hot dish with ground cumin and pepper, and use.

3.2.2. **Alternatively for the digestion**: you make bundles of beets; wipe them clean but do not wash them, sprinkle soda in the middle of them and tie up each bundle. Put them in water and when they are cooked, flavour the dish with (some of) the water and *passum* or *caroenum*, and sprinkle on cumin and pepper and a little oil. When it has boiled, you grind (cooked) polypody and broken nuts with *liquamen*. Tip this into the hot dish, cover it up; take it off the heat and use immediately.

---

[1] We take *sive sponduli* to be a variant spelling of the same term, which may date back to an early period in the compilation, hence its not being translated.

[2] *pulmentaria* is a term for any food eaten with bread, a relish to accompany bread as the main part of the meal, and is generally strongly flavoured.

[3] The root of the tree or oak fern. Its purgative qualities are well known.

[3.2.3] **aliter betacios Varrones**: Varro: betacios sed nigros quorum detersas radices et mulsu decoctas cum sale modico et oleo, uel sale aqua et oleo in se coctas; iusculum facere et potari; melius etiam si in eo pullus sit decoctus.

[3.2.4] **aliter ad uentrem**: apios uirides cum suis radicibus lauabis et siccabis

5 ad solem. deinde albamen et capita porrorum simul elixabis in caccabo nouo ita ut aqua ad tertias deferueat, id est ut ex III eminis aquae una remaneat. postea teres piper, liquamen et aliquantum mellis humore temperabis, et aquam apiorum decoctorum colabis in mortario et superfundes apio. cum simul feruuerit appones et si libitum fuerit apios adicies.

10 **III. ASPHARAGOS.** aspharagos siccabis, sursum in calidam summittas.

IV. CVCVRBITAS.

[3.4.1] **callosiores reddes gustum ad cucurbitas**: coctas expressas in patinam conpones. adicies in mortarium pipere cuminum silfi modice (id est laseris radicem), rutam modicum; liquamine et aceto temperabis; mittes defreto

15 modicum ut coloretur; ius exinanies in patenam. cum ferbuerit iterum ac tertio, depones et piper minutum asparges.

[3.4.2] **aliter cucurbitas iure colocesiorum**: cucurbitas quoques ex aqua in modum colocasiorum; teres piper cuminum rutam; suffundes acetum, liquamen temperabis in caccabum cui adicies <oleum modicum> et eas cucurbitas incisas

---

3. coctas *Gi*: cocta *VE*: cocto *Tor*: coctos *Sch* 5. albamen *Hum*: albam *VE* | ca.cabo *V*
6. id est... remaneat *del. Hum* 8. apio *VE*: porro *GiVo* 10. siccabit *E* |
sursum in calidam *CGSG*: sursum in calidam sursum in calidam *VE*: rursum in calidam
RGO | summitas *V*: summittes *GiVo* 11-12. CVCVRBITAS. callosiores reddes
gustum ad cucurbitas *CGSG*: callossiores reddes cucurbitas gustum de cucurbatas cucurbitas
V, E1: callosiores reddes cucurbitas gustum ad cucurbitas *E2*: CVCVRBITAS. gustum de
cucurbitis *GiVo*: CVCURBITAS. gustum de cucurbitas *André* callosiores reddes *transferred
to end of 3.3 Sch* 13. piper *ζ*: piperem *Milham* | id est laseris radicem *del. Hum*
14. rutae *GiVo* | defritum *Sch* 15. patinam *V* | ferbuerit *CGSG*: feruuerit *V*: ferbuerint *E*
19. temperabis <mittes> *Gi* | <oleum modicum> *André*: <olei guttas> *Bra3*: ...*GiVo*

3.2.3. **Alternatively Varro's beets**: Varro: wipe the roots of black beets and cook then in *mulsum* with a little salt and oil, or make a broth for drinking by cooking them in salted water and oil. It is even better if a chicken is cooked in it first.

3.2.4. **Alternatively for the digestion**: you wash green celery with its root and dry it in the sun. Next boil it with the white part and the head of leek in a new pan[1] until the water has reached a third of its volume, that is, out of three measures of water, one remains. Next pound pepper, moisten with *liquamen* and a little runny honey, strain the liquor from the boiled celery into the mortar and pour it back over the celery. When all has come to the boil serve it and, if you like, add the celery.

3.3. ASPARAGUS. Dry the asparagus, put it upright in hot water.[2]

3.4. GOURD.

3.4.1. **To make tougher-skinned gourds tasty**:[3] arrange cooked and well-drained[4] gourds in a dish. Put in a mortar pepper, cumin, and a little *silphium,* which is *laser* root,[5] a little rue, flavour it with *liquamen* and vinegar, put in a little *defrutum* to give it colour. Pour this sauce into the dish; when it has come to the boil three times, take it off and sprinkle with ground pepper.

3.4.2. **Alternatively gourd in a sauce for taro**:[6] cook the gourd in water in the manner of taro. Pound pepper, cumin and rue, pour on vinegar and flavour with *liquamen*. (Put into) a pan, to which you add a little oil; put the gourd itself, well

---

[1] In this recipe the liquor is taken in the first instance as a digestive drink, and the celery can be served as well if desired.

[2] The MSS read *sursum*, 'upright'; as all good cooks know, that is precisely how asparagus is cooked. It is hard to understand why all editors and translators since Schuch (though not, it should be noted, Vehling – the only chef) changed the Latin to make it read *rursum* ('again') as if cooking asparagus twice would make it better!

[3] The line *callosiores reddes* is put in the preceding recipe for asparagus in earlier editions and translations. Both MSS clearly end the asparagus recipe at *summitas* and begin the gourd recipe in red with *callosiores*; as our text makes clear, we think that confusion arose when the title *cucurbitas* was misplaced in the text and then a doublet involving mis-spelling was introduced.

[4] We think it likely that the gourd was peeled, given that it is supposed to be tough. The term *expressas* denotes squeezing or wringing to extract the cooking water.

[5] This may be a later gloss, but even so it indicates that the cook who wrote this recipe understood what *silphium* was, but he (or a later compiler) needed to clarify, for the benefit of other users, that *laser* root was meant. See the Glossary.

[6] The root or corm of the taro, *Colocasia esculenta v. antiquorum*. See the Glossary.

expressas; in ius mittes ut ferueant; amulo obligas; piper asparges et inferes.

[3.4.3] **cucurbitas more Alexandrino**: elixatas cucurbitas exprimis; sale asparges; in patina conpones. teres piper cuminum coriandri semen mentam uiridem lasaris radicem; suffundes acetum; adicies cariotam nucleum, teres;
5 melle acetum liquamine defrito et oleum temperabis et cucurbitas perfundes. cum ferbuerint piper asparges et inferes.

[3.4.4] **aliter cucurbitas elixatas**: ex liquamine oleo mero.

[3.4.5] **aliter cucurbitas frictas**: oenogaro simplici et piperem.

[3.4.6] **aliter cucurbitas elixatas et frictas**: in patina conpones; cuminatum
10 superfundes; modico oleo super adiecto feruere facies et inferes.

[3.4.7] **aliter cucurbitas frictas**: tritas piper ligusticum cuminum origanum cepam uinum liquamen et oleum; amulo obligabis in patina et inferes.

[3.4.8] **aliter cucurbitas cum gallina**: duracina tubera piper careum cuminum silfi, condimenta uiridia: mentam apium coriandrum puleium caroetam mel
15 uinum liquamen oleum et acetum.

V. CITRIVM. sil montanum silfi mentam siccam acetum liquamen.

VI. CVCVMERES.

[3.6.1] **cucumeres rasos**: siue ex liquamine siue ex enogaro sine ructu et grauitudine teneriores senties.
20 [3.6.2] **aliter cucumeres rasos**: elixabis cum cerebellis elixis cumino et melle modico apii semen liquamine et oleo; obis obligabis. piper asparges et inferes.

[3.6.3] **aliter cucumeres**: piper puleium mel uel passum liquamen et acetum. interdum et silfi accedit.

---

2. *?elixatus E1*   4. laseris *E* | caroetam *V*   5. aceto *Hum* | oleo *Hum*   6. feru-
uerint *V*   8. frictas frictas *V* | pipere *ζ*   9. patena *E* | compones *V*   10. *E writes* et
inferes *below last line of the page*   12. patena *E*   13. piperem *GiVo*   14. menta
V | mentam cepam apium *E1* | puleum *V1* | caroetam *André*: caromentam *E*: caromemtam
V   15. et *om. E*   16. CITRVM *E (cf. index,* cidrium *VE)*   18. enegaro *E1*
20. cerebellis elixabis *E1* | *?*cucumino *V1*: cuminum *André*   21. semine *Hum* | obis *CGSG*:
bis *VE*: ouis *Sch*   22. et acetum et acetum *V*

drained and chopped, into the sauce and allow it to boil. Thicken with starch, sprinkle with pepper and serve.

3.4.3. Gourd in an Alexandrian style: boil the gourd and press the water out, sprinkle with salt and arrange in a dish. Pound pepper, cumin, coriander seed, green mint, *laser* root; pour on vinegar and add dates and pine nuts and pound them. Flavour with honey, vinegar, *liquamen*, *defrutum* and oil. Pour over the gourd and when it has come to heat, sprinkle with pepper and serve.

3.4.4. Alternatively for boiled gourd: (serve) in some *liquamen*, oil and unmixed wine.

3.4.5. Alternatively for fried gourd: (serve) with simple *oenogarum* and pepper.

3.4.6. Alternatively for boiled and fried gourd: put the gourd in a dish and pour on a cumin sauce, add a little oil, bring to the heat and serve.

3.4.7. Alternatively for fried gourd: grind[1] pepper, lovage, cumin, oregano, onion, wine, *liquamen,* and oil, thicken with starch in the dish and serve.

3.4.8. Alternative sauce for gourd with chicken: peaches, truffles, pepper, caraway, cumin, *silphium*; green herbs: mint, celery, coriander, pennyroyal; dates, honey, wine, *liquamen,* oil and vinegar.

3.5. CITRON MELON:[2] (serve with) mountain sesely, *silphium*, dry mint, vinegar and *liquamen*.

3.6. COOKING 'CUCUMBERS'.[3]

3.6.1. Peeled cucumbers: you will find them more digestible, producing no wind or heaviness, if you cook them in some *liquamen* or *oenogarum*.

3.6.2. Another way with peeled cucumbers: boil them with boiled brains, with cumin and a little honey, with celery seed*, liquamen,* and oil. Thicken with eggs, sprinkle with pepper and serve.

3.6.3. Another recipe for cucumbers: pepper, pennyroyal, honey or *passum, liquamen* and vinegar. Sometimes *silphium* is added.

---

[1] *trito* noted as a Late Latin variant of *tero* in Oribasius (cf. Souter, *Glossary of Late Latin*, ad loc.); purée of fried gourd (André, *FR*) is an unlikely concept.

[2] This is not the citron fruit but a kind of gourd or melon; see the Glossary.

[3] This is likely to be the 'chate melon' or 'cooking cucumber', rather than the juicy variety known today. See the Glossary.

VII. PEPONES ET MELONES. piper puleium mel uel passum liquamen acetum. interdum et silfi accedit.

VIII. MALVAS. maluas minores in oenogaro ex liquamine oleo acetum: maluas maiores in oenogaro piper liquamine careno uel passo.

5   **IX. CIMAS ET COLICLOS.**
[3.9.1] **cimas**: cuminum salem uinum uetus et oleum.
[3.9.1a] si uoles, addes piper et ligusticum mentam rutam coriandrum folia coliclorum liquamen uinum oleum.
[3.9.2] **aliter**: culiculos elixatos mediabis; summa foliarum teres cum coriandro
10   cepa cumino piper passo uel careno et oleo modico.
[3.9.3] **aliter**: cauliculi elixati in patina conpositi condiuntur liquamine oleo mero cumino. piper asparges; porrum cuminum coriandrum uiridem super concides.
[3.9.4] **aliter**: cauliculi conditi ut supra cum elixis porris quoquantur.
[3.9.5] **aliter**: cauliculos condies ut supra admisces olibas uirides et simul
15   ferueant.
[3.9.6] **aliter**: culiculis conditis ut supra; superfundes alicam elixam cum nucleis et uua passa super asparges.

X. PORROS.
[3.10.1] **porros maturos fieri**: pugnum salis aquam et oleum mixtum facies et
20   ibi quoques et eximes. cum oleo liquamine mero et inferes.
[3.10.2] **aliter porros**: opertos foliis coliculorum et in prunis quoques; ut supra et inferes.

1. PEMONES *V* | uel *om. VI*   3. in oenogaro *CGSG*: de grano *VE*: oenogaro *Hum*: de garo *Tor*: eleogaro *André* | aceto *GiVo*   4. oenogaro *Hum*: oenogara *VE* | pipere *Hum*
5. CAVLICVLOS *GiVo*   6. et *om. E*   7. menta *V*   8. coliclorum *CGSG*: colicorum *VE*: cauliculorum *GiVo*   10. pipere *Hum*   11. culiculi *V* | exati *V* | conposita *V* 12. piper *Hum*: super *VE*   13. culiculi *V* | coquantur *E* 14. culiculos *V* | admiscis *V*   16. culiculos *V* | super fundes *E*   17. super *VE*: piper *Vo*   20. liquamine liquamine *VE* | et *del. FR*   21. apertos *V*

3.7. LONG AND ROUND SWEET MELONS: pepper, pennyroyal, honey or *passum, liquamen,* vinegar. Sometimes *silphium* is added.[1]

3.8. MALLOWS: (cook) young mallow leaves in an *oenogarum* with *liquamen*, oil and vinegar. Larger mallow leaves are (cooked) in an *oenogarum* made of pepper, *liquamen, caroenum* or *passum*.[2]

3.9. YOUNG GREENS AND CABBAGE.[3]
3.9.1. **Young greens**: cumin, salt, old wine, and oil.
<3.9.1a.> If you wish, you add pepper, lovage, mint, rue, coriander, cabbage leaves, *liquamen*, wine, oil.
3.9.2. **Alternatively**: cut boiled cabbages in half; pound the tips of the leaves with coriander, onion, cumin, pepper*, passum* or *caroenum* and a little oil.
3.9.3. **Alternatively**: arrange boiled cabbages in a dish and flavour with *liquamen*, oil, pure wine, cumin. Sprinkle with pepper and chop over them leek, cumin and green coriander.
3.9.4. **Alternatively**: cabbages flavoured as above may be cooked with boiled leeks.
3.9.5. **Alternatively**: flavour cabbages as above; mix with green olives and let them boil together.
3.9.6. **Alternatively**: cabbages are flavoured as above; pour over *alica* boiled with pine nuts and sprinkle raisins over them.

3.10. LEEKS.
3.10.1. **To cook mature leeks**: stir a handful of salt into water and oil, cook them in it and strain them. (Dress with) oil, *liquamen* and pure wine, and serve.
3.10.2. **Another leek recipe**: wrap the leeks in the leaves of cabbage and cook them in the hot coals. Serve them as above.

---

[1] This recipe is almost identical to 6.3, missing only *et. melones* might refer to watermelons (we are indebted to Andrew Dalby for this suggestion).
[2] The MSS both read *degrano*, which is meaningless. An *oenogarum* or *oxygarum* seems to be intended, with *ex* before the list of ingredients from which it is made. See the Glossary for a general discussion.
[3] See the Glossary for *cymae et coliculi*. *FR*, following Brandt, interpreted the *folia coliculorum* in recipe 1 as the beginning of a new recipe. This is not represented in the MSS where the red capitals clearly indicate the start of a recipe which we think contains a variant. The next recipe also includes pounded cabbage leaves as a normal ingredient of a sauce.

[3.10.3] **aliter porros**: in lacte coctos; ut supra et inferes.

[3.10.4] **aliter porros**: in aquam elixati erunt. fabe nondum condite plurimum admisce conditure in qua eos manducaturus es.

XI. BETAS.

5   [3.11.1] concides porrum coriandrum; cuminum uuam passam farinam et omnia in medullam mittes; ligabis et <elixas>. ita inferes ex liquamine oleo et aceto.

[3.11.2] **aliter betas elixas**: ex sinapi oleo modico et aceto bene inferuntur.

XII. OLISERA.

olisera in fasciculum redacta manuale ex liquamine oleo et mero bene inferuntur, uel cum piscibus assis.

10 ### XIII. RAPAS SIVE NAPOS.

[3.13.1] rapas siue napos elixatos exprimes. deinde teres cuminum plurimum rutam minus laser Particum mel acetum liquamen defritum et oleum modice; feruere facies et inferes.

[3.13.2] **aliter**: rapas siue napos elixas inferes; oleum super istillabis. si uoles
15   acetum adde.

XIIII. RAFANOS.

rafanos cum piperato ita ut piper cum liquamine teras.

1. lacte *CGSG*: baca *VE*: aqua *André*: caccabo *Hum* | et *om. V*   2. <si> in aqua *Sch*
5. *lacuna after* cuminum *André* | farinam *VE*: Varianam *Sch*   6. <elixas> *CGSG*
7. et inapi *V*   8. manuale *CGSG, cf. Pliny,* HN. *19.16*: manu *VE*: a manu *Vo* | et oleo *V1*
12. ratam *V* | parthicum *E*   16. tereas *V*

3.10.3. **Another leek recipe**: cook them in milk; serve them as above.[1]

3.10.4. **Another leek recipe**: boil the leeks in water; stir plenty of unseasoned beans into the sauce you are going to eat them with.

3.11. BEETS.

3.11.1. Chop leeks, coriander, (mix with) cumin, raisins and flour. Put the mixture in the middle (of the beet leaves); tie up and (boil). Serve in a sauce of *liquamen*, oil and vinegar.[2]

3.11.2. **Another recipe for boiled beets**: they are served nicely in a sauce of mustard, a little oil and vinegar.

3.12. ALEXANDERS: the alexanders are gathered into handy little bundles and are nicely served in a sauce of *liquamen*, oil, pure wine, or they can be served with grilled fish.

3.13. TURNIPS OR SWEDES.

3.13.1. Squeeze the water out of boiled turnips or swedes. Then pound plenty of cumin, a little rue, Parthian *laser*, honey, vinegar, *liquamen, defrutum* and a little oil. Bring to a simmer and serve.

3.13.2. **Alternatively**: serve the turnips and swedes boiled; drizzle oil over them, add vinegar if you wish.

3.14. RADISHES: serve them with a pepper sauce, in which you pound pepper with *liquamen*.

---

[1] The text is a little confused here. The term *in baca coctos* ought to represent a cooking medium of some sort rather than an extra ingredient. Water would appear to be unlikely as it would repeat recipe 3.9.1 almost entirely. Brandt's suggestion of olives seems not to be accurate given the terminology at 3.9.5 for cabbage. *lacte* is our suggestion as a cooking liquor as it is culinarily apt for leeks.

[2] This recipe is ambiguous: are beet roots or greens implied? We have opted for greens (*FR* prefer roots) because they have to be tied up. The phrase *in medullam mittes* means something like 'put it in the middle or heart of' and we think refers to stuffing the leaves. There is no mention of the cooking process, and we have assumed they should be boiled.

XV. HOLVS MOLLE.

[3.15.1] **holus molle ex olisatro**: coctum ex aqua nitrata expressum concides minutatim, et teres piper ligusticum satureiam siccam cum cepa sicca liquamen oleum et uinum.

[3.15.2] **aliter olus molle**: apium quoques ex aqua nitrata, exprimes et concides minutatim. in mortario teres piper ligusticum origanum cepam uinum liquamen et oleum. quoques in pultario et sic apium commisces.

[3.15.3] **aliter holus molle ex foliis lactucarum**: cum cepis quoques ex aqua nitrata; expressum concides minutatim; in mortario teres piper ligusticum apii semen mentam siccam cepam liquamen oleum et uinum.

[3.15.4] **aliter: holus molle ne arescat**: summa quaeque anputantur et purgamenta et caules madefactos in aqua absenti contegito.

XVI. HERBAE RVSTICAE. liquamine oleo aceto a manu uel in patina piper cumino bacis lentisci.

XVII. VRTICAE. urticam feminam sole in ariete posito aduersus aegritudinem sumes si uoles.

XVIII. INTVBAE ET LACTVCAE.

[3.18.1] intuba ex liquamine et oleo modico medere cepa concisa. pro lactucis uero hieme intibę ex enbammate uel melle et aceto acri.

[3.18.2] **lactucas**: cum oxyporio et aceto et modico liquamine ad digestionem et inflationem et ne lactucæ ledant: cumini uncias II; gengiber unciam I; rutae uiridis unciam I; dactilorum pinguium scripulos XII; piperis unciam I; mellis uncias

---

2. coctum *Sch*: cocto *VE*   3. minutatim *GiVo, see 3.15.2*: minutum *VE*   5. holus *E* | coques *E*   7. coques *E*   8. coques *E* | exaques ex aqua *E1*   9. expressum *GiVo*: expressa *VE*   11. aliter *del. Sch* | quæque *E* | amputantur *E*   13. HERBĘ RVSTICĘ *E* | pipere *GiVo*   15. urticæ urticam *runs on from XVI in E: all subsequent chapters in E are numbered one short as a result* | aduersis *V*   17. INTVBĘ VEL LACTVCĘ *E*: INTVBA ET LACTVCAE *Hum*   18. et liquamine oleo *V* | medere *VE*: comedere *Sch*: modicaque *Tor*: modice *Hum*: mero *Bra3* | cępa *E*   19. intibę *V*: incube *E1*: intube *E2*: intuba *ζ* | embammate *V* | agri *V*   20. exyporio aceto *V (om.* et) | digestione *V* 21. lactucę *V* | cuminum uncias *E* | gengiber *V* : gingiber *E1*: gingiberis *E2*: zingiberis *GiVo* | rutæ *E*

3.15. VEGETABLE MASH.

3.15.1. **Vegetable mash from alexanders**: cook them in water with soda, strain them and chop finely, and then pound pepper, lovage, dry savory with dried onion,[1] *liquamen,* oil and wine.

3.15.2. **Another vegetable mash recipe**: cook celery in some water with soda, squeeze out the water and chop finely. In a mortar pound pepper, lovage, oregano, onion, wine, *liquamen,* and oil. Cook in a pan and then stir the celery in.[2]

3.15.3. **Another vegetable mash recipe made with lettuce leaves**: cook them with onions in water with soda. Squeeze the water out and chop finely. In a mortar pound pepper, lovage, celery seed, dry mint, onion, *liquamen,* oil, and wine.

3.15.4 **Another recipe: to stop soft greens from shrivelling**: remove all the tips and the blemished parts and steep the leaves in water with absinthe and cover them.[3]

3.16. RUSTIC GREENS: (serve) with *liquamen,* oil and vinegar as a salad or (cook) in a dish with pepper, cumin and mastic berries.[4]

3.17. NETTLES: when the sun is in Aries you may pick stinging nettles against sickness if you like.

3.18. ENDIVE AND LETTUCE.

3.18.1. Remedy (the bitterness of) endive with a dressing of *liquamen,* a little oil, and chopped onion. But instead of lettuce in winter serve endive in a sauce or with honey and sharp vinegar.[5]

3.18.2. **Lettuce**: (serve) with an *oxyporium,* with vinegar and a little *liquamen* for the digestion and to ease wind and to prevent the lettuce from doing harm: 2 oz. cumin, 1 oz. ginger, 1 oz. green rue, 12 scruples date flesh, 1 oz. pepper, 9

---

[1] See the Glossary under *cepa* for a discussion of dried onions.

[2] *pultarius*: a cooking pot originally used for *puls*, a wheat porridge, but here a general term for cooking vessel.

[3] *holus molle* can mean both a purée and tender leaves. In this context it must be the latter. *FR* tied themselves in knots trying to interpret this recipe in terms of a purée.

[4] *a manu* 'by hand', but used here to signify a cold salad eaten with the hands, while the *patina* signifies that the herbs are to be cooked and might need a spoon.

[5] *enbammate*: a Greek term for sauce. See Pliny, *HN*. 20.147. One would expect a dative with *medere* in a classical text.

VIIII. cuminum aut Aethiopicum aut Siriacum aut Libicum. tundes cuminum et postea infundes in aceto. cum siccauerit postea melle omnia conprehendes; cum necesse fuerit dimidium coclearum <cum> aceto et liquamine modico misces aut post cenam dimidium coclearum accipies.

XVIIII. CARDVI.

[3.19.1] **carduos**: liquamine oleo et ouis concisis.

[3.19.2] **aliter carduos**: rutam mentam coriandrum feniculum omnia uiridia teres; addes piper ligusticum mel liquamen et oleum.

[3.19.3] **aliter carduos elixos**: piper cuminum liquamen et oleum.

[XX. SFONDILI VEL FUNDILI.

[3.20.1] **sfondili fricti**: ex oenogaro simplici.

[3.20.2] **aliter sfondili elixi**: ex sale oleo mero coriandro uiridi conciso et piper integro.

[3.20.3] **aliter sfondilos elixos**: perfundes ammulato infra scripto: apii semen rutam mel piper; teres; passum liquamen et oleum modice; amulo obligas; piper asparges et inferes.

[3.20.4] **aliter sfondilos**: teres cuminum rutam liquamen caroenum modice oleum coriandrum uiridem et porrum et sfondilos inferes pro salso.

[3.20.5] **aliter sfondilos elixatos**: predurabis; mittes in caccabum oleum liquamen piper; passum colorabis et obligas.

[3.20.6] **aliter**: sfondilos oleum liquamine conplebis uel oleo et sale; assabis; piper asparges et inferes.

1. æthiopicum *E* | tundis *E*   2. infundis *E* | cōprehendes *V*   3. nece fuerit *V* | coclearum *JBHall*: cloclearum *V*: coclearium *E*: cocleare *GiVo* | <cum> *add. GiVo* 4. coclearum *JBHall*: coclearem *E*: cloclearem *V*: cocleare *GiVo*   6. liquamen *Milham* 7. feniculum *R*: fenicum *VE*   10. SFONDILI VEL FVDILI *V1 (*FVNDILI *V2)*: SPHONDILI VEL FVNDILI *E*: uel fundili *del.GiVo NB: this whole chapter should really be placed in Book IX,* Talassa   11. sphondili *E*   12. sphundili *E1*: sphondili *E2* | sale *om. E1*   14. sphondilos *E* | elixo *V, E1*   15. piper² *om. E1*   16. asperges *E* 18. uiride *GiVo* | spondilos *E*   19. spondilos *E* | mictes *V*   20. passo *GiVo* 21. sphondilos *E* | oleo *GiVo* | liquamen *Milham* | cōplebis *V*

oz. honey, Ethiopian, Syrian, or Libyan cumin. Pound the cumin after you have steeped it in vinegar. When it has dried mix all the ingredients with the honey.[1] When required mix ½ teaspoon with the vinegar and a little *liquamen* or take ½ teaspoon after dinner.

3.19. CARDOON.
3.19.1. **Cardoon**: (serve) with *liquamen*, oil, and chopped boiled egg.
3.19.2. **Another cardoon recipe**: pound rue, mint, coriander, fennel, all green; add pepper, lovage, honey, *liquamen* and oil.
3.19.3. **Alternatively for boiled cardoons**: pepper, cumin, *liquamen*, and oil.

3.20. MUSSELS.[2]
3.20.1. **Fried mussels**: (serve) in a simple *oenogarum*.[3]
3.20.2 **Another recipe for boiled mussels**: (serve) in some salt, oil, pure wine, chopped green coriander and whole peppercorns.
3.20.3. **Another recipe for boiled mussels**: drench them with the thick sauce written below: celery seed, rue, honey, pepper; pound; *passum*, *liquamen*, a little oil; thicken with starch, sprinkle with pepper and serve.
3.20.4. **Another recipe for mussels**: pound cumin, rue, *liquamen*, *caroenum*, a little oil, green coriander and leeks, and serve the mussels instead of salted fish.
3.20.5. **Another recipe for boiled mussels**: fry them; put in a pan oil, *liquamen*, pepper; colour with *passum* and thicken.
3.20.6. **Alternatively**: fill up the mussels with oil and *liquamen* or oil and salt. Grill, sprinkle with pepper and serve.

---

[1] When it has dried? One can imagine the cumin seeds being soaked in vinegar first and then dried and pounded – hence the order in the translation. This method is employed above, at 1.32.
[2] This section is obviously misplaced. *spondyli* in both Latin and Greek originally meant 'vertebrae'. It also can mean artichoke (hence its position here), and is used to refer to the inner fleshy part of a shellfish because of its similarity in appearance to vertebrae, and so became the term for mussels. See Pliny, *HN*. 32.151, 154; Seneca, *Ep*. 95. 26, 28. The title appears to indicate differing pronunciation of the Greek *sphondylos/spondylos* in Attic and Ionian dialect respectively.
[3] Probably an unthickened sauce: see Glossary, *oenogarum*.

[3.20.7] **aliter**: sfondilos elixatos conteres et neruos eorum eximes. deinde cum eis alicam elixatam et oua conteres, liquamen, piper. esicia ex his facies cum nucleis et pipere. in omento assabis, oenogaro continges et pro esiciis inferes.][112]

5 **XXI. CAROETAE SEV PASTINACE.**

[3.21.1] caroetae fricta oenogaro inferuntur.[113]

[3.21.2] **aliter caroetas**: sale oleo puro et aceto.

[3.21.3] **aliter caroetas**: elixatas concisas in cuminato oleo modico quoques et inferes; cuminatum coliculorum facies.[114]

10 # EXPLICIT APICI CEPVROS DE OLERIBVS LIBER TERTIVS

1. sphondilos *E*   2. alica *V* | et pipere *VE*: et piper *Milham*   3. omento *Hum*: augmento *VE* | oenogairo *V*   5. CAROEOTAE *V* | PASTINACI *E*   6. caroetę *E* | frictae *Hum* | oenagaro *E*   8. coques *E*   9. coliculorum *Milham*: coliorum *VE*: colicorum *Tor*: colorium *Sch*   10. APICI *V*: EPICII *E* | DE OLERIBVS *del. Sch* 11. III *E*

3.20.7. **Alternatively**: pound boiled mussels which have been bearded. Next pound with them cooked *alica* and eggs, *liquamen* and pepper. You make forcemeat from the mixture with pine nuts and pepper. Roast them wrapped in caul fat. Sprinkle with *oenogarum* and serve instead of forcemeat.

3.21. CARROTS OR PARSNIPS.

3.21.1. Fried carrots are served with *oenogarum*.

3.21.2. **Another carrot recipe**: salt, pure oil and vinegar.

3.21.3. **Another carrot recipe**: boil the carrots and chop them into a cumin sauce with a little oil, finish cooking and serve. Make the cumin sauce as for cabbage.[1]

HERE ENDS BOOK THREE OF APICIUS,

'VEGETABLE DISHES'

[1] The sauces at 3.9.1 or 3.9.3 would do.

BOOK FOUR

INCIPIT \<EIVSDEM\> PANDECTER LIBER QVARTVS

I. sala cattabia. II. patine piscium olerum pomorum. III. minutal de piscibus uel esiciis. IIII. tisana uel sucum. V. gustum.

5 **I. SALA CATTABIA.**

[4.1.1] **sala cattabia**: piper mentam apium puleium aridum caseum nucleos pineos mel acetum liquamen ouorum uitella aquam recentem. panem ex posca maceratum exprimes; caseum bubulum, cucumeres in caccabulo conpones, interpositis nucleis. mittes concisi capparis minuti iocusculis gallinarum; ius

10 perfundes; super frigidam collocabis et sic appones.

[4.1.2] **aliter sala cattabia Apiciana**: adicies in mortario apii semen puleio aridum mentam aridam gengiber coriandro uiridem uuam passam enucleatam mel acetum oleum et uinum. conteres. adicies in caccabolo panis Picentini frustra, interpones pulpas pulli glandulas edinas caseum Vestinum nucleos pineos

15 cucumeres cepas aridas minute concisas; ius supra perfundes; insuper niuem sub ora, \<piper\> asparges et inferes.

[4.1.3] **aliter sala cattabia**: panem Alexandrinum excauabis; in posca macerabis. adicies in mortarium piper mel mentam alium coriandrum uiridem caseum bubulum sale conditum aquam oleum; insuper niuem et inferes.

---

1. \<EIVSDEM\> *add. CGSG*　　2. IIII *E*　　4. salacat tabia *E*: sala caccabia *Hum*: sala cottabia *Bas*: gala cattabia *Wilson* | patine *from heading to II, below*: pastine *VE* | olerum *André*: holerum E: oleum *V*　　5-6. salacat tabia salacat tabia *E*　　6. nucleos ζ: nucleo *VE* 7. aquam ζ: quam *VE*　　9. interponesitis *E1* | locusculis *V*: ...locusculis *sugg. Vo* 10. perfundes *Sch*: profundes *VE* | super super *V*　　11. salacat tabia *E* | puleium *GiVo* 12. gingiber *E*: zingiber *GiVo* | coriandrum *E*　　13. caccabulo *E* | picemtini *V* 14. frusta *GiVo* | uescinum *Bas* | pineos nucleos *E*　　15. concissas *V* | fundes *E1*, per *add. E2* | niuem *P*: nuem *VE*　　16. hora *E* | \<piper\> *CGSG*　　17. salacattabia *E* | elexandrinum *E1*　　18. mel *om. V*　　19. insuper ...inferes *below last usual line E* | niuem *Bas*: uinum *VE*

BOOK FOUR OF THE SAME, 'COMPOUND DISHES', BEGINS

1. *Sala cattabia.* 2. *Patinae* of fish, vegetables and fruit. 3. *Minutal* of fish and meat. 4. Barley soup or liquor. 5. Hors-d'oeuvre.

4.1. *SALA CATTABIA.*

4.1.1. ***Sala cattabia*:**[1] pepper, mint, celery seed, dried pennyroyal, cheese, pine nuts, honey, vinegar, *liquamen,* yolks of eggs, fresh water. Squeeze dry bread soaked in some *posca*;[2] (put this), cow's cheese and cucumber into a small pot,[3] interlayered with pine nuts. Put in finely-chopped capers with little chicken livers. Pour the sauce over it, stand it in cold water and set it forth.

4.1.2. **Another *sala cattabia* in the style of Apicius:** put in a mortar celery seed, dry pennyroyal, dry mint, ginger, green coriander, de-seeded raisins, honey, vinegar, oil and wine. Pound together. Put in a small pot pieces of *Picentine* bread[4] interlayered with chicken meat, goats' sweetbreads, *Vestine* cheese, pine nuts, cucumber, finely chopped dried onions.[5] Pour the sauce over (the ingredients); stand (the pot) in snow for an hour, sprinkle with pepper and serve.

4.1.3. **Another *sala cattabia*:** hollow out an Alexandrian loaf. Soak (the crumb) in *posca.* Put in a mortar pepper, honey, mint, garlic,[6] green coriander, cows' cheese, salt, spiced wine, water and oil. Stand (the pot) in snow and serve.

---

[1] These recipes are clearly salads. All the ingredients that would normally need cooking, such as the meat, are assumed to have been prepared in advance. How the bread is placed in the mould is difficult to determine. If one were simply to stir the softened bread into the ingredients, then the term *interpones* meaning 'interlayer' would be unnecessary. The bread should either line the mould, as with a summer pudding, or be placed in layers with the salad ingredients. We prefer the former simply because the dressing, no matter how well ground, cannot filter down through the ingredients if there is a barrier of bread or for that matter of cucumber slices. It then becomes apparent that the salad could be turned out and it can be, quite successfully.

[2] *posca,* a mixture of sour wine and water. Pliny, *HN.* 28.56.

[3] *cucumeres*: here possibly a modern juicy variety rather than the cooking cucumber; see the Glossary.

[4] Pliny, *HN.* 18.27.106. This is a very light, spongy bread made using *alica* (semolina). See the Glossary for a detailed discussion. A substitute would be a French *pain au levain*.

[5] See the Glossary under *cepa* for a discussion of the question of dried onions.

[6] It is very rare to see garlic in high-status food. See Horace *Ep.* 3 for an ancient comment on its powerful effects.

II. PATINE PISCIVM OLERVM POMORVM.

[4.2.1] **patina cotidiana**: cerebella elixata teres cum piper cuminum laser cum liquamine carenum lacte et obis. ad ignem lenem uel ad aquam calidam coques.

[4.2.2] **aliter patina uersatilis**: nucleos nuces fractas; torres eas et teres cum melle pipere liquamine lacte et obis; olei modicum.

[4.2.3] **aliter patina**: tyrsum lactuce teres cum pipere liquamine careno aquam oleo; quoques; ouis obligabis; piper asparges et inferes.

[4.2.4] **aliter patina fusilis**: accipies olisatra, purgas lauas quoques; refrigerabis, restringues. accipies cerebella IIII, eneruabis, quoques. adicies in mortario piper scripulos VI, suffundes liquamen, fricabis; postea adicies cerebella, fricabis iterum; adicies olisatra et simul conteres; postea franges oua VIII, adicias ciatum liquaminis uini ciatum passi ciatum; contrita simul temperabis; patinam perungues; inpones in termospodio. postea quod coctum fuerit piper asparges et inferes.

[4.2.5] **aliter patina de asparagis frigida**: accipies asparagos purgatos, in mortario fricabis; aqua suffundes, perfricabis; per colum colabis, et mittes fecitulas curatas; teres in mortario piperis scrupulos sex, adicies liquamen; fricabis; uini ciatum I passi ciatum I; mittes in caccabum olei uncias tres; illic ferueant. perungues patinam; in ea oua VI cum enogaro misces; cum suco asparagis inpones cineri calido. [mittes inpensam super scriptam] tunc ficetulas conpones, quoques; piper asparges et inferes.

---

1. OLERVM *André*: HOLERVM *E*: OLEVM *V*   2. patinam *E* | laser *E*, -a- *marked for deletion in error*   3. careno *ζ*| obis *V2*: ouis *V1,E* | leuem *E1* | ad quam *E* | callidam *V*
5. torres *Hum*: teres *VE*   7. lactucæ *E* | aqua *Tor*   8. coques *E* | aspargis *E*
9. coques *E*   10. coques *E*   14. inter mos podio *V*: intermo spodio *E2*: interimo spodio *E1* | quod *VE*: cum *GiVo* | aspargis *E*   16. aspargis *E*
18. ficedulas *Hum*: ficetulas *Sch* | curatas *Hum*: curtas *VE* | scripulos *E* | sex *Hum*: sed *VE*
19. ciatum uni passi *V* | III *E*   21. asparagi *π*| inpensas *E* | mittes ...scriptam *del. CGSG*
22. conpo.nes *E:* compones *V* | coques *E* | aspergis *E*

---

[1] See the Introduction p. 79 and the Glossary for a discussion of these egg-based dishes.

[2] The first reference to a water bath or bain-marie. See Introduction, p. 73ff., for a discussion of cooking methods in general.

[3] 'Thicken it with eggs' is a frequent instruction in this chapter. The addition of eggs to a mixture identifies the dish as a *patina*, it seems, though eggs are not a prerequisite. The finished dish could be like scrambled egg or an omelette in appearance.

4.2. *PATINAE* OF FISH, VEGETABLES AND FRUIT[1]

4.2.1. Everyday *patina*: pound boiled brains with pepper, cumin, *laser*, with *liquamen, caroenum*, milk and eggs. Cook over a slow fire or in hot water.[2]

4.2.2. Another *patina*, omelette-style: roast pine nuts and broken nuts and pound them with honey, pepper, *liquamen*, milk and eggs; add a little oil.

4.2.3. Another *patina* recipe: pound lettuce stalks with pepper, *liquamen, caroenum*, water and oil. Cook it, thicken it with eggs, sprinkle with pepper and serve.[3]

4.2.4. Another soft *patina*: take alexanders, trim, wash, cook, refresh and wring them out. Take 4 brains, remove the sinews and cook them. Put in a mortar 6 scruples of pepper, pour on *liquamen* and pound; next add the brains and pound again; add the alexanders and pound all together. Next break 8 eggs (into the mix), add a *cyathus* of *liquamen*, a *cyathus* of wine, and a *cyathus* of *passum*. Blend thoroughly with the pounded mixture. Grease a dish, (pour in the mixture), place in the hot embers; then afterwards when it is cooked sprinkle with pepper and serve.[4]

4.2.5. Another *patina*, of asparagus (served) cold: take prepared asparagus,[5] pound in a mortar, pour on water and pound thoroughly; strain through a colander. Put prepared figpecker to one side. Pound in a mortar 6 scruples of pepper, add *liquamen,* grind again. Add a *cyathus* of wine, a *cyathus* of *passum*; pour into a pan (with) 3 oz. of oil. Let it come to heat there. Grease a dish. In it mix 6 eggs with *oenogarum*; put this with the asparagus liquor in hot embers. Then arrange the figpeckers, cook, sprinkle with pepper and serve.[6]

---

[4] Alexanders (*Smyrnium olusatrum)* resembles celery and was often used in place of celery in medieval times. It has a slightly more bitter flavour, but so did celery until recently. The young shoots and stalks are used in this recipe. The term *restringere* has the meaning of 'bind up', which could hardly be relevant in this dish where a purée is intended. Here it means 'wring out' as one would spinach.

[5] The term *purgatos* lit. 'cleaned', has the added meaning of 'peel and prepare generally', hence our use of this term here.

[6] There is some confusion here as to how many sauces are required. We believe that the *oenogarum* has already been added to the mixture and that *mittes impensam super scriptam*, 'add the sauce written above', is a gloss, probably taken from 4.2.9, where it is in the correct context and makes perfect sense. See the Glossary, *oenogarum*, for a discussion of the problems in this recipe. *FR* dealt with the confusion by altering the word-order so that the sauce is added before the dish goes in the embers. The technique here differs from that found e.g. at 4.2.9 in that here the *patina* with its contents is put into the hot embers whereas later the dish is heated up and the mixture is then added.

[4.2.6] **aliter patina de asparagis**: adicies in mortario asparagorum præcisuras quae proiciuntur; teres, suffundes uinum, colas. teres piper ligusticum coriandrum uiridem satureiam cepam uinum liquamen et oleum; sucum transferes in patellam perunctam et si uolueris oua dissolues ad ignem ut obliget. piper minutum
5 asparges.

[4.2.7] patinam ex rusticis siue tannis siue sinapi uiridi siue cucumeres siue coliculis ita facies: si uolueris substernes pulpas piscium uel pullorum.

[4.2.8] **aliter patina de sabuco calida et frigida**: accipies semen de sabuco, purgabis, ex aqua dequoques; super colum exsiccabis; patinam perunges et in
10 patinam conpones ad surcellum. adicies piperis scripulos VI, suffunde liquamen. postea adicies liquaminis ciatum I uini ciatum passi ciatum. teres. tum in patinam mittes olei uncias IIII, pones in termospodio et facies ut ferueat. cum ferbuerit franges postea oua VI, agitabis et patinam sic obligabis; cum obligaberis piper asparges et inferes.

15 [4.2.9] **patinam decoris**: accipies rosas et exfoliabis; album tolles; mittes in mortarium, suffundes liquamen, fricabis. postea mittes liquaminis ciatum I semis et sucum per colum colabis. accipies cerebella quattuor, eneruabis et teres piperis scripulos VIII; suffundes ex suco, fricabis. postea oua VIII frangis, uini ciatum unum semis et passi ciatum I, olei modicum. postea patinam perunges et eam
20 impones cinere calido, et sic inpensam supra scriptam mittes. cum cocta fuerit in termospodio piperis puluerem super asparges et inferes.

1. praecisurasque *V*   3. transferens *E*   5. asperges *E*   6. *Bra3 put* 4.2.19 *before* 4.2.7* | rusticis *VE*: ruscis *post Heraeum Bra3* | tamnis *Vo* | cucumere *π*   8. sabulo calida *E* | de sambuco *E*   9. decoques *E* | super colum *Wilson*: speculum *VE*: paulum *Sch*: per colum *André*   10. compones *V* | liquamen <fricabis> *Hum*: liquamen <teres> *André* 11. tum *Bra3*: tantum *VE*: tandem *Sch*   12. oleum *E* | intermospodio *E*: inter mos podio *V* | feruuerit *V*   13. obligaueris *V*   15. decoris *VE*: de rosis *Hum* | rosas *Tor*: rosis *VE* | tollis *E*   17. collum *E1*   18. et suco *E*   19. perunges et eam perunges et eam *V* 20. inpones *E* | cineri *ζ*   21. intermo spodio *E*: inter mospodio *V* | asperges *E*

---

[1] The trimmings of asparagus are the coarse, hard root-ends of the stems. They tend to be full of flavour but quite tough. It is strange that their flavour is extracted without cooking them. *FR* use asparagus tip instead of the ends. The *si uolueris*, 'if you want', also seems odd, as without the eggs you just have a sauce. These words may be introduced from the phrases which follow, which are interpreted as a separate recipe by other editors, but which have no rubric initial in *VE*; hence our bracketing the number here, to maintain the numbering found elsewhere.

[2] It seems odd from a modern perspective, but it appears that the raw greens are pounded to extract the juice, which is then used to flavour the *patina*.

[3] *semen de sabuco* must refer to the berry, presumably because the fruit is so small.

4.2.6. Another *patina* of asparagus: put in a mortar the trimmings of asparagus which are thrown away, pound them, pour on wine and strain them. Pound pepper, lovage, green coriander, savory, onion, wine, *liquamen* and oil. Pour the liquor into a greased dish and if you want stir eggs in over the fire so that it thickens, sprinkle with ground pepper.[1]

(4.2.7.) This is how you make a *patina* from wild herbs, black briony, mustard greens, or cucumber or spring greens. If you want, put a layer of fish or chicken beneath.[2]

4.2.8. Another hot or cold *patina* of elderberries: take elderberries,[3] wash them in some boiled water,[4] strain them through a colander and shake them dry. Grease a dish, and arrange the elderberries in the dish in a circle.[5] Put (in a mortar) 6 scruples of pepper, pour on *liquamen*; next add 1 *cyathus* of *liquamen*, a *cyathus* of wine and a *cyathus* of *passum,* pound; then pour into the dish 4 oz. of oil. Put in the hot ashes and allow it to come to heat; when it is simmering break 6 eggs into it, stir it and thus you thicken the *patina*. When you have thickened it, sprinkle with pepper and serve.

4.2.9. Deluxe *patina*:[6] take roses and remove all the petals; remove the white parts and put (the rest) in a mortar, pour on *liquamen* and pound. Next add 1½ *cyathi* of *liquamen* and strain the liquor through a colander. Take 4 brains, remove the sinews and pound (with) 8 scruples of pepper. Pour on the (rose) liquor, pound again. Next break 8 eggs, add 1½ *cyathi* of wine, 1 *cyathus* of *passum* and a little oil. Next grease a dish and put it into the hot embers and pour in the mixture written above. When it is cooked in the hot embers, sprinkle on finely ground pepper and serve.[7]

---

[4] Lit. 'wash (them), cook some water'. For *aquam decoctam* see Pliny, *HN.* 31.40.

[5] *FR* interpret the MSS reading *ad surcellum* 'with a little stick', which seems unlikely to us: we think that it is an alternative spelling of *ad circellum*, 'in a circle' (to cover the dish), so that they can be cooked in the relatively small amount of fluid.

[6] *FR*, together with André and Vollmer, follow Hummelberg in printing *de rosis* when both MSS say *decoris*. We are of the opinion that if the MSS make sense, their reading should be kept. *Decoris* can be interpreted as indicating a 'luxury' or 'fine' *patina*, which of course it was, given that roses were being used.

[7] *thermospodium* is the Greek for 'hot embers'. We do not think it is a piece of equipment, as other commentators have suggested. Recipe 4.2.9 uses both the Latin and the Greek term for 'hot embers', apparently for clarity's sake. Later recipes in this chapter (4.2.33, 36) suggest that this form of cooking could involve the ashes being above and below the *patina* dish. However in this case we think that the *patina* has the appearance of an omelette. See the Glossary, *thermospodium*, and the Introduction, p. 79, for further discussion of this recipe.

[4.2.10] **patina de cucurbitas**: cucurbitas elixas et frictas in patina conpones; cuminatum superfundes modico oleo super adiecto; feruere facias et inferes.

[4.2.11] **patina de apua**: abuam lauas, ex oleo maceras; in cummana conpones, adicies oleum liquamen uinum; alligas fasciculos rute et origani et subinde fasciculos apababdiabis; cum cocta fuerit proicies fasciculos et piper asperges et inferes.

[4.2.12] **patina de abua sine abua**: pulpas piscis assi uel elixi minutatim facies ita abundanter ut patinam qualem uoles implere possit. teres piper et modicum rute, suffundes liquamen quod satis erit et olei modicum et conmisces in patina cum pulpis sic et oua cruda confracta, ut unum corpus fiat. desuper leuiter conpones urticas marinas ut non cum ouis misceantur. inpones ad uaporem ut cum ouis ire non possint et cum siccauerint super aspargis piper tritum et inferes. ad mensam nemo agnoscet quid manducet.

[4.2.13] **patinam ex lacte**: nucleos infundes et siccas; echinos recentes iam preparatos habebis. accipies patinam et in eam conpones singula infra scriptam: mediana maluarum et betarum et porros maturos; apios holus molles et uiridia elixa; pullum carptum ex iure coctum; cerebella elixa; lucania; oua dura per medium incisa; mittes longaones porcinos ex iure Terentino farsos coctos concisos; iecinera pollorum, pulpas piscis ascelli fricti, urticas marinas, pulpas hostreorum, caseos recentes. alternis conpones nucleos et piper integrum asparges. ius tale perfundes: piper ligusticum apii semen silfi; quoques, at ubi cocta fuerit lactem colas cui cruda oua conmisces ut unum corpus fiat et super

1. de cucurbitis *Hum*   3. compones *V*   4. adligas *E* | fasciculos rute et origanum et subinde fasciculos rute et origani et subinde fasciculos *V* | origani *P, V second time*: origanum *V first time, E*   5. apababdiabis *V*: apababtidiabis *E*: apobaptizabis *Bra3*: apobaptidiabis *André*: †apa babtidiabis† *FR* | cum *LC*: dum *VE*   8 qualem *T*: quale *VE*   9. erat *E1* | cōmisces *V* | intina cum *V*   10. corpus unum *E*   11. cōpones *V* | et cum *Hum* 12. ire possint *V* | aspergis *E*   14. echinos *Bas*: eos *VE* | iam preparatos *CGSG*: inpreparatos *VE*: iam praeparatos *Bas*   15. habebis *ζ*: habetis *V*: abetis *E* | compones *V* | scripta *ζ* 16. ?holis *V* | molle *ζ*   17. carptum ex *Sch*: raptum et *VE* | lucanicas *Sch* 18. coctus *E*   19. pullorum *ζ* | aselli *Hum*   20. cōpones *V*   21. coques *E* | ad ubi *V*   22. commisces *V*

4.2.10. *Patina* **of gourd**: boil the gourd, then fry it and arrange the pieces in a dish. Pour on a cumin sauce with a little oil on top. Bring to heat and serve.

4.2.11. *Patina* **of small fry**: wash the small fry and marinade in oil, arrange in an earthenware dish. Add oil, *liquamen*, and wine; bind up bundles of rue and oregano and straightaway push the bundles under the surface. When it is cooked, discard the bundles, sprinkle with pepper and serve.

4.2.12. *Patina* **of small fry without small fry**: flake the flesh of fish, either grilled or boiled, in sufficient quantity to fill the dish you choose. Pound pepper and a little rue, pour on sufficient *liquamen* and a little oil and stir the fish together in the dish with raw eggs so that a smooth emulsion is produced. Gently place sea-anemones on top so that they do not mix in with the egg mixture. Place in a gentle rising heat so that they do not sink into the mixture. When they have dried out sprinkle with ground pepper and serve. At the table no one will know what they are eating.[1]

4.2.13. *Patina* **with milk**: soak pine nuts and then dry them. Have fresh sea-urchins prepared in advance. Take a dish and arrange some of the following in it:[2] hearts of mallow and beet and mature leek, celery, young greens[3] and boiled greens, chicken meat cooked in a sauce, boiled brains, *lucanicae,* hard-boiled eggs cut in half. Put in pork sausages stuffed with a Terentine mix,[4] cooked and sliced; chicken livers, flaked fried hake, sea-anemones, oyster flesh, fresh cheese. Arrange these in alternate layers with pine nuts and sprinkle on whole pepper. Pour on the following sauce: pepper, lovage, celery seed, *silphium*; cook it;[5] when it is cooked, strain into it milk to which you have added raw eggs so

[1] *ad uaporem* is normally translated as 'in the steam' but this cannot be its meaning here or elsewhere as the sea-urchins are expected to cook *and dry out.* Here it can only mean 'a gently rising heat'. See recipes 2.2.2; 4.2.12; 9.10.1 for other instances where *ad uaporem ignis* is used, and Introduction, pp. 93-94, for a discussion of this method of cooking .

[2] The phrase *singula infra scripta* literally means 'the items listed below,' or, bringing out the separative force, 'each item individually,' but one is surely not expected to use all the items in this list of ingredients; equally, using just one seems implausible. A happy medium would be that you would use what you want or like to use or what you have available – logically, a selection of the meats, fish and vegetables on the list. The *mittes* after the eggs suggest the rest of the items on the list may have been considered more optional.

[3] For *holus molle* recipes see 3.15.

[4] See 8.1.10 where a Terentine stuffing mix is described. It contains pepper, laurel berries, rue, asafoetida, *liquamen* and oil.

[5] There may have to be a little oil and *liquamen* added here before the spices are cooked. However, this may be a direct indication that all the spices were dry-roasted first.

illa omnia perfundes. cum cocta fuerit <conpones> echinos recentiores, piper asparges et inferes.

[4.2.14] **patinam Apicianam sic facies**: frustra suminis cocti pulpas piscium pulpas pulli ficetulas uel pectora turdorum cocta et quaecumque optima fuerint.

5 haec omnia concides diligenter preter ficetulas. oua uero cruda cum oleo dissoluis. teres piper ligusticum; suffundes liquamen uinum passum et in caccabum mittis ut calefiat et amulo obligas. antea tamen pulpas concisas uniuersas illuc mittes et sic bulliat; at ubi coctum fuerit leuabis cum iure suo et in patella alternis de trulla refundes cum piperis grana integra et nucleis pineis, ita ut per singula

10 coria substernas diploidem in laganum similiter; quotquot lagana posueris tot trullas imples, desuper adicies; unum uero laganum fistula percuties et super inpones. piper asparges. ante tamen illas pulpas ouis confractis obligabis et sic in caccabum mittes cum inpensam. patellam aeneam qualem debes habere infra ostenditur.

15 [4.2.15] **patina cotidiana**: accipies frustra suminis coctum pulpas piscium coctas pulpas pulli coctas; haec omnia concides diligenter. accipias patellam aeneam, oua confringes in caccabum et dissolues. adicies in mortarium piper ligusticum, fricabis; suffundes liquamen uinum passum oleum modice; reexinanies in caccabum, facies ut ferueat; cum ferbuerit et obligas, pulpas quas subcultrasti

20 in ius mittis. substerne diploides patinam aeneam et trullam plenam pulpae et disparges oleum; laganum pones similiter; quotquot lagana posueris tot trullas

1. <conpones> *CGSG*: <addes> *Vo* | echinos *Tor*: echino *V*: enchono *E1*: enchino *E2*
2. asperges *E*   3. PATINAM patinam *V* | <accipies> frusta *Vo*
4. quæcum que *E*   5. hæc *E* | dissoluendis *E1*   6. et *om. E1*   8. ad ubi *V*
8-9. detrullare fundes *E*   10. diploidem dein *Sch* | quotquot *RC*: quoquo *V1*: quodquo *E, V2*
11. imples *VE*: impensae *Hum*   12. impones *V*   13. inpensam *E*: impensam *V1*: in pensam *V2*: impensa *Milham* | patelam æneum *E*   15. frusta *GiVo* | coctum *V*: coctam *E*: cocta *DG*: cocti *Sch*   16. hæc *E* | concides *Hum*: condies *VE* | accipies *E*
17. mortario *E*   19. feruuerit *V* | et *om. R*   20. substernere *V* | diploides *LT*: diplodies *VE*: *lacuna after* diploides *GiVo* | æneam *E* | pulpe *E*   21. quodquo *V*

that a smooth emulsion is produced, and pour this over everything. When it is cooked, arrange fresh sea-urchins, sprinkle with pepper and serve.

4.2.14. You make an Apician *patina* like this:[1] pieces of cooked udder, flaked fish, chicken meat, figpeckers or cooked breast of thrush and whatever finest quality things there may be. Dice all these carefully apart from the figpeckers. Beat up raw eggs in oil. Pound pepper, lovage, pour on *liquamen*, wine, *passum*; put into a pan so that it warms through and thicken it with starch. Before this, however, put all the chopped meat in and bring it to the boil. When this is cooked, take it out with its sauce and ladle it into a dish in alternate layers with whole peppercorns and pine nuts in such a way that, with each layer, you spread out a double layer like a *laganum*. Fill as many ladles as *lagana* you put in, and put (the mixture) on top. Then pierce one *laganum* with a reed and put it on top. Sprinkle with pepper. Beforehand, you should have thickened the meat mixture with the broken eggs and put it in the pan with the seasonings. The kind of bronze dish you ought to have is shown below.

4.2.15. Everyday *patina*: take pieces of cooked udder, cooked and flaked fish and cooked chicken meat; cut all this up carefully. Take a bronze dish; break eggs into a pan and whisk them. Put into a mortar pepper and lovage, grind them; pour on *liquamen*, wine, *passum* and a little oil. Tip it into the pan (with the eggs), bring it to heat; when it has simmered and thickened, put the meat you have cut up into the sauce. Spread out a double layer and a full ladle of meat mixture in the bronze dish[2] and sprinkle it with oil. Then lay down another *laganum*, adding one ladleful of mixture for each *laganum*. Pierce one *laganum* with a reed from

---

[1] This recipe has often been described as the forerunner of modern lasagne; see the Glossary, *lagana*. However, a closer inspection reveals that the 'Everyday *patina*' is turned out and free-standing and is unlikely to be cooked again. We also believe it was designed to be served in layers as opposed to wedges. The central problem revolves around the meaning of the *diplois* in relation to the *lagana*. It means a 'double-layered cloak' or 'robe' in its original Greek sense: cf. Isidore, *Orig.* 19.24.11. It is our belief that, in this instance, *lagana* are a kind of pre-cooked flat bread. The cook who dictated this recipe – it strikes us as having the characteristics of oral instruction – had great trouble expressing himself logically. He twice forgot to put instructions in the correct order and had to add them later. He struggles to express in Latin the physical actions that are necessary to make the dish. He says that each layer should, in effect, be a 'double layer' and that on top of each layer only one ladleful of mix is used. We can visualize two scenarios: (a) each *laganum* is folded in half and a ladleful of mixture is placed in the centre, like a soft taco; (b) each layer is made up of two separate *lagana*, with mixture between the two. In both scenarios, each layer represents a portion that is lifted off the pile with the reed.

[2] This *patina* is presumably the same dish as the *patella* mentioned at the outset.

inpense adicies. unum laganum fistula percuties a superficie; uersas in discum, insuper superficiem pones, piper asperges et inferes.

[4.2.16] **patina uersatilis uice dulci**: nucleos pineos nuces fractas et purgatas attorrebis. eas teres cum melle pipere liquamine lacte ouis modico mero et oleo.

[4.2.17] **patellam thirotarricam ex quocumque salso uolueris**: quoques ex oleo, exossabis, et cerebella cocta pulpas piscium iocuscula pullorum oua dura caseum mollem excaldatum. haec omnia calefacies in patella; teres piper ligusticum origanum rutæ bacam uinum mulsum oleum; patella ad lentum ignem ut quoquatur. ouis crudis obligabis, adordinabis, cuminum minutum asparges et inferes.

[4.2.18] **patellam esiciatam**: esicia de tursione: eneruabis, concides minutatim. teres piper ligusticum origanum petrosilenum coriandrum cuminum rutæ bacam mentam siccam ipsum turtionem; isicia deformabis uinum liquamen oleum; quoques. coctum in patellam collocabis. ius in ea facies: piper ligusticum satureiam cepam uinum liquamen oleum. patellam pones ut quoquatur, ouis obligabis, piper asparges et inferes.

[4.2.19] **patellam ex olisatro**: elixas ex aqua nitrata, exprimis in patella; teres piper ligusticum coriandrum satureiam cepam uinum liquamen acetum oleum; transferes in patellam, quoques, amulo obligas; thimum et piper minutum asparges; et de quacumque erba si uolueris facies ut supra.

[4.2.20] **patina de apua fricta**: apua lauas oua confringes et cum apua commisces. adicies liquamen uinum oleum; facies ut ferueat, et cum ferbuerit,

1. lagana *D*: lagas   1-2. a superficie; uersas in discum, insuper superficiem pones *CGSG*: a superficie uersas in discum insuper insuperficiem pones *V*: a superficie uersas in discum in superficiem pones *E*: in superficiem pones, a superficie uersas in discum *André*: a superficie insuper[ficiem] pones *Bra3 with* uersas in discum *placed at the end of the recipe following*   3. dulce *E*   4. attorrebis *D*: atorrebas *VE*   5. oleo <uersas in discum> *GiVo from the previous recipe*   6. coques *E*   7. pulpas *V1*: pulpis *V2,E*   8. hæc *E* | patella *VE*: patellam *Milham*   9. rute *V* | ignem <pones> *GiVo*   10. coquatur *E* | craudis *V1* | cuminum c minutum *V1*   12. esiciatam *CGSG*: siccam *VE*: isiciatam *Milham*: esitiatam *Gi* esicia *VE*: isiciam *Sch*: siculam *Vo* | tursione *André*: tursone *VE*: thursione *π*   13. petrosilinum *E* | rute *V*   14. deformabis *VE*: de <eo> formabis *Bra3*: <in>de formabis *Vo*   15. coques *E* | conlocabis *E*   16. <adicies> uinum *Gi* | <in> patellam *Hum* | coquatur *E*   18. in patellam *E*   20. coques *E*   22. apuam lauas *Hum* | cum apua *LT*: cum apia *VE* | feruuerit *V*

the top; turn out on to a round dish, and put this top layer in place. Sprinkle with pepper and serve.[1]

4.2.16. **A sweet omelette-style *patina***: roast pine nuts and skinned broken nuts. Pound them with honey, pepper, *liquamen*, milk and eggs, a little pure wine and oil.[2]

4.2.17. **Salt fish and cheese *patella* using any salt fish you like:**[3] cook (the salt fish) in oil and remove the bones. (Take) cooked brains, the flesh of the fish, (cooked) chicken-livers, hard-boiled eggs, soft cheese washed in warm water. Heat up all these things in a dish. Pound pepper, lovage, oregano, rue berries, wine, *mulsum* and oil. The dish is placed on a gentle heat so that it cooks. Thicken with raw eggs, arrange (on a serving dish),[4] sprinkle with finely ground cumin and serve.

4.2.18. **Forcemeat *patella***: porpoise forcemeat: remove the sinews and chop finely. Pound pepper, lovage, oregano, parsley, coriander, cumin, rue berries, dried mint, the porpoise-meat itself. Form the forcemeat with wine, *liquamen* and oil. Cook it. Put the cooked forcemeat in a dish and make the following sauce for it: pepper, lovage, savory, onion, wine, *liquamen*, oil. Set the *patella* to cook, thicken with eggs, sprinkle with pepper and serve.

4.2.19. ***Patella* of alexanders**: boil in water with soda. Squeeze them dry and arrange in a dish. Pound pepper, lovage, coriander, savory, onion, wine, *liquamen*, vinegar and oil. Put this into the dish. Cook it and thicken with starch. Sprinkle with thyme and ground pepper. You may also use the above recipe for any pot-herb if you wish.

4.2.20. ***Patina* of fried small fry**: wash the small fry, break eggs and mix them with the fish. Take[5] *liquamen*, wine and oil and bring it to heat and, when it is

---

[1] One would have hoped for an illumination in the second recipe, but sadly there is none. The final stage of the recipe is also ambiguous. The reed and the final top *laganum* are clearly a form of finishing off.

[2] *versatilis*, lit. 'that turns around', and by inference, 'turns out'. A metal *patina* would have been used. See *The Classical Cookbook*, p. 139, and *Cooking Apicius*, recipe 59, for SG's modern recipe of this dish. It seems to be an omelette in all but name and can be made quite easily in a frying-pan.

[3] *tyrotaricham*: a Greek term for a cheese and salt fish dish which was familiar to Cicero, who identifies it as plain, ordinary food. cf. Cicero, *Ad. fam.* 9.16.7, 9; *Ad Att.* 4.8.1.

[4] *adordinabis*: these savoury scrambled egg dishes look unappetizing, but taste better than they look. Note the lack of *liquamen* in a salt fish dish.

[5] Lit. 'add', but not to the fish, which are put in later.

mittes apuam. cum duxerit subtiliter uersas. facies ut coloret, oenogarum simplex perfundes, piper asparges et inferes.

[4.2.21] **patina ex lagitis et cerebellis**: friges oua dura; cerebella elixas et eneruas, cizeria pullorum quoques; haec omnia diuides preter piscem; conpones in patina præmixta; salsum coctum in medio pones. teres piper ligusticum, suffundes <liquamen et passum> ut dulcis sit. piperatum mittes in patinam, facies ut ferueat; cum ferbuerit, ramo rutae agitabis et amulo obligabis.

[4.2.22] **patina mullorum loco salsi**: mullos rades, in patina munda conpones; adicies <olei quod satis est et salsum interpones. facies> ut ferueat; cum ferbuerit mulsum mittes aut passum; piper asparges et inferes.

[4.2.23] **patina piscium loco salsi**: pisces qualeslibet curatos friges, in patinam conpones; adicies olei quod satis est et salsum interpones; facies ut ferueat; cum ferbuerit mittes mulsam et ius agitabis.

[4.2.24] **patina piscium**: pisces qualeslibet rades et curatos mittes; cepas siccas ascalonas uel alterius generis concides in patinam et pisces super conpones. adicies liquamen oleum, <facies ut ferueat;> cum coctum fuerit salsum coctum in medio pones; addendum acetum. <piper> asparges et coronam bubulam.

[4.2.25] **patellam Lucretianam**: cepas pallachanas purgas; uiridia earum proicies; in patinam concides; liquaminis modicum oleum et aquam. dum quoquitur salsum crudum in medium ponis; at ubi cum salso prope cocta fuerit melle cocleare asparges, aceti et defreti pusillum; gustas; si fatuum fuerit,

---

3. lagatis *V1*   4. cizeria *E*: cizema *V*: gigeria *Hum*: gizeria *Milham* | coquis *E*: coques *Hum* | hæc *E* | compones *V*   6. <liquamen et passum> *CGSG*: <passum> *Hum* | dulcis *VE*: dulce *GiVo*   7. feruuerit *V* | rutæ *E*   8. mullos *E,V2*: mullo *V1* | compones *V*   9. <olei …facies> *Sch from recipe following* | feruuerit *V*   11. patina *V*: patinam *E* | locos alsi *V*   12. compones *V*   13. feruuerit *V* | ius agitabis *L2*: insagitabis *VE, L1*   14. curatos *Hum*: duratos *VE*   15. ascalonias *D* | compones *V*   16. <facies ut ferueat> *CGSG*   17. <piper> *CGSG* | bubulem *E1*   18. palachanas *E*   19. ex aquam *E1*   20. coquitur *E*   21. cocleare *V2,E*: clocleare *V1* | defreti *E*: defrethi *V* | pussillum *E* | fuerit *Hum*: efuerit *VE*

---

[1] *lagita* fish: otherwise unknown. *FR* cite Guégan who equates it with *lacerta*, or horse-mackerel; the Greek *lagion* means 'leveret', and is a diminutive of *lagōs*, which is used of this animal and also of the sea-hare (so *Liddell and Scott*, and the *Thesaurus Linguae Graecae*, ad loc.), which was known for its highly poisonous qualities: cf. Aelian 2.45, Pliny, *HN*. 9.155, 32.8. D'Arcy Wentworth Thompson, *A Glossary of Greek Fishes* (Oxford, 1947), ad loc., refers to Horace *Sat.* 2.2.22, but comments that the fish is 'quite unknown'.

simmering, put in the small fry mixture. When it holds together, carefully turn it over. Ensure it has colour. Pour on plain *oenogarum*, sprinkle with pepper and serve.

4.2.21. *Patina* of *lagita*[1] fish and brains: fry eggs until firm, boil brains and remove the sinews, cook chicken giblets. Cut up all these things apart from the fish. Arrange this mixture in a dish. Place the cooked, salted fish in the middle. Pound pepper, lovage; pour on *liquamen* and *passum* so that it is sweet. Pour this pepper sauce over the dish, bring to heat; when it is simmering, stir it with a sprig of rue and thicken it with starch.

4.2.22. *Patina* of mullet making use of salt fish:[2] scale mullets and place them in a clean dish, add sufficient oil and intersperse salted fish. Bring to heat; when it is simmering, put in *mulsum* or *passum*, sprinkle with pepper and serve.

4.2.23. *Patina* of fish making use of salt fish: prepare any fish you like, fry it and place in a dish, add sufficient oil and intersperse salted fish. Bring to heat; when it is simmering, add *mulsum* and stir the sauce.

4.2.24. *Patina* of fish: scale any fish you like, clean and put to one side. Chop dried Ascalonian onions, or another type of onion, into a dish and put the fish on top. Add *liquamen* and oil, bring it to heat; when it is cooked, place cooked salt fish in the middle; vinegar should be added; sprinkle with pepper and a circle of savory.[3]

4.2.25. *Patella* in the style of Lucretius: peel *pallachana* onions[4] and throw the green parts away; chop them into a dish with a little *liquamen*, oil and water. While it is cooking put raw salt fish in the middle. When all this, with the salt fish, is nearly cooked, dribble on a spoon of honey and a tiny amount of vinegar

---

[2] The obvious and literal sense of *loco salsi* is 'instead of' or 'taking the place of', but both fresh fish and salt fish are included in this recipe and the following one. Clearly the salt fish is used to bulk up the fresh fish and make it appear that guests are getting more fresh fish, which was much more expensive. The use of the term is highly idiosyncratic, to say the least, but cf. *LS* II.C. The required sense is 'making a place for salt fish', hence our rendering it 'making use of salt fish'.

[3] *coronam bubulam*: see Pliny, *HN.* 19.165, where he tells us that *cunila bubula* is known as *satureia* or savory. It is difficult to visualize the 'crown'; presumably the dried savory is sprinkled in a circle around the dish as one would use chopped parsley today as a garnish or alternatively the sprigs are tied in a circle.

[4] *cepae pallachanae*: as these 'onions' are peeled, the earlier identification of them with 'chive' is unfortunately impossible. See the Glossary, *cepa*.

liquamen adicies; si salsum, mellis modicum, et coronam bubulam aspergis et bulliat.[150]

[4.2.26] **patinam de lagitis**: lagitas rades lauas; oua confringis et cum lagitis conmiscis; adicies liquamen uinum oleum; facies ut ferueat. cum ferbuerit
5   oenogarum simplex perfundis; piper asperges et inferes.[151]

[4.2.27] **patina zomoteganona**: crudos quoslibet pisces in patina conpones: adicies oleum liquamen uinum coctum fasciculum porri coriandri; dum quoquitur teres piper ligusticum origanum fasciculum de suo sibi fricabis; suffundes ius de suo sibi; oua cruda dissolues, temperas, exinanies in patinam; facies ut obligetur.
10   cum tenuerit piper asparges et inferes.[152]

[4.2.28] **patina solearum**: soleas battues et curatas conpones in patina; adicies oleum liquamen uinum; dum quoquitur teres piper ligusticum origanum; fricabis; suffundes ius, oua cruda, ut unum corpus facias; super soleas refundes, lento igni quoques. cum duxerit piper aspargis et inferes.[153]

15   [4.2.29] **patina de piscibus**: piperis unciam garoeni eminam conditi eminam olei uncias II.[154]

[4.2.30] **patina de pisciculis**: uuam passam piper ligusticum origanum cepam uinum liquamen oleum; transferes in patellam; cum cocta fuerit adicies in ipsam pisciculos coctos; amulo obligas et inferes.[155]

20   [4.2.31] **patina de piscibus denticem auratam et mugillem**: accipies pisces curatos, subassabis; postea eos in pulpas carpes; deinde hostrea curabis. adicies in mortarium piperis scripulos VI, suffundes liquamen, fricabis; postea adicies liquaminis ciatum unum, uini ciatum unum, mittes in caccabum et olei uncias III et hostrea. oenogarum facies feruere; cum ferbuerit patinam perungis et pulpam

---

1. asparges *E* | et *Sch*: ut *VE*   4. commiscis *V* | ferbuerit *E2*: feruburit *E1*: feruuerit *V*
5. oenagarum *V*   6. zomoteganona *V*: zomoteganone *E*: zomoteganon *GiVo* | compones *V*
7. coctum *del. Bra3* | coquitur *E*   8. ligusticum *Milham*: libustici *E2,V*: libestici *E1*:
ligustici *GiVo* | origanum *CGSG*: origani *E*: horigani *V* | de suo sibi *del. Bra3* | frigabis *V*
9. obliget *V1*   10. asparges *GiVo*: aspargas *V*: aspergis *E*   11. compones *V*
12. coquitur *E*   13. ut *VE*: et *Hum, edd.* | facias *CGSG*: facies *VE*   14. coques *E*
15. garoeni *VE*: caroeni *ζ*   17. uuas *V*   20. denticem auratam et mugillem
VE: dentice aurata et mugile *Hum*   21. carpes *Hum*: carpeas *VE*   23. et *ζ*: ea *VE*
24. ostrea *ζ* | feruuerit *V* | et pulpam *CGSG*: et in pulpam *VE*

and *defrutum*; taste; if it is bland, add *liquamen*; if it is salty, add a little honey,[1] and sprinkle with a circle of savory, and bring it to the boil (first).

4.2.26. ***Patina* of *lagita* fish**: scale and wash the *lagita* fish. Break eggs and mix them with the *lagita* fish. Add *liquamen*, wine and oil; bring it to heat; when it is simmering, pour on plain *oenogarum,* sprinkle with pepper and serve.

4.2.27. ***Patina zomoteganon*:**[2] arrange any raw fish you like in a dish, add oil, *liquamen* and boiled wine[3] and a bundle of coriander and leek. While it is cooking, pound pepper, lovage, oregano and the bundle itself; pound again, and pour on the cooking liquor; stir raw eggs in and balance the flavours. Tip it all out into the dish, allow it to thicken. When it is firm, sprinkle with pepper and serve.

4.2.28. ***Patina* of sole**: beat the sole, clean and arrange in a dish, add oil, *liquamen* and wine. While it is cooking, pound pepper, lovage, oregano; pound again, pour on the cooking liquor and raw eggs so that you make a smooth emulsion. Pour back over the sole and cook on a gentle fire. When it has set, sprinkle with pepper and serve.

4.2.29. ***Patina* of fish**: 1 oz. pepper, ½ pt. *garoenum,* ½ pt. spiced wine, 2 oz. oil.[4]

4.2.30. ***Patina* of small fry**: (pound) raisins, pepper, lovage, oregano, onion, wine, *liquamen,* oil; transfer to a dish; when it is cooked, add the cooked small fry to it; thicken with starch and serve.

4.2.31. ***Patina* of dentex, gilthead bream, and grey mullet**: take the fish, prepare them and grill them a little, then flake the meat (from the bone); next prepare oysters. Put in a mortar 6 scruples of pepper, moisten with *liquamen* and grind; after this add 1 *cyathus* of *liquamen*, 1 *cyathus* of wine, put into a pan with 3 oz. oil and the oysters. Bring (this) *oenogarum* to heat; when it is simmering,

---

[1] A clear and concise description of how *liquamen* functions in Roman food. It is a flavour-enhancer, doing far more than salt to enhance the natural flavours of the dish, but when used with salt fish its dominant flavour of salt needs taming with honey.

[2] *zomoteganon* from Greek *zomos*, 'broth', and *teganon*, 'frying-pan'. Lit. 'fish cooked in sauce in a pan'; see also *Excerpta Vinidarii* 11 and 13 and their notes.

[3] Probably a form of *caroenum*; see the Glossary.

[4] This is clearly not a *patina* and appears to be an *oenogarum* sauce that might flavour one, though the absence of *liquamen* or *garum* is odd. The MSS reading of *garoeni* is therefore particularly of interest. We have retained the spelling and suggest that it represents a mixture of wine such as *caroenum* with a fish sauce.

supra scriptam mittes et [in] condituram de ostreis; facies ut ferueat; cum ferbuerit franges oua X, infundes super ostrea. cum strinxerint, piper asparges et inferes.

[4.2.32] **patina de pisce lupo**: teres piper cuminum petrosilenum rutam cepam mel liquamen passum olei guttas.

5 [4.2.33] **patina de sorbis calida et frigida**: accipies sorbas, purgas; in mortario fricabis, per colum colabis. cerebella eneruabis quattuor cocta; mittes in mortario piperis scripulos VIII, suffundes liquamen, fricabis; adicies sorba, in se contemperabis; frangis oua VIII, adicies ciatum liquaminis, uinum. patinam mundam perunges et in termospodio pones, et sic eam inpensam mittes, ut 10 subtus supra termospodium habeat. cum cocta fuerit piper minutum aspargis et inferes.

[4.2.34] **patina de persicis**: persica duriora purgabis, frustratim concides; elixas in patina conpones, olei modicum superstillabis et cum cuminato inferes.

[4.2.35] **patina de piris**: pira elixa et purgata e medio; teres cum pipere cumino 15 melle passo liquamine oleo modico. ouis missis patinam facies; piper super aspargis et inferes.

[4.2.36] **patina urticarum calida et frigida**: urticam accipies, lauas, colas per colum, exsiccabis in tabula; eam concides. teres piperis scripulos X, suffundes liquamen, fricabis. postea adicies liquaminis ciatos duos, olei uncias VI. caccabus 20 ferueat; cum ferbuerit coctam tolles ut refrigescat; postea patinam mundam perungues, franges oua octo et agitabis. perfundes, subtus supra cinerem calidam habeat. coctam piper minutum asparges et inferes.

[4.3.37] **patina de cidoneis**: mala cydonia cum porris melle liquamine oleo defricto quoques et inferes; uel elixata ex melle.

---

1. in *del. Bra3* | feruuerit *V*   2. X *CGSG*: XL *V*: quadraginta *E*: XI *Sch* | asperges *E*
3. petrosilinum *E*   8. franges *GiVo* | uinum *VE*: unum *ζ*   9. in termospodio *E*: inter
mospodio *V* | ut *CGSG*: ac *VE*   10. asparges *GiVo*   12. persicis *E*: piscis *V* | persica
ζ: persicca *VE*   13. compones *V*   15. super *om. E1*   18. culum *V* | condies *E*
20. feruuerit *V* | coctam *Milham*: coctum *VE*   21. VIII *V* | agitas *E*   22. coctum *V1*:
<cum> cocta <fuerit> *GiVo*   24. defricto *André*: defricato *VE*: defrito *Bra3* | coques *E*

---

[1] The sorb apple is in fact a form of berry or drupe related to the rowan. In the UK they are invariably sour and remain hard but in southern Italy they ripen sufficiently to be eaten raw. See Davidson, *Oxford Companion to Food*, s.v. 'Rowan'. As we have seen in the asparagus recipes at 3.2.5 and 6, cooking is considered unnecessary to extract the flavour and juices of many vegetables and fruits. We must therefore assume that the sorb apples here are relatively ripe.

grease a dish and put in the fish flesh written above and the oysters in their spiced sauce. Bring it to heat; when it is simmering, break 10 eggs and pour them over the oysters. When they have set, sprinkle with pepper and serve.

4.2.32. *Patina* **of pike**: pound pepper, cumin, parsley, rue, onion, honey, *liquamen, passum* and some drops of oil.

4.2.33. *Patina* **of sorb apples served hot or cold**: take the apples, prepare them and pound them in a mortar and pass them through a sieve.[1] Take the sinews out of 4 cooked brains. Put in a mortar 8 scruples of pepper, moisten with *liquamen* and pound, add the sorb apple purée (and the brains), blend thoroughly. Break in 8 eggs, add a *cyathus* of *liquamen* and some wine.[2] Grease a clean dish and put it in the hot ashes, pour the mixture in, allow the hot ashes to be above and below (the dish).[3] When it is cooked, sprinkle with finely ground pepper and serve.

4.2.34. *Patina* **of peach**: clean fairly firm peaches and cut into pieces, boil them and arrange in a dish, dribble a little oil over the top and serve with a cumin sauce.

4.2.35. *Patina* **of pears**: core and boil the pears, pound them with pepper, cumin, honey, *passum, liquamen*, and a little oil. Add eggs to make a *patina*, sprinkle with pepper and serve.

4.2.36. Nettle *patina* **served hot or cold**: take nettles, wash them, drain through a colander and dry them on a board; chop them up. Pound 10 scruples of pepper, moisten with *liquamen*, pound again. Next add 2 *cyathi* of *liquamen*, 6 oz. of oil, put in a pan and bring it to heat. When it is simmering, take out the cooked nettles and let them cool. Then grease a clean dish and break 8 eggs and beat them. Pour them (over the cooked nettles in the dish).[4] Let it have hot ashes above and below. Sprinkle finely ground pepper over the cooked dish and serve.

4.2.37. *Patina* **of quince**: cook quinces with leeks, honey, *liquamen*, oil, *defrutum*, and serve, or boil them in some honey.

[2] *FR* preferred *unum* here and thought it referred to the number of *cyathi* of *liquamen*. We prefer the MSS reading of 'wine', which is necessary to dilute the brains and egg mixture and to balance the *liquamen*.

[3] The instruction here is for ashes to be below and above the dish. See Introduction, p.78, for an illustration of the equipment that might be used.

[4] According to other similar recipes the cooking liquor is used in the final dish; here, however, the quantity of *liquamen* in the cooking liquor is sufficient to flavour the whole dish.

III. MINVTAL DE PISCIBVS VEL ISICIIS.

[4.3.1] **minutal marinum**: pisces in caccabum <mittes,> adicies liquamen oleum uinum cocturam. porros capitatos coriandrum minutatim concides, esiciola de pisce minuta facies et pulpas pisces cocti concarpis, urticas marinas bene lotas
5   mittes. haec omnia cum cocta fuerint, teres piper ligusticum origanum; fricabis; liquamen suffundes, ius de suo sibi, exinanies in caccabum. cum ferbuerit tractam confringes, obligas, cum ferbuerit, agitas; piper aspargis et inferes.

[4.3.2] **minutal Terentinum**: concides in caccabum albamen de porris minutatim; adicies oleum liquamen cocturam, esiciola ualde minuta, et sic temperas ut
10   tenerum sit; esicium Terentinum facies: inter esiciam confectionem inuenies. ius tale facies: piper ligusticum origanum fricabis, suffundes liquamen, ius de suo sibi, uino et passo temperabis; mittes <in> caccabum; cum ferbuerit, tractam confringes, obligas, piper aspergis et inferes.

[4.3.3] **minutal Apicianum**: oleum liquamen uinum porrum capitatum mentam
15   pisciculos esiciola minuta testiculos caponum glandulas porcellinas. hæc omnia in se quoquantur. teres piper ligusticum coriandrum uiridem uel semen; suffundis liquamen, adicies mellis modicum et ius de suo sibi, uino et melle temperabis; facies ut ferueat; cum ferbuerit tractam confringes, obligas, coagitas; piper aspargis et inferes.

20   [4.3.4] **minutal Matianum**: adicies in caccabum oleum liquamen cocturam; concides porrum coriandrum, esicia minuta; spatulam porcinam coctam tessellatim concides cum sua sibi tergilla. facies ut simul quoquantur; media coctura mala Maziana purgata intrinsecus concisa tessellatim mittes; dum coquitur

---

2. <mittes> *add. Hum*   4. pulpas pisces *V2,E*: pulpasces *V1* | concarpis *Bra3*: concapis *VE*
5. hæc *E*   6. feruuerit *V*   7. feruuerit *V*: cum ferbuerit *om. D, del. Hum* |
coagitas *GiVo* | piper] per *V1* | asparges *GiVo*   9. ualde minuta *Sch*: uel deminuta *VE*
12. <in> *CGSG* | feruuerit *V* | tractam *Hum*: tracta *VE*   13. piper *ζ*: piperis *VE* | asparges *GiVo*
15. caponum *D*: capronum *VE*   16. quoquantur *CGSG*: quoquatur *VE*: coquantur *ζ*
18. facias *V* | feruuerit *V*   19. asparges *GiVo*   21. ?cocttam *E1*
22. coquantur *E*   23. matiana *ζ*

---

[1] *cocturam*: this noun is rendered 'cooking', 'melting' or 'style of cooking' in *LS*. It may have derived from a future participle assuming *aquam*, meaning literally 'water which will cook something'. Cf. E. Espinilla Buisán, 'Les mots en *-tio*, *-tura*, *-tus* dans la prose technique de S. I. Frontin: De Aquaeductu Vrbis Romae', in *Latin Vulgaire, Latin Tardif* IV, ed. L. Callebat (Hildesheim, Zurich, New York, 1998), 643-54, at pp. 648-9. Here and below it seems to refer to

4.3. *MINUTAL* OF FISH AND MEAT.

4.3.1. **Sea food *minutal***: put the fish in a pan, add *liquamen*, oil, wine, stock;[1] chop leek[2] and coriander finely, make finely ground fish forcemeat and flake the flesh of the cooked fish, and put in well-washed sea-urchins. When all these are cooked, pound pepper, lovage, oregano, pound again, pour on *liquamen* and some of the cooking liquor and put it back into the pan. When it has come to the boil, crumble a *tracta* in,[3] thicken it, and stir it when it comes to the boil (again); sprinkle with pepper and serve.

4.3.2. **Terentine *minutal***: finely chop into a pan the white part of leek, add oil, *liquamen* and stock and very finely ground forcemeat; you blend the forcemeat so that it is delicate: you make Terentine forcemeat: you will find the recipe under 'forcemeat'.[4] Make the sauce like this: pound pepper, lovage, oregano, pour on *liquamen*, some of the cooking liquor, flavour with wine and *passum*; pour into the pan; when it is simmering, crumble a *tracta* in and thicken, sprinkle with pepper and serve.

4.3.3. **Apician *minutal***: oil, *liquamen*, wine, leek, mint, small fry, finely ground forcemeat, capon testicles, suckling pig sweetbreads; cook all these things together. Pound pepper, lovage, green coriander or seed; pour on *liquamen*, add a little honey and some of the cooking liquor, flavour with wine and honey. Bring it to heat; when it is simmering, crumble a *tracta* in, thicken it, stir it, sprinkle with pepper and serve.

4.3.4. **Matian *minutal*:**[5] put in a pan oil, *liquamen*, stock; chop in leek and coriander, ground forcemeat, diced cooked shoulder of pork with its crackling. Allow all this to cook together. In the middle of the cooking put in cored and

---

water which has already been used for this purpose, hence 'stock'. The *VE* reading preserved at 4.3.7a below, *coctura porrorum*, would mean 'water used for cooking leeks', but given the frequent occurrence of leeks as an ingredient in all the recipes in this section save 4.3.6 and 8, we have adopted the emendations *cocturam* and *porrum*.

[2] *porrum capitatum*: see the Glossary for a definition. For the purposes of reconstruction it is indistinguishable from modern leek.

[3] A thin sheet of pastry. See the Glossary for a more complete definition of *tracta*.

[4] No such recipe exists in Chapter 2. Other commentators have seen two separate kinds of *isicia* in this recipe. We believe only one was intended.

[5] Matian apples: Columella 5.10.9. These apples are said to have been developed by either Gaius Matius, or his son; the former was friend to Cicero and Caesar, while the latter was friend to Augustus. The latter was also responsible for a cookery book: see Columella 11.4.2 and Introduction, p. 53.

teres piper cuminum coriandrum uiridem uel semen mentam laseris radicem; suffundis acetum mel liquamen defritum modice et ius de suo sibi; aceto modico temperabis, facies ut ferueat; cum ferbuerit, tractam confringes et ex ea obligas; piper asparges et inferes.

5   [4.3.5] **minutal dulce ex cytriis**: adicies in caccabo oleum liquamen cocturam porrum capitatum concides coriandrum minutatim; spatulam porcinam coctam et esiciola minuta; dum coquitur, teres piper cuminum coriandrum <uiridem> uel semen, rutam uiridem, laseris radicem; suffundis acetum <mel liquamen> defritum ius de suo sibi; aceto temperabis. facies ut ferueat; cum ferbuerit citrium
10   purgatum intro foras tessellatim concisum et elixatum in caccabum mittes. tractam confringes et ex ea obligas; piper aspargis et inferes.

    [4.3.6] **minutal ex praecoquiis**: adicies in caccabo oleum liquamen uinum; concides cepam ascaloniam aridam; spatulam porcinam coctam tessellatim concides. his omnibus coctis teres piper cuminum mentam siccam anetum; suffundis
15   mel liquamen passum acetum modice ius de suo sibi; temperabis; praecoqua enucleata mittis, facies ut ferueant donec percoquantur. tractam confringes, ex ea obligas, piper aspargis et inferes.

    [4.3.7a] **minutal ex iecineribus et pulmonibus leporis**: inuenies inter lepores quemadmodum facies.
20   [4.3.7b] **<aliter minutal dulce>**: adicies <in> caccabum liquamen uinum oleum cocturam, porrum et coriandrum concisum. esicia minuta, spatulam porcinam coctam tessellatim concisam et in eundem caccabum inmittes. dum coquitur teres piper ligusticum origanum; ius de suo sibi uino et passo temperabis. facies ut ferueat; cum ferbuerit tractam confringes et ex ea obligas; piper aspargis et inferes.
25   [4.3.8] **minutal ex rosis**: eodem iure supra scripto sed passum plus adicies.

2. suffundis *VE*: suffundes *GiVo*   3. feruuerit *V*   4. aspargis *E*   5. citriis *E* | cocturam *SC*: cocturum *VE*   7. et esiciola *CGSG*: et siciola *VE*: et isiciola *GiVo*: esiciola *André*: isiciola *Milham* |cuminum *P*: cumino *VE* | <uiridem> *Tor*   8. *3 letters erased after* uel *V* | rutam *ξ*: ruta *VE* | coriandrum uiridem uel semen rutam laseris *Milham* | radicem radicem *E1* | <mel liquamen> *CGSG*   9. feruuerit *V*   10. purgutum *E*   11. tractum *E2*: tractatum *E1* | ex a *E1* | asparges *GiVo* | inferæs *E*   12. praecoquiis *Sch*: praecoques *VE*: praecoquis *Hum* | caccabum *GiVo*   12-13. concedes *E1*   13. ascoliniam *V* | tessellatim his *V1*   14. hominibus *E* | cumiinum *E1* | ?sictam *E1*   15. praecoqua *Hum*: pręcoqui *VE*   16. tractam *Tor*: fracta *VE* | confringis *E*   18-20. inuenies…dulce *del. André*   20. <aliter minutal dulce> *Bra3* | adies *E* | <in> *GiVo*   21. cocturam *Hum*: coctura *VE* | porrum *Sch*: porrorum *VE*   22. inmettes *E1*   23. ligustium *E* 24. feruuerit *V* | tractam *D*: fractam *V,E2*: frattam *E1*   25. adicias *E*

diced Matian apples. While it is cooking pound pepper, cumin, green coriander or seed, mint, *laser* root; pour on vinegar, honey, *liquamen*, a little *defrutum,* and some of the cooking liquor; flavour with a little vinegar, bring it to heat; when it is simmering, crumble a *tracta* and thicken with some of it, sprinkle with pepper and serve.

4.3.5. **A sweet *minutal* of gourd**: put in a pan oil, *liquamen*, stock, chopped leek, finely chopped coriander, cooked pork shoulder and finely ground forcemeat. While it is cooking, pound pepper, cumin, green coriander or seed, fresh rue, *laser* root; pour on vinegar, honey, *liquamen*, *defrutum*, some of the cooking liquor and flavour with vinegar.[1] Bring it to heat; when it is simmering, put into the pan the gourd which has been peeled, de-seeded, diced and boiled. Crumble a *tracta* and thicken with some of it. Sprinkle with pepper and serve.

4.3.6. ***Minutal* of apricots**: put oil, *liquamen* and wine in a pan, chop in dried ascalonian onions and diced cooked shoulder of pork. When all this is cooked, pound pepper, cumin, dry mint, dill; pour on honey, *liquamen*, *passum*, a little vinegar, some of the cooking liquor; balance the flavours. Put in stoned apricots, bring them to a simmer until they are thoroughly cooked. Crumble a *tracta* and thicken with some of it. Sprinkle with pepper and serve.

4.3.7a. ***Minutal* of hare's livers and lungs**: You will find a recipe for this under 'hare'.[2]

4.3.7b. **Another sweet *minutal***: put in a pan *liquamen*, wine, oil, stock; chop in leek and coriander. You also put in the same pan ground forcemeat and diced cooked shoulder of pork. While it is cooking, pound pepper, lovage, oregano, some of the cooking liquor, flavour with wine and *passum*. Bring to heat; when it is simmering, crumble a *tracta* and thicken with some of it. Sprinkle with pepper and serve.

4.3.8. **Rose-coloured *minutal***: use the same sauce as above but put more *passum* in.

---

[1] This recipe is supposed to be sweet, yet the text includes no honey and in fact has vinegar twice. We have therefore added honey and *liquamen* to balance it.
[2] See 8.8.5.

IIII. TISANAM VEL SVCVM.

[4.4.1] **tisanam uel sucum.** tisanam sic facies: tisanam lauando fricas quam ante diem infundes. inpones supra ignem calidum; cum bullierit mittes olei satis et aneti modicum fasciculum, cepam siccam satureiam et coloefium ut ibi coquantur propter sucum. mittes coriandrum uiridem et salem simul tritum et facies ut ferueat; cum bene ferbuerit, tolles fasciculum et transferes in alterum caccabum tisanam sic ne fundum tangat propter conbusturam. ligas et colas in caccabolo supra acronem coloefium. teres piper ligusticum pulei aridi modicum cuminum et silfi frictum; ut bene tegatur suffundis acetum defritum liquamen, refundis in caccabum, sed coloefium acronem facias ut ferueat super ignem lentum.

[4.4.2] **tisanam barricam**: infundis cicer lenticulam pisa; defrixas tisanam et cum leguminibus elixas. ubi bene bullierit olei satis mittis et super uiridia concidis: porrum coriandrum anetum feniculum betam maluam culiculum molle; et uiridia minuta concisa in caccabum mittis. colicolos elixas et teres fenicoli semen satis, origanum silfi ligusticum; postquam tribueris liquamine temperabis et super legumina refundis, et agites. colicolorum minutas super concidis.

V. GVSTVM.

[4.5.1] **gustum uersatile**: albas betas minutas porros requietos apios uulbos cocleas elixas; gizeria pullorum aucellas esicia coques ex iure. perungis patinam

---

1-2. TISANAM VEL SVCVM *del.GiVo* 3. antediem *V* | impones *V* | callidum *V1*
4. coloefium *Tor*: coloethum *or* coloedium *E*: coloedium *V* 5. salem *Hum*: sale *VE*
6. ferbuerit *E with* q *in red above the line before this word*: feruuerit *V* 7. combusturam
V | lyas *Hum*: lias <bene> *GiVo* 8. supra *VE*: super *GiVo* | coloefium *Tor*: coloefrium *VE*
9. cuminum cuminum *V* | *GiVo move* ut bene tegatur *to after* supra acronem coloefium:
André puts the words after coloefium acronem | silfi *VE*: sil *GiVo* | suffundis <mel> acetum
GiVo 10. sed *VE*: super *GiVo* 12. barricam *VE*: taricham *Hum*: farricam *Sch*
| defricas *Hum* 13. mitis *E1* 14. feniculum *λ*: nuculum *VE* | coliculum *Hum*
15. uiridia *Hum*: uiridi *VE* | coliculos *Hum* | elixas *π*: elixos *VE* | fenicolo *V1*: feniculi *E*
16. triueris *Hum* 17. et agites *André*: iagites *VE*: et agitas *Hum*: agites *Bra3*:
agitas *GiVo* | coliculorum *Hum* 19. requietos *ξ*: requetos *V*: requietas *E* | bulbos *E*
20. coclios *E* | alixas *E* | gizeria pullorum *Milham*: gingibera pullorum *V*: lapullorum *E*: gigeria
pullorum *Hum* | perungis *LT*: proungis *VE*

4.4. BARLEY SOUP OR LIQUOR.

4.4.1 **Barley soup or liquor.** You make a barley soup like this: soak barley overnight and wash and rub (it free of husk). Put it over hot coals (in a pan). When it is boiling, add sufficient oil and a small bundle of dill, dried onion, savory and a knuckle ham bone so they may cook there to produce a liquor. Put in green coriander and salt, which have been pounded together. Bring it to heat; when it is simmering well, take out the bundle and transfer the barley soup to another pan, making sure that the bottom of the pan does not touch (the coals) and so burn: you smooth it and strain it into the pan, over the top of the ham bone. Pound pepper, lovage, a little dried pennyroyal, cumin and pounded *silphium*; so that it is well covered, pour on vinegar, *defrutum*, *liquamen*; pour back into the pan; but bring the ham bone to heat over a slow fire.[1]

4.4.2. **Thick barley soup**:[2] soak chick peas, lentils and peas; crush barley and boil it with the vegetables. When they are well boiled add sufficient oil and chop (these) greens into it: leek, coriander, dill, fennel, beet (leaves), mallow, tender cabbage. Chop the greens finely and put them in the pan. Boil (more) cabbage and pound a sufficient quantity of fennel seed, oregano, *silphium* and lovage. After you have ground them, flavour with *liquamen* and pour back over the vegetables and stir. Chop the cabbage finely and sprinkle over.

4.5. HORS-D'OEUVRE.

4.5.1. **A 'turned out' hors-d'oeuvre**: boil chopped white beet, stored leeks, celery, bulbs and snails. Cook in stock chicken gizzards, small birds, and forcemeat. Grease a dish and line it with mallow leaves. Arrange the mixed

---

[1] This recipe gave us considerable problems. Many previous editors have found it baffling too and made frequent emendations of the MSS in order to make sense of it. In this instance we found that leaving the text as it reads and taking out all previous attempts at correction solved many of the problems that we found. A *tisana* is defined as a 'drink made from barley-groats' (so *LS* II) or 'barley gruel' used as a medicinal drink (Dalby, *Food in the Ancient World*, p. 46); it is distinct from *polenta*, in which the barley was roasted. The ham bone is added as means of flavouring and not as an integral part of the dish. *FR* interpreted the *coloefium* as a leg of pork, which is not sustainable in a *tisana* recipe. See the Glossary under *coloefium* for a detailed discussion.

[2] *barricham*: possibly related to the Greek *barus,* 'heavy', hence 'thick', however it could equally be scribal error. As André points out (p. 174, note ad loc.), it is a *hapax legomenon* (it occurs nowhere else), and the other conjectures illustrate its difficulty: *taricham* (Hummelberg) means 'salty', and *farricham* (Schuch) 'of *far*, or spelt.' André's own tentative suggestion is (*bar*)*baricam*, 'barbarian', because (he claims) Greeks made *tisanae* with lentils and wheat, but do not seem to have included chick peas in them.

et folia maluarum substernis et praemixta olera conponis sic ut laxa <sint>; permisces bulbos intunsos damascenas cocleas esicia; lucanicas breues concidis; liquamine oleo uino aceto; ponis ut ferueat; cum ferbuerit teres piper ligusticum zingiber pyretrum modicum, fricabis, suffundis <liquamen et uinum; mittes in caccabum; omnia perfundes> et facies ut bulliat patina. oua conplura confringis et ius mortarii reliquum conmoues; conmiscis, patinam obligabis. dum ducit oenogarum ad eam sic facies: teres piper ligusticum; fricabis; suffundis liquamen et uinum, passo temperabis uel uino dulce; temperabis in caccabolo; mittis olei modicum, facies ut ferueat; cum ferbuerit amulo obligas; patinam uersas in lancem (folia maluarum ante tollis), oenogaro perfundis insuper; piper aspargis et inferes.

[4.5.2] **gustum de oleribus**: condies bulbos liquamine oleo et uino; cum cocti fuerint <addes> iecinera porcelli et gallinarum et ungellas et aucellas diuisas. haec omnia cum bulbis ferueant; cum ferbuerint, teres piper ligusticum; suffundis liquamen uinum et passum ut dulce sit; ius de suo sibi suffundis, reuocas in bulbos. cum ferbuerint ad momentum amulo obligas.

[4.5.3] **gustum de cucurbitis farsilibus**: cucurbitas a latere subtiliter ad modum tesselle oblonge decidas et excauas et mittis in frigidam. inpensam ad eam sic facies: teres piper ligusticum origanum; suffundis liquamen; cerebella cocta teres, oua cruda dissolues et mittes ut unum corpus efficias. liquamine temperabis, et cucurbitas supra scriptas non plene coctas ex ea inpensa inples. de tessella sua recludis, surclas et coctas exhimes et frigis. oenogarum sic facies: teres piper ligusticum, suffundis uinum et liquamen; passo temperabis, olei modicum; mittis in caccabum et facies ut ferueat. cum ferbuerit amulo obligas et cucurbitas frictas oenogaro perfundis et piper aspargis et inferes.

1. filia *E* | perẹmixta *E1* | componis *V* | <sint> *CGSG*: <mentum habeant> *GiVo*   2. pulbos *E* | intunsos *Milham*: inuersos *VE*: tusos *André*   3. ferbuerit *E2*: feruuerit *V, E1*   4. piretrum *E*   4-5. <liquamen…perfundes> *CGSG*: *lacuna André*   5. confrigis *E1*   6. reliqum *E1* | commoues *V* | ducit *Hum*: ducis *VE*   8. dulce *V, E2*: dulces *E1*: dulci *Milham*   8-9. olei modicum mittis *E*   9. ferbuerit *E2*: feruuerit *V, E1* | uersa *E*   10. perfundis *GiVo*: profundis *VE*   12. holeribus *E* | et *om. E1*   13. fuernnt *E1* | <addes> *CGSG* | iecira *E1* | aucellas *Hum*: scellas *VE*: ascellas *GiVo*   14. hẹc *E* | bulbis ferueant *ζ*: bubis ferueat *VE* | ferbuerit *E2*: feruuerit *V, E1*   16. ferbuerit *E2*: feruuerit *V, E1*   17. cucurbitis *ζ*: cucurbatas *VE*   18. decidas *VE*: decidis *GiVo* | eam *VE*: eas *Sch*   21. coctas et ex ea inpensa *V* | imples *V*   22. exhimes *V*: eximes *E*: eximis *GiVo*   24. facias *E* | feruuerit *V*   25. perfundis] per- *over an erasure V*

vegetables loosely. Mix together (in a pan) pounded bulbs, damsons, the snails and the forcemeat; chop in small pieces of *lucanica*, *liquamen*, oil, wine and vinegar; bring this to heat. When it is simmering, pound pepper, lovage, ginger, a little Spanish camomile, pound again, pour on <*liquamen* and wine, put in the pan, then pour everything> into the dish and make it boil. Break plenty of eggs into the mortar and mix with the remaining sauce. Stir into the dish and thicken. While it is thickening, make an *oenogarum* for it like this: pound pepper, lovage, pound again, pour on *liquamen* and wine. Flavour with *passum* or with sweet wine. Blend it in a little pan; put in a little oil and bring to heat; when it is simmering, thicken with starch. Turn the *patina* out on to a serving dish and remove the mallow leaves, before pouring the *oenogarum* on the top; sprinkle with pepper and serve.[1]

4.5.2. **A vegetable hors-d'oeuvre**: flavour bulbs with *liquamen*, oil, and wine. When they are cooked add young pig's and chicken livers and chopped meat from chicken legs and small birds. Bring all these things to heat with the bulbs; when they are simmering, pound pepper, lovage, pour on *liquamen*, wine, and *passum* so that it is sweet. Pour on some of the cooking liquor and pour back over the bulbs. As soon as it simmers, thicken it with starch.

4.5.3. **Hors-d'oeuvre of stuffed gourds**: carefully cut out a rectangle from the side of the gourds and hollow them out and put (to cook) in cold water. Make the stuffing for them like this: pound pepper, lovage, oregano, pour on *liquamen*; pound cooked brains, stir in raw eggs and make all into a smooth mixture. Flavour with *liquamen*, and stuff the above-mentioned par-boiled gourds with this mixture. Put back the rectangle, tie them up, cook them, remove and fry them.[2] Make an *oenogarum* like this: pound pepper, lovage, pour on wine and *liquamen*, flavour with *passum* and a little oil, put in a pan and bring to heat. When it is simmering, thicken it with starch and pour the *oenogarum* over the fried gourds and sprinkle with pepper and serve.

---

[1] A very complex recipe with some omissions which lead to confusion. The gizzards and small birds are not apparently used. The forcemeat cooked *ex iure* is surely the same ingredient as the later forcemeat added to the first sauce, as are the snails. It is likely that a line of text has been omitted; our conjecture attempts to supply what may be lacking. We have translated *temperabis* with two separate meanings within the same sentence quite intentionally. See the Introduction, p. 87, for a discussion of the verb.

[2] A confusing statement. Presumably the gourds are then boiled, to set the filling, and sliced before frying. The slice is very attractive with the *oenogarum* poured over.

[4.5.4] **gustum de praecoquiis**: duracina primotica pusilla precoquiis purgas, enucleas, in frigidam mittis; in patina conponis; teres piper mentam siccam; suffundis liquamen; adicies mel passum uinum et acetum; refundis in patina super precoquia, olei modicum mittis et lento igni ferueat. cum ferbuerit, amulo obligas, piper aspargis et inferes.

5

EXPLICIT APICI PANDECTER LIBER QVARTVS

1. precoquiis *V2*: praecoquiis *GiVo*: prēcoquiis *E*: pretoquiis *V1* | duracina *GiVo*: dureina *V*: dure ina *E* | *GiVo delete* duracina primotica *as a gloss*; *André del. these words plus* pusilla   2. conponis *E2*: conteres *E1*: compones *V*   3. patina *VE*: patinam *GiVo*   4. feruuerit *V*   6. APICII *E*   7. IIII *VE*

4.5.4. **Hors-d'oeuvre of apricots**: take firm, early or undersized fruits, wash them, remove the stone and put them (to cook) in cold water and then arrange them in a dish. Pound pepper, dried mint; pour on *liquamen*; add honey, *passum*, wine and vinegar; pour over the apricots in the dish, add a little oil and let it come to heat over a gentle fire. When it is simmering, thicken it with starch, sprinkle with pepper and serve.

HERE ENDS BOOK FOUR OF APICIUS, 'COMPOUND DISHES'

BOOK FIVE

INCIPIT EIVSDEM OSPREON LIBER QVINTVS

I. pultes. II. lenticula. III. pisa. IIII. concicla. V. tisana et alica. VI. fabaciae uirides et Baianae. VII. fenum Grecum. VIII faseoli et cicer.

5 **I. PVLTES.**

[5.1.1] **pultes Iuliane sic coquuntur**: alicam purgatam infundis, coques, facies ut ferueat. cum ferbuerit, oleum mittis; cum spissauerit, ligas diligenter. adicies cerebella duo cocta et selibram pulpe quasi ad esicia liate: cum cerebellis teres et in caccabum mittis. teres piper ligusticum feniculi semen, suffundis liquamen et
10 uinum modice. mittis in caccabum supra cerebella et pulpam; ubi satis ferbuerit, cum iure misces. ex hoc paulatim alicam condies, et ad trullam permisces et lias ut quasi sucus uideatur.

[5.1.2] **pultes cum iure oenococti**: pultes oenococti iure condies; **copadia**: similam siue alicam coctam hoc iure condies, et cum copadiis porcinis adponis
15 oenococti iure conditis.

[5.1.3] **pultes tractogalatae**: lactis sextarium et aquae modicum mittes in caccabo nouo et lento igni ferueat. tres orbiculos tracte siccas et confringis et partibus in lac summittis ne uratur. aquam miscendo agitabis. cum cocta fuerit, ut est super ignem, mittis melle. ex musteis cum lacte similiter facies, salem et
20 oleum minus mittis.

1. OSPREON *Ven*: OSPREO *E*: OSTREO *V*　　　2. V *E*　　　3. conchicla *Hum* | V tisana et alica *displaced to end of list (after* cicer) *E1* | fabaciae *GiVo, section VI below*: fabacia *VE*
4. fenogrecum *E1*: fenugrecum *E2*　　　5. PVLTES *at end of first line of text E*
6. alicam purgatam *Ven*: alica purgata *VE*　　　7. ferbuerit *E1*: feruuerit *V, E2* | pissauerit *E1* | ligas *VE*: lias *Sch*: obligas *Hum*　　　10. ferbuerit *Hum*: fuerit *VE*
13. pultes oenococti *GiVo*: pultes benococti *V*: pultes bene cocti *E*: pultes oenogari cocti *P, Tor*: pultes aenococti *Bra2*　　　16. tractogalatae *Hum*: tractogale *V*: tractogalę *E* | aquę *E* | mittis *E*
17. orbiculos *Hum*: sorbiculos *VE*　　　18. neu.ratur *V* | agitabis *P*: sagittabis *VE*
19. ignem *VE*: inguen *Sch*: agninam *GiVo*

206

BOOK FIVE OF THE SAME, 'PULSES', BEGINS

1. Pottage. 2. Lentils. 3. Peas. 4. *Conchicla*. 5. Barley and wheat soup. 6. Green beans and Baian beans. 7. Fenugreek. 8. Cow peas and chick peas.

5.1. POTTAGE.

5.1.1. **Julian pottage is cooked like this**: soak cleaned *alica*, cook it, bring it to heat. When it is simmering add oil; when it becomes thick, carefully stir it smooth. Add 2 cooked brains and ½ lb. of meat ground as if for forcemeat: pound it with brains and put in a pan. Pound pepper, lovage, fennel seed; pour on *liquamen* and a little wine. Put in the pan over the brains and meat: when they have simmered enough, stir them with the sauce. Gradually blend the *alica* with this, and mix it and smooth it so that it is pourable, so that it seems like soup.

5.1.2. **Pottage with a wine-based stock**: flavour the pottage with a wine-based stock. **Pork delicacies**: blend cooked fine wheat or *alica* with this sauce and serve with pork delicacies flavoured with the sauce made from wine-based stock.[1]

5.1.3. **Pottage made with *tracta* and milk**: put a pint of milk and a little water in a new pan and let it heat on a gentle fire. Dry 3 discs of *tracta* and crumble them and put them, little by little, into the milk so that it does not burn. Stir it while adding water. When it is cooked, add honey while it is still over the fire.[2] You can make this in a similar way with milk and sweet-wine cakes. Put in salt and a little oil.[3]

---

[1] This recipe repeats itself endlessly; the final phrase may be a (totally superfluous) gloss. In Book 7 we have translated *copadia* as 'morsels of meat'. *FR* follow Brandt's suggestion: *aenococti*, 'bronze-pan cooked', but we fail to see what difference it would make to the dish though it may be the origin of an early cooking method. See *Excerpta Vinidarii* 13 and note.

[2] *FR* follow Giarratano and Vollmer, rejecting the MSS reading *super ignem* for the conjecture *super agninam* 'over lamb', and have therefore misunderstood the recipe somewhat.

[3] *minus* is awkward, but this recipe clearly does not contain salt and oil, so 'less' makes no sense; perhaps 'less than usual' is meant. Athenaeus 113d records that oil can be added to *tracta*. Cato, *De agricultura* 121 calls them *mustacei*.

[5.1.4] **pultes**: alicam purgatam infundis, quoques. dum ferbuerit, oleum mittis. cum spissauerit, adicies cerebella duo cocta et selibram pulpe quasi ad esicia liate: cum cerebellis teres et in caccabum mittes. teres piper ligusticum feniculi semen, suffundis liquamen et meri modicum, et mittis in caccabum supra cerebella et

5 pulpam. ubi satis ferbuerit, cum iure miscis. ex hoc paulatim alicam condies. sed ius ut quasi sucus uideatur.

II. LENTICVLA.

[5.2.1] **lenticula ex spondilis siue fondilis**: accipies caccabum mundum, adicies in mortarium piper cuminum semen coriandri mentam rutam puleium,

10 fricabis, suffundis acetum, adicies mel, liquamen et defritum, aceto temperabis, reexinanies in caccabo. spondilos elixatos teres et mittes ut ferueant. cum bene ferbuerint, obligas. adicies in boletari oleum uiridem.

[5.2.2] **lenticulam de castaneis**: accipies caccabum nouum, et castaneas purgatas diligenter mittis. adicies aquam et nitrum modice, facies ut coquatur. cum

15 coquitur, mittis in mortario piper cuminum semen coriandri mentam rutam laseris radicem puleium, fricabis. suffundis acetum mel liquamen, aceto temperabis, et super castaneas coctas refundis. adicies oleum, facies ut ferueat. cum bene ferbuerit, tutunclabis ut in mortario teres. gustas, si quid deest, addes. cum in boletar miseris, addes oleum uiridem.[1]

20 [5.2.3] **aliter lenticulam**: coquis. cum despumauerit, porrum et coriandrum uiridem supermittis. <teres> coriandri semen puleium laseris radicem, mentam et rute semen, suffundis acetum, adicies melle, liquamine, uino, defrito temperabis, adicies oleum, agitabis. si quid opus fuerit, mittis. amulo obligas, insuper oleum uiridem mittis, piper aspargis et inferes.

1. alica *V* | coques *E* | cum *Hum* | feruuerit *V*   2. selebram *E1*   5. ferbuerit *Hum*: fuerit *VE* | misces *V1*   6. sed ius *VE*: et lias *GiVo*   8. spondilis siue fondilis *CGSG*: fondilos siue fondilis *VE*: sfondylis [siue fondilis] *GiVo*: sfondilis [siue fondilis] *André*: sphondylis [siue fondilos] *Milham*   9. imortarium *E* | mentam *P*: menta *VE* | rutam *P*: rutae *V*: rute *E* | puleium *P*: pulei *VE*   11. in caccabo ζ: in in caccabo *E*: in caccabos *V* | spondilos *CGSG*: spyondilos *E*: pyondilos *V*: sfondylos *GiVo*: sfondilos *André*: sphondylos *Milham* | mittis *V* 12. ferbuerit *E* | uiridem *V,E1*: uiridi *E2*   13. *VE begin this recipe at* de castaneis de castaneis *P*: de castaneis de castaneis *VE*   14-15. cum coquatur *E*   15. mentæ *E* | rutam *R*: rutae *V*: rutæ *E*   18. feruuerit *V* | tutunclabis *VE*: tudiclabis *Hum*: turundabis *Sch*: tutundabis *TP* | ut...teres *del. Vo* | guttas *E*   19. addis *E*   20. despumauerit *GiVo*: despumaueris *VE*   21. uiride *GiVo* | <teres> *Gi*   21-22. mentam et rute semen *CGSG*: semen mente et rute *VE*: mentam et rutam *André*   22. uino *CGSG*: aceto *VE*

5.1.4. **Pottage**: soak cleaned *alica,* cook it. While it is simmering, add oil; when it becomes thick add 2 cooked brains, ½ lb. meat, ground as if for forcemeat: pound with the brains and put in a pan. Pound pepper, lovage, fennel seed, pour on *liquamen*, a little pure wine and put in the pan over the brains and meat. When they have simmered enough, stir them with the sauce. Gradually blend the *alica* with this. But the sauce should look like a soup.

5.2. LENTICULA[1]

5.2.1. **Lentils with mussels**: take a clean pan, (put the lentils in and cook them). Put in a mortar pepper, cumin, coriander seed, mint, rue, pennyroyal, and pound them. Pour on vinegar, add honey, *liquamen*, and *defrutum*, flavour with vinegar. Empty the mortar into the pan. Pound cooked mussels, put them in and bring to heat; when it is simmering well, thicken. Pour green oil over it in the serving dish.

5.2.2. **Lentils with chestnuts**: take a new pan and put in carefully peeled chestnuts. Add water and a little soda, put it to cook. When it is cooking, put in a mortar pepper, cumin, coriander seed, mint, rue, *laser* root, pennyroyal, and pound them. Pour on vinegar, honey, *liquamen*, flavour with vinegar and pour it over the cooked chestnuts. Add oil, bring it to heat. When it is simmering well, pound it with a stick as you pound in a mortar.[2] Taste it; if there is anything lacking, add it. When you have put it in the serving dish, add green oil.

5.2.3. **Another lentil dish**: cook (the lentils); when they have been skimmed, add in leek and green coriander. Pound coriander seed, pennyroyal, *laser* root, mint and rue seed. Pour on vinegar, add honey, *liquamen*, wine,[3] flavour with *defrutum*, add oil and stir. If it needs anything, add it. Thicken with starch, pour on green oil, sprinkle with pepper and serve.

---

[1] In 5.2.1, we assume that lentils are cooked separately and added with the sauce. However, in 5.2.2 the Latin is expressed in a slightly different way, with *de castaneis* instead of *ex spondilis*, which may indicate that in 5.2.2 chestnuts are used alone to make a purée, which might therefore be a transferred meaning of *lenticula*.

[2] On *tutunclabis*, found here and in 5.3.6, see Introduction, p. 88 n. 2.

[3] We have removed a vinegar from this recipe and replaced it with wine.

III. PISA.

[5.3.1] **pisum**: coques. cum despumauerit, porrum coriandrum et cuminum supra mittis. teres piper ligusticum careum [hoc est carauitam] careum anetum ocymum uiridem; suffundis liquamen, uino et liquamine temperabis, facies ut
5   ferueat. cum ferbuerit, agitabis. si quid defuerit mittis, et inferes.

[5.3.2] **pisam farsilem**: coques, cui oleum mittis. abdomen, et mittis in caccabum liquamen et porrum capitatum, coriandrum uiridem; inponis ut coquatur. esicia minuta facies quadrata, et coques simul turdos uel aucellas uel de pullo conciso, et cerebella prope cocta cum iuscello coques. lucanicas assas, petasonem elixas,
10   porros ex aqua coques, nucleorum eminam frigis. teres piper ligusticum origanum gengiber, ius abdominis fundis, lias. angularem accipies qui uersari potest et omentis tegis. oleo perfundis, deinde nucleos aspargis et supra pisam mittis ut tegas fundum angularis, et sic conponis supra petasonis pulpas porros lucanicas concisas. iterum pisam supermittis. item alternis abtabis obsonia quousque
15   impleatur angularis. nouissime pisam admittis ut intus omnia contineat. coques in furno uel lento igni inponis, ut ducat ad se deorsum. oua dura facies, uitella eicies, in mortario mittis cum pipere albo nucleis melle uino candido et liquamine modico. teres et mittis in uas ut ferueat. cum ferbuerit, pisam mittis in lancem et hoc iure perfundis. hoc ius candidum appellatur.

20   [5.3.3] **pisum Indicum**: pisum coques. cum despumauerit, porrum et coriandrum concidis et mittis in caccabum ut ferueat, et accipies sepias minutas, sic quomodo

---

2. pisam *GiVo*   3. carauita *V*: caruitam *E* | hoc est carauitam *del. Sch*   4. liquamene *V1*
5. feruuerit *V*   6. <pisam> coques *Gi* | <accipies> abdomen *Vo*   8. deconciso *E1*
9. pro pecocta *V*   10. porros *Hum*: porro *VE*   11. gingiber *E* | qui uersari *Bas*:
conuersari *E*: couersari *V*   12. perfundis *Gi*: profundis *VE* | et supra *Hum*: ut supra *VE*
13. componis *V*   14. aptabis *TC*   15. pisam *P*: pis *VE*: pisa *TC* | mittis *Hum*
17. mitis cum *E* | liquamines *E1*   18. feruuerit *V*   19. ocius *V*   20. pisam
indicum *V*: pisam Indicam *GiVo*

---

[1] The peas used for these recipes seem to be dried (and more specifically marrowfat) peas. All the recipes need to be skimmed and they also naturally form a thick pease-pudding-like consistency which can be beaten smooth.

[2] The gloss *hoc est carauita* seems only to clarify the term *careum* with a later word for this spice.

[3] Literally, 'stuffed pea'; our rendering describes the dish rather than being a close translation.

[4] It seems extremely improbable that the meat is cooked only in *liquamen*. We think that 'water' is assumed as the cooking medium (as with the peas).

[5] The production of forcemeat cubes implies that the forcemeat has been cooked first; see the Glossary, *isicia*.

5.3. PEAS[1]

5.3.1. **Peas**: cook them; when they have been skimmed, put in leek, coriander and cumin. Pound pepper, lovage, caraway,[2] dill, green basil; pour on *liquamen*, flavour with wine and *liquamen*. Bring it to heat. When it is simmering, stir it. If it lacks anything, add it and serve.

5.3.2. **Pease mould**:[3] cook peas and add oil to them. Put some belly pork in a pan with *liquamen*, (water),[4] leek and green coriander. Put it to cook. Make cubes of finely-ground forcemeat,[5] and at the same time cook thrushes or other little birds or chicken meat and also par-cooked brains in stock.[6] Roast some *lucanicae*; boil some pork shoulder and cook leeks in water; dry-roast a pint of pine nuts. Pound pepper, lovage, oregano, ginger, pour on some of the cooking liquor from the belly pork; make it smooth.[7] Take an angular mould[8] which can be turned out and line it with caul fat. Pour on oil, then sprinkle with pine nuts and put some peas on top of that so that you cover the bottom of the mould and then lay on top some of the pork, leek and chopped *lucanicae*. Put in another layer of peas; keep putting in alternate layers of the ingredients until the mould is full. Last of all put in a layer of peas to seal everything in.[9] Cook in an oven or put it on a slow fire so that it sets from the top down.[10] Hard-boil some eggs and put aside the yolks. Put (the whites) in a mortar with white pepper, pine nuts, honey, white wine, and a little *liquamen*. Pound it and put it in a pan to heat; when it is simmering, turn the pease mould out on to a serving dish and pour the sauce over it. This sauce is called 'white sauce'.

5.3.3. **Indigo peas**:[11] cook the peas; when you have skimmed them, put chopped leek and coriander in the pan and cook them; then take some small cuttlefish

---

[6] There seem to be too many instructions to 'cook' at this point; perhaps *coques* has been inserted in error at the end of this sentence.

[7] The term *lias*, 'make it smooth', must include the assumed instruction to thicken first. This sauce is not mentioned again but is no doubt intended to be poured over the various layers of meat and vegetables.

[8] i.e. a deeper-than-normal dish with straight sides.

[9] 'Seal everything in': it is possible to do this with peas, but more caul fat (i.e. that hanging over the sides) might be meant.

[10] This is an indication that a lid or some kind of *testa* is intended so that hot coals can be utilized to transfer heat down as well as up. See the Introduction, p. 78 fig. 5, p. 82, for an illustration and discussion. *FR* could not understand the term *ad se deorsum* and left it untranslated.

[11] The term *indicum* here means 'indigo', and refers to the dark blue/green colour of the dish when the ink from the cuttlefish is added, and not that the dish was Indian in style, as *FR* suggest.

sunt cum atramento suo, ut simul coquantur. adicies oleum liquamen et uinum,
fasciculum porri et coriandri, facies ut coquantur. cum coctum fuerit, teres piper
ligusticum origanum, carei modicum, suffundis ius de suo sibi, uino et passo
temperabis. sepias minutatim concidis et in pisum mittis. piper asparges <et

5   inferes>.

[5.3.4] **pisum**: coques, agitabis et mittis in frigidam. cum refrigerauerit, deinde
agitabis. concidis cepam minutatim et albamentum oui, oleo et sale condies, aceti
modicum adicies. in boletari uitellum oui cocti colas, insuper oleum uiridem
mittis et inferes.

10 [5.3.5] **pisam Vitellianam siue fabam**: pisam coques, lias. teres piper ligusticum
gengiber, et super condimenta mittis uitella ouorum quę dura coxeris; mellis
uncias III, teres, liquamen uinum et acetum. haec omnia mittis in caccabum et
condimenta quae triuisti. adiecto oleo ponis ut ferueat. condies pisam, lias; si
aspera fuerit melle mittis et inferes.

15 [5.3.6] **aliter pisa siue faba**: ubi dispumauerit teres mel liquamen carenum
cuminum rutam apii semen oleum et uinum. tutunclabis. cum pipere trito et
cum esiciis inferes.

[5.3.7] **aliter pisam siue fabam**: despumatam subtrito lasare Partico liquamen
et careno condies. oleum modice superfundis et inferes.

20 [5.3.8] **pisam adulteram uersatilem**: coques pisam. cerebellam uel aucellas
uel turdos exossatos a pectore lucanicas iecinera gizeria pullorum in caccabum
mittis, liquamen, oleum; fasciculos porri capitati, coriandrum uiridem concidis,
et cum cerebellis coques. teres piper, ligusticum et liquamen . . .

[5.3.9] **pisam siue fabam Vitellianam**: pisam siue fabam coques. cum
25 despumauerit mittis porrum coriandrum et flores maluarum. dum coquitur, teres
piper ligusticum origanum feniculi semen, suffundis liquamen et uinum, <mittis>
in caccabum, adicies oleum. cum ferbuerit, agitas. oleum uiridem insuper mittis
et inferes.

---

4. aspargis *E*   4-5. <et inferes> *add. Gi*   6. pisum *V*: ipsum *E*: <aliter> pisum *Gi* |
deinde *VE*: denuo *GiVo*: *lacuna André*   7. ouinoleo *E1*   8. boletari *Hum*: boletam *VE*
11. gingiber *E*   12. teres *om. E* | uinum] uirium *E1* | aceta *V* | hęc *E*
13. condimenta *E2*: condimitti/mentum *E1*: condimentum *V* | quæ *E*   15. despumauerit *Hum*
16. ruta *V* | tutunclabis *VE*: tudiclabis *Hum*: turundabis *Sch*   19. modicę *E*
20. cerebella *Hum*   21. peccatore *E1*   22. fascilos *E* | porri *corr.* porro *E*
23.... *lacuna André*   24. siue fe fabam *E1*   26. <mittis> *Gi*

just as they come with their ink sacs and cook them straightaway. Add some oil, *liquamen*, wine, and a bundle of leek and coriander. Allow it to cook through; when it is cooked, pound pepper, lovage, oregano, a little caraway, pour on the cooking liquor and flavour with wine and *passum*. Chop the small cuttlefish and put them in the peas. Sprinkle with pepper and serve.

5.3.4. **Peas**: cook them, stir them and put the pan in cold water; when it has gone cold, stir again. Chop onion finely with cooked white of egg, season with oil and salt and add a little vinegar. (Put in the pan.) Pass cooked egg yolk through a sieve on to the peas in their serving dish. Pour green oil on top and serve.

5.3.5. **Vitellian peas or beans**: cook the peas and beat them smooth. Pound pepper, lovage, ginger; put on top of the spices egg yolk which you have hard-boiled, 3 oz. honey; pound again; *liquamen*, wine, and vinegar. Put all this in a pan with the spices you have pounded. Having added some oil, bring it to heat. Season the peas with this; stir them smooth; if they are sharp add some honey and serve.

5.3.6. **Another pea or bean recipe**: when you have skimmed them, pound honey, *liquamen*, *caroenum*, cumin, rue, celery seed, oil and wine.[1] Pound with a stick. Serve with ground pepper and with forcemeat.

5.3.7. **Another pea or bean recipe**: when they have been skimmed, season them with finely ground Parthian *laser*, *liquamen* and *caroenum*. Pour on a little oil and serve.

5.3.8. **'Disguised' pease mould**: cook peas; then you put in a pan brains, little birds, breasts of thrushes, *lucanicae*, liver, chicken gizzards; add *liquamen*, oil, a bundle of leek, chopped green coriander, and cook them with the brains. Pound pepper, lovage and *liquamen*...[2]

5.3.9. **Vitellian peas or beans**: cook the peas or beans; when you have skimmed them, put in leek and coriander and mallow flowers. While it is cooking, pound pepper, lovage, oregano, fennel seed; pour on *liquamen* and wine, put in the pan, add oil. When it is simmering, stir it, pour green oil on top and serve.

[1] We have translated the ingredients in the order in which they occur in the text, but for practical purposes the dry ingredients would be ground first, then the *liquamen* put in, and the other liquids would be added last.

[2] The rest is missing but it is probable that recipe 5.3.2 will contain the basic method.

IIII. CONCICLA.

[5.4.1] **cum faba**: coques. teres piper ligusticum cuminum coriandrum uiridem; suffundis liquamen; uino et liquamen in ea temperabis, mittis in caccabum, adicies oleum. lento igni ferueat et inferes.

5   [5.4.2] **conciclam Apicianam**: accipies cumanam mundam, ubi quoques pisum, cui mittis lucanicas concisas esiciola porcina pulpas petasonem. teres piper ligusticum origanum anetum cepam siccam coriandrum uiridem; suffundis liquamen; uino et liquamine temperabis. mittis in cumanam cui adicies oleum, pungis ubique et cumbibat oleum; igni lento quoques ita ut ferueat et inferes.

10   [5.4.3] **conciclam de pisa simplici**: pisam coques. cum dispumauerit, fasciculum porri et coriandri mittis. dum coquitur,   teres piper ligusticum origanum, fasciculum de suo sibi; fricabis; suffundis <liquamen; uino et> liquamine temperabis, mittis. super adicies oleum et lento igni ferueat, et inferes.

    [5.4.4] **concicla Commodiana**: pisam quoques. cum dispumauerit, teres piper 15   ligusticum anetum cepam siccam; suffundis liquamen; uino et liquamine temperabis. mittis in caccabum ut cumbibat. deinde oua IIII solues, in sextarium pise mittis, agitas, mittis in cumana, ad ignem ponis ut ducat, et inferes.

    [5.4.5] **aliter conciclam sic facies**: concidis pullum minutatim, liquamine oleo et uino ferueat. concidis cepam coriandrum minutum, cerebella eneruas, mittes in 20   eundem pullum. cum coctus fuerit, leuas et exossas. concides minutatim cepam et coriandrum, colas ibi pisam coctam non conditam. accipies conciclarem, pro modo conponis uarie. deinde teres piper, cuminum, suffundis ius de suo sibi. item in mortario oua duo dissolues; temperas, ius de suo sibi suffundis. pise integre elixe uel nucleis adornabis, et lento igni feruere facies et inferes.

1-2. CONCICLA cum faba *VE*: CONCICLA concicla cum faba *TC*   3. uinum *Milham* | liquamine temperabis *Hum*   4. feruæat *E*   5. coques *E*   9. et cumbibat *VE*: ut combibat *Hum* | lecto *V* | quoques *V,E1*: coques *E2*   10. dispumauerit *VE*: despumauerit *TP*   11. coandri *E* | qcuoquitur *E*   12. fasciculum <suffundis ius> de suo sibi fricabis liquamine *André* | <liquamen uino et> *Hum*   13. mittis <in caccabum> *Hum*: mittis <in cumanum> *Gi*   14. coques *E* | dispumauerit *V,E2*: ?dispumauent *E1*: despumauerit *TP*   16. cumbibat *V*: bibat *E*: combibat *Hum* | dein *E1* | soues *E1*   17. cumana *VE*: cumanam *GiVo*   18. condis *E1*   19. cepam *ξ* cepa *VE* | cerebella eneruas *Bra3*: cerebella eneruatas *E*: cerebellae neruatas *V*   20. leuas *Sch*: lauas *VE* | exsossas *E* 22. componis *V* | uariae *V*   24. nuncleis *E*

---

[1] See the Glossary for a discussion of these pea dishes.

[2] The peas at this stage will be very thick, thick enough even to make them difficult to stir – hence the need to disperse the sauce in this way.

[3] *mittis* seems to be a self-sufficient instruction for the ancient cook; Hummelberg's addition of

5.4. *CONCHICLA.*[1]

5.4.1. **With beans**: cook them. Pound pepper, lovage, cumin, green coriander, pour on *liquamen*, balance their flavour with wine and *liquamen*. Pour into the pan, add oil. Bring to heat on a gentle fire and serve.

5.4.2. **Apician *conchicla***: take a clean Cumaean clay pot in which you cook the peas; add to it chopped *lucanicae*, pork forcemeat, pork shoulder meat. Pound pepper, lovage, oregano, dill, dried onion, green coriander, pour on *liquamen*, flavour with wine and *liquamen*. Put this in the pot to which you add some oil. Poke holes into it all over and let it absorb the oil (and sauce).[2] Cook it over a gentle fire so that it comes to heat and serve.

5.4.3. **Plain pea *conchicla***: cook the peas; when you have skimmed them, put in a bundle of leeks and coriander. While it is cooking, pound pepper, lovage, oregano, the bundle itself, pound again, pour on *liquamen,* flavour with wine and *liquamen*; put (in the pan).[3] Pour oil over the top; let it come to heat over a gentle fire and serve.

5.4.4. **Commodian *conchicla***: cook peas; when you have skimmed them, pound pepper, lovage, dill, dried onion; pour on *liquamen*; flavour with wine and *liquamen*. Put in the pan so that the peas soak up the flavourings. Then break in 4 eggs to every 1 pt. of cooked peas and beat them together. Put the mixture in a Cumaean clay dish and place on a fire so that it sets, and serve.

5.4.5. **You make another *conchicla* recipe like this**: chop a chicken into small pieces and bring them to heat in *liquamen*, oil and wine. Chop onion and coriander finely, take the sinews from brains and put in with the chicken. When they are cooked, take them out and remove the meat from the bone. Chop onion and coriander finely and strain on to them cooked peas which have not been seasoned. Take a *conchicla* serving dish and arrange the various ingredients appropriately. Then pound pepper, cumin, pour on some of the cooking liquor (from the chicken). Next break 2 eggs into the mortar and blend, pouring on (more) cooking liquor. Garnish with whole boiled peas or pine nuts. Put on a gentle fire to heat, and serve.[4]

in caccabum is helpful but strictly unnecessary.

[4] The recipe does not include instructions to pour the sauce over the peas, but this kind of laconic instruction is not unusual. The repeat of *ius de suo sibi* may be the result of dittography but we have decided to retain it. There is also a partial repetition in *concidis...minutum* and *concides ...coriandrum*. Having thought about the practicalities of the recipe, we decided that the meats go at the bottom of the dish, the peas on the top and the sauce with the eggs over the whole so that it sets, giving a pale skin to the finished dish.

[5.4.6] **aliter concicla**: conciclatus pullus uel porcellus: exossas pullum a pectore, femora eius iungis in porrectum, surculo alligas, et inpensam [concicla farsilis] paras, et farcies alternis pisam lotam, cerebella, lucanicas et cetera. teres piper ligusticum origanum et gengiber; liquamen suffundis; passo et uino temperabis.

5 facies ut ferueat, et cum ferbuerit, mittis modice; et inpensam cum condieris, alternis in pullo conponis, omento tegis et in operculo deponis et in furnum mittis ut coquantur paulatim, et inferes.

V. TISANAM ET ALICAM.

[5.5.1] **[tisanam et alicam] alicam uel sucum tisane sic facies**: tisanam uel

10 alicam lauando fricas, quam ante diem infundis. inponis supra ignem calidum. cum bullierit, mittis olei satis et aneti modicum fasciculum, cepam siccam satureiam et coleuium ut ibi coquantur propter sucum. mittis coriandrum uiridem et salem simul tritum et facies ut ferueat. cum bene ferbuerit, tollis fasciculum et transferes in alterum caccabum tisanam sic ne fundum tangat

15 propter combusturam. ligas bene et colas in caccabo super acronem colouium. teres piper ligusticum pulei aridi modicum cuminum silfi frictum; ut bene tegatur suffundis mel acetum defritum liquamen, refundis in caccabum; sed coloefrium acronem facies ut ferueat super ignem lentum.

[5.5.2] **aliter tisanam**: infundis cicer lenticulam pisam. defricas tisanam et cum

20 leguminibus elixas. ubi bene bullierit, olei satis mittis et super uiridia concidis: porrum coriandrum anetum feniculum <betam maluam coliculum> mollem. haec uiridia minuta concisa in caccabum mittis; coliculos elixas et teres feniculi

1. concicla *VE*: *om.* T: *del. GiVo* | exossas *Hum*: exossatus *VE*: exossabis *Sch*   2-3. concicla farsilis *del. Sch*   3. farties *E (?and V)* | piper V2, *ζ*: *om.V1, E*   4. gingiber *E* 5. ferbuerit *E2*: feruuerit *V, E1* | inpensam *CGSG*: ipsam *VE*: pisam *Hum*: impensam *Sch* | cum dieris *E1*   6. componis *V* | in o/perculo *corr.* in/operculo *E* 8. ALIQVAM *V*   9. tisanam et alicam *del. Hum*   9-10. uel acam *E*. 10. ignem calidum cum *CGSG, see 4.4.1*: ignem uel dum cum *VE*: ignem ualidum cum *Svennung*: uel dum *del. gloss. GiVo*   12. coleuinum *E1*: coloefium *Tor*   14. altero *V* 15. ligas *VE*: lias *Sch*: lyas *Hum* | colouinum *E1*: coloefium *Tor*   16. silfi *GiVo*: sil *VE* 16-18. ut bene tegatur teres piper ligusticum …frictum *Bra3*: sil frictum. suffundis mel …acronem ut bene tegatur. facies ut ferueat *André*: *Milham writes* facies ut ferueat *twice, following both Bra3 and André*   17. sed *VE*: super *GiVo* | coloefrium *CGSG*: coloefrim *VE*: coloefium *Tor* 18. acronem *ζ*: acromen *VE*   19. defri casti sanam *E*   21. <betam maluam coliculum> *Hum from 4.4.2* | hẹc *E*   22. minuta *Mar*: mina *VE* | cociculos *E1*

5.4.6. Another *conchicla* recipe: a *conchicla* of chicken or piglet: bone the chicken from the breast, then stretch the thighs out and tie them together with binding, and prepare[1] the stuffing. Stuff it in layers with (cooked) washed peas, brains, *lucanicae* and other ingredients. Pound pepper, lovage, oregano and ginger; pour on *liquamen*; flavour with *passum* and wine. Bring to heat and, when it is simmering, put a little in the stuffing; and when you have flavoured it, place in the chicken in layers. Wrap the chicken in caul fat, place in a covered dish and put in the oven so that it may cook slowly, and serve.

5.5. BARLEY OR *ALICA* SOUP.[2]

5.5.1. You make *alica* or barley soup like this: soak barley or *alica* overnight and rub it (free of husk). Put it over a hot fire; when it is boiling, put in sufficient oil and a small bundle of dill, dried onion, savory and a knuckle ham bone so that they may cook there to produce a liquor. Put in green coriander and salt which have been pounded together and bring it to heat. When it is simmering, remove the bundle and transfer the barley soup to another pan in such a way that the bottom of the pan does not touch (the coals) and so burn. Smooth it well and pass it through a sieve into the pan, over the top of the ham bone. Pound pepper, lovage, a little dry pennyroyal, cumin and pounded *silphium*.[3] So that it is well covered pour on honey, vinegar, *defrutum*, *liquamen*. Pour back into the pan; but bring the ham bone to heat over a gentle fire.

5.5.2. Another barley soup: soak chick peas, lentils and peas; crush barley and boil it with the vegetables. When they are well boiled, add sufficient oil and chop (these) greens into it: leek, coriander, dill, fennel, beet (leaves), mallow, tender cabbage; chop the greens finely and put them in the pan. Boil (more) cabbage and pound a good quantity of fennel seed, oregano, *silphium* and lovage. After

---

[1] We bracket *concicla farsilis*, 'pease mould', which may be a mis-placed part of the title, as in *pisam farsilem*, 5.3.2.

[2] The repetition of *tisanam et alicam* is most likely scribal error.

[3] With some variations (addition of honey, use of *caccabo* for *caccabulo*), this is a repeat recipe from 4.4.1. See note on that recipe. There, *silfi frictum* clearly means *silphium* (so Vehling). This phrase appears here as *silfrictum* in the MSS. *Pace FR*, who follow Brandt, we do not think that the interpretation of *sil* to indicate sesely (cf. *sil montanum*, 3.5; *silis Gallici*) is warranted, much less *tordyle grillé* (André).

semen satis, origanum silfi ligusticum. postquam triueris, liquamine temperas et super legumina refundis. agitas. coliculorum minutas super concidis.

VI. FABACIAE VIRIDES ET BAIANAE.

[5.6.1] **fabaciae uirides**: ex liquamine oleo coriandro uiridi cumino et porro conciso cocte inferuntur.

[5.6.2] **aliter**: fabaciæ fricte ex liquamine inferuntur.

[5.6.3] **aliter**: fabaciae ex sinapi trito melle nucleis ruta cumino; ex aceto inferuntur.

[5.6.4] **Baianas**: elixas minutatim concidis. ruta apio uiridi porro aceto oleo liquamine careno uel passo modico inferes.

VII. FENUM GRECUM. fenum Grecum ex liquamine oleo et uino.

VIII. FASEOLI ET CICER.

[5.8.1] **faseoli uirides et cicer**: ex sale cumino oleo et mero modico inferuntur.

[5.8.2] **aliter faseolus siue cicer**: frictos ex oenogaro et pipere gustabis. et elixati sumpto semine cum ouis in patella, feniculo uiride piper et liquamine et careno modico pro salso inferuntur, uel simpliciter, ut solet.

EXPLICIT APICI OSPREON LIBER
QVINTVS

3.FABACIĘ *E* | BAIANĘ *E*: BAGANAE *V*   4. fabacię *E*   5. concis *E*
6. fabacię *V*   7. fabaciæ *E* | ex aceto *VE*: et aceto *Hum*   9. bainas *E1* | opio
uiridi *E*   11. GREGVM *V*   12. FASIOLI *V*   13. faseoleo *E1*
15. fasiolus *E* | piperere *V* | elixati *Hum*: elixatis *V, E2*: elaxatis *E1*   16. sumto *E* | uiridi *Hum*
17. pro sal *VI* | simpliter *E* | ut *Tor*: et *VE*   18. APICII *E* | OSPREON *Ven*: OSPREO *VE*
19. V *V*

you have ground them, flavour them with *liquamen* and pour back over the vegetables and stir. Chop the cabbage finely and sprinkle over.[1]

5.6. GREEN BEANS AND BAIAN BEANS.
5.6.1. **Green beans**: serve cooked in a dressing of *liquamen*, oil, green coriander, cumin, and chopped leek.

5.6.2. **Alternatively**: fry the beans and serve them in *liquamen*.

5.6.3. **Alternatively**: serve the beans (cooked) in some pounded mustard, honey, pine nuts, rue, cumin; serve with vinegar.

5.6.4. **Baian beans**:[2] boil and chop finely. Serve in a sauce of rue, green celery, leek, vinegar, oil, *liquamen*, *caroenum* or a little *passum*.

5.7. FENUGREEK: dress fenugreek with *liquamen*, oil and wine.

5.8. BLACK-EYED PEAS AND CHICK PEAS.
5.8.1. **Fresh black-eyed peas or chick peas**: serve with salt, cumin, oil, and a little pure wine.

5.8.2. **Another black-eyed pea or chick pea recipe**: fried, they will taste nice in some *oenogarum* and pepper. They are served boiled in place of salt fish[3] with their seeds set to one side,[4] with eggs in a patella, with green fennel, pepper, *liquamen*, and a little *caroenum*, or plainly, as is common.

HERE ENDS BOOK FIVE OF APICIUS, 'PULSES'

---

[1] This recipe is almost word-for-word that found at 4.4.2. See the Introduction, p. 22, for a discussion of the implications of duplication of recipes.

[2] It is not known what sort of beans 'Baian' ones were, but the name may have passed from Latin via Old French *baien* into English, 'bean' (so Dalby, *Food in the Ancient World*, p. 49). The *Oxford English Dictionary*, however, states that bean comes from Old Norse. Presumably a variety of broad bean is meant.

[3] Or perhaps 'as a relish'.

[4] Or possibly 'with the seeds removed'. It is also possible that the removed seeds, with the eggs, are the replacement for the salt fish.

BOOK SIX

INCIPIT \<EIVSDEM> TROPETES LIBER SEXTVS

I. in struthione. II. in grue uel anatae perdice turture palumbo columbo et diuersis auibus. III. in turdis. IIII. in fecetulis. V. in pauo. VI. in fasiano. VII. in ansere.
5 VIII. in pullo.

I. IN STRVTIONE.

[6.1.1] **in strutione elixo**: piper mentam cuminum assum apii semen dactilos uel careotas mel acetum passum liquamen et oleum modice, et in caccabo facies ut bulliat. amulo obligas, et sic partes strutionis in lance perfundis, et desuper piper
10 aspargis. si autem in condituram coquere uolueris, alicam addis.

[6.1.2] **aliter in struthione elixo**: piper ligusticum tymum aut satureiam, mel sinape acetum liquamen et oleum.

II. IN GRVE VEL ANATAE PERDICE TVRTVRE PALVMBO COLVMBO ET DIVERSIS AVIBUS.

15 [6.2.1] **gruem uel anatem**: lauas uel ornas et includis in olla. adicies aquam salem anetum. dimidia coctura dequoques dum obduretur; leuas et iterum in caccabum mittis cum oleo et liquamine, cum fasciculo origani et coriandri. prope cocturam defritum modice mittis ut coloret. teres piper ligusticum cuminum coriandrum laseris radicem rutam carenum mel; suffundis ius de suo sibi, aceto
20 temperas. in caccabo reexinanies ut calefiat. amulo obligabis. inponis in lance et ius perfundis.

---

1. \<EIVSDEM. *CGSG* | TROPETIS *E (but cf. explicit to VI)*: TROPHETES *Ven*: AEROPETES *GiVo*   2. VI *E*   3. I in struthione *om. V, which then numbers* in grue. . .turture *as* I *and* palumbo. . .auibus *as* II, *and so on, in these chapter headings but not where they appear in the body of the text* | stutione *corr.* strutione *E* | anatẹ perdicẹ turturæ *E* | columbo *om. Milham* | *NB. in the text which follows, the contents of III, IIII, V and VI are missing from the MSS*
4. ficedulis *GiVo*: ficetulis *André* | fassiano *E*   6. INSTRVTIONE *V*: INSTRVCTIONE *E*
7. mentam *Hum*: menta *VE*   9. lace *E*   10. conditurum *E1*   11. in *PJ*: *om. VE*   12. sinape *corr.* sinaper *E*   13. ANATẸ *E* | COLVMBO *om. E*
15. anate *V* | uel *VE*: et *Gi*   16. lauas *E*   18. coleret *E*   20. reinanies *V1* | lamce *V*

BOOK SIX OF THE SAME, 'FOWL', BEGINS[1]

1. Sauces for ostrich. 2. Sauces for crane or duck, partridge, turtle-dove, wood-pigeon, dove and various other birds. 3. Sauces for thrushes. 4. Sauces for figpeckers. 5. Sauces for peacock. 6. Sauces for pheasant. 7. Sauces for goose. 8. Sauces for chicken.[2]

6.1. SAUCES FOR OSTRICH.

6.1.1. **Sauce for boiled ostrich**: pepper, mint, roasted cumin, celery seed, long or round dates,[3] honey, vinegar, *passum*, *liquamen* and a little oil. Put in a pan and bring to the boil. Thicken it with starch and in this state pour over the pieces of ostrich on a serving dish and sprinkle with pepper. If however you want to cook (the ostrich) in the sauce then add *alica*.

6.1.2. **Another sauce for boiled ostrich**: pepper, lovage, thyme or savory, honey, mustard, vinegar, *liquamen*, and oil.

6.2. SAUCES FOR CRANE OR DUCK, PARTRIDGE, TURTLE-DOVE, WOOD-PIGEON, DOVE, AND VARIOUS OTHER BIRDS.

6.2.1. **Crane or duck**: wash and dress (the bird) and put in a large cooking pot; add water, salt, dill; cook it until it is firm, half way through the cooking process; take it out and put it in another pan with oil and *liquamen* and with a bundle of oregano and coriander. When it is almost cooked add a little *defrutum* to add colour. Pound pepper, lovage, cumin, coriander, *laser* root, rue, *caroenum*, honey; pour on some of the cooking liquor, flavour with vinegar. Pour this back into the pan so that it warms through. Thicken with starch. Put the bird on a serving dish and pour the sauce over.

---

[1] The Latin is obscure: it perhaps comes from Greek *trophē* 'nurture or keeping of animals' and *trophopoios* 'rearing, bringing up' (Manetho 4. 244); cf. Columella 8.2.6, where he says that the normal Greek term for the raising of birds is *ornithotrophoia*.

[2] Sections 3, 4, 5 and 6 of this chapter are missing. They may have fitted into an entire gathering of text which has been omitted. The omission is also shown clearly by the marginal numbers next to the chapter headings in *VE*; only I, II and VIII survive. Previous editors have attempted to adjust the extant recipes to fit the surviving headings at the start of the book. We have re-numbered their sections 3, 4, 5, 6 consecutively as section 2.

[3] Lit. 'finger-dates' and 'nut-shaped dates'. This is the only occasion in which a choice of date is given. *dactylus* means 'date' in general, while *caryota* was the name for a variety native to Syria and Egypt. Cf. Pliny, *HN*. 15.116.

[6.2.2] **in grue in anate uel in pullo**: piper cepam siccam ligusticum cuminum apii semen pruna uel damascena enucleata mustum acetum liquamen defritum oleum et coques. gruem cum coquis, caput eius aquam non contingat, sed sit foris ab aqua. cum cocta fuerit, de sauano calido inuolues gruem et caput eius trahe
5   cum neruis: sequetur ut pulpe uel ossa remaneant; cum neruis enim manducare non potest.

[6.2.3] **gruem uel anatem ex rapis**: lauas, ornas et in olla elixabis cum aqua sale et aneto dimidia coctura. rapas quoque, ut exbromari possint. leuabis de olla et iterum lauabis, et in caccabum mittis anatem cum oleo et liquamine et
10   fasciculo porri et coriandri. rapam lotam et minutatim concisam desuper mittis, facies ut quoquatur. modica coctura mittis defritum ut coloret. ius tale parabis: piper cuminum coriandrum laseris radicem; suffundis acetum et ius de suo sibi; reexinanies super anatem ut ferueat. cum ferbuerit, amulo obligabis et super rapas adicies. piper aspargis et adponis.

15   [6.2.4] **aliter in gruem uel anatem elixam**: piper ligusticum cuminum coriandrum; siccam mentam origanum nucleos; careotam liquamen oleum mel sinape et uinum.

[6.2.5] **aliter gruem uel anatem**: assas, eas de hoc iure perfundis: teres piper ligusticum origanum liquamen mel aceti modicum et olei. ferueat bene. mittis
20   amulum et supra ius rotulas cucurbitę elixe uel colocasiæ ut bulliant. si sunt et ungellae quoques et iecinera pullorum. in boletari piper minutum adspargis et inferes.

[6.2.6] **aliter in grue uel anate elixa**: piper ligusticum apii semen erucam et coriandrum mentam careotam; mel acetum liquamen defritum et sinape. idem
25   faciet et [si] in [caccabo] assas.

1. capam *E* | cumiminum *E*   2. uel *del. Hum.* | mustum *VE*: mulsum *GiVo*. 3. gruem ζ: grue *VE* | aquam *CGSG*: aqua quam *VE* | tingat *V*   4. ab aquam *V* | callido *V*
5. ut in pulpe *V*   6. postest *E1*   7. elixabis *BPJ*: exiliabis *VE*   8. lauabis *E*
9. anetem *V1*   13. ferbuerit *E2*: feruuerit *V, E1*   15. grue *E* | anatem in elixam ligusticum piper cuminum *V*   16. siccam *CGSG*: siccum *VE*   20. cucurbite *V* |
colocas *V*   21. ungellę *E*: ungellas *Sch* | coques *E*: *this word put after* pullorum *Milham* | iocinerea *E1*: iocinera *E2* | boletario *E*   23. alixa *E* | eruca *V*   24. coriandrum ζ: coriandri *VE* | menta *V* | cariotam *E* | defrictum *V*   25 14. faciet *VE*: facies *λ* | si *del. CGSG* | caccabo *del. CGSG*

6.2.2. Sauce for crane, duck or chicken: pepper, dried onion, lovage, cumin, celery seed, stoned plums or damsons, must, vinegar, *liquamen*, *defrutum*, oil; cook this. When you cook the crane its head should not touch the water but should stand clear of the water. When it is cooked, wrap the crane in a hot towel and pull the head off with its sinews: the result will be that the flesh and bones will be left behind; it is impossible to eat it with its sinews left in.

6.2.3. Crane or duck with turnip: wash and dress (the bird) and boil in a large cooking pot in water, salt and dill until it is half cooked. Cook some turnips by bringing them to the boil and draining them immediately.[1] Lift the bird from the pot and wash it again and put it in a pan with oil and *liquamen* and a bundle of leek and coriander. Rinse the turnip, chop it finely and put it in on top, then set it to cook. When it is cooked a little more, add *defrutum* to add colour. Prepare this kind of sauce: pepper, cumin, coriander, *laser* root; pour on vinegar and some of the cooking liquor, pour back over the duck and bring to heat. When it is simmering, thicken with starch and add turnip over the top. Sprinkle with pepper and serve.[2]

6.2.4. Another recipe for boiled crane or duck: pepper, lovage, cumin, coriander, dried mint, oregano, pine nuts, dates, *liquamen*, oil, honey, mustard and wine.

6.2.5. Another recipe for crane or duck: roast them and pour this sauce over them: pound pepper, lovage, oregano, *liquamen*, honey, a little vinegar, and oil; simmer thoroughly. Put in starch and (add) into the sauce slices of boiled gourd or taro so that they boil together. If available, add cooked chicken legs and chicken livers. Sprinkle with finely ground pepper in a dish and serve.

6.2.6. Another recipe for boiled crane or duck: pepper, lovage, celery seed, rocket and coriander, mint, date, honey, vinegar, *liquamen*, *defrutum* and mustard. It is equally suitable for roast (birds).[3]

---

[1] *exbromare*. See 2.2.9, and the Introduction, p. 92, for a fuller discussion of this obscure term.

[2] Some of the diced and cooked turnip is likely to have been held back for this purpose. Duck braised with turnips in a sweetened sauce is a classic French recipe.

[3] The MSS read '*et si in caccabo assas*'. A *caccabus* is a cooking pot for liquids and regardless of whether *assas* means 'roast' or 'grill', neither action can be performed in a such a vessel. There is no evidence that *assas* could ever mean 'braise', as *FR* have suggested: it is a dry form of cooking. It is quite possible that someone has taken *assas* to be a 2nd sing. verb, rather than a 'recipe accusative', and made up the putative sense with *si* and *caccabo* without comprehending that you cannot roast in the equivalent of a Roman saucepan (though note the use of *caccabina* for dishes similar to *patinae* in the *Excerpta Vinidarii* 2 and 3, which may explain the confusion).

[6.2.7] **in perdice et attagena et in turture elixis**: piper ligusticum apii semen mentam mirtae bacas uel uuam passam mel uinum acetum liquamen et oleum. uteris frigido.

[6.2.8] **perdicem**: cum pluma sua elixas ibi et madefactam depilabis. perdices coctura: occisa perdix potest ex iure coqui, ne indurescat. si dierum fuerit, elixa quoqui debet.

[6.2.9] **in perdice et attagena et in turture**: piper ligusticum mentam rutae semen; liquamen merum et oleum. calefacies.

[6.2.10] **in palumbis columbis auibus in altile et in fenicoptero. in assis**: piper ligusticum coriandrum careum cepam siccam mentam oui uitellum careotam mel acetum liquamen oleum et uinum.

[6.2.11] **aliter in elixis**: piper careum apii semen petrosilenum condimenta mortaria; careotam mel acetum uinum oleum et sinape.

[6.2.12] **aliter**: piper ligusticum petrosilenum apii semen rutam nucleos; careotam mel acetum liquamen sinape et oleum modice.

[6.2.13] **aliter**: piper ligusticum laser uiuum; suffundis liquamen; uino et liquamine temperabis, et mittis super columbum uel palumbum. piper adspersum inferes.

[6.2.14] **ius in diuersis auibus**: piper cuminum frictum ligusticum mentam uuam passam enucleatam aut damascena; mel modice. uino myrto temperabis, aceto liquamine et oleo. calefacies et agitabis apio et satureia.

[6.2.15] **aliter ius in auibus**: piper petrosilenum ligusticum mentam siccam cneci flos; uino suffundis, adicies ponticam uel amigdala tosta, mel modicum; uino et aceto; liquamine temperabis. oleum in pultarium super ius mittis, calefacies, ius agitabis apio uiridi et nepeta. incaraxas et perfundis.

1. perdiciẹ *E* | adtagenea *E1*: adtagena *E2* | *Vo. added* in perdice *after* elixis   2. mirtae *André*: myrtae *Sch*: mirtam et *VE, E2 clarifying poorly-written* r *in E1* | mel *Hum*: uel *VE*   4. elixas ibi et *V*: elixias ibi et *E*: elixabis et *Hum*   4-5. perdices coctura *del. GiVo*   5. si III dierum *Bra1*   6. coqui *V*   7. rutæ *E*   9. palumbus *E* | auibus …fenicoptero *del. Sch*   10. coriamdrum *V1*   11. oleum et uinum *V2* *?over an erasure*   12. in λ: *om. VE* | condimenta *Hum*: condimentam *E*: condimentum *V*   13. mortaria *V*: moretaria *E* | cariotam *E*   14. alite *E1* | ruta *V* | cariotam *E*   15. modicẹ *E*   16. laserum uinum *V* | liquamine *V*   17. adspersum *V*: adspersum *corr.* asspersum *(or vice versa?) E*   20. damascenam *V* | myrto *VE*: myrtheo *Hum*: myrteo *Milham*   21. liquamen *V* | et satureia *om. E1*   22. petroselinum *E* | cneci *Sch*: eneci *VE*: aneti *P, Hum*   23. modicum <cum> uino *GiVo*   24. et ceto *E1* | liquamen *Milham*   25. *?*apiio *E1* | uirido *corr.* uiride *E*

6.2.7.[1] **Sauce for boiled partridge, francolin,**[2] **and turtle-dove**: pepper, lovage, celery seed, mint, myrtle berries or raisins, honey, wine, vinegar, *liquamen*, and oil. Use cold.[3]

6.2.8. Partridge: boil it with its feathers on and pluck it there and then while it is wet. How to cook partridge: freshly killed partridge can be cooked with its sauce so that it does not become tough. If it has been killed for more than a day it must be boiled.

6.2.9. Sauce for partridge, francolin and turtle-dove: pepper, lovage, mint, rue berries, *liquamen*, pure wine and oil. Warm it up.

6.2.10. Wood-pigeon, pigeon, fattened birds and flamingo. Sauce for roasted birds: pepper, lovage, coriander, caraway, dried onion, mint, egg yolk, date, honey, vinegar, *liquamen*, oil and wine.

6.2.11. Another sauce for boiled birds: pepper, caraway, celery seed, parsley; these are the mortar spices;[4] date, honey, vinegar, wine, oil and mustard.

6.2.12. Another sauce: pepper, lovage, parsley, celery seed, rue, pine nuts, date, honey, vinegar, *liquamen*, mustard, and a little oil.

6.2.13. Another sauce: pepper, lovage, fresh *laser*; pour on *liquamen*; flavour with wine and *liquamen* and pour over the turtle-dove or pigeon. Sprinkle with pepper and serve.

6.2.14. Sauce for various birds: pepper, roasted cumin, lovage, mint, de-seeded raisins or damsons, a little honey. Flavour with myrtle wine, vinegar, *liquamen* and oil. Bring it to heat and stir it with a stick of celery and savory.

6.2.15. Another sauce for birds: pepper, parsley, lovage, dried mint, safflower; pour on wine, add roasted hazelnuts or almonds, a little honey, wine, vinegar; flavour it with *liquamen*. Pour oil over the sauce in the pan, warm it through, stir the sauce with green celery and catmint. Make cuts in the flesh and pour the sauce on.[5]

---

[1] See p. 223 n. 2 above for an explanation of the numbering here.

[2] Common in the ancient Mediterranean as far west as Italy, but now confined to the Near East. A marsh bird: see Dalby, *Food in the Ancient World*, p. 150.

[3] The spices are roasted but the rest of the ingredients are unheated.

[4] *mortaria*: the term is also found at 10.2.11. We do not think this is related to the mixture at 1.45. The interesting point is that the ingredients that come after the *condimenta mortaria* in both recipes are not spices but other fruits and liquids: the position of the term is all-important and allows it to define rather than designate an ingredient. We therefore feel that the term is a definition of what has come before. See the Glossary, *condimentum*.

[5] See 6.8.2 for a more detailed method: the bird is par-boiled, cut and then roasted with the sauce.

[6.2.16] **ius candidum in auem elixam**: piper ligusticum cuminum apii semen ponticam uel amigdalam tostam uel nuces depilatas, mel modicum, liquamen acetum et oleum.

[6.2.17] **ius uiride in auibus**: piper careum spicam Indicam cuminum folium, condimenta uiridia omne genus, dactilum; mel acetum uinum modice, liquamen et oleum.

[6.2.18] **ius candidum in ansere elixo**: piper careum cuminum apii semen tymum cepam laseris radicem nucleos tostos; mel acetum liquamen et oleum.

[6.2.19] **ad aues hyrcosas omni genere**: piper ligusticum tymum mentam aridam caluam careotam; mel acetum uinum liquamen oleum defritum sinape. auem sapidiorem et altiliorem facies et ei pinguedinem seruabis si eam farina oleo subacta contextam in furnum miseris.

[6.2.20] **aliter auem**: in uentrem eius fractas oliuas nouas mittis et consutam sic elixabis; deinde coctas oliuas eximes.

[6.2.21] **in fenicoptero**: fenicopterum eliberas, lauas, ornas, includis in caccabum; adicies aquam salem anetum et aceti modicum. dimidia coctura alligas fasciculum porri et coriandri ut coquatur. prope cocturam defritum mittis, coloras. adicies in mortarium piper cuminum coriandrum laseris radicem mentam rutam, fricabis. suffundis acetum, adicies caroenum, ius de suo sibi perfundis. reexinanies in eundem caccabum, amulo obligas. ius perfundis et inferes. idem facies et in psittato.

[6.2.22] **aliter**: assas auem, teres piper ligusticum apii semen sesamum frictum petrosilenum mentam cepam siccam careotam; melle uino liquamine aceto oleo, et defrito temperabis.

[6.2.23] **aues omnes ne liquescant**: cum plumis elixare omnibus melius erit. prius tamen extenterantur per guttur uel inania sublata.

2. amygdala tosta *GiVo* | depeletas *V*   3. accetum *E*   4. uirede *E1* | spicam Indicam *Sch*: spica indica *VE*   5. condimenti *E1* | acętum *E* | modicę *E*   9. hircosas *P* | omni genere *T1*: omnigere *VE* | menta *E*   10. liqumeno leum *E1* | defritum *GiVo*: defrictum *VE*   11. altiliorem *Sch*: altiorem *VE* | pinguidinem *E* | farina *Hum*: farinam *VE*   12. subacta *Hum*: subactam *VE* | contectam *Hum*   13. consutam *ξ*: cosutam *VE*   14. dein decoctas *V* | eximes *ξ*: eximens *VE*   15. eliberas *VE*: elixas *Hum*   17. ut coquatur *VE*: et coquatur *GiVo*   19. caroenum *CGSG*: caroetam *V*: careotam   23. cepam *V2*: cepi *V1*: capem *E* | careotam *V*: careotatm *E* | mele *E1*   25. elixare *Gi*: elixate *VE*: elixatae *Hum*: elixato *Sch*   26. inania sublata *CGSG*: in abias sublata *VE*: in ambiges sublatae *Hum*: a naui ac sub latera *Bas*: e naui assublatae *Bra3*

6.2.16. White sauce for boiled bird: pepper, lovage, cumin, celery seed, roasted hazelnuts or almonds or (any) skinned nut,[1] a little honey, *liquamen*, vinegar and oil.

6.2.17. Green sauce for birds: pepper, caraway, Indian nard, cumin, *folium,* any kind of green herb, date, honey, vinegar, a little wine, *liquamen* and oil.

6.2.18. White sauce for boiled goose: pepper, caraway, cumin, celery seed, thyme, onion, *laser* root, roasted pine nuts, honey, vinegar, *liquamen* and oil.

6.2.19. Sauce for any kind of well-hung bird: pepper, lovage, thyme, dried mint, *calua* nut,[2] date, honey, vinegar, wine, *liquamen*, oil, *defrutum*, mustard. You will make the bird richer and more flavoursome and you will retain its juices if you put it in the oven covered in a paste made of flour and oil.

6.2.20. Another recipe for bird: stuff its cavity with broken fresh olives, sew it up and boil it. Then take the cooked olives out.[3]

6.2.21. Sauce for flamingo: pluck, wash and dress the flamingo and put in pan; add water, salt, dill, and a little vinegar. Half-way through the cooking, bind up a bundle of leek and coriander to cook with it. Near the end of the cooking, add *defrutum* for colour. Put in a mortar pepper, cumin, coriander, *laser* root, mint, rue; pound. Pour on vinegar, add *caroenum*, pour on some of the cooking liquor. Pour back into the same pan, thicken with starch. Pour the sauce over the bird and serve. You also make the same sauce for parrot.

6.2.22. Another recipe: roast the bird, pound pepper, lovage, celery seed, roasted sesame seed, parsley, mint, dried onion, date, honey, wine, *liquamen*, vinegar, oil, and flavour it with *defrutum*.

6.2.23. To prevent all kinds of birds from going bad: it is better to boil all types of bird with their feathers. Beforehand however the cavity should be opened[4] at the neck end and the innards removed.

[1] *nuces* can refer to 'walnuts' but we are dealing with a white sauce here and they do not seem appropriate, especially as they are to be 'skinned'; to translate *depilatas* as 'shelled' is otiose – how else could they be used? Hazelnuts, whose brown skin could be rubbed off, might be appropriate. See the Glossary on 'nuts'.

[2] An otherwise unknown type of smooth-shelled nut: see Cato, *De agricultura* 8.2.

[3] Previous translations have implied that the olives should be thrown away. This is not very economical or sensible! The term *eximes* simply means 'remove them'. We would suggest that the dish would be finished with any of the sauces above or below, and the olives served in it or by the side of the bird.

[4] *extenterare* is also found at 7.5.3, 8.1.3, 8.7.1, and 8.7.5; the last two references are to a piglet and the others to bay berries. Adams, *Pelagonius*, p. 511, notes that 'it is an old-established verb, well-established … as early as Plautus'. See Introduction, p. 92.

< III, IIII, V, VI DESVNT >

<VII. IN ANSERE.>

anserem elixum calidum ex iure frigido Apiciano: teres piper ligusticum
coriandri semen mentam rutam; refundis liquamen et oleum modice, temperas.
5   anserem elixum feruentem sabano mundo exsiccabis, ius perfundis et inferes.

VIII. IN PULLO.

[6.8.1] **elixo ius crudum**: adicies in mortarium aneti semen mentam siccam
laseris radicem; suffundis acetum; adicies careotam, refundis liquamen senapis
modicum et oleum, defrito temperas et sic mittis.

10   [6.8.2] **pullum anetatum**: mellis modice, liquamine temperabis. leuas pullum
coctum et sabano mundo siccas; caraxas et ius scissuris infundis ut conuiuat, et
cum conuiuerit assabis et suo sibi iure pinnis tangis. piper aspersum inferes.

[6.8.3] **pullum Particum**: pullum aperies a naui et in quadrato ornas. teres
piper ligusticum carei modicum, suffunde liquamen, uino temperas. conponis
15   in cumana pullum et condituram super pullum facies. laser uiuum in tepida
dissoluis, et in pullum mittis simul et quoques. piper aspersum inferes.

[6.8.4] **pullum oxizomum**: olei acetabulum maiorem, <uini> satis modice,
liquaminis acetabulum minorem, aceti acetabulum perquam minorem, piperis
scripulos sex, petrosilenum scripulum, porros fasciculum.

20   [6.8.5] **pullum Numidicum**: pullum curas, elixas, leuas, laser ac piper <aspergis>
et assas. teres piper cuminum coriandri semen laseris radicem rutam careotam
nucleos; suffundis acetum mel liquamen et oleum; temperabis. cum ferbuerit,
amulo obligas, pullum perfundis, piper aspergis et inferes.

---

2. <VII. IN ANSERE> *Hum*   3. ex *G*: et *VE*   4. liquamine *E1*   7. VIII
in l/h marg. V | IN PVLLO <in pullo> *Hum*   8. sinapis *Hum*   9. defricto *V*
10. <aliter> pullum anethatum *Bra2* | modico et *GiVo* | leuas *Sch*: lauas *VE*   11. combibat *Hum*
12. cum conuiuerit V: cum uiuerit *E*: cum combiberit *Hum* | pinnis *VE*: penitus *Vo* | tangis *P*: tongis *V*:
ton.gis *E*: pertangis *Hum*   13. particum *E*: partium *V*   14. componis *V*   15. pulum
E1 | laser uiuum *Vo*: laser et uinum *VE* | in tepida *Bas*: interidas *VE*: radas *Sch*   16. coques *E*
17. oleum *E* | <uini> *CGSG*: <laseris> *Gi*: *lacuna André*   19. scripulis sex *V* | petrosilinum *E*
| scripulum *MD*: scriptulum *VE*   20. NVMIDVM *V* | leuas *Bra2*: lauas *VE* | laser ac *André*:
laseras *VE*: lasere ac *GiVo* | <aspergis> *GiVo*   22. ferbuerit *E2*: feruuerit *V, E1*

---

[1] *temperas* is normally translated as 'blend' but it can also mean to balance the flavours of a dish
with *liquamen* or some form of Roman wine. *Temperas* here stands alone; the *liquamen* and a little

(Sections 3, 4, 5, 6 are missing)

6.7. GOOSE.

Hot boiled goose in a cold Apician sauce: pound pepper, lovage, coriander seed, mint, rue; pour on *liquamen* and a little oil; balance the flavours.[1] Dry the hot boiled goose with a clean towel, pour the sauce on and serve.

6.8. CHICKEN.

6.8.1. **Uncooked sauce for boiled chicken**: put dill seed, dried mint, and *laser* root into a mortar, pour on vinegar, add date, pour on *liquamen*, a little mustard and oil, flavour with *defrutum* and use as it is.

6.8.2. **Chicken in dill sauce**: flavour (the above sauce) with a little honey and *liquamen*. Take the cooked chicken out of the pan and dry it with a clean towel. Make cuts in the flesh and pour the sauce into the cuts so that it absorbs it; and when it has absorbed it, roast it and baste it with the sauce using its feathers. Serve sprinkled with pepper.

6.8 3. **Parthian chicken**: draw the chicken from the rear and cut it into quarters. Pound pepper, lovage, a little caraway, pour on *liquamen*, flavour with wine. Arrange the chicken pieces in a ceramic dish, put the sauce over the chicken. Dissolve fresh *laser* in warm water[2] and put it straightaway on the chicken and cook it. Sprinkle with pepper and serve.

6.8.4. **Chicken in a sour sauce**: a generous cup of oil, just enough wine,[3] a small cup of *liquamen*, a very small cup of vinegar, 6 scruples of pepper, 1 scruple of parsley, and a bundle of leek.

6.8.5. **Numidian chicken**: prepare the chicken, (par-)boil it and lift it out; sprinkle with *laser* and pepper and roast it. Pound pepper, cumin, coriander seed, *laser* root, rue, date, pine nuts; pour on vinegar, honey, *liquamen* and oil; balance the flavours. When it comes to heat, thicken with starch, pour over the chicken, sprinkle with pepper and serve.

---

oil in the recipe are governed by *refundis* and so it appears to have been used in the simple sense of 'blend'; however the sauce has no sweetness or sharpness at all, which is very odd in a Roman sauce. Consequently we have translated the word with the added meaning 'balance the flavours', i.e. with a sweet wine or sharp vinegar as required.

[2] See the Glossary, *laser*, for discussion of the term *uiuum*.

[3] *satis modice* is an odd combination of qualifying instructions, which we interpret as being 'enough but a little'.

[6.8.6] **pullum laseratum**: pullum aperies a nabi, lauabis, ornabis et in cumana ponis. teres piper ligusticum laser uiuum, suffundis liquamen, uino et liquamine temperabis, et mittis pullum. coctus si fuerit, piper aspersum inferes.

[6.8.7] **pullum paroptum**: laseris modicum, piperis scripulos sex, olei
5 acetabulum, liquaminis acetabulum, petrosileni modice.

[6.8.8] **pullum elixum ex iure suo**: teres piper cuminum timi modicum feniculi semen mentam rutam laseris radicem; suffundis acetum, adicies careotam et teres. melle aceto liquamine et oleo temperabis. pullum refrigeratum et mittis siccatum, quem perfusum inferes.

10 [6.8.9] **pullum elixum cum cucurbitis elixis**: iure supra scripto, addito sinape, perfundis et inferes.

[6.8.10] **pullum elixum cum cologasiis elixis**: supra scripto iure perfundis et inferes. farcies inelixum etiam oliuis columbaribus, non ualde ita ut laxamentum habeat ne dissiliat dum quoquitur in ollam submissus in sportellam. cum bullierit,
15 frequenter leuas et ponis ne dissiliat.

[6.8.11] **pullus Vardanus**: pullum quoques iure hoc: liquamine oleo uino fasciculum porri coriandri satureiae; cum coctus fuerit teres piper; nucleos ciatos duos et ius de suo sibi subfundis et fasciculos proicies. lac temperas et reexinanies [in] mortarium supra pullum, ut ferueat. obligas eundem aluamentis
20 ouorum tritis, ponis in lance et iure supra scripto perfundis. hoc ius candidum appellatur.

[6.8.12] **pullum Frontonianum**: pullum praedura, condies liquamine oleo mixto, cui mittis fasciculum aneti porri satureiae et coriandri uiridis, et quoques. ubi coctus fuerit leuabis eum, in lance defrito perungues, piper aspargis et inferes.

---

1. RASSERATVM *V* | aperies *Hum*: asperges *VE* | in ⹂ *om. VE*   5. petroselini *E* | modicę *E*
8. melle *VE*: mel *Hum* | et oleo *D*: ex oleo *VE* | siccatum mittis *Hum*   11. perfundis
Hum: piper fundis *VE*   12. cologasiis *VE*: colocasiis *TP*   13. farcies inelixum
etiam *CGSG*: facit et in elixam et in *VE*: facis et in elixa et in *Vo*: *lacuna after* et in *André*,
with two recipes combined | columbaribus *V*: columbaribis *E*: columbadibus *Hum*: *lacuna after*
this word Vo   14. coquitur *E* | olla *T* | sportella *GiVo*   15. leuas *Sch*: lauas *VE*
16. Varianus *Hum* | coques *E*   17. <cui mittis> fasciculum *GiVo* | satureiae *Hum*: satureia *VE*
18. suffundis *E*   19. in *del. Sch*   21. apellatur *E1*   22. Frotitonianum
E1   23. satureiae ⹂ satureia *VE* | coques *E*   24. leuabis *Hum*: lauabis *VE*

---

[1] We have emended the MSS readings considerably here: the text is very corrupt. We assume that *columbaribus* is an odd spelling for *oliuae columbades*, 'olives in brine', hence 'preserved olives',

6.8.6. Chicken in a *laser* sauce: draw the chicken from the rear, wash it and dress it and arrange in a ceramic dish. Pound pepper, lovage, fresh *laser*, pour on *liquamen*, flavour with wine and *liquamen* and put over the chicken. When it is cooked, serve sprinkled with pepper.

6.8.7. Roast chicken: a little *laser*, 6 scruples of pepper, a cup of oil, a cup of *liquamen*, a little parsley.

6.8.8. Chicken boiled in its own sauce: pound pepper, cumin, a little thyme, fennel seed, mint, rue, *laser* root; pour on vinegar, add date and pound. Flavour with honey, vinegar, *liquamen* and oil. Cool and dry the chicken and serve in the sauce.

6.8.9. Boiled chicken with boiled gourds: pour the sauce written above, with the addition of mustard, over the chicken and serve.

6.8.10. Boiled chicken with boiled taros: pour over the sauce written above and serve. You can also stuff the un-boiled bird with preserved olives,[1] but not with too many, so that some space remains and it does not burst while it is cooking in the pot, lowered there in a basket. When it is boiling lift it out and replace it frequently so that it does not burst.[2]

6.8.11. Vardanian chicken:[3] cook the chicken with this sauce: a bundle of leek, coriander and savory, in *liquamen*, oil, wine; when it is cooked, pound pepper, two cups of pine nuts, and pour on the cooking liquor and discard the bundle. Blend with milk and pour the contents of the mortar over the chicken and bring it to heat. Thicken it with beaten white of egg. Place the chicken on a serving dish and pour the sauce written above over it. This is called a white sauce.

6.8.12. Frontonian chicken: sear the outside of the chicken, flavour with a mixture of *liquamen* and oil, to which you add a bundle of dill, leek, savory and green coriander and cook it. When it is cooked, lift it out, drizzle *defrutum* over it on the serving dish, sprinkle with pepper and serve.

---

from the Greek *kolumbades elaai*. See for example Athenaeus 56b; Dalby, *Food in the Ancient World*, p. 238.

[2] 6.8.10 has been interpreted as two recipes by *FR* and André. It is very poorly preserved, yet does make more sense gathered together as one recipe. It seems to be referring to a galantine rather than to a whole chicken. An un-boned chicken would not be in danger of bursting, while one completely free of bone and possibly stitched together would certainly need this special treatment. See recipe 6.8.15 of this chapter where there are obscure instructions at the end of the recipe to bone the capon or chicken required.

[3] Presumably named after a 'Vardanus'; see Appendix 3.

[6.8.13] **pullus tractogalatus**: pullum quoques liquamine oleo uino, cui mittis fasciculum coriandri, cepam. deinde cum coctus fuerit leuabis eum de iure suo et mittis in caccabum nouum lac et salem modicum, mel et aquae minimum, id est tertiam partem. ponis ad ignem lentum ut tepescat; tractum confringis et

5   mittis paulatim; assidue agitas ne uratur. pullum illic mittis integrum uel carptum, uersabis in lance, quem perfundis ius tale: piper ligusticum origanum; suffundis mel et defritum modicum et ius de suo sibi. temperas. in caccabulo facies ut bulliat. cum bullierit, amulo obligas et inferes.

[6.8.14] **pullus farsilis**: pullum sicut in iure cuminato. a ceruice expedies. teres

10   piper ligusticum gengiber pulpam cesam aliquam elixam, teres cerebellum ex iure coctum. oua confringis et commiscis ut unum corpus efficias. liquamine temperas et oleum modice; mittis piper integrum, nucleos abundantes. fac inpensam et imples pullum uel porcellum ita ut laxamentum habeat. similiter in capo facies. ossibus eiectis coques.

15   [6.8.15] **pullus leocozumus**: accipies pullum et ornas ut supra. aperies illum a pectore. †...accipiat aquam et oleum Spanum abundans. agitatur ut ex se amulet et humorem consumat...† postea, cum coctus fuerit, quodcumque porri remanserit inde leuas. piper aspargis et inferes.

EXPLICIT TROPETES LIBER SEXTUS

1. quoques *V, E1*: coques *E2* | oleum *V*   2. leuabis *Hum*: lauabis *VE*   3. aquę minimum *E*: aquam eminimum *V*   4. id est . . partem *del. Bra2*   5. adsiduę *E* | carptum *Hum*: cariotum *VE*   7. defritum *Hum*: defrito *VE*   9. farsilis *Hum*: fusilis *VE* | sicut in iure cuminato *CGSG*: sicut ilique cuminatum *VE*: sicuti liquaminatum *Bra3* | acer uice *VE*   10. gingiber *E* | pulpam *P*: pulpem *V2,E*: pulpe *V1* | aliquam *VE*: alicam *ζ*   14. capo *Ven*: capso *VE*   15. *VE place* pullus leocozomus *after* a pectore: *Lis puts these words before* accipies | *obeli and lacunae CGSG*   16. spanus *E* 17. amulet *Bas*: ambulet *VE* | porro *P, GiVo*   18. leues *E*   19. VI *E*

---

[1] The first sauce in this recipe seems to be rather thick: the suggestion that it might burn implies as much. The chicken and first sauce are poured out together in one go implying that it binds the chicken into one mass. The second sauce is also thickened with starch but would be relatively clear and cover the first one with a glossy sheen.

[2] Our conjecture here attempts to make *some* sense of the MSS reading *sicut ilique cuminatum*. The problem with the recipe is that neither cumin nor a sauce are indicated in the recipe itself, and if we try to imitate the pattern of instructions found in other recipes, a sauce is needed. *cuminatum* is also referred to in 1.29, 2.4.6, 3.21.3, 4.2.10. *FR*, André and Milham all follow Brandt, who

6.8.13. Chicken cooked with milk and *tracta*: cook the chicken in *liquamen*, oil, and wine, to which you add a bundle of coriander, and onion. Then when it is cooked, lift it from the cooking liquor. Then put in a new pan milk, a little salt, honey and a little water: that is, a third of the volume. Put it on a gentle fire so that it warms through. Crumble *tracta* and sprinkle them in gradually, stir constantly so that it does not burn. Put the chicken in whole or jointed. Turn out on to a serving dish and pour on this kind of sauce:[1] pepper, lovage, oregano; pour on honey and a little *defrutum* and some of the cooking liquor. Balance the flavours. Bring to the boil in the pan. When it has boiled, thicken with starch and serve.

6.8.14. Stuffed chicken:[2] the chicken (is prepared) as if (served) with a cumin sauce. Draw the chicken from the neck, pound pepper, lovage, ginger, chopped meat, boiled *alica,* pounded brains cooked in stock; break eggs and stir them all to make a smooth mixture. Flavour with *liquamen* and a little oil, add whole peppercorns and plenty of pine nuts. Make the stuffing and fill the chicken or piglet in such a way that some space remains. You can do the same with a capon. Cook with the bones taken out.

6.8.15. Chicken in a white sauce:[3] take a chicken and dress as above. Open the bird at the breast. †...let it have water and plenty of Spanish oil,[4] shake it so that it thickens itself and takes away the humours....† Afterwards, when it is cooked, take out any leek that happens to remain. Sprinkle with pepper and serve.[5]

HERE ENDS BOOK SIX, 'FOWL'

also found the Latin here unintelligible and changed it to an otherwise unknown (and equally unintelligible) *liquamen* sauce. The offending phrase may be a gloss; certainly there seems no logical connection between cumin sauce and the way that the bird is prepared.

[3] From *leukos*, the Greek for 'white'.

[4] *Spanus* is Late Latin for *Hispanus* (found in the sixth-century poet Dioscurides, 4.45) but the form is also found as a substitute for *Hispanus* in Greek as early as the second century AD (Plutarch, *Sertorius* 11, etc.).

[5] This recipe has lost its central section and is beyond retrieval. The title bears no relation to the method, which is itself fragmentary. *consumere* has the meaning of 'use up' and might make sense if the dressing of oil and water is thickened by being shaken together, but this hardly seems possible if it is inside the chicken! The MSS *ambulet* is either a Late Latin variant spelling for *amulet*, with –mb– formed after the manner of words such as *plumbum* or *columba*, or an unfortunate misreading. The chicken's cavity was presumably stuffed with leek before cooking.

BOOK SEVEN

INCIPIT EIVSDEM POLITELES LIBER SEPTIMVS

I. uulue steriles callum libelli coticule et ungellae. II. sumen. III. ficatum. IIII. ofelle. V. assature. VI. in elixam et in copadiis. VII. uentricula. VIII. lumboli et
5   renes. VIIII. perna. X. iecinera siue pulmones. XI. dulcia domestica et melce. XII. uului. XIII. fungi farnei uel uoleti. XIIII. tubera. XV. in colacasio. XVI. cocleas. XVII. oua.

I. VVLVE STERILES CALLVM LIBELLI COTICULE ET VNGELLE.
[7.1.1] **uuluæ steriles**: laser [uuluas et apices politeles liber VII] Cirenaicum
10   uel Particum, aceto et liquamine temperato adpones.

[7.1.2] **in uulua [et] sterile**: piper apii semen mentam siccam laseris radicem mel acetum et liquamen.

[7.1.3] **uulue [et] steriles**: piper et liquamine cum lasere Partico adponis.

[7.1.4] **uulue steriles**: piper liquamine et condito modico adponis.
15   [7.1.5] **callum, libelli, coticulæ, ungelle**: cum piper liquamine lasere adponis.

[7.1.6] **uuluam ut tostam facies**: in cantabro inuolue et postea in muria mitte et sic quoque.

II. SUMEN.
[7.2.1] sumen elixas, de cannis surclas, sale adspargis et in furnum mittis uel
20   in graticulam. subassas. teres piper ligusticum; liquamen mero et passo; amulo obligas et sumen perfundis.

1-2. LIBER OCT SEPTIMVS *V*: LIBER VII *E*   3. uulue *CGSG, see usage in 7.1*: uulua *VE*: uuluae *GiVo* | labelli *André* | coticule *V1* | ungelle *E*   4. lumbi *E*   5. iocinera *E* 6. bulbi *E* | boleti *E* | in colocasio *Milham*: incola casio *V*: incola cassia *E*: in colocasia *André*   8. COCTICVLE *V1* | VNGELLE *E*: VNGVLE *V*   9. uulue *V* | laser uuluas et apices politeles liber VII *V,E1, del. E2*   10. Parthicum *E*   11. et *om. D* | sterili *GiVo* | mentem *E1*   13. et *om. D* | piper et *VE*: pipere *Milham* | cum *om. V* | laceri *V* | Parthico *E*   14. uuluae steriles *E2*: uulue et steriles *V,E1* | pipere *E*   15. cocticule *V* | cum *om. V* | pipere *E*   16. facias *D* | muriam *GiVo*   17. quoque *V, E1*: coque *E2* 20. craticulam *E*

---

¹ *libellus* is unknown as a foodstuff in ancient texts, and is more familiar as a 'little book' or a 'leaf' of papyrus, the reed-like plant used by the Egyptians for making writing material. However, we think it refers to the type of tripe known today as 'leaf, book or bible' tripe which is the third

BOOK SEVEN OF THE SAME, 'LUXURY DISHES', BEGINS

1. Sterile wombs, crackling, beef tripe, ribs, trotters. 2. Udders. 3. Fig-fattened liver. 4. *Ofellae.* 5. Grills or roasts. 6. Sauces for boiled meat and meat morsels. 7. Stomach. 8. Testicles and kidneys. 9. Ham. 10. Liver and lights. 11. Home-made sweets and curds. 12. Bulbs. 13. Ash-tree fungi or mushrooms. 14. Truffles. 15. Sauce for taro. 16. Snails. 17. Eggs.

7.1. STERILE WOMBS, CRACKLING, BEEF TRIPE,[1] RIBS AND TROTTERS.

7.1.1. **Sterile wombs**: *laser* from Cyrenaica or Parthia; serve it flavoured with vinegar and *liquamen.*

7.1.2. **Sauce for sterile womb**: pepper, celery seed, dry mint, *laser* root, honey, vinegar and *liquamen.*

7.1.3. **Sterile wombs**: serve with pepper, *liquamen*, Parthian *laser.*

7.1.4. **Sterile wombs**: serve with pepper, *liquamen*, and a little spiced wine.

7.1.5. **Crackling, beef tripe, ribs, trotters**: serve with pepper, *liquamen* and *laser.*

7.1.6. **To make roast womb**:[2] roll the womb in bran after you have put it in brine and then cook it.[3]

7.2. UDDER.

7.2.1. Boil the udder, bind it with reeds, sprinkle with salt and put it in the oven or on the gridiron. Roast it a little. Pound pepper, lovage, *liquamen*, pure wine, and *passum,* thicken with starch and pour over the udder.

---

true stomach of a ruminant, also called *omasum* or *psalterium.*

[2] We have translated this term as 'roasted' but it usually occurs in relation to browning nuts or seeds and in this case may refer to the womb being grilled or pan-fried.

[3] The Latin appears to say that the womb is rolled in bran and then soaked in brine, which is totally illogical and a waste – the bran would simply wash off. The brine would act as a cleansing agent prior to the application of the bran, which would presumably form a crust if it was roasted. In the translation we have reversed the order in which the instructions occur, taking *postea* as the equivalent of *postquam*, even though it rather tortures the Latin to do so. It is quite possible that the cook could write or speak nothing but tortured Latin! See also 7.7.2, and the Introduction, p. 91.

[7.2.2] **sumen plenum**: teritur piper careum hecinus salsus; consuitur et sic quoquitur. manducatur cum allece sinape.

III. FICATUM.

[7.3.1] **in ficato oenogarum**: piper timum ligusticum; liquamen uinum modice
5 oleum.

[7.3.2] **aliter**: ficatum precidis ad cannam, infundis in liquamine, piper ligusticum bacas lauri duas. inuolues in omento et in graticula assas et inferes.

IIII. OFELLE.

[7.4.1] **ofellas Ostienses [in ofillam]**: designas ofellas in cute, ita ut cutis sic
10 remaneat. teres piper ligusticum anetum cuminum silfium bacam lauri unam; suffundis liquamen, fricas; in angularem refundis simul cum obellis. ubi requieuerint in condimentis biduo uel triduo, ponis, surclas decusatim, et in furnum mittis. cum coxeris, ofellas quas designaueras separabis, et teres piper ligusticum, suffundis liquamen et passum modicum ut dulce fiat. cum ferbuerit,
15 ius amulo obligas, ofellas satias et inferes.

[7.4.2] **ofellas Apicianas**: ofellas exossas, in rotundum conplicas, surclas, ad furnum admoues. postea preduras, leuas; ut humorem exspuant in graticula igni lento exsiccabis ita ne urantur. teres piper ligusticum ciperis cuminum; liquamen et passo temperabis. cum hoc iure ouellas in caccabum mittis. cum coctæ fuerint,
20 leuas et siccas sine iure, piper asperso et inferes. si pingues fuerint, cum surclas, tollis cutem. potest et de abdomine huiusmodi ofellas facere.

[7.4.3] **ofellae aprogeneo more**: ex oleo liquamine condiuntur et mittitur eis condimentum cum cocte fuerint. et super adicitur his cum in foco sunt conditura, et denuo bulliunt: piper tritum condimentum mel liquamen; amulum cum iam

---

1. consuitur *Hum*: quosuitur *VE*   2. cum allece *Ven*: cum malleco *VE*   4. timu *E*
6. ad *V*: ut *E* | <teres> piper *Gi*   7. omento *Hum*: aucmento *VE* | craticula *E*
9. Ostienses *Hum*: otienses *VE* | in ofillam *del. Bas* | designas *C*: designans *VE*   11. ofellis *π*
12. requieuerint *λ*: requieuerit *VE*   17. leuas ut *CGSG*: leuas et *VE*: leuas et <ut>
Gi | exspuant *Tor*: exspuat *E*: expuat *V* | craticula *E*   18. urantur *Hum*: uratur *VE*
19. ouellas *V, E2*: ?ouellae *E1*: ofellas *TP* | cocte *V*   22. aprogineo *Sch*

---

[1] See the Glossary for a definition.
[2] *in ofillam,* 'for an ofella', is clearly a gloss.
[3] That is, meat is cut into squares, while the skin is left whole.
[4] See Columella 12.56.1 for a parallel to 'cross-shaped'.

7.2.2. Full (stuffed) udder: pepper, caraway and salted sea-urchins are ground (and stuffed inside); it is sewn up and cooked like this. It is eaten with *allec* and mustard.

7.3. FIG-FATTENED LIVER.

7.3.1. An *oenogarum* for fig-fattened liver: pepper, thyme, lovage, *liquamen*, a little wine and oil.

7.3.2. Alternatively: punch holes in the liver with a reed, marinade in *liquamen*, pepper, lovage and 2 laurel berries. Wrap in caul fat and grill on a gridiron and serve.

7.4. *OFELLAE.*[1]

7.4.1. Ostian *ofellae*:[2] mark out the *ofellae* pieces on the skin, leaving the skin uncut.[3] Pound pepper, lovage, dill seed, cumin, *silphium*, one bay berry; pour on *liquamen*, pound again. Pour into the roasting dish with the *ofellae*. When it has marinated for two to three days, lay it out and tie it up in a cross-shape[4] and put it in the oven. When you have cooked it, separate the *ofellae* which you have marked out, and then pound pepper, lovage, pour on *liquamen* and a little *passum* so that it becomes sweet. When it is simmering, thicken the sauce with starch, smother the *ofellae* and serve.

7.4.2. Apician *ofellae*: bone (the meat for) the *ofellae,* roll up, tie it and put it in the oven. After it has been browned, take it out and dry-roast it on a gridiron over a gentle fire so that it gives of its juices, without letting it burn. Pound pepper, lovage, sweet rush,[5] cumin, *liquamen*, and flavour with *passum*. Put the *ofellae* in a pan with this sauce. When they are cooked, take them out, drain the sauce from them, sprinkle with pepper and serve. If they are fatty, take the skin off when you bind them up. It is also possible to make *ofellae* of this kind from belly pork.[6]

7.4.3. Wild-boar style *ofellae*: they are seasoned with oil and *liquamen* and the spice mix is added to them when they are cooked. In addition, these seasonings are added when they are on the hearth and then they are brought back to the boil:

[5] See note on 1.6.

[6] We have translated *ofellae* as 'it' at the start of this recipe and 'they' at the end to show where a single piece of meat becomes treated as individual finished pieces; note that the Latin uses plural forms throughout. See 7.4.1.

bulliunt. et sine liquamine et oleo elixantur; cocuntur et sic piper <inferuntur>. perfunduntur ius supra scriptum et sic bulliunt.

[7.4.4] **aliter ofelle**: recte friguntur ut pene ossa rodantur. liquaminis summi ciatum, aquae ciatum, aceti ciatum, olei ciatum. simul mixtis et inmissis in patellam fictilem frigis et inferes.

[7.4.5] **aliter ofellas**: in sartagine abundanti oenogaro. piper asparges et inferes.

[7.4.6] **aliter ofellas**: ofelle prius sale et cumino infuse in aquam recte friguntur.

V. ASSATURE.

[7.5.1] **assaturam**: assam a furno simplicem salis plurimi conspersam cum melle inferes.

[7.5.2] **aliter assaturas**: petrosilene scripulos sex, laser scripulos sex, gingiberis scripulos sex, <condimenti> lauri bacas <scripulos> quinque, [condimenti] laseris radicem scripulos sex, origani scripulos sex, ciperis scripulos sex, costi modice, piretri scripulos tres, apii seminis scripulos sex, piperis scripulos XII, liquaminis et olei quod sufficit.

---

1. cocuntur *V*: coquuntur *E* | <inferuntur> *CGSG*   2. <mittis> ius *Vo*   3. ossa rodantur *E*: asso rodantur *V*: assae reddantur *Hum*   3-4. summi ciatum *André*: summi ciato *VE*: sumis cyathum *Hum*   4. aquae ciatum aceti *V*: aquæ aceti *(om.* ciatum*) E* | mixtis *Ven*: mixti *VE*   11. simplicem *after* assaturam *Bra3* | sale *Tor* | plurimo *Tor* | conspersa *E* 13. laser *VE*: assareos *GiVo, FR*   14. <condimenti> *CGSG from before* laseris | bagas *E* | <scripulos> *CGSG*   15. VI origani *E*   16. III *E* | api seminis *V2*: apii eminis *V1* | VI piperis *V*

---

[1] *condimentum*: see the Glossary for a general discussion. In this instance the spice-mix might be the same as the *condimentum aprunum* found at 8.1.1. The spices used for boar may well have been available to purchase in a pre-mixed form, though the actual spices used would differ depending on the spice-seller. A pre-mixed combination of spices comprising black cumin, coriander, mustard seed and fennel was found in a warehouse of a Roman London street. See the Glossary, *condimentum*, n. 37, and see P. Rowsome, *Heart of the City* (English Heritage/Museum of London Archaeological Service, 2000), p. 22.

ground pepper, spice-mix,[1] honey, *liquamen*; starch when it is boiling well. They are also boiled without *liquamen* and oil; they are cooked and served as they are with pepper. They are covered with the sauce written above and brought to the boil like this.

7.4.4. Another *ofellae* recipe: they are fried well so that the bones are almost exposed. A *cyathus* of finest *liquamen*, a *cyathus* of water, a *cyathus* of vinegar, a *cyathus* of oil; mix them together, put them in a ceramic dish, boil fiercely and serve.[2]

7.4.5. Another *ofellae* recipe: (cook) in a frying-pan with plenty of *oenogarum*. Sprinkle with pepper and serve.

7.4.6. Another *ofellae* recipe: marinade the *ofellae* first in salt and cumin and then boil fiercely in water.[3]

7.5. ROASTED MEATS.

7.5.1. Roasted meat: take unseasoned, roasted meat from the oven, sprinkle with plenty of salt and serve with honey.

7.5.2. Another roast meat recipe: 6 scruples of parsley, 6 scruples of *laser*, 6 scruples of ginger, 5 scruples of bay berry spice,[4] 6 scruples *laser* root,[5] 6 scruples oregano, 6 scruples of sweet rush, a little *costum*, 3 scruples pyrethrum, 6 scruples celery seed, 12 scruples pepper, sufficient *liquamen* and oil.

[2] The term *frigere*, 'to fry', would not normally be used in relation to liquids today, but its use seems to be normal here. In 7.4.6 the *ofellae* are 'fried' or boiled rapidly in water! We retain the reading of MS E, which literally means 'so that the bones are almost gnawed', a very picturesque way of describing what happens as the meat shrinks away from the bones. The *cyathus* here is therefore a quantity of roughly 1½ fl.oz rather than simply a cup. See the Introduction, pp. 83ff., for measurements generally.

[3] See the Introduction, p. 90, for a discussion of *frigere*.

[4] In the MSS the position of *condimenti* in this list is puzzling. It cannot mean 'other spices' or define what has gone before or after it as we interpret the word elsewhere. By coincidence, another reference to bay berries also has a puzzling *condimentum* before it. At 2.4, *lucanicae* sausages have *condimentum bacae lauri*. Bay berries have pea-sized hard kernels in a flimsy skin which soon dries and falls off. They could be pre-ground to save time as they are rather large to be easily ground at the time. Other recipes call for whole bay-berries (7.3.1; 8.6.11; 8.7.9). At 8.1.10 the seeds are ground at the time. We suggest that a weight of the spice is expected here and that the omission of the scruple is the result of scribal corruption. See the Glossary for a discussion of *condimentum* generally.

[5] In this recipe *laser* root and *laser* appear together, clearly representing two different types of the spice, the resin and the root. See the Glossary.

[7.5.3] **aliter assaturas**: mirte sicce bacam extenteratam cum cumino pipere mel liquamen defrito et oleo teres, et feruefactum amulas. carnem elixam sale subassatam perfundis, piper adspargis et inferes.

[7.5.4] **aliter assaturas**: piperis scripulos sex, ligusticum scripulos sex, petrosileni scripulos sex, apii semen scripulos sex, aneti scripulos sex, laseris radicem scripulos sex, asareos scripulos sex, piretri modice, ciperis scripulos VI, carei scripulos sex, cumini scripulos VI, gengiberis scripulos sex, liquaminis eminam, olei acetabulum.

[7.5.5] **assaturas in collare**: elixatur et infunditur in fretali piper condimentum mel liquamen, et attorretur in clibano quousque coquatur. elixum uero collare, si uoles, sine conditura assas, et siccum calidum perfundis.

VI. IN ELIXAM ET COPADIA.

[7.6.1] **ius in elixam omnem**: piper ligusticum origanum rutam silfium cepam siccam uinum carenum mel acetum olei modicum; persiccatam et sabano expressam elixam perfundis.

[7.6.2] **ius in elixam**: piper petrosilenem liquamen acetum careotam cepullam olei modicum. perfundis calido iure.

[7.6.3] **ius in elixam**: teres piper rutam aridam feniculi semen cepam careotam liquamen et oleum.

[7.6.4] **ius candidum in elixam**: piper liquamen uinum rutam cepam nucleos conditum, modicum de buccellis maceratis unde stringat, oleum. cum coxerit, ius perfundis.

[7.6.5] **aliter ius candidum in elixam**: piper careum ligusticum timum origanum cepullam dactilum mel acetum liquamen oleum.

[7.6.6] **in copadiis ius album**: piper cuminum ligusticum rute semen damascenas. infundis uinum, oenomeli et aceto temperabis. <agitabis> timo et origano.

1. extenteratam *D*: extenteratum *VE*: extemperatam *P* | cumine *E*   2. mel *om. VI*
3. aspargis *E*   5. petrosilenum *V* | semen *V* | VI aneti *V*   6. VI peretri *V*
7. carei scripulos VI *V* | cuminis *E* | gingiberis *E*   7-8. VI liquaminis olei eminam
olei acetabulum *V*   9. elixantur *E1*   10. attorretur *Hum*: atteritur *VE*
11. callidum *V*   12. IN ELIXAM IN ELIXAM *E*   14. persiccatam *Hum*:
persiccatum *VE*   16. petroselinum *ζ*   26. <agitabis> *Hum* | prigano *V*

7.5.3. Another sauce for roast meat: pound squashed,[1] dried myrtle berries with cumin, pepper, honey, *liquamen, defrutum* and oil, bring to the boil and thicken. Pour it over boiled meat, which has also been roasted a little with salt. Sprinkle with pepper and serve.

7.5.4. Another sauce for roasted meat: 6 scruples pepper, 6 scruples lovage, 6 scruples parsley, 6 scruples celery seed, 6 scruples dill, 6 scruples *laser* root, 6 scruples hazelwort, a little Spanish camomile, 6 scruples sweet rush,[2] 6 scruples caraway, 6 scruples cumin, 6 scruples ginger, ½ pt. *liquamen*, 1 *acetabulum* of oil.

7.5.5. Roasted neck joint: the joint is boiled, placed in a roasting dish with pepper, spices, honey, *liquamen*, and roasted in a *clibanus* until it is cooked. If you wish you may roast the boiled neck joint without the sauce and pour it on while it is hot and dry.

7.6. SAUCES FOR BOILED MEAT AND MEAT MORSELS.[3]

7.6.1. Sauce for any boiled meat: pepper, lovage, oregano, rue, *silphium*, dried onion, wine, *caroenum*, honey, vinegar, a little oil; wring the boiled meat out in a towel, dry it thoroughly and pour on the sauce.

7.6.2. Sauce for boiled meat: pepper, parsley, *liquamen*, vinegar, date, onion,[4] a little oil; pour on the hot sauce.

7.6.3. Sauce for boiled meat: pound pepper, dried rue, fennel seed, onion, date, *liquamen* and oil.

7.6.4. White sauce for boiled meat: pepper, *liquamen*, wine, rue, onion, pine nuts, spiced wine, and small pieces of bread soaked in the liquor so that it thickens, oil. When it is cooked, pour on the sauce.

7.6.5. Another white sauce for boiled meat: pepper, caraway, lovage, thyme, oregano, onion, date, honey, vinegar, *liquamen*, oil.

7.6.6. White sauce for meat morsels: pepper, cumin, lovage, rue seeds, damsons, pour on wine, flavour with *oenomeli*,[5] and vinegar. Stir with a sprig of thyme and oregano.

---

[1] For *extenterare*, see also 6.2.23 above, where it is used in relation to a chicken carcass. 'Squashed' seems to be the best rendition of a process which we assume involved opening up the berry and then letting it dry.

[2] See note on 1.6.   [3] See the Glossary for a discussion of *copadia*.

[4] *cepulla*: see the Glossary, *cepa*. This diminutive form of *cepa* has the general meaning of 'onion' and does not represent a distinct variety in our view.

[5] *oenomeli*: the Greek term for a wine and honey mixture, hence *mulsum*.

[7.6.7] **aliter ius candidum in copadiis**: piper timum cuminum apii semen feniculum mentam bacam myrte uuam passam. mulso temperas. agitabis ramo satureie.

[7.6.8] **ius in copadiis**: piper ligusticum careum mentam nardostacium folium, oui uitellum, mel mulsam acetum liquamen et oleum. agitabis satureia et porro, amulabis.

[7.6.9] **ius album in copadiis**: piper ligusticum cuminum apii semen timum, nucleos infusos, nuces infusas et purgatas, mel acetum liquamen et oleum.

[7.6.10] **ius in copadiis**: piper apii semen careum satureiam cnechi flos cepullam amigdala tosta careotam liquamen oleum sinapis modicum. defrito coloras.

[7.6.11] **ius in copadiis**: piper ligusticum petrosilenem cepullam amigdala tosta dactilum mel acetum liquamen defritum oleum.

[7.6.12] **ius in copadiis**: oua dura incidis; piper cuminum petrosilenem porrum coctum, mirte uacas, plusculum mel, acetum liquamen oleum.

[7.6.13] **<ius> in elixam anetatum crudum**: piper aneti semen mentam siccam laseris radicem; suffundis acetum, adicies cariotam mel liquamen sinapis modicum; defrito oleo temperabis. et hoc in collare porcino.

[7.6.14] **ius in elixam allegatam**: piper ligusticum careo apii semen timum cepullam dactilum allecem colatum. melle et uinum temperas. apium uiridem incisum super aspargis, oleum mittis et inferes.

VII. VENTRICVLA.

[7.7.1] uentrem porcinum bene exinanies, aceto et sale, postea aqua lauas, et sic hanc inpensam imples: pulpam porcinam tonsam tritam, ita ut eneruiata conmisceas cerebella tria et oua cruda, cui nucleos infundis et piper integrum mittis et hoc iure temperas: teres piper ligusticum silfium anesum gengiber rute modicum, liquamen optimum et olei modicum. reples aqualiculum sic ut laxamentum habeat, ne dissiliat in coctura. surclas ambas et in ollam bullientem

---

4. careum *TC*: careo *VE*   5 satureiam *V*   6. amulabis ζ   9. cneci *E*
| cepulam *GiVo*   11. petroselinum ζ| cepulam *GiVo*   13. incidis *VE*:
concidis *Sch* | petroselinum ζ   14. myrte *E* | uacas *VE*: bacas *C*: baccas *T*: bacam *P*
15. ius *add. P* | elixum *E* | anetatum *André*: anetatam *VE*: anetathum *Tor*   16. careotam *E*
17. collari *Hum*   18. allecatum *Hum* | careum *Hum*   19. cepulam *GiVo* | uino *E*
22. aqa *V1*   23. hac impensa *Tor* | tonsam *V2*: tonsa *V1*: tunsa *E*: tunsam *P* | tritam
V2: trita *V1, E*   24. cōmisceas *V*   25. gingiber *E*   26. aqualiculum *Tor*:
aqualicum *VE*

7.6.7. Another white sauce for meat morsels: pepper, thyme, cumin, celery seed, fennel, mint, myrtle berries, raisins; flavour with *mulsum*. Stir with a sprig of savory.

7.6.8. Sauce for meat morsels: pepper, lovage, caraway, mint, spikenard, *folium*, egg yolk, honey, *mulsum*, vinegar, *liquamen* and oil. Stir it with savory and leek, and thicken it.

7.6.9. White sauce for meat morsels: pepper, lovage, cumin, celery seed, thyme, soaked pine nuts, soaked and skinned nuts,[1] honey, vinegar, *liquamen* and oil.

7.6.10. Sauce for meat morsels: pepper, celery seed, caraway, savory, safflower, onion, roasted almonds, date, *liquamen*, oil, a little mustard. Colour it with *defrutum*.

7.6.11. Sauce for meat morsels: pepper, lovage, parsley, onion, roasted almonds, dates, honey, vinegar, *liquamen*, *defrutum*, oil.

7.6.12. Sauce for meat morsels: chop hard-boiled eggs, pepper, cumin, parsley, cooked leek, myrtle berries, a generous amount of honey, vinegar, *liquamen*, oil.

7.6.13. Uncooked dill sauce for boiled meat: pepper, dill seed, dry mint, *laser* root; pour on vinegar, add date, honey, *liquamen*, a little mustard, flavour with *defrutum* and oil. This also goes with neck of pork.

7.6.14. *Allec* sauce for boiled meat: pepper, lovage, caraway, celery seed, thyme, onion, date, strained *allec*; flavour with honey and wine. Sprinkle with chopped green celery, add some oil and serve.

7.7. STOMACH.

7.7.1. Carefully empty out a pig's stomach, wash it with salt and vinegar and afterwards with water and stuff it with the following mixture: pound pork meat thoroughly, mix this with three brains that have had their sinews removed and raw eggs. Tip in some pine nuts and put in whole peppercorns, and flavour it with this sauce: pound pepper, lovage, *silphium*, anise, ginger, a little rue, the best *liquamen*, and a little oil. Fill the stomach, leaving a little space so that it does not burst during cooking. Tie up both ends and put into a boiling pot. Lift it out and pierce it with a needle to release the air. When it is half way through

---

[1] The nuts are probably soaked in wine. As well as enhancing their flavour, the process should help to remove the bitter skins.

summittis. leuas et pungis acu, ne crepet. qua dimidias coctum fuerit, leuas et ad fumum suspendis ut coloretur, et denuo eum perelixabis ut coqui possit. deinde liquamine mero oleo modico, et cultello aperies et eum liquamine et ligustico adponis.

5 [7.7.2] **uentrem ut tostum facias**: in cantabro inuolue postea in muriam mittis et sic quoque.

VIII. LUMBI ET RENES.

lumbuli assi ita fiunt: aperiuntur in duas partes ita ut expansi sint, et aspergitur eis piper tritum, nuclei et coriandrum concisum minutatim factum et semen feniculi tritum. deinde lumboli recluduntur et [assi] consuuntur et inuoluuntur omento et sic predurantur in oleo et liquamine, inde assantur in clibano uel craticula.

IX. PERNA.

[7.9.1] pernam, ubi eam cum caricis plurimis elixaueris et tribus lauri foliis, detracta cute tessellatim incidis et melle conplebis. deinde farinam oleo subactam contexes et ei coreum reddis ut, cum farina cocta fuerit, eximas furno et ut est inferes.
[7.9.2] **perne cocturam**: ex aqua cum caricis cocta simpliciter. ut solet, inlata cum buccellis, caroeni uel condito. melius si cum musteis.
20 [7.9.3] **petasonem ex musteis**: petasonem elixas cum bilibre ordei et caricis XXV. cum elixatus fuerit, decarnas et aruillam illius candenti uatillo uris et melle contingis. quod melius, missum in furnum, melle oblinas. cum colorauerit,

---

1. crepet cum ad dimidias *Hum*   2. coloretur *V1*: coleretur *V2, E*   3. eum *VE*: cum *RG*
6. coque *E*   10. lumboli *TC*: lumbuli *E*: lumbolis *V* | ecluduntur *V* | assi *del. Gi*: passi *Sch*
| cosuuntur *V*   15. tessellatim *Tor*: tessellam *VE* | complebis *V*   16. contexes *Sch*:
conteres *VE* | est ei *V* | corium *Ven*   16-17. et ut est inferes *CGSG*: et ut est et feres *E*: ut est
et inferes *V*   19. caroeno *P* | si cum *Bas*: sicut *VE*   20. peta sonem *E, twice* | bilibri
GiVo | cacis *V*   21. aruillam *Bas*: armillam *VE*   22. oblinas *Sch*: obligas *VE*

the cooking, lift it out and hang in the smoke to give it colour, and then finish boiling it so that it may be cooked. Then add *liquamen*, wine and a little oil, cut it open with a knife and serve with *liquamen* and lovage.[1]

7.7.2. **To make roast stomach**: roll the stomach in bran after you have put it in brine and then cook it.[2]

7.8. TESTICLES AND KIDNEYS.

You make roasted testicles in this way:[3] they are opened up in two parts and stretched out, and ground pepper, pine nuts, finely chopped coriander and pounded fennel seed are sprinkled on them. Then the testicles are closed up again and sewn together and wrapped in caul, and in this state they are fried in oil and *liquamen* and then roasted in a *clibanus* or on a gridiron.

7.9. HAM.

7.9.1. Boil the ham with plenty of dried figs and 3 bay leaves, remove the skin, score the meat in a grid pattern and fill the cuts with honey. Then coat it with a dough made with oil and give it a covering, so that when the dough is cooked you take it out of the oven and serve it as it is.

7.9.2. **Cooked ham**: simply cook it in some water with figs. The normal way of serving this is with pieces of dry bread and *caroenum* or spiced wine. It is better with sweet wine cakes.[4]

7.9.3. **Cured shoulder of pork with sweet wine cakes**: boil the shoulder of pork with 2 lb. of barley and 25 figs. When it is boiled, bone the joint and crisp the fat with honey on a red-hot frying-pan. It is better if you coat it in honey and

---

[1] The end of the recipe is confused: it may be that the *'liquamen*, wine and a little oil' are added to the cooking liquor; and the second amount of *liquamen* with the lovage is a dressing. Alternatively, the *'liquamen*, wine and a little oil' are a simple *oenogarum*, as an alternative to the second amount of *liquamen* and lovage.

[2] See 7.1.6, *uuluam ut tostam facies,* where the same instruction is used. See also the Introduction, p. 91.

[3] *lumbus and renes* both have the general meaning of 'loins' (cf. Adams, *Pelagonius* pp. 379-81), but it is *renes* which means 'kidney'. The question then is what is meant by *lumbus*. It can also refer to the sexual organs and it is therefore likely that pork or lamb testicles are intended, though thankfully it seems that the recipe can be used with kidneys as well.

[4] See Cato, *De agricultura* 121: a mixture of flour, must, anise, cumin, lard, cheese and grated laurel bark. The must has to act as a fermenting agent. See the Glossary for Picentine bread, where flour and must is allowed to ferment for nine days.

mittis in caccabum passum piper fasciculum rute merum, temperas; cum fuerit temperatum, dimidium in petasonem perfundis et aliam partem piperati, buccellas musteorum fractas perfundis. cum sorbuerint, quod mustei recusauerint petasoni refundis.

5   [7.9.4] **laridi coctura**: tectum aqua cum multo aneto coques, oleum modicum distillabis et modicum salis.

X. IECINORA SIVE PVLMONES.

[7.10.1] **iecinera haedina uel agnina sic coques**: aquam mulsam facies, et oua; partem lactis admiscis eis ut incisa iecinera sorbeant. coques; ex oenogaro piper
10   asperso et inferes.

[7.10.2] **aliter [iecinera] in pulmonibus**: ex lacte lauas pulmones et colas quod capere possunt, et infringis oua dua cruda, salis grana pauca, mellis ligulam, et simul conmiscis et imples pulmones. elixas et concidis. teres piper, suffundis liquamen passum merum. pulmones confrigis et hoc oenogaro perfundis.

XI. DVLCIA DOMESTICA ET MELCE.

15   [7.11.1] **dulcia domestica**: palmulas uel dactilos excepto semine, nuce uel nucleis uel piper tritum infercies. sales foris contingis, frigis in melle cocto, et inferes.

[7.11.2] **aliter dulcia**: musteos Afros optimos rades et in lacte infundis. cum
20   biberint, in furnum mittis, ne arescant, modice. eximes eos calidos, melle perfundis, conpungis ut bibant. piper aspargis et inferes.

---

2. impetasonem *V* | alia parte *Hum*   3. sorbuerint…recusauerint *Hum*: sorbuerit…recusauerit *V*
7. IECINORA *V,E2* : IECINERA *E1*   8. hædina *E* | agnina *π*: agmina *VE*
9. ex *Bra3*: et *VE*   11. iecinera *del. Hum*   12. dura *E*   13. cōmiscis *V*
14. confrigis *André*: confringis *VE*: conpungis *Sch* | oenogaræ *V*   16. excepto *Hum*: et
cepto *VE*: excoepto *P*   17. sale *Hum*   19. musteo safros *V*: musteos apios *Hum*
20. callidos *V1*   21. aspergis *E*

---

[1] There is no *liquamen* in this recipe. This is quite odd, and even if the shoulder of pork is cured and quite salty the pepper sauce should have some. We think that the term *temperas* here has the meaning of 'bring the sauce to a balance with the normal ingredients' i.e. *liquamen*. The term clearly has a more complex meaning than the physical act of mixing or blending, as in previous English translations. See the Introduction, p. 87.

[2] *iecerina* is erroneously inserted here; it would give the sense 'another liver recipe: for lights'.

put it in the oven. When it is brown, put *passum*, pepper, a bundle of rue, and pure wine in a pan, balance the flavours; when you have the balance right, pour half of it over the meat and pour the rest of the pepper sauce over broken pieces of sweet wine cakes. When they have soaked up as much as they can, pour the remainder over the ham.[1]

7.9.4. **Cooked bacon**: cook it covered in water with plenty of dill, drizzle with a little oil and a little salt.

7.10. LIVER AND LIGHTS.

7.10.1. **You cook kid's or lamb's liver like this**: make up *mulsum*, water and eggs and stir in a little milk, make cuts in the liver so that it may absorb the sauce. Cook it; serve in some *oenogarum* with sprinkled pepper.

7.10.2. **Another recipe for lights**:[2] wash the lights in some milk and strain out what they are able to hold. Break 2 raw eggs, add a few grains of salt, a spoonful of honey, stir together and fill the lights with it. Boil them and slice them. Pound pepper, pour on *liquamen*, *passum*, pure wine. Fry the slices of lights and pour on this *oenogarum*.

7.11. HOME-MADE SWEETS AND CURDS.

7.11.1. **Home-made sweets**: take the stone from palm dates or ordinary dates and stuff them with nuts or pine nuts or ground pepper. Roll in salt, fry them in cooked honey and serve.

7.11.2. **Another sweet recipe**: peel best-quality African honey apples[3] and put them in milk. When they have soaked it up, put them in the oven for a little while without letting them dry out, take them out when they are hot and pour honey on them, puncturing them so that it soaks in. Sprinkle with pepper and serve.

---

[3] The term *musteos afros* ought to be translated as 'African sweet wine cakes'. However, we think that it may be a masculine variant form of *mala mustea*, 'must apple'. 'The must apple was named from its quickness in ripening but is now called the honey apple from its flavour' (Pliny, *HN*. 15.15.51); see also Cato, *De agricultura* 73, where it is a distinct apple rather than a quince, and Varro, *RR*. 1.49, where Pliny found his references for the name-change. It seems highly unlikely that an African cake would be imported. The term may however refer to a particular African recipe for wine cakes. One would not expect cakes to need peeling or scraping, but as the recipe below uses the same term *rasos* to mean take the crust off, we have to concede that a cake is possible. An African apple, on the other hand, is quite likely to be available, would need to be peeled or scraped and, more to the point, would need puncturing in order for the honey to be absorbed.

[7.11.3] **aliter dulcia**: siligineos rasos frangis et buccellas maiores facies. in lacte infundis, frigis [et] in oleo, mel superfundis et inferes.

[7.11.4] **dulcia piperata**: <teres piper,> mittis mel merum passum rutam. eo mittis nucleos nuces alicam elixatam. concisas nuces auellanas tostas adicies
5 et inferes.

[7.11.5] **aliter dulcia**: piper nucleos mel rutam et passum teres; cum lacte et tractam coques. coagulum coque cum modicis ouis. perfusum melle, <pipere> aspersum inferes.

[7.11.6] **aliter dulcia**: accipies similam, coques in aquam calidam ita ut
10 durissimam pultem facias, deinde in patellam expandis. cum refrixerit, concidis quasi dulcia et frigis in oleo optimo. leuas, perfundis mel, piper aspargis et inferes. melius feceris, si lac pro aquam miseris.

[7.11.7] **tiropatinam**: accipies lac, aduersus quod patinam estimabis, temperabis lac cum melle quasi ad lactantia, oua quinque ad sextarium mittis, si ad eminam,
15 oua tria. in lacte dissoluis ita ut unum corpus facias, in cumana colas et igni lento coques. cum duxerit ad se, piper adspargis et inferes.

[7.11.8] **oua sfongia ex lacte**: oua quattuor, lactis eminam, olei unciam in se dissoluis, ita ut unum corpus facias. in patellam subtilem adicies olei modicum; facies ut bulliat, et adicies inpensam quam comparasti. una parte cum fuerit
20 coctum, in disco uertes, melle perfundis, piper adspargis et inferes.

[7.11.9] **melcas**: cum pipere et liquamine, uel sale, oleo et coriandro.

XII. BVLVOS.

[7.12.1] buluos oleo liquamine aceto inferes, modico cumino adsperso.
25 [7.12.2] **aliter**: buluos tundis atque ex aqua coques, deinde oleo frigis. ius sic facies: timum puleium piper origanum mel acetum modice et, si placet, et modice liquamen. piper aspargis et inferes.

---

1. bucellas *E* | ?malores *E*   2. et *del. André*   3. <aliter> dulcia *Gi* | piperato *Sch* |
<teres piper> *CGSG: lacuna André*   4. adiciæs *V*   7. tracta *GiVo* | <pipere> *CGSG*
9. coques *E2*: coques et *V, E1* | aqua *E* | calidam *CGSG*: callidam *V*: calida *E*
10. durissima pulte *V* | facies *V*   11. aspergis *E*   12. aqua *ζ*   13. quod *om.*
V: quod aduersus *Vo* | extimabis *V*   14. imina *V*   15. cumana *Hum*: cuminata *VE*
17. sfongia *V2*: fongia *V1*: sfhongia *E*: spongia *GiVo*   19. quam comparasti *V2*: comparasti
V1: quam parasti *E*   21. melcas cum *Bra3*: mel castum *E*: melcastum *V* | piper et liquamen *V*
24. olei *V* | infere *V* | cuuino *E1*   25. atque *Hum*: aquo *VE*: a quo *André*
26. thimum *E*

7.11.3. **Another sweet recipe**: take the crust off a white loaf and break it into quite large pieces. Soak in milk, fry in oil, pour on honey and serve.

7.11.4. **Peppered sweets**: pound pepper; add honey, wine, *passum*, and rue. Add to the mixture pine nuts, nuts and boiled *alica*. Add chopped roasted hazelnuts and serve.

7.11.5. **Another sweet recipe**: pound pepper, pine nuts, honey, rue, and *passum*. Cook with milk and *tracta*. Cook the thickened mixture with a little egg. Serve drenched in honey and sprinkled in pepper.

7.11.6. **Another sweet recipe**: take coarse wheat flour,[1] cook in hot water in such a way that you make a very thick porridge, then spread it out in a dish. When it has cooled down, cut it up like sweets and fry in best-quality oil; take them out, pour on honey, sprinkle with pepper and serve. A better result is obtained if you use milk instead of water.

7.11.7. **Cheese *patina***: take some milk and choose a dish of sufficient size to hold it; flavour the milk with honey as though for milk pudding. Put in 5 eggs to a pint or 3 to ½ pint.[2] Dissolve them in the milk so that you have a smooth emulsion. Strain it into a Cumaean clay dish and cook over a slow fire; when it has set, sprinkle with pepper and serve.

7.11.8. **Egg and milk sponge**: stir together 4 eggs, ½ pt. milk and 1 oz. oil so that you have a smooth emulsion. Add a little oil to a thin *patella,* heat until it sizzles and then add the mixture you have prepared. When it is cooked on one side, turn it into a round serving dish, pour on honey, sprinkle with pepper and serve.

7.11.9. **Curds**:[3] (serve with) pepper and *liquamen,* or salt, oil and coriander.

7.12 BULBS.[4]

7.12.1. Serve bulbs in oil, *liquamen*, vinegar, sprinkle with a little cumin.

7.12.2. **Alternatively**: pound the bulbs and cook in some water, then fry in oil. Make the sauce like this: thyme, pennyroyal, pepper, oregano, honey, a little vinegar and also, if you like, a little *liquamen*. Sprinkle with pepper and serve.

---

[1] Or possibly a coarse semolina.

[2] The classical French recipe for cream caramel has virtually the same ratio of egg to milk.

[3] See *Geoponica* 18.21, where *melcae* are curds made using vinegar as the curdling agent.

[4] See Pliny, *HN.* 19. 93ff. on general consumption of many different kinds of flowering bulbs such as the lily, especially the hyacinth, arum lily and squill. *Bulbi* refers specifically to grape hyacinth; see Dalby, *Food in the Ancient World*, p. 63. It should be noted that other types of bulb listed by Pliny are harmful when eaten!

[7.12.3] **aliter**: buluos elixos in pultorium pressos mittis timum origanum mel acetum defritum caroetam liquamine, oleum modice. piper adspargis et inferes. Varro: 'si quid de buluis dixi, in aquam qui Veneris ostium quaerunt, deinde ut legitimis nuptiis in cena ponuntur, sed et cum nucleis pineis aut cum erucę sucum et pipere'.

[7.12.4] **aliter**: puluos frictos oenogaro inferes.

XIII. FVNGI FARNEI VEL BOLETI.

[7.13.1] **fungi farnei**: elixi calidi exsiccati in garo, piper accipiuntur, ita ut piper cum liquamine teres.

[7.13.2] **in fungis farneis**: piper carenum acetum et oleum.

[7.13.3] **aliter fungi farnei**: elixi ex sale oleo mero coriandro conciso inferuntur.

[7.13.4] **boletos fungos**: carenum, fasciculum coriandri uiridis. ubi ferbuerint, exempto fasciculo inferes.

[7.13.5] **boletos aliter**: caliculos eorum liquamine uel sale aspersos inferunt.

[7.13.6] **boletos aliter**: tirsos eorum concisos in patellam, ouam perfundis addito pipere ligustico modico melle; liquamine temperabis. oleum modice.

XIIII. TVBERA.

[7.14.1] tubera radis, elixas, sale aspargis et surculo infiges. subassas, et mittes in caccabum oleum liquamen carenum uinum piper et mel. cum ferbuerit, amulo obligas. tubera exornas et inferes.

[7.14.2] **aliter tubera**: elixas et asperso sale in surculis adfigis et subassas, et mittes in caccabum liquamen oleum uiridem carenum uinum modice et piper confractum et mellis modicum, et ferueat. cum ferbuerit, amulo obligas et tubera

---

1. elixas *Hum* | pultorium *V*: pulturium *E*: pultarium *D*			2. liquamen et *Sch*
3-5. Varro…pipere *del. Sch*	3. de puluis *E* | quærunt *E*		4. eruce *E*
5. suco *E*	6. buluos *E*	8. callidi *V1* | exsiccati oenogaro *Hum*	
9. teras *Hum*	13. ferbuerit *V*	14. ex emto *E*	15. buletos *E* | inferum *E*
16. buletos *E* | ouam *VE*: uuam *P, Sch*: nouam *Hum*			19. radix *E* | aspergis *E*
20. feruerit *V*			

---

[1] The use of *pressos* here is unusual, but it cannot mean 'wring out' or 'dry out' as *exprimere* does at (for example) 3.4.1, 3.15.2, 3.15.3; the bulbs are likely to have been small and could be tightly packed at the base of the *pultarium*; the recipe implies that this dish was used for service as well as for cooking.

7.12.3. **Alternatively**: boil the bulbs and press them into a porridge-pan.[1] Put in thyme, oregano, honey, vinegar, *defrutum*, date, *liquamen*, and a little oil. Sprinkle with pepper and serve. Varro: 'If I have said anything about bulbs, those who seek the harbour of Venus should have them cooked in water, and they can be served at dinner when a marriage takes place, but they can also be served with pine nuts or with the juice of rocket and pepper.'[2]

7.12.4. **Alternatively**: fry the bulbs and serve in *oenogarum*.

7.13. ASH-TREE FUNGI OR MUSHROOMS.

7.13.1. **Ash-tree fungi**: boil and serve while hot and dry in *garum* and pepper, so long as you pound the pepper with *liquamen*.[3]

7.13.2. **Sauce for ash-tree fungi**: pepper, *caroenum*, vinegar and oil.

7.13.3. **Another ash-tree fungi recipe**: boil and serve in salt, oil, wine and chopped coriander.

7.13.4. **Mushrooms**: *caroenum*, a bundle of green coriander. When they have boiled remove the bundle and serve.

7.13.5. **Another recipe for mushrooms**: their stalks are served sprinkled with salt or *liquamen*.

7.13.6. **Another mushroom recipe**: chop their stems and put in a dish, pour egg over them, adding pepper, lovage, a little honey, flavour with *liquamen*, add a little oil.[4]

7.14. TRUFFLES.

7.14.1. **Truffles**: peel them, boil, sprinkle with salt and skewer them. Grill them lightly, and put in a pan oil, *liquamen*, *caroenum*, wine, pepper, and honey. When it is simmering, thicken with starch. Un-skewer the truffles and serve.

7.14.2. **Another truffle recipe**: boil them, sprinkle with salt and skewer them. Grill them lightly. Put in a pan *liquamen*, green oil, *caroenum*, a little wine, and cracked pepper and a little honey. Bring it to heat; when it is simmering, thicken

---

[2] Brandt, *Untersuchungen*, p. 93, assumes this to be an addition in the *Apicius* text drawn from a Menippean Satire *peri edesmatōn*. It is not clear exactly which words are drawn from Varro.

[3] The one-and-only reference to *garum* on its own, and apparently defined as *liquamen* in the body of the recipe. See the Glossary for further discussion.

[4] The MSS read *in patellam ouam perfundis* which makes adequate sense; the adoption of *nouam* by *FR* still requires the object of *perfundis* to be the mushroom stalks, which cannot be 'poured' in any sense. The term has to refer to a liquid of some kind, and eggs are the only option.

conpunges ut conbibant illud. exornas. cum bene sorbuerint, inferes. si uolueris, eadem tubera omento porcino inuolues et assabis et sic inferes.

[7.14.3] **aliter tubera**: oenogarum: piper ligusticum coriandrum rutam liquamen mel uinum oleum modice. calefacies.

5 [7.14.4] **aliter tubera**: piper mentam rutam mel oleum uinum modicum. calefacies et inferes.

[7.14.5] **aliter tubera**: elixa cum porro, deinde sale piper coriandro conciso mero oleo modico inferes.

[7.14.6] **aliter tubera**: piper cuminum silfi mentam apium rutam mel acetum
10 uel uinum salem uel liquamen et oleum modice.

XV. IN COLOCASIO.

in colocasio: piper cuminum rutam mel liquamen, olei modicum. cum ferbuerit, amulo obligas.

XVI. COCLEAS.

15 [7.16.1] **cocleas lacte pastas**: accipies cocleas, fongizabis, membranam tolles ut possint prodire. adicies in uas lac et sale uno die, ceteris diebus in lac per se, et omni hora mundabis stercus. cum paste fuerint ut non possint se retrahere, <extrahes> et ex oleo friges. mittes oenogarum. similiter et pulte pasci possunt.

20 [7.16.2] **cocleas**: sale puro et oleo assabis. cocleas lasere liquamine pipere oleo suffundis.

[7.16.3] **cocleas assas**: liquamine pipere cumino, suffundis assidue.

[7.16.4] **aliter**: cocleas uiuentes in lac siligineum infundes. ubi paste fuerint, coques.

---

1. conpunges *P*: conpungens *VE* | et conbibant *E* | sorbuerint *Sch*: ferbuerint *VE*   3. <in> tubera *Bra2* | oenogaro *Sch*   4. modice oleum *E1*   7. piper *V*: pipere *E* 8. oleo modico *Bra1*: obomo *VE*: optimo *Hum*   15. sfongizabis *Ven*: spongizabis *Hum* 16. salem *GiVo* | in² *del. Sch*   17. omni hora *M*: ommora *VE*   18. <extrahes> *CGSG*: *lacuna André* | pulte *Hum*: pulpas *VE*: pultae *Milham*: pulpa *GiVo*   22. adsidue *E* 23. infundis *V1*

with starch, then pierce the truffles so that they can soak up the sauce. Un-skewer them (into the sauce) and serve them when they have soaked up the sauce well. If you want, you can wrap them in caul, roast them and serve like that.

7.14.3. Another truffle recipe: *oenogarum*: pepper, lovage, coriander, rue, *liquamen*, honey, wine, a little oil; warm it up.[1]

7.14.4. Another truffle recipe: pepper, mint, rue, honey, oil, a little wine. Warm it up and serve.

7.14.5. Another truffle recipe: serve them boiled with leek and then salt, pepper, chopped coriander, pure wine and a little oil.

7.14.6. Another truffle recipe: pepper, cumin, *silphium*, mint, celery, rue, honey, vinegar or wine, salt or *liquamen* and a little oil.

7.15. SAUCE FOR TARO.

Sauce for taro: pepper, cumin, rue, honey, *liquamen*, a little oil; when it has come to heat, thicken with starch.

7.16. SNAILS.

7.16.1. Milk-fed snails: take the snails, wipe them over with a sponge, take off their membranes so that they can come out (of their shells). Put them in a pot with milk and salt for the first day, and in milk alone for the remaining days, continually removing the waste matter. When they are so well fed that they cannot go back in their shells, pull them out and fry in some oil. Serve in *oenogarum*. They can also, in a similar way, be fed on porridge.[2]

7.16.2. Snails: roast them in pure salt and oil. Pour on to the snails a sauce of *laser*, *liquamen*, pepper and oil.

7.16.3. Roasted snails: pour a sauce of *liquamen*, pepper, and cumin generously over them.

7.16.4. Alternatively: tip the living snails into floured milk. When they are fattened, cook them.

---

[1] See 1.31 for a duplication of this recipe.

[2] The MSS read *pulpas*, 'meat', but it is unlikely that meat was fed to snails. *FR* retain this reading, but Humelberg's suggestion *pulte* is far more plausible: porridge would be a far more logical food for snails, confirmed by recipe number 4 of this section, which uses floured milk. Milham's reading *pultae* cannot be derived from *puls*. We see no warrant for *FR*'s tentative suggestion *sapa*.

XVII. OVA.

[7.17.1] **oua frixa**: enogarata.

[7.17.2] **oba elixa**: liquamine oleo mero, uel ex liquamine pipere lasere.

[7.17.3] **in ouis apalis**: piper ligusticum nucleos infusos; suffundes mel acetum,
5   liquamine temperabis.

EXPLICIT APICI POLITELES LIBER

SEPTIMVS

2. enogarata *V2, E*: .enogarata *V1*: oenogarato *Sch*: oenogaro *Hum*   3. oba elixa *CGSG*:
obelixa *VE*: oua elixa *Hum*   6. APICII *E* | POTELES *V*   7. VII *VE*

7.17. EGGS.

7.17.1. **Fried eggs**: serve in *oenogarum*.

7.17.2. **Boiled eggs**: serve in *liquamen*, oil, wine, or in *liquamen*, pepper and *laser*.

7.17.3. **Sauce for soft-boiled eggs**: pepper, lovage, soaked pine nuts; pour on honey, vinegar, flavour with *liquamen*.

HERE ENDS BOOK SEVEN OF APICIUS,

'LUXURY DISHES'

BOOK EIGHT

INCIPIT EIVSDEM TETRAPVS LIBER OCTAVVS

I. in apro. II. in ceruo. III. in caprea. IIII. in ouifero. V. bubula siue uitulina. VI. in edo et agno. VII. in porcello. VIII. leporem. VIIII. glires.

5 **I. IN APRO.**

[8.1.1] **aper ita conditur**: sfungiatur, et sic aspergitur ei sal, cuminum tritum, et sic manet. alia die mittitur in furnum. cum coctus fuerit, perfunditur piper tritum condimentum aprunum mel liquamen carenum et passum.

[8.1.2] **aliter in apro**: aqua marina cum ramulis lauri aprum elixas quousque
10 madescat. corium ei tolles. cum sale sinape aceto inferes.

[8.1.3] **aliter in apro**: teres piper ligusticum origanum; bacas mirte extenteras, coriandrum, cepas; suffundes mel uinum liquamen oleum modice; calefacies, amulo obligas. aprum in furno coctum perfundes. hoc et in omne genus carnis ferine facies.

15 [8.1.4] **in aprum assum iura feruentia facies sic**: piper cuminum frictum apii semen mentam timum satureiam cneci flos, nucleos tostos uel amigdala tosta, mel uinum liquamen acetum, oleum modice.

[8.1.5] **aliter in aprum assum iura feruentia**: piper ligusticum apii semen mentam tymum nucleos tostos uinum acetum; liquamen et oleum modice.
20 cum ius simplex bullierit, tunc triturae globum mittes et agitas cepam et rutae fasciculos. si uolueris pinguius facere, obliga, si uis, albo ouorum liquido; moues paulatim, aspargis piper tritum et inferes.

[8.1.6] **ius in aprum elixum**: piper ligusticum cuminum silfi origanum nucleos cariotam mel sinape acetum liquamen et oleum.

---

2. VIII *VE*   3. capria *E*   4. aedo *E* | clires *V, but see section VIIII below*   6. sfongiatur
π: spongiatur *Hum* | sale *V*: sal et *Sch*   7. tritum *VE*: frictum *Sch from 8.1.4*   8. aprunum
GiVo: aprinum *E*: aprimum *V* | condimentum aprunum *del. Sch*   11. myrte *E* | extenteratas *Hum*
12. calefacies *Ber*: salefacies *VE*   14. farine *E* | facias *E*   15. iura *P*: iure *VE*
16. cneci *O2*: enechi *VE*   17. acetum *Bra2*: acetabulum *VE*   20. triturae *E* | rutæ *E*
21. pingui ius *V* | si uis *V, E2*: si uos *E1*: obligauis ius *Hum*   22. aspergis *E*

---

[1] It is not clear what these spices might be. *FR* interpret *condimentum* to mean the juices from the meat. See the Glossary.

[2] *in apro* is normally translated as 'sauce for...' but no sauce as such is indicated here.

HERE BEGINS BOOK EIGHT OF THE SAME, 'QUADRUPEDS'

1. Sauces for wild boar. 2. Sauces for venison. 3. Sauces for wild goat. 4. Sauces for wild sheep. 5. Beef or veal. 6. Sauces for kid or lamb. 7. Sauces for piglet. 8. Hare. 9. Dormice.

8.1. SAUCES FOR WILD BOAR.

8.1.1. Wild boar is seasoned like this: it is sponged clean, and salt and ground cumin are sprinkled over it and it is left. The next day it is put in the oven. When it is cooked pour on a sauce of ground pepper, wild boar seasoning,[1] honey, *liquamen, caroenum* and *passum*.

8.1.2. **Another recipe[2] for wild boar**: boil the boar in seawater with sprigs of bay until it is tender. Take the skin off. Serve it with salt, mustard, and vinegar.

8.1.3. **Another sauce for wild boar**: pound pepper, lovage, oregano, de-seeded myrtle berries, coriander, onion; pour on honey, wine, *liquamen*, a little oil; warm it through and thicken with starch. Pour on to the boar, previously cooked in the oven. This can be used for all kinds of wild meat.

8.1.4. **You make hot sauce for roast boar like this**: pepper, roasted cumin, celery seed, mint, thyme, savory, safflower, roasted pine nuts or roasted almonds, honey, wine, *liquamen*, vinegar, a little oil.

8.1.5. **Another hot sauce for roast boar**: pepper, lovage, celery seed, mint, thyme, roasted pine nuts, wine, vinegar, *liquamen* and a little oil. When the simple sauce has boiled then put in the ground spice ball and stir it with a bundle of onion and rue. If you want to make it richer, thicken it if you like with egg white, stir gently, sprinkle with ground pepper and serve.[3]

8.1.6. **Sauce for boiled boar**: pepper, lovage, cumin, *silphium*, oregano, pine nuts, date, honey, mustard, vinegar, *liquamen*, and oil.

---

[3] *FR* were confused by the description of this sauce as 'simple', and interpreted the *ius simplex* as the cooking liquor from the roasting pan! In our opinion the wine, *liquamen*, vinegar and oil constitute the 'simple sauce', while the spices and nuts make up the spice ball. It is interesting to note the use of the spice ball and to wonder whether this method was more frequently used than first appears from the recipes. See also 8.8.4, where the instructions for the spice ball are more clearly outlined. On the *ius simplex* see Horace, *Satires* 2.4.64-5 and for *oenogarum simplex* see *Apicius* 3.4.2, 3.20.1, 4.2.20 etc.

[8.1.7] **ius frigidum in aprum elixum**: piper careum ligusticum, coriandri semen frictum, aneti semen, apii semen, tymum origanum cepulam mel acetum sinape liquamen oleum.

[8.1.8] **aliter ius frigidum in aprum elixum**: piper ligusticum cuminum aneti semen et timum origanum, silfi modicum, eruce semen plusculum; suffundes merum, condimenta uiridia modica, cepa, pontica uel amigdala fricta, dactilum mel acetum, merum modicum; coloras defrito; liquamen oleum.

[8.1.9] **aliter in apro**: teres piper ligusticum origanum apii semen laseris radicem cuminum feniculi semen rutam liquamen uinum passum. facies ut ferueat. cum ferbuerit, amulo obligas. aprum intro foras <infundes> et inferes.

[8.1.10] **perna apruna ita impletur recentior**: per articulum pernae palum mittes ita ut cutem a carne separes, ut possit condimentum accipere per cornulum ut uniuersa impleatur. teres piper bacam lauri rutam. si uolueris laser adicies, liquamen optimum, carenum et olei uiridis guttas. cum impleta fuerit, constringitur illa pars qua impleta est ex lino et mittitur in zemam. elixatur in aquam marinam cum lauri turionibus et aneto.

II. IN CERVO.

[8.2.1] **ius in ceruum**: teres piper ligusticum careum origanum apii semen laseris radicem feniculi semen; fricabis, suffundes liquamen uinum passum oleum modice. cum ferbuerit, amulo obligas. ceruum coctum intro foras tanges et inferes. in platone similiter et in omne genus uenationis eadem conditura uteris.

[8.2.2] **aliter**: ceruum elixabis et subassabis. teres piper ligusticum careum apii semen; suffundes mel acetum liquamen oleum. calefactum amulo obligas et carnem perfundes.

---

2. thymum *E* | ponticas *GiVo* | <tanges> *Bas*   3. et oleum *E1*   5. thimum *E* | euruce *E1*   6. cepam *Milham*   7. defrito *ξ*: defricto *VE*   10. feruuerit *E* | <infundes> *CGSG*: 11. aprina *E* | recentior *CGSG*: recentina *VE*: Terentina *Sch* | pernæ *E*   12. ut² *VE*: et *Sch*   14. guttas *V2*: gustas *V1, E*   16. aqua marina *GiVo*   21. platonem *GiVo*   23. sub assabis *VE*

---

[1] The *perna apruna* may already be partly salted and smoked before it is flavoured and boiled. Schuch's emendation is based on the Terentine flavourings found in recipe 8.7.1, where a similar liquor is introduced to a suckling pig via a reed pipe; however we are dealing here with a ham, which if salted and hung for some time would have too tough a skin for the procedure described to be carried out. This is why we prefer our conjecture *recentior*, 'fresh' or 'fairly fresh', implying

8.1.7. Cold sauce for boiled boar: pepper, caraway, lovage, roasted coriander seed, dill seed, celery seed, thyme, oregano, onion, honey, vinegar, mustard, *liquamen* and oil.

8.1.8. Another cold sauce for boiled boar: pepper, lovage, cumin, dill seed and thyme, oregano, a little *silphium*, rather more rocket seed; pour on pure wine, a little green herb, onion, roasted hazelnuts or almonds, date, honey, vinegar, a little pure wine; colour with *defrutum*; *liquamen* and oil.

8.1.9. Another sauce for boar: pound pepper, lovage, oregano, celery seed, *laser* root, cumin, fennel seed, rue, *liquamen*, wine, *passum*. Bring it to heat; when it is simmering, thicken with starch. Pour the sauce into and over the boar and serve.

8.1.10. Wild boar ham is stuffed like this when fresh:[1] insert a stick in the knuckle end of the ham in such a way that you separate the skin from the meat, so that it is able to receive the flavourings through a little funnel, so that it is filled all the way round. Pound pepper, bay berries, and rue. If you want, add *laser*, best-quality *liquamen*, *caroenum*, and some drops of green olive oil. When it is filled, that end through which it was filled is tied up with some linen thread and it is put in a cauldron. It is boiled in seawater with sprigs of bay and dill.

8.2. SAUCES FOR DEER.

8.2.1. Sauce for deer: pound pepper, lovage, caraway, oregano, celery seed, *laser* root, fennel seed; pound again, pour on *liquamen*, wine, *passum* and a little oil. When it has come to heat, thicken with starch. Pour the sauce into and over the deer and serve. You may use the same flavourings in the same way for broad-horned deer[2] or any other kind of game.

8.2.2. Alternatively: boil and then lightly roast the deer. Pound pepper, lovage, caraway, celery seed; pour on honey, vinegar, *liquamen*, oil. Warm it through, thicken with starch and pour over the meat.

---

that the skin is still pliant, crucial because the problem with this kind of 'stuffing' is the absolute need for the skin to be free of holes. Any cut or tear will allow the so-called 'stuffing' to run out, and particularly so if the meat is boiled. It may just be possible that chopped meat, so obvious in a stuffing, is taken for granted in these recipes though it is not likely under the skin. See recipe 4.3.2 where a *Minutal Terentinum* contains a forcemeat similarly named, though in this instance we are told to find the recipe in Book 3, where unfortunately it fails to appear; see also Brandt, *Untersuchungen*, pp. 92ff..

[2] Probably fallow deer, *Dama dama*, as *FR* render this term.

[8.2.3] **ius in ceruo**: piper ligusticum cepulam origanum nucleos cariotas mel liquamen sinape acetum oleum.

[8.2.4] **ceruine conditura**: piper cuminum condimentum petrosilenum cepam rutam mel liquamen mentam passum carenum et oleum modice. amulo obligas cum iam bulliit.

[8.2.5] **iura feruentia in ceruo**: piper ligusticum petroselinum cuminum [suffundes] nucleos tostos aut amigdala; <suffundes> mel acetum uinum oleum modice liquamen et agitabis.

[8.2.6] **embambam in ceruinam assam**: piper nardostacium folium apii semen cepam aridam rutam uiridem mel acetum liquamen adlectum caretam uuam passam et oleum.

[8.2.7] **aliter in ceruum assum iura feruentia**: piper ligusticum petroselinum damascena macerata uinum mel acetum liquamen oleum modice. agitabis porro et satureia.

III. IN CAPREA.

[8.3.1] **ius in caprea**: piper ligusticum careum cuminum petroselinum rutae semen mel sinape acetum liquamen et oleum.

[8.3.2] **ius in caprea assa**: piper condimentum rutam cepam mel liquamen passum oleum modice, amulum iam bulliet.

[8.3.3] **aliter ius in caprea**: piper condimentum petroselinum origanum modicum rutam liquamen mel passum et olei modicum. amulo obligabis.

IIII. IN OVIFERO (hoc est ouis siluatica).

[8.4.1] **ius in ouifero feruens**: piper ligusticum cuminum mentam siccam timum silfi; suffundes uino, adicies damascenam macerata mel uinum liquamen acetum, passum ad colorem, oleum. agitabis fasciculo origani et mentae siccae.

3. petrosilinum *E*   3-4. cepa ruta *V*   4. amulos *E1*   6. petrosilinum *E*
7. <suffundes> *moved here from before* nucleos *Hum*   9. embamma *Tor*
10. adlectum *CGSG*: adiectum *V*: adiectam *E*: *other editors obelize*   12. ceruo massum *V* |
petrosilinum *E*   16. petrosilinum *E* | rutę *E*   20. petrosilinum *E*   22. hoc
est ouis siluatica *del. Hum*   24. uinum *Hum* | merata *E1*: mecerata *E2*   25. mente
sicce *V*

8.2.3. Sauce for deer: pepper, lovage, onion, oregano, pine nuts, dates, honey, *liquamen*, mustard, vinegar, oil.

8.2.4. Sauce for venison: pepper, cumin, spices,[1] parsley, onion, rue, honey, *liquamen*, mint, *passum*, *caroenum* and a little oil. Thicken with starch when it comes to the boil.

8.2.5. Hot sauce for deer: pepper, lovage, parsley, cumin, roasted pine nuts or almonds; pour on honey, vinegar, wine, a little oil, *liquamen*, and give it a stir.

8.2.6. Sauce for roast venison: pepper, spikenard, *folium*, celery seed, dried onion, green rue, honey, vinegar, choice *liquamen*, date, raisins, and oil.

8.2.7. Another hot sauce for roast deer: pepper, lovage, parsley, softened damsons,[2] wine, honey, vinegar, *liquamen* and a little oil. Stir it with leek and savory.[3]

8.3. WILD GOAT.

8.3.1. Sauce for wild goat: pepper, lovage, caraway, cumin, parsley, rue seed, honey, mustard, vinegar, *liquamen* and oil.

8.3.2. Sauce for roast wild goat: pepper, spices,[4] rue, onion, honey, *liquamen*, *passum*, a little oil, starch when it boils.

8.3.3. Another sauce for wild goat: pepper, spices, parsley, a little oregano, rue, *liquamen*, honey, *passum* and a little oil. Thicken with starch.

8.4. SAUCES FOR WILD SHEEP (THAT IS, SHEEP FROM THE WOODS).

8.4.1. Hot sauce for wild sheep: pepper, lovage, cumin, dry mint, thyme, *silphium*; pour on wine, add softened damsons, honey, wine, *liquamen*, vinegar, *passum* to colour it, oil. Stir with a bundle of oregano and dry mint.

---

[1] It is not clear what is meant here. See the Glossary under *condimentum* for a discussion. In this instance, and also below at 8.3.2 and 3, the cook must expect us to add other spices of our own choice, though this seems to us a very odd way to record a recipe.

[2] *macerata*: does this term tell us that all dried fruit should be macerated before being added to a sauce? In many cases *caryotae/dactyli* and *uua passa* appear in the recipes among the liquors where any attempt to pound dried fruit in an already liquid mixture would be impossible. If they were already in a mashed state they could easily be added with the other liquids.

[3] An odd piece of advice given that leek would be very ineffectual as a stirrer.

[4] *condimentum* is particularly odd here as there are no other spices apart from the pepper and the rue, and these are not sufficient for a good Roman sauce! There ought to be other seasonings and one wonders why the recipe was ever saved.

[8.4.2] **ius in uenationibus omnibus elixis et assis**: piperis scripulos VIII, rutam ligusticum apii semen iuniperum timum mentam aridam scripulos senos, pulei scripulos III. haec omnia ad leuissimum puluerem rediges et in uino commisces et teres. adicies in uasculum melle quod satis erit, et his uteris cum oxigaro.

[8.4.3] **ius frigidum in ouifero**: piper ligusticum thimum cuminum frictum nucleos tostos mel acetum liquamen et oleum. piper aspergis.

V. BVBVLA SIVE VITELLINA.

[8.5.1] **uitellina fricta**: piper ligusticum apii semen cuminum origanum cepam siccam uuam passam mel acetum uinum liquamen oleum defritum.

[8.5.2] **uitulinam siue bubulam cum porris <uel> cidoneis uel cepis uel colocaseis**: liquamen piper laser et olei modicum.

[8.5.3] **in uitulinam elixam**: teres piper ligusticum careum apii semen; suffundes mel acetum liquamen oleum. calefacies, amulo obligas et carnem perfundes.

[8.5.4] **aliter in uitulina elixa**: piper ligusticum feniculi semen origanum nucleos careotam mel acetum liquamen, sinapi et oleo.

VI. IN AEDO VEL AGNO.

[8.6.1] **copadia hedina siue agnina**: pipere liquamine coques, cum faseolis faratariis liquamine pipere lasere, cum inbracto bocellas panis et oleo modico.

[8.6.2] **aliter hedinam siue agninam excaldatam**: mittes in caccabum copadia. cepam coriandrum minutum succides; teres piper ligusticum cuminum liquamen oleum uinum. coques; exinanies in patina; amulo obligas.

[8.6.3] **aliter hedinam siue agninam excaldatam**: <agnina> a crudo trituram mortario accipere debet; caprina autem cum coquitur accipit trituram.

[8.6.4] **hedum siue agnum assum**: edi cocturam: ubi eum ex liquamine et oleo coxeris, incisum infundes in pipere lasere liquamine oleo modice. et in graticula assabis: eodem iure continges. piper asparges et inferes.

---

3. hæc *E* | in uino *E*: in uno *V* 4. uas/.culum *E* 10. <uel> *Gi* 15. et om. *E* | oleum *Hum* 16. HEDO *E* 18. cum inbracto *V*: cum bracto *E*: cuminum tritum *Hum*: cumino fricto *André* | buccellas *T* 19. mittis *E* 22. aliter… excaldatam *del.Vo* | <agnina> *Hum* | trituram *Hum*: tritura *VE* 24 hedi *E* | edi cocturam *del. Sch* 25. craticula *TP* 26. asperges *E*

---

[1] That is, fish sauce and vinegar which have probably been cooked together.

[2] The term *faseoli faratarii* seems to imply a 'starchy' pea, or perhaps 'pea flour' is intended. Lit. 'with flour-filled beans'.

8.4.2. **Sauce for all kinds of boiled and roast game**: 8 scruples pepper, rue, lovage, celery seed, juniper berries, thyme, 6 scruples dry mint, 3 scruples pennyroyal. Reduce all these to a very fine dust and mix with wine and pound again. Add to this in a vessel sufficient honey and use it with *oxygarum*.[1]

8.4.3. **Cold sauce for wild sheep**: pepper, lovage, thyme, roasted cumin, roasted pine nuts, honey, vinegar, *liquamen* and oil. Sprinkle with pepper.

8.5. BEEF OR VEAL.

8.5.1. **Fried veal**: pepper, lovage, celery seed, cumin, oregano, dried onion, raisins, honey, vinegar, wine, *liquamen*, oil, *defrutum*.

8.5.2. **Veal or beef with leek or quince, or onion, or taro**: *liquamen*, pepper, *laser*, and a little oil.

8.5.3. **Sauce for boiled veal**: pound pepper, lovage, caraway, celery seed, pour on honey, vinegar, *liquamen*, oil. Warm it through, thicken with starch and pour on to the meat.

8.5.4. **Another recipe for boiled veal**: pepper, lovage, fennel seed, oregano, pine nuts, date, honey, vinegar, *liquamen*, mustard and oil.

8.6. SAUCES FOR KID OR LAMB.

8.6.1. **Kid or lamb pieces**: cook with pepper and *liquamen*, (or) with cow peas,[2] *liquamen*, pepper, *laser*, (or) as a relish[3] on pieces of bread with a little oil.

8.6.2. **Another recipe for boiled kid or lamb**: put the pieces of meat in a pan. Finely chop onion and coriander; pound pepper, lovage, cumin, *liquamen*, oil, wine. Cook it; tip into a dish; thicken with starch.

8.6.3. **Another recipe for boiled kid or lamb**: lamb must receive the seasonings from the mortar when it is raw, whereas kid receives the seasonings while it is cooking.

8.6.4. **Roast kid or lamb**: to cook a goat: when you have cooked it in some *liquamen* and oil, make an incision in the skin and pour on pepper, *laser*, *liquamen*, and a little oil. You can also roast it on a gridiron; brush it with the same sauce, sprinkle with pepper and serve.

---

[3] André, followed by Milham, printed *cumino fricto* here, but the MSS read *cum bracto* (*E*) and *cum inbracto* (*V*), possibly cognate with Greek *embrechō*, 'moisten in' (André 1974, pp. 206-7), and therefore 'something which moistens' bread, i.e. relish: that which is eaten with bread. See *embractum* in 9.11. It is not clear whether the relish is another item or that the *copadia* are in fact the relish itself.

[8.6.5] **aliter hedum siue agnum assum**: piperis semunciam, asereos scripulos VI, gengiberis modicum, petroselini scripulos VI, laseris modice; liquaminis optimi eminam, olei acetabulum.

[8.6.6] **hedus siue agnus syringiatus (id est mammotestis)**: exossatur diligenter a gula sic ut uter fiat et intestina eius integra exinaniantur ita ut in caput intestina sufflentur et per nouissimam partem stercus exinanibitur. aqua lauantur diligenter et sic inplentur admixto liquamine et ab humeris consuitur et mittitur in cliba-num. cum coctus fuerit, perfunditur ius bulliens: lacte piper tritum liquamen carenum defritum modice sic et oleum, et iam bullienti mittis amulum. uel certe mittitur in retiaculo uel in sportella et diligenter constringitur et bullienti zemae cum modico salis summittitur. cum bene illic tres undas bullierit, leuatur et denuo bullit cum humore supra scripto. bulliente conditura perfunditur.

[8.6.7] **aliter hedus siue agnus syringiatus**: lactis sextarium unum, mellis uncias IIII, piperis unciam I, salis modicum laseris modicum. ius [in] ipsius: oleum acetabulum liquaminis acetabulum mellis acetabulum dactilos tritos octo, uini boni eminam, amulum modice.

[8.6.8] **hedus siue agnus crudus**: oleo piper fricabis et asparges fores salem purum multo cum coriandri semen. in furnum mittis, assatum inferes.

[8.6.9] **hedum siue agnum Tarpeianum**: antequam coquatur ornatus consuitur. piper rutam satureiam cepam timum modicum et liquamine colles hedum, macerabis. in furno, in patella quae oleum habeat cum percoxerit, perfundes in patella inpensam: teres satureiam cepam rutam dactilos liquamen uinum carenum oleum. cum bene duxerit inpensam, in disco pones, piper asparges et inferes.

5

10

15

20

---

1. asareos *Hum*   2. gingiberis *E* | petroselini *Hum*: petroselinis *VE*   4. syringiatus *GiVo (cf. 8.6.7)*: syringladus *VE* | mammotestus *E*: mammocoetis *Sch*: mammochestes *Heraeus*: mammothreptus *Dufresne*: amnocistis *Bas* | id est est mammotestis *del. Hum* | exossatur *E*: exsorsatur *V*   5. a gula *Tor*: agilla *VE* | sicut *E* | uter *om. V*   6. sufflentur *L*: suffletur *VE*   7. implentur *V*   9. defritum *Hum*: defrictum *VE*   10. zemae *Sch (cf. 8.7.3, 4)*: zema *VE*   11. modice *E1*   14. ius [in] ipsius *André*: ius in ipsius *VE*: ius spissius *Sch*: ius in ipsum *Gi*: ius †ipsius† *Milham*   15. liquaminis acetabulum mellis acetabulum *after* tritos octo *E1, marked for del. and recopied at foot of page E2*   17. pipere *E* | asperges *E* | foris *E*   18. semine *E*   19. Tarpeianum *R*: tatarpeianum *VE* | coquatur *P*: coquantur *VE*   20. thimum *E*   21. <mittis> in furno *André*: <mittes> in furno *Milham* | quæ *E*   23. asperges *E*

8.6.5. Another roast kid or lamb recipe: ½ oz. pepper, 6 scruples of hazelwort,[1] a little ginger, 6 scruples of parsley, a little *laser*, ½ pt. best *liquamen*, 1 *acetabulum* of oil.

8.6.6. Hollowed-out kid or lamb (that is, swollen-skinned):[2] carefully bone the carcass from the neck end so that it is like a bag. The entire intestinal tract should be emptied out in this way: blow into the intestines at the top end so that the excrement is expelled from the very bottom. It is washed carefully with water and filled with *liquamen*, the lamb is sewn up at the shoulder and put in the oven. When it is cooked this boiling sauce is poured on: milk, ground pepper, *liquamen*, *caroenum*, a little *defrutum*, a little oil too, and when it is boiling add starch. Or alternatively it is tied up carefully, put in a net or basket and lowered into a pan of boiling water with a little salt. When it has come to the boil well and truly three times, it is taken out and boiled once more in the sauce written above. Then pour the boiling sauce over it.

8.6.7. Another hollowed-out kid or lamb: 1 pt. milk, 4oz. honey, 1oz. pepper, a little salt, a little *laser*, some of the cooking liquor, 1 *acetabulum* of oil, 1 *acetabulum* of *liquamen*, 1 *acetabulum* of honey, 8 pounded dates, ½ pt. good wine, a little starch.[3]

8.6.8. Rare kid or lamb: rub with oil and pepper, and sprinkle plenty of pure salt and coriander seed all over the outside. Put in the oven. Serve roasted.

8.6.9. Tarpeian kid or lamb: before (the carcass) is cooked it should be trussed and dressed. Soak the goat in a mixture of pepper, rue, savory, onion, a little thyme, and *liquamen*. Marinade it. When it has finished cooking in the oven in a dish with some oil, pour into the dish (and over the lamb) this mixture: pound savory, onion, rue, dates, *liquamen*, wine, *caroenum*, oil. When the mixture has been well absorbed, place on a serving dish, sprinkle with pepper and serve.

---

[1] Wild spikenard.

[2] This appears to be an early gloss from a commentator attempting to define the title, though it is obscure in the extreme, and (so far as we have been able to ascertain) unknown anywhere else: *mammosus* means 'full-breasted' or 'swollen'; *testa* means 'shell' or 'outer covering'. The reference is to the resulting appearance of the carcass. For a modern instance of this method of skinning an animal see Carlo Levi, *Christ stopped at Eboli*, (Penguin edition, 1982), p. 51. André comments (*Apicius*, p.198), 'la glose semble incompréhensible, malgré les corrections proposées'.

[3] Previous editors have been confused by the MSS reading *ius in ipsius*. *FR* suggested that it is the beginning of another sauce and that the first half of the recipe is the cooking liquor for the meat. We prefer André's deletion of *in*, interpreting *ius ipsius* as some of the liquor in which the carcass has been boiled, as in the alternative method suggested in 8.6.6.

[8.6.10] **hedum siue agnum Particum**: mittes in furnum; teres piper rutam cepam satureiam damascena enucleata laseris modicum uinum liquamen et oleum [uinum]. feruens colluitur in disco, ex aceto sumitur.

[8.6.11] **hedo laureato ex lacte**: hedum curas, exossas, interanea eius cum
5 coagulo tolles, lauas. adicies in mortarium piper ligusticum laseris radicem, bacas lauri duas, piretri modicum, cerebella duo uel tria. haec omnia teres, suffundes liquamen, temperabis ex sale. super trituram colas lactis sextarios duos, mellis ligulas duas. hac inpensa intestina reples et super hedum conponis in giro, et omentum <uel> carta cooperies; surclas. in caccabum uel patellam
10 conpones hedum; adicies liquamen oleum uinum. cum ad mediam cocturam uenerit, teres <piper> ligusticum, et ius de suo sibi suffundes. mittes defriti modicum, teres, reexinanies in caccabum. cum percoctus fuerit exornas, amulo obligas et inferes.

VII. IN PORCELLO.

15 [8.7.1] **porcellum farsilem duobus generibus**: curas, a gutture extenteras, a ceruice ornas. antequam praedures, subaperies auriculam sub cutem, mittes inpensam Terentinam in uesicam bubulum et fistolam auiarii rustro uesicae alligabis per quam exprimes in aurem quantum ceperit. post a carta præcludes et infiblabis et praeparabis aliam inpensam. sic facies: teres piper ligusticum
20 origanum laseris radicem modicum; suffundes liquamen adicies cerebella cocta oua cruda alicam coctam, ius de suo sibi <si> fuerit; aucellas, nucleos piper integrum; liquamine temperas. imples porcellum carta obduras et fiblas. mittes in fornum. cum coctus fuerit exornas, perunges et inferes.

[8.7.2] **aliter porcellum**: salem cuminum laser.

1. Particum *Sch*: pasticum *VE*   2. damascenae nucleata *V* | leseris *V*   3. oleum *P*: oleum uinum *VE*   4. hedo *VE*: haedum *GiVo*: haedus *Tor* | laureato *CGSG*: laurum *VE*: laureum *Sch*: laureatum *GiVo*: laureatus *Tor* | exorsas *E*   5. coagulo *LBTP*: quagulo *VE* 6. piretri *CGSG*: pirethi *VE*: pirethri *André*: pyrethri *Ber* | hæc *E* | teres *om. E1* 8. componis *V*   9. omentum *V2, E2*: mentum *E1*: omento *V1* | <uel> *Gi* | cooperies *T*: cooperes *VE*   10. cōpones *V* | cocturam *P*: cora *VE*   11. piper add. *π* | defrito *V* 15. generibus *GiVo*: generis *VE*   16. praedures *Hum*: perdures *VE*   17. bubulam *Rot* | rostro *TP* | uesicæ *E*   18. post a charta *GiVo*: posta carta *V*: post acarta *E*: postea charta *π*   21. <si> *Sch* | fuerint *GiVo*   22. obturas *Lis*: obducas *Sch* | fibras *E1* | mittes *π*: mitteres *V*: mitteris *E*   23. furnum *V*

8.6.10. **Parthian kid or lamb**: put it in the oven. Pound pepper, rue, onion, savory, stoned damsons, a little *laser*, wine, *liquamen*, and oil. Pour lots of the boiling sauce over the meat on a serving dish. Eat it with some vinegar.

8.6.11. **'Crowned' kid in a milk sauce**: prepare and bone the kid. Take out the intestines and stomach. Wash them. Put in a mortar pepper, lovage, *laser* root, 2 bay berries, a little Spanish camomile and 2 or 3 brains. Pound all this, pour on *liquamen*, balance the flavour with salt.[1] Pour 2 pt. milk and 2 spoons of honey over the pounded mixture. Fill the intestines with this mixture and arrange them in a spiral over the kid. Wrap it in either caul or papyrus and bind it up. Put the kid in a pan or dish, add *liquamen*, oil, wine. When it is half way through cooking, pound pepper, lovage, and pour on some of the cooking liquor, put in a little *defrutum*, pound again, empty it back into the pan. When it is completely cooked, arrange (the kid on a dish), thicken the sauce with starch and serve.[2]

8.7. RECIPES FOR PIGLET.

8.7.1. **Piglet stuffed in two ways**: prepare the piglet: open it out at the gullet and draw it from the neck. Before you brown it, open up the skin below the ear flap. Put Terentine stuffing in an ox bladder and fasten a bird-keeper's reed pipe to the mouth of the bladder; squeeze through this into the ear as much as it can hold. Next cover it up with a sheet of papyrus and pin it in place. Then prepare the second stuffing like this: pound pepper, lovage, oregano a little *laser* root, pour on *liquamen*, add cooked brains, raw eggs, cooked *alica*, some cooking liquor if available, little birds, pine nuts, whole peppercorns, flavour with *liquamen*. Stuff the piglet. Cover with papyrus and pin in place.[3] Put in the oven. When it is cooked, arrange it and smear with oil and serve.

8.7.2. **Another piglet recipe**: salt, cumin, *laser*.

---

[1] An interesting use of *liquamen* and salt in the same recipe. It is quite rare for obvious reasons. *temperabis* is clearly here a term for adjusting the salt balance.

[2] The kid is 'crowned' with its own stuffed intestines. Elsewhere in *Apicius* the intestines are filled or stuffed and then put back inside the carcass: see above, 8.6.6, where the intestines are just filled with *liquamen*, and the more complex recipe preserved in the *Excerpta Vinidarii* 28. In this instance, 'the sausages' in a spiral are placed on top and the whole is wrapped in caul or papyrus to hold it together when it is cooked. Presumably caul would be used for roasting the dish and papyrus for boiling.

[3] A suckling pig could easily be wrapped entirely in papyrus, or the papyrus might simply be used to cover the opening.

[8.7.3] **porcellum liquaminatum**: de porcello eicis utriculum ita ut alique pulpe in eo remaneant. teres piper ligusticum origanum, suffundes liquamen, adicies uinum, cerebellum, oua duo, misces in se. porcellum praeduratum imples, fiblabis, in sportella feruenti olle summittis. cocto fiblas tolles ut ius ex ipso manare possit. piper aspersum inferes.

[8.7.4] **porcellum elixum farsilem**: de porcello utriculum eicies, preduras. teres piper ligusticum origanum, suffundes liquamen; cerebella cocta quod satis sit, similiter oua dissolues, liquamine temperabis; farcimina cocta integra precides. sed ante porcellum preduratum liquamine delauas, deinde imples, infiblas. in sportella feruenti olle summittes. coctum sfongizas, sine pipere inferes.

[8.7.5] **porcellum assum tractomelinum**: porcellum curatum a gutture extenteras, siccas. teres piperis unciam, mel uinum, inpones ut ferueat; tractam siccatam confringes et partibus caccabo permisces. agitabis surculo lauri uiridis. tam diu coques donec lenis fiat et inpinguet. hac inpensa porcellum inples, surculas, obduras carta, in furnum mittes, exornas et inferes.

[8.7.6] **porcellum lacte pastum elixum calidum iure frigidum crudo Apiciano**: adicies in mortarium piper ligusticum coriandri semen mentam rutam, fricabis; suffundes liquamen, adicies mel uinum et liquamine <temperabis>. porcellum elixum feruentem sauano mundo siccatum perfundes et inferes.

[8.7.7] **porcellum Vitellianum**: porcellum ornas quasi aprum, sale asparges, in furno assas. adicies in mortarium piper ligusticum, suffundes liquamen, uino et passo temperabis. in caccabo cum olei pusillum ferueat, et porcellum assum iure asperges ita ut sub cute ius recipiat.

[8.7.8] **porcellum Flacianum**: porcellum ornas in modum apri, sale asperges et in furnum mittes. dum coquitur adicies in mortarium piper ligusticum careum apii semen laseris radicem rutam uiridem, fricabis; suffundes liquamen, uino et passo temperabis. in caccabum; cum olei modicum ferueat; amulo obligas. porcellum coctum ab ossibus tanges, apii semen teres ita ut fiat puluis, asperges et inferes.

1. aliquem *E*   3. uinum *VE*: unum *LT*   5. manare *Hum*: manere *VE*   7. suffendes *E1*
10. sfongizas *CGSG*: sfongias *VE*: spongizas *GiVo*   11. tractomelinum *Sch*: tractomel in- *E*: tracto mel in- *V*: tractomelitum *Hum*: tractomellinum *André* | agutture *E*   12. tractam *Hum*: tactam *VE*   14. imples *V*   15. obturas *Lis*   16. frigidum *del. Sch*: frigido *GiVo*
17. menta ruta *V*   18. liquamen *V*: liquidum *E* | <temperabis> *Gi*   19. sauano *V2, E*: sauono *V1* | profundes *E*   20. asperges *E*   22. olei *V*: oleo *E* | pusillum *V*: pussillum *E*: pusillo *GiVo*   23. ita et *V* | cute eius *V*   25. mittis *E*   26. liquamen *λ*: liquamine *VE*   27. passio *V* | caccabo *GiVo* | modico *GiVo*   28. fiat] faciat *E1*

8.7.3. Piglet in *liquamen*: gut the piglet's belly in such a way that some of the offal remains. Pound pepper, lovage, oregano, pour on *liquamen*, add some wine, a brain and 2 eggs, stir together. Brown the piglet, stuff it and pin it up, place in a basket and put it in a vessel of boiling water. When it is cooked, take the pins out so that the juice can run out. Sprinkle with pepper and serve.

8.7.4. Stuffed boiled piglet: gut the piglet and brown it. Pound pepper, lovage oregano, pour on *liquamen*, add as much cooked brains as is necessary, likewise stir in eggs, flavour with *liquamen*. Cook the stuffing in one piece and slice it. But first sear the piglet (on a fire and) wash it down in *liquamen* and then stuff it and pin it up. Place in a basket and put it in a pan of boiling water. When it is cooked, sponge it down and serve without pepper.

8.7.5. Roast piglet in a *tracta* and honey sauce: gut the prepared piglet from the neck, open it out and dry it. Pound 1 oz. pepper, honey, wine, bring it to heat in a pan. Crumble a dried *tracta* and stir it into the pan a little at a time. Stir with a twig of green bay, cooking it until it becomes smooth and thickens. Fill the piglet with this stuffing, bind it up, cover with papyrus, put in the oven, arrange (on a serving dish) and serve.

8.7.6. Milk-fed piglet, boiled and served hot with a cold uncooked Apician sauce: put in a mortar pepper, lovage, coriander seed, mint, rue; pound them. Pour on *liquamen*, add honey and wine and flavour with *liquamen*. Wipe the boiled piglet with a clean cloth while it is still hot, pour on the sauce and serve.

8.7.7. Vitellian piglet: dress the piglet like a boar. Sprinkle with salt and roast in the oven. Put in a mortar pepper, lovage, pour on *liquamen*, flavour with wine and *passum*. Bring it to heat in a pan with a tiny amount of oil. Drizzle the sauce over the roasted piglet so that the sauce seeps beneath the skin.

8.7.8. Flaccian piglet: dress the piglet in the manner of a boar. Sprinkle with salt and put in the oven. While it is cooking, put in a mortar pepper, lovage, caraway, celery seed, *laser* root, green rue; pound them. Pour on *liquamen*, flavour with wine and *passum*. In a pan, bring it to heat with a little oil. Thicken with starch. Smother the cooked piglet (thoroughly with the sauce) 'down to the bone'.[1] Pound celery seed to a fine powder, sprinkle and serve.

---

[1] *porcellum coctum ab ossibus tanges*: 'touch the cooked piglet (with the sauce) down to the bone' i.e. smother it well and truly, let it penetrate, seep, flow everywhere. This seems to be a culinary turn of phrase for 'totally covered'. There is no indication that the cooked pig is cut or slashed open so that the sauce can penetrate. In fact recipe 9 uses the same words even though the piglet does not in fact have any bones!

[8.7.9] **porcellum laureatum**: porcellum exossas, quasi oenogaratum ornas, preduras. laurum uiridem in medio franges satis, in furnum assas et mittes in mortarium piper ligusticum careum apii semen laseris radicem bacas lauri; fricabis; suffundes liquamen et uino et passo temperabis. adicies in caccabo cum olei modicum ut ferueat. obligas. porcellum lauro eximes et ius ab ossa tanges et inferes.

[8.7.10] **Frontinianum porcellum**: exossas, preduras, ornas. adicies in caccabum liquamen uinum, obligas fasciculum porri aneti. media cocturam mittes defritum. coctum leuas et siccum mittes. piper asparges et inferes.

[8.7.11] **porcellum oenococtum**: porcellum preduras, ornas. adicies in caccabum oleum liquamen uinum aquam; obligas fasciculum porri coriandri; media coctura colorabis defrito. adicies in mortarium piper ligusticum careum origanum apii semen laseris radicem, fricabis; suffundes liquamen, ius de suo sibi; uino et passo temperabis. exinanies in caccabum, facies ut ferueat; cum ferbuerit amulo obligas. porcellum compositum in patina perfundes, piper asparges et inferes.

[8.7.12] **porcellum Celsinianum**: ornas, infundes pipere ruta cepa satureia sub cute suo et oua infundes per auriculam et ex pipere liquamine uino modico in acetabulum temperas et sumes.

[8.7.13] **porcellum assum**: teres piper rutam satureiam cepam, ouorum coctorum media, liquamen uinum oleum conditum. bulliat. conditura porcellum in boletari perfundes et inferes.

[8.7.14] **porcellum hortolanum**: porcellus hortolanus exossatur per gulam in modum utris. mittitur in eo pullus esiciatus particulatim concisus, turdi ficetulæ, esicia de pulpa sua, lucanicae, dactili exossati, fabriles bulbi, cocleae exemptae, malue bete porri apium, coliculi elixi, coriandrum piper integrum, nuclei, oua

2. furno *GiVo*   4. uino passo *E (om.* et*)*   5. modico *GiVo* | ossis *P*: ossibus *GiVo*
8. coctura *π*   9. leuas *André*: lauas *VE* | asperges *E*   10. oeno coctum *E* |
preduras *π*: produras *VE*   14. feruuerit *V*   15. oblizas *V* | conpositum *E* | asperges *E*
16-17. sub cute suo *Milham*: sicuto suo *VE*: sub cute sua *André*   18. acetabolum *E* |
temperas *π*: teriperas *VE*   22. hortulanum *Milham*   23. particulatim *LR*:
particulam *VE* | ficetule *E*   24. lucanicæ *E* | cocleæ exemptæ *E*

[1] *hortulanum*: 'of or pertaining to the garden' and by inference a simple peasant style, indicated by the number of vegetables, produce of a market garden. Alternatively, as *FR* note, there may (by emending the text to read *hortalanum*) be a reference to the M. Hortensius Hortalus mentioned by Tacitus, *A*. 2.37, and Suetonius, *Tib.* 47.

8.7.9. **Piglet in bay sauce**: bone the piglet, dress it as though for cooking in *oenogarum* and brown it. Break up a sufficient quantity of green bay into the cavity. Roast in the oven. Put into a mortar pepper, lovage, caraway, celery seed, *laser* root, bay berries, pound them. Pour on *liquamen* and flavour with wine and *passum*. Put into a pan with a little oil and bring to heat, thicken it. Take the bay out of the piglet and smother the piglet down to the bone with the sauce and serve.

8.7.10. **Frontinian piglet**: Bone, brown and dress the piglet. Put in a pan (with) *liquamen*, and wine. Bind up a bundle of leek and dill (and put it in). In the middle of the cooking add *defrutum*. When it is cooked take it out and dry it, put (it on a dish). Sprinkle with pepper and serve.

8.7.11. **Piglet cooked in wine**: brown the piglet and dress it. Put in a pan oil, *liquamen*, wine, water; bind up a bundle of leek and coriander. In the middle of the cooking colour it with *defrutum*. Put in a mortar pepper, lovage, caraway, oregano, celery seed, *laser* root; pound them. Pour on *liquamen* and some of the cooking liquor, flavour with wine and *passum*. Empty this into a pan and bring to heat. When it is simmering thicken with starch. Arrange the piglet on a dish, pour on the sauce, sprinkle with pepper and serve.

8.7.12. **Celsinian piglet**: dress the piglet. Insert (a mixture of) pepper, rue, onion, savory, under its skin and pour eggs into the ear cavity. Blend a sauce of pepper, *liquamen*, a little wine in a cup and serve it up.

8.7.13. **Roast piglet**: pound pepper, rue, savory, onion, the yolks of hard boiled-eggs, *liquamen*, wine, oil, spiced wine; bring it to the boil. Pour the finished sauce over the piglet in a serving dish and serve.

8.7.14. **Garden-style piglet**:[1] garden-style piglet is boned through the gullet to form a bag. Into it is put: chicken forcemeat cut into pieces,[2] (meat from) thrushes and figpeckers, forcemeat from the pig, *lucanicae* sausages, stoned dates, forge-dried bulbs,[3] snails removed from their shells, mallows, beets, leeks, celery, boiled cabbage, coriander, whole peppercorns, pine nuts, and 15 eggs are

---

[2] For *particulatim* see Glossary, *isicia*.

[3] Bulbs and onions are often described as dried in many of the recipes. This corresponds to the normal state of onions today; the first few layers of skin are dried but they are still juicy inside. These bulbs, on the other hand, may have been fully dried given that a forge is going to generate much more heat than a bulb would be used to when it is dried out of doors. Pliny, *HN.* 14.16, gives a reference to grapes dried in a forge.

XV superinfunduntur; liquamen piperatum, oua mittantur tria, et consuitur et praeduratur. in furno assatur. deinde a dorso scinditur et iure hoc perfunditur: piper teritur ruta liquamen passum mel oleum modicum. cum bullierit amulum mittitur.

[8.7.15] **ius frigidum in porcellum ita facies in elixum**: teres piper careum anetum, origanum modice, nucleos pineos; suffundes acetum liquamen careotam mel, sinape factum; superstillabis oleum, piper asparges et inferes.

[8.7.16] **porcellum Traianum sic facies**: exossas porcellum et aptabis sicuti enococtum et ad fumum suspendes et adpendeas, et quantum adpendeas tantum salis in ollam mittes et elixas ut coquatur, et siccum in lance inferes salso recente.

[8.7.17] **in porcello lactante**: piperis unciam I, uini eminam, olei optimi acetabulum maius, liquaminis acetabulum, aceti acetabulum minus.

VIII. LEPOREM.

[8.8.1] **leporem madidum**: in aqua precoquitur modice, deinde conponitur in patina ac coquendus oleo in furno et cum prope sit coctus ex alio oleo. pertangito de conditura infra scripta: teres piper <ligusticum> satureiam cepam rutam apii semen liquamen laser uinum et modice olei. aliquotiens uersatur, in ipsa percoquitur conditura.

[8.8.2] **item aliam ad eum inpensam**: cum prope tolli debeat, teres piper dactilum laser uuam passam caroenum liquamen oleum; suffundes, et cum bullierit piper asparges et inferes.

[8.8.3] **leporem farsum**: nucleos integros amigdala, nuces siue glandes concisas, piperis grana solida, pulpa de ipso lepore; et ouis fractis obligatur; de omento porcino in furno. sic iterum inpensam facies: rutam piper satis cepam satureiam

1. super infunduntur *E* | consuitur *V1,E2*: cosuitur *E1,V2*   *2.* preduratur *E*

5. in elixum ita facies *λ, Hum*   6. ?origænum *E1*   7. asperges *E*

8. Traianum *GiVo*: traganum *VE* | abtabis *E*   9. enococtum *E*: eno coctum *V*

10. sic cum *V* | efferes *V* | <pro> salso recente *Bas*   13. acetabulum maius liquaminis minus *E2*: acetabulum aceti acetabulum maius liquaminis minus *E1*   15. componitur *V*

16. ac. *del. Sch*   17. ligusticum *add. λ*   20. alia *E* | eum *Sch*: eam *VE*

22. asperges *E*   24. pulpam *Hum*   25. porcino <inuolutum assatur> in *André*: porcino <obduratur> in *Bra3*

poured in over the top; peppered *liquamen*, and 3 eggs are put in,[1] it is sewn up and browned. It is roasted in the oven. Then it is split open along its back and this sauce is poured on: pepper is pounded (with) rue, *liquamen*, *passum*, honey, a little oil. Starch is added when it has come to the boil.

8.7.15. **You make a cold sauce for piglet in this way when it is boiled**: pound pepper, caraway, dill, a little oregano, pine nuts, pour on vinegar, *liquamen*, dates, honey, made-up mustard. Drizzle some oil over, sprinkle with pepper and serve.

8.7.16. **You make Trajan-style piglet like this**:[2] bone the piglet, prepare it as for 'Piglet cooked in wine sauce',[3] and hang it in the smoke, and then weight it and put its own weight of salt in a vessel. Boil it so that it cooks and serve it dry on a dish like freshly-salted pork.[4]

8.7.17. **Sauce for suckling pig**: 1 oz. pepper, 1 pt. wine, a generous cup of best-quality oil, a cup of *liquamen*, a smaller cup of vinegar.

8.8. HARE.

8.8.1. **Moist hare**: it is cooked for a little while in water and then arranged on a dish in order to be cooked in the oven with oil, and when it is nearly cooked add some more oil. Smother it with the sauce written below: pound pepper, lovage, savory, onion, rue, celery seed, *liquamen*, *laser*, wine and a little oil. Turn it over a few times; it finishes cooking in the sauce.

8.8.2. **Another sauce for the same**: when it is nearly ready to be taken out, pound pepper, date, *laser*, raisins, *caroenum*, *liquamen*, oil; pour over, when it has come to the boil, sprinkle with pepper and serve.

8.8.3. **Stuffed hare**: whole pine nuts, chopped almonds, hazelnuts or acorns, whole grains of pepper, meat from the hare itself: it is bound together with broken eggs. (Stuff the hare, wrap) in pig's caul and put in the oven. Once again make the sauce like this: rue, sufficient pepper, onion, savory, dates, *liquamen*,

---

[1] What are the 'three more eggs' doing here? It seems to us like a suggestion made in the margin of a MS which is later brought into the text and therefore not part of the original recipe.

[2] The MSS both read *traganum*. *Tragum* is derived from the Greek *tragos*, a wheat product made into porridge which has no association here. *Tragus* is the Greek for 'goat', which clearly cannot be connected to this recipe. The emendation to *Traianum* seems sound.

[3] Probably 8.7.11.

[4] *inferes salso recente*: FR adopted Baseggio's conjecture *pro salso* and translated it as 'instead of salt fish'. *salsum* usually means salted fish, but surely not in this context.

dactilos liquamen caroenum uel conditum; diu conbulliat donec spisset et sic perfunditur. sed lepus in piperato liquamine et lasere maneat.

[8.8.4] **ius album in assum leporem**: piper ligusticum cuminum apii semen oui duri medium. trituram colligis et facies globum ex ea. in caccabolo quoques

5 liquamen uinum oleum acetum modice cepullam concisam, postea globolum condimentorum mittes et agitabis origano uel satureia. si opus fuerit, amulas.

[8.8.5] **aliter in leporem ex sanguine et iecinere et pulmonibus leporinis minuta**: adicies in caccabum liquamen et oleum, cocturam; porrum et coriandrum minutatim concides, iecinera et pulmones in caccabum mittes. cum cocta

10 fuerit, teres piper cuminum coriandrum laseris radicem mentam rutam puleium; suffundes acetum; adicies iecinera leporum et sanguinem, teres. <adicies> mel et <ius> de suo sibi, aceto temperabis, exinanies in caccabum; pulmones leporum minutatim concisos in eundem caccabum mittes, facies ut ferueat. cum ferbuerit, amulo obligas, piper asparges et inferes.

15 [8.8.6] **aliter leporem ex suo iure**: leporem curas, exossas, ornas; mittes in caccabo, adicies oleum liquamen cocturam, fasciculum porri coriandrum anetum. dum coquitur adicies in mortarium piper ligusticum cuminum coriandri semen laseris radicem cepam aridam mentam rutam apii semen, fricabis; suffundes liquamen, adicies mel, ius de suo sibi, defrito aceto temperabis. facies ut ferueat;

20 cum ferbuerit, amulo obligabis. exornas, ius perfundes, <piper> asparges et inferes.

[8.8.7] **leporem Passenianum**: leporem curas, exossas, extensum ornas, suspendes ad fumum. cum coloraberit, facies ut dimidia coctura coquatur. leuas, asparges salem, assum oenogaro tanges: adicies in mortarium piper ligusticum,

25 fricabis; suffundes liquamen, uinum et liquamine temperabis. in caccabum adicies oleum modicum, facies ut ferueat; cum ferbuerit, amulo obligas. leporem assum a dorso tangis, piper asparges et inferes.

[8.8.8] **leporem esiciatum**: eadem conditura condies pulpam, nucleos infusos admisces, omento teges uel carta; colliges lacinias et surcula.

---

2. et lasere *om. E*   4. ex ea *Hum*: extra *VE* | caccabolo *V2*: caccabulo *E*: caccabo *V1*
9. minutal *Hum*   10. fuerint *LT*   11. <adicies> *Hum*   12. <ius> *Hum*
14. asperges *E*   16. adicies…cocturam *om. V1, added in a diff. hand* (oleo *V2*)
20. <piper> *Hum* | asperges *E*   23. colorauerit *E* | facies et *E* | leuas *Gi*: lauas *VE*
24. asperges *E* | assum *CGSG*: massam *VE*: assas *Bra3* | oenogaro *Hum*: oenogara *VE*
25. uino *GiVo*   26. feruuerit *E*   27. asperges *E*   28. eadem *TP*: eandem
VE | conditura *VE*: coctura *P, Hum*: condituram *Milham*   29. omente *V*

caroenum, or spiced wine. Let it boil a long time until it thickens and then pour it on. But let the hare rest in peppered *liquamen* and *laser*.[1]

8.8.4. White sauce for roast hare: pepper, lovage, cumin, celery seed, a hard-boiled egg yolk. Gather the pounded mixture and make a ball of it. Heat in a pan *liquamen*, wine, oil, a little vinegar, chopped onion, then put in the ball of spices and stir with oregano or savory. Thicken if needed.[2]

8.8.5. Another recipe for hare with the blood and chopped liver and lights of a hare:[3] put in a pan *liquamen*, oil, stock; finely chop in leek and coriander, then put the liver and lights in the pan. When it has cooked, pound pepper, cumin, coriander, *laser* root, mint, rue, pennyroyal, pour on vinegar, add the liver and the blood of the hare and pound again. Add honey and some of the cooking liquor, flavour with vinegar, empty into a pan; chop the hare's lungs finely and put them in the same pan and bring it to heat; when it is simmering thicken with starch, sprinkle with pepper and serve.

8.8.6. Another recipe for hare in its own sauce: prepare the hare, bone it and dress it and put in a pan. Add oil, *liquamen*, stock, a bundle of leek, coriander and dill. While it is cooking, put in a mortar pepper, lovage, cumin, coriander seed, *laser* root, dried onion, mint, rue, celery seed; pound them; pour on *liquamen*, add honey, some of the cooking liquor, flavour with *defrutum* and vinegar. Bring it to heat; when it is simmering, thicken with starch. Arrange it, pour on the sauce, sprinkle with pepper and serve.

8.8.7. Passenian hare: prepare the hare, bone it, and dress it stretched out; hang it in the smoke. When it has taken on some colour, see that it is part-boiled. Take it out, sprinkle with coarse salt, roast (the hare) and cover with (this) *oenogarum*: put in a mortar pepper, lovage; pound them, pour on *liquamen*, flavour with wine and *liquamen*. Put in a pan with a little oil, bring it to heat; when it is simmering, thicken with starch. Cover the roasted hare along its back, sprinkle with pepper and serve.

8.8.8. Hare forcemeat: flavour the meat with the same spices, mix in soaked pine nuts, wrap in caul or papyrus. Gather up the edges and tie them.

[1] This instruction is not very clear. Is the hare marinated in the *liquamen* and *laser* before it is stuffed or allowed to stand in the liquor after cooking? Note also that walnuts instead of acorns may be intended. On acorns used as a foodstuff, see S. Mason, 'Acornutopia? Determining the Role of Acorns in Past Human Subsistence', in *Food in Antiquity*, 12-24.

[2] See 8.1.5 for a similar use of a spice ball.

[3] There is no need to emend to *minutal* (Hummelberg), given that the MSS reading *minuta* in the title is confirmed by the instructions contained in the recipe itself.

[8.8.9] **leporem farsilem**: leporem curas, ornas quadratum, inponis. adicies in mortarium piper ligusticum origanum, suffundes liquamen, adicies iecinera gallinarum cocta, cerebella cocta, pulpam concisam, oua cruda tria, liquamine temperabis. omento teges aut carta et surclas. lento igni subassas. adicies in mortarium piper ligusticum, fricabis, suffundes liquamen, uino et liquamine temperabis, facies ut ferueat; cum ferbuerit, amulo obligas et leporem subassatum perfundes. piper asparges et inferes.

[8.8.10] **aliter leporem elixum**: ornas, adicies in lance oleum liquamen acetum passum; cepam concides et rutam uiridem, thimum subcultratum et sic adpones.

[8.8.11] **leporis conditura**: teritur piper ruta cepula et iecur leporis; liquamen caroenum passum olei modicum. amulum cum bullit.

[8.8.12] **leporem sicco sparsum**: et hunc precondies sicut hedum Tarpeianum: antequam coquatur ornatus suitur. piper rutam satureiam cepam thimum modicum liquamine colues, postea in furnum coques. et inpensam tali circumsparges: piperis semunciam rutam cepam satureiam, dactilos IIII, uuam passam. mustum coloratum super uatillum, uinum oleum liquamen carenum. frequenter tangitur ut condituram suam omnem tollat; postea ex pipere sicco in disco sumitur.

[8.8.13] **aliter leporem conditum**: coques ex uino liquamine aqua sinape modicum aneto porro cum capillo suo. cum se coxerit condies: piper satureia cepae rutundum dactilos, damascenæ duo, uinum liquamen caroenum, olei modice. stringatur amulo, modicum bulliat. conditura lepus in patina perfunditur.

---

4. aut carta et surclas *CGSG*: et carta et surclas *V*: et surclas et carta *E*   6. feruuerit *V*
7. asperges *E*   8. aliter leporem elixum *O*: leporem aliter elixum *VE* | oenas *E*
10. adponis *V*   11. iecor *E*   13. leporem <pipere> sicco *Gi*   14. coquantur *E*
15. furnum <mittes> coques *Gi* | impensa *GiVo* | talem *TP*   16. mustum *CGSG*: ius tam
VE: ius cum *Hum*: ustam *Bra2*: iusculum *Gi*   17. coloratur *Hum*: caloratum *Sch*:
coloratam *Bra2*   20. modico *GiVo* | pipere *E* | cepæ *E*   21. damascenę *V*
22. conditura *Sch*: conditur *VE* | lep *V1*

8.8.9. **Stuffed hare**: prepare the hare, cut into neat portions[1] and put to one side. Put in a mortar pepper, lovage, oregano; pour on *liquamen,* add cooked chicken livers, cooked brains, chopped meat, 3 raw eggs, flavour with *liquamen*. (Stuff the hare pieces), wrap in caul or papyrus and tie up. Grill on a gentle fire. Put in a mortar pepper, lovage; pound them, pour on *liquamen*, flavour with wine and *liquamen*. Bring it to heat; when it is simmering, thicken with starch and pour over the lightly grilled hare. Sprinkle with pepper and serve.

8.8.10. **Another recipe for boiled hare**: arrange on a serving dish (with) oil, *liquamen*, vinegar, *passum*; chop on onion and green rue, finely chopped thyme, and serve it like this.

8.8.11. **Seasoning for hare**: pepper, rue, onion and the liver of the hare are ground; *liquamen, caroenum, passum,* a little oil. Starch when it boils.

8.8.12. **Hare basted dry**:[2] you can also season this like Tarpeian kid:[3] before it is cooked it is dressed and trussed. Drench it (in a mixture of) pepper, rue, savory, onion, a little thyme, *liquamen*; afterwards cook it in the oven. You can also sprinkle this round it: ½ oz. pepper, rue, onion, savory, 4 dates, raisins, must reduced over a brazier for colouring, wine, oil, *liquamen, caroenum*. It is basted frequently so that it takes up all the sauce; then it is taken out and served dry with pepper on a round dish.

8.8.13. **Another recipe for spiced hare**: cook in some wine, *liquamen*, water, a little mustard, dill, leeks with their tops. When it has cooked, season with pepper, savory, slices of onion, dates, 2 damsons, wine, *liquamen, caroenum,* a little oil; it should be thickened with starch; let it boil a little. Pour the sauce over the hare in a dish.

---

[1] *quadrare* has the basic meaning of 'square off', hence 'put in order'; it cannot mean 'truss' here (i.e. square up the whole carcass) since separate pieces of hare are used later. Perhaps the sense is to 'square the pieces up' (as in 'quartering' the carcass). However, the term *quadra* is used elsewhere of pieces of cheese (Martial 12.32.18) or of placenta (Martial 6.75.1, 9.90.17-18), where 'wedge' or 'slice' would be an appropriate rendering, as both items were typically round in shape.

[2] *sicco*: the meaning of 'dry' here is obscure; we think that it refers to the nature of the dish when it is cooked, i.e. that (as the final sentence of the recipe makes clear) the basting is continued until all the sauce is used up, hence our rendering 'basted dry'. The ablative is frequently used to indicate the manner of serving. Giarratano's addition of *pipere*, copied from the final sentence, is unnecessary; in any case, pepper is quite naturally dry.

[3] See 8.6.9.

VIIII. GLIRES.

glires isicio porcino, item pulpis ex omni membro glirium trito, cum pipere nucleis lasere liquamine farcies; glires et sutos in tegula positos mittes in furnum, aut farsos in clibano coque.

5

EXPLICIT APICI TETRAPVS LIBER

OCTAVVS

2. trito *VE*: tritis *Hum*   3. inte gula *V*   4. coques *P*   6. VIII *VE*

8.9. DORMICE.

Stuff the dormice with pork forcemeat and also with the flesh from all parts of the dormouse, pounded with pepper, pine nuts, *laser* and *liquamen*. Sew them up and arrange them on a tile and put them in the oven or cook them, stuffed, in a *clibanus*.[1]

HERE ENDS BOOK EIGHT OF APICIUS, 'QUADRUPEDS'

[1] See Introduction, p. 80 figs. 7, 8 and pp. 82-3, for discussion of these portable baking covers.

BOOK NINE

INCIPIT EIVSDEM TALASSA LIBER
NONVS

I. in locusta. II. in torpidine. III. in lolligine. IIII. in sepiis. V. in polipo. VI. in ostreis. VII. omne genus conciliorum. VIII. in echino. VIIII. in metulis. X. in sarda cordula. XI. embractum Baianum.

I. IVS IN LOCVSTA.

[9.1.1] **ius in locusta et cammari**: indura cepam pallacanam concisam. ius: piper ligusticum careum cuminum careotam mel acetum uinum liquamen oleum defritum. hoc ius adicito sinapi in elixuris.

[9.1.2] **locustas assas sic facies**: aperiuntur locustae ut adsolet cum testa sua et infunditur eis piperatum coriandratum et sic in graticula assantur. cum siccauerint, adicies ius in graticula quotiens siccauerint, quousque assantur.

[9.1.3] **locusta elixa**: cum cuminato bene inferes: piper ligusticum petroselinum mentam siccam, cuminum plusculum, mel acetum liquamen. si uoles, folium et malabatrum addes.

[9.1.4] **aliter lucusta**: esicia de cauda eius sic facies: folium nociuum prius demes et elixas, deinde pulpam concides, cum liquamine pipere et ouis esicia formabis.

[9.1.5] **in lucusta elixa**: piper cuminum rutam mel acetum liquamen et oleum.

[9.1.6] **aliter in locusta**: piper ligusticum cuminum mentam rutam nucleos mel acetum liquamen et uinum.

2. VIIII *VE*   4. metulis *V*: metullis *E*: mitulis *GiVo*   7. cammari *André*: cappari *VE*: cammaris *Bra3*   7-8. concisam ius piper ligusticum *CGSG*: concisam eius piper ligusticum *V2,E*: concisam ius ligusticum piper *V1*: concisam …ligusticum *del. Hum*: concisam facies ei ius piper ligusticum *Gi*: concisam †eius piper ligusticum *FR (adicies piper Rosenbaum in note)*: concisam <...> [e] ius *André*: concisam ... e ius, piper, ligusticum *Milham*
9. elixaturis *Hum*   10. lucustas *E* | locuste *E*   12. ius *Gi*: eis *VE*
13. bene inferes *transposed from here to the end of 9.1.2, after* assantur *Hum*: bene <et> inferes *GiVo* | petrosilinum *E*   15. malabatrum *Sch*: malabratum *VE*: malabathrum *Hum*
16. locusta *E* | esicia *om. V1* | caudae ius *V* | folium *VE*: folliclum *Sch*: follem *Vo, in apparatus* | nociuum *Vo, in note*: noci uuam *VE*: nardi uuam *Hum*: *del. Sch*   17. cocindes *V*
19. locusta *E* | ruta *V* | oleum *V, E2*: uinum *E1*   21. uinum *V, E2*: oleum *E*

HERE BEGINS BOOK NINE OF THE SAME, 'THE SEA'

1. Sauces for spiny lobster. 2. Sauces for electric ray. 3. Sauces for squid. 4. Sauces for cuttlefish. 5. Sauces for octopus. 6. Sauces for oysters. 7. All types of shellfish. 8. Sauces for sea-urchins. 9. Sauces for mussels. 10. Sauces for bonito and baby tuna. 11. Relish from Baiae.

9.1. SAUCE FOR SPINY LOBSTER.[1]

9.1.1. **Sauce for spiny lobster and crayfish**: fry a chopped *pallacana* onion. Sauce: pepper, lovage, caraway, cumin, date, honey, vinegar, wine, *liquamen*, oil, *defrutum*. Add this sauce to mustard if you are going to boil them.

9.1.2. **You make grilled spiny lobsters like this**: cut open the spiny lobsters in the normal way in their shells, and a pepper sauce with coriander is poured on and they are grilled like this on a gridiron. As they dry out add sauce to them on the gridiron; do it every time they dry out until they are roasted.

9.1.3. **Boiled spiny lobster**: serve well with cumin sauce: pepper, lovage, parsley, dry mint, plenty of cumin, honey, vinegar, *liquamen*; if you want, add *folium* and *malabathrum*.[2]

9.1.4. **Another spiny lobster recipe**: you make forcemeat from its tail like this: first remove the harmful leaf parts[3] and boil it. Then chop the meat and make a forcemeat with *liquamen*, pepper and eggs.

9.1.5. **Sauce for boiled spiny lobster**: pepper, cumin, rue, honey, vinegar, *liquamen*, and oil.

9.1.6. **Another sauce for spiny lobster**: pepper, lovage, cumin, mint, rue, pine nuts, honey, vinegar, *liquamen*, and wine.

---

[1] See the Glossary under Seafood for the precise identification of these crustacea.

[2] *folium* and *malabathrum* have been identified as the same thing, i.e the leaf of cinnamon, by Andrew Dalby: see the Glossary. This recipe seems to indicate that they are different items. Also see section 7 of this chapter where this recipe is repeated.

[3] *folium nociuum*: the leaf-shaped parts that were believed to be dangerous. According to Alan Davidson, *Mediterranean Seafood*, p. 178, only the pouch that acts as a gastric mill where grit collects needs to be removed.

II. IN TVRPEDINE.

[9.2.1] **in turpedine**: teritur piper ruta cepulla arida. mel liquamen passum, uinum modice, olei boni guttas. cum bullire coeperit, amulo obligas.

[9.2.2] **in turpidine elixa**: piper ligusticum petroselinum mentam origanum, oui 5 medium, mel liquamen passum uinum oleum. si uoles, addes sinape acetum. ius calidum. si uolueris uuam passam addes.

III. IN LOLLIGINE.

[9.3.1] **in lolligine in patina**: teres piper rutam mel modicum liquamen carenum, olei guttas.

10 [9.3.2] **in lolligine farsile**: piper ligusticum coriandrum apii semen oui uitellum mel acetum liquamen uinum et oleum. obligabis.

IIII. IN SEPIIS.

[9.4.1] **in sepia farsile**: piper ligusticum apii semen careum mel liquamen uinum condimenta coctiua. calefacies et sic aperies sepiam et perfundes.

15 [9.4.2] **sic farcies eam sepiam coctam**: cerebella elixa eneruiata teres cum pipere, cui commisces oua cruda quod satis erit, piper integrum, esicia minuta, et sic consues et in bullientem ollam mittes ita ut coire inpensa possit.

[9.4.3] **sepias elixas a balneo**: in frigidam missas, cum pipere lasere liquamine nucleis oua, aut condies ut uoles.

20 [9.4.4] **aliter sepias**: piper ligusticum cuminum coriandrum uiridem mentam aridam oui uitellum mel liquamen uinum acetum et oleum modicum, et ubi bullierit, amulo obligas.

V. IN POLIPO.

[9.5] **in polipo**: pipere liquamine lasere. inferes.

1. IN TVRPEDINE *V*: TORPEDINE *E*   2. torpedine *E* | <addes> mel *Gi*   3. ceperit *E*
4. torpidine *E*   5-6. ius calidum si uolueris *CGSG, cf.10.1.2*: si calidum uolueris *E*: si
callidum uolueris *V*   9. gutas *E*   10. farsili *Hum* | coriandum *λ*: coliandrum *VE*
13. farsili *Hum*   15. farcies *Tor*: fācies *E*: facies *V* | elixa *TP*: lixa *VE*
16. commistes *V1* | piper *T*: pipere *VE*   17. sic consues *Hum*: sic cosues *E*: sicco sues
V | in pensa *E*   18. a balneo *André*: abalieno *VE*: a balineo *Milham* | *lacuna after*
missas *André*   19. aut condies *CGSG*: et condies *VE*: oua <adicies> et condies *Gi*
21. acetum oleum *E1*

9.2. SAUCES FOR ELECTRIC RAY.

9.2.1. **Sauce for electric ray**: pepper, rue and dried onion are ground; honey, *liquamen*, *passum*, a little wine, some drops of good oil. When it begins to boil, thicken with starch.

9.2.2. **Sauce for boiled electric ray**: pepper, lovage, parsley, mint, oregano, yolk of egg, honey, *liquamen*, *passum*, wine, oil. If you want, add mustard and vinegar. Serve the sauce hot. If you want, add raisins.

9.3. SAUCES FOR SQUID.

9.3.1. **Sauce for squid in a *patina***: pound pepper, rue, a little honey, *liquamen*, *caroenum*, some drops of oil.

9.3.2. **Sauce for stuffed squid**: pepper, lovage, coriander, celery seed, egg yolk, honey, vinegar, *liquamen*, wine and oil. Thicken it.

9.4. SAUCES FOR CUTTLEFISH.

9.4.1. **Sauce for stuffed cuttlefish**: pepper, lovage, celery seed, caraway, honey, *liquamen*, wine; these are the cooking spices.[1] Warm it through, open up the cuttlefish and pour the sauce on.

9.4.2. **This is how you stuff the cooked cuttlefish**: take the sinews from boiled brains, pound them with pepper, with which you mix enough raw eggs, whole peppercorns, and chopped forcemeat, and so you sew them up and put them in a pan of boiling water so that the stuffing can set.

9.4.3. **Boiled cuttlefish to serve after bathing**: start them off in cold water,[2] serve with pepper, laser, *liquamen*, pine nuts, egg. or season them how you like.

9.4.4. **Another cuttlefish recipe**: pepper, lovage, cumin, green coriander, dried mint, egg yolk, honey, *liquamen*, wine, vinegar, and a little oil, and when it boils thicken with starch.

9.5. SAUCE FOR OCTOPUS.

Sauce for octopus: pepper, *liquamen*, *laser*, and serve.

---

[1] *condimenta coctiua*: see the Glossary under *condimenta* for a discussion. Here if green herbs were meant then *uiridia* would be so much less ambiguous. Our instinct is that these words represent a definition of what has been listed and is to be equated with the similar *condimenta mortaria* found at 6.2.11 and 10.2.11.

[2] Lit. 'put them into cold water', i.e. bring them to a cooking temperature from cold.

VI. IN OSTREIS.

[9.6] **in ostreis**: piper ligusticum oui uitellum acetum liquamen oleum et uinum. si uolueris et mel addes.

VII. IN OMNE GENVS CONCILIORVM.

[9.7] **in omne genus conciliorum**: piper ligusticum petroselinum mentam siccam, cuminum plusculum, mel liquamen. si uoles folium et malabatrum addes.

VIII. IN ECHINO.

[9.8.1] **in echino**: accipies pultarium nouum, oleum modicum, liquamen uinum dulce piper minutum. facies ut ferueat; cum ferbuerit in singulos echinos mittes, agitabis; ter bulliat. cum coxeris piper asparges et inferes.

[9.8.2] **aliter echino**: piper costum modice mentam siccam mulsum liquamen spicam Indicam et folium.

[9.8.3] **aliter echino**: colum mittes in aqua calida, coques; leuas, in patella conpones; addes folium piper mel liquamen olei modice oua et sic obligas. in termospodio coques, piper asparges et inferes.

[9.8.4] **in echino salso**: echinum salsum cum liquamen optimum; careno pipere temperabis et adpones.

[9.8.5] **aliter**: echinis salsis liquamen optimum admisces, et quasi recentes apparebunt ita ut a balneo sumi possint.

VIIII. IN METVLIS.

[9.9.] **in metulis**: liquamen porrum concisum cuminum passum satureiam uinum; mixtum facies aquatius et ibi mitulos quoques.

2. et uinum *om. E1*   5. petrosilinum *E*   8. ENICHO *E1*   9. echino *V2, E*: enicho *E1*   10. feruuerit *E*   11. ter *VE:* iterum *Hum* | asperges *E* 12. echino *V2, E*: enicho *E1*: <in> echino *Hum* | mulsam *E* | liquamen *Hum*: liquamine *VE* 14. echino *V*: echinum *E2*: enichum *E1*: in echino *P* | colum *VE*: solum *Tor*: totum *Ven*: lotum *Bas* | callida *V*   15. compones *V*   15-16. inter mos podio *V*: intermo spodi° *E* 16. asperges *E*   17. enicho *E1* | enichum *E1*   19. enichinis *E1* | salsis *Sch in note*: salis *VE*   20. apparebunt *E*: aptabunt *V* | possit *E1*   21-22. MITVLIS...mitulis *GiVo* 23. aquatius *Hum*: aquati ius *VE* | quo ques *V*: coques *E*

9.6. SAUCE FOR OYSTERS.

Sauce for oysters: pepper, lovage, egg yolk, vinegar, *liquamen*, oil, and wine. You can also add honey if you like.

9.7. SAUCE FOR ALL KINDS OF SHELLFISH.

Sauce for all kinds of shellfish: pepper, lovage, parsley, dry mint, plenty of cumin, honey, *liquamen*. You can also add *folium* and *malabathrum* if you like.

9.8. SAUCES FOR SEA-URCHINS.

9.8.1. **Sauce for sea-urchins**: take a new porridge pan, add a little oil, *liquamen*, sweet wine, ground pepper; bring it to heat. When it is simmering put the sea-urchins in one at a time. Stir them and bring them to the boil three times. When they are cooked, sprinkle with pepper and serve.

9.8.2. **Another recipe for sea-urchins**: pepper, a little *costum*, dry mint, *mulsum*, *liquamen*, spikenard and *folium*.

9.8.3. **Another recipe for sea-urchins**: put the central (parts of the sea-urchins) in hot water, cook them, lift them out and arrange in a dish.[1] Add *folium,* pepper, honey, *liquamen*, a little oil, egg so that it thickens. Cook in the hot embers, sprinkle with pepper and serve.

9.8.4. **Sauce for salted sea-urchins**: serve the salted sea-urchins with the best *liquamen*, flavour with *caroenum* and pepper, and serve.

9.8.5. **Alternatively**: mix best quality *liquamen* with the sea-urchins and they will look as though they are fresh, so that they can be served after the baths.

9.9. SAUCE FOR MUSSELS.

Sauce for mussels: *liquamen*, chopped leek, cumin, *passum*, savory, wine; dilute the mixture with water and cook the mussels in it.

---

[1] Sea-urchins contain a number of orange or pink ovaries, or 'corals', which are the only parts of the creature that are eaten: see Davidson, *Mediterranean Seafood*, p. 217. They are not normally cooked, but eaten live like oysters. *Colum* literally means 'the gut', but this must be what is referred to here.

X. IN SARDA CORDVLA MVGILE.

[9.10.1] **in sardis**: sardam farsilem sic facere oportet: sarda exossatur et teritur puleium cum piperis grana, mentam nuces mel; impletur et consuitur. inuoluitur in carta et sic supra uaporem ignis in operculo conponitur. conditur ex oleo
5 careno allece.

[9.10.2] **sarda ita fit**: coquitur sarda et exossatur. teritur pipere ligustico timo origano ruta careota melle, et in uasculo ouis incisis. ornatur inpensa: uinum modice acetum defritum et oleum uiridem.

[9.10.3] **ius in sarda**: piper origanum mentam cepam aceti modicum et
10 oleum.

[9.10.4] **ius in sarda**: piper ligusticum mentam aridam cepam coctam mel acetum oleum. perfundes, asperges ouis duris concisis.

[9.10.5] **ius in cordula assa**: piper ligusticum apii semen mentam rutam careotam mel acetum uinum et oleum. conuenit et in sarda.

15 [9.10.6] **ius in mugile salso**: piper ligusticum cuminum cepa menta ruta calua careotam mel acetum sinape et oleum.

[9.10.7] **aliter ius in mugile salso**: piper origanum eruca mentam ruta calua careotam mel oleum acetum et sinape.

[9.10.8] **ius in siluro in pelamide et in tinno salsis**: piper ligusticum cuminum
20 cepam mentam rutam caluam careotam mel acetum sinape oleum.

[9.10.9] **ius in mulo tarico**: piper rutam cepam dactilum sinapi trito conmisces echino oleo et sic perfundes piscem frictum uel assatum.

[9.10.10] **salsum sine salso**: iecur quoques; teres et mittes piper aut liquamen aut salem; addes oleum. iecur leporis aut hedi aut agni aut pulli, et si uolueris in
25 formella piscem formabis. oleum uiridem supra adicies.

---

2. sarda *TP*: sardam *VE*   3. puleium *TP*: pulpeium *VE* | cum *VE*: cuminum *Hum* | menta *Hum* | cosuitur *E*   4. cōponitur *V*   5. allece *Hum*: allego *VE*   6. pipere *VE*: piper cum *Hum*: piper ex *Sch*   7. rutam careotam *V*   13. ius cordula *V* | semen *V*: sepe *E* | caroetam *E*   14. conuenit in sarda *E*   15. cepe *E1* | cepam mentam rutam caluam *GiVo*   16. careotam *VE*: caryota *Milham* | oleum *V2, E*: oleo *V1* 17. origano *E* | erucam *GiVo* | rutam *E* | caluam *GiVo*   19. pelapide *V*   21. mullo *ζ*| sinape *λ* | cōmisces *V*   23. coques *V* | mittes *TP*: inities *VE* | piper et liquamen *Bra2*

---

[1] Pliny, *HN*. 9.47 explains that *cordula* are baby tuna up to 6 months old; from 6 months to one year they were called *pelamydes* (see 10.1.13), and that when over a year old they were called *thynnus*.
[2] *supra uaporem ignis*: there is little doubt that this term refers to the fire's vapours or heat and not that of steam coming from a bath, as *FR* interpret. Were it to be steam, there would be little

9.10. SAUCES FOR BONITO, BABY TUNA,[1] MULLET.

9.10.1. **Sauce for bonito**: stuffed bonito should be made like this: the bonito are boned and pennyroyal is pounded with grains of pepper, mint, hazelnuts, honey. They are stuffed and sewn up. They are wrapped in papyrus and placed in a covered pan above the heat of the fire.[2] They are flavoured with oil, *caroenum* and *allec*.

9.10.2. **Bonito are cooked like this**: the bonito are cooked and boned. They are pounded with pepper, lovage, thyme, oregano, rue, date, honey, and (are put in) a little vessel with chopped egg. They are dressed with this mixture: a little wine, vinegar, *defrutum*, and green oil.

9.10.3. **Sauce for bonito**: pepper, oregano, mint, onion, a little vinegar, and oil.

9.10.4. **Sauce for bonito**: pepper, lovage, dried mint, cooked onion, honey, vinegar, oil. Pour on the sauce and sprinkle with chopped hard-boiled eggs.

9.10.5. **Sauce for roasted baby tuna**: pepper, lovage, celery seed, mint, rue, date, honey, vinegar, wine, and oil. Also suitable for bonito.

9.10.6. **Sauce for salted mullet**: pepper, lovage, cumin, onion, mint, rue, smooth nuts,[3] date, honey, vinegar, mustard and oil.

9.10.7. **Another sauce for salted mullet**: pepper, oregano, rocket, mint, rue, smooth nuts, date, honey, oil, vinegar and mustard.

9.10.8. **Sauce for salted sheatfish, young tuna and tuna**: pepper, lovage, cumin, onion, mint, rue, smooth nuts, date, honey, vinegar, mustard, oil.

9.10.9. **Sauce for preserved grey mullet**:[4] mix pepper, rue, onion and date with pounded mustard, sea-urchins and oil and then pour over the fried or grilled fish.

9.10.10. **Salt fish without salt fish**: cook liver, pound it and add pepper and either *liquamen* or salt. Add oil. Use hare's or kid's or lamb's or chicken's liver, and if you like you can shape it like a fish in a mould. Pour green oil over it.

---

purpose to the combination of papyrus and covered pan: the steam could not penetrate to the fish in these circumstances. The fish will in fact steam in its own juices, but that requires the normal heat of a fire.

[3] See the Glossary on 'nuts'; *calua* cannot mean 'walnuts' here, as the description 'smooth' can hardly apply to them.

[4] *tarichos*, Greek for 'salted' or 'preserved' meat or fish. The grey mullet is larger and more suitable for salting than the red.

[9.10.11] **aliter uice salsi**: cuminum piper liquamen teres et passum modice uel caroenum et nuces tritas plurimas misces et simul conteres et salsare defundes. oleum modice superstillabis et inferes.

[9.10.12] **aliter salsum**: **in salso**: cuminum tantum quantum quinque digitis tollis, piperis ad dimidium eius et unam spicam alei purgatam; teres, liquamen superfundes, oleum modice superstillabis. hoc egrum stomachum ualde reficit et digestionem facit.

XI. EMBRACTVM BAIANVM.

[9.11] **embractum Baianum**: ostreas minutas sfondilos orticas in caccabum mittes; nucleos tostos concisos rutam apium piper coriandrum cuminum passum liquamen careotam oleum.

EXPLICIT APICI TALASSA LIBER NONVS

2. caroenum *R*: caroeni *VE* | salsare defundes *E*: salsa redefundes *V*: salsario defundes *Sch*: salsari defundes *GiVo*: <in> salsare defundes *André*   4. in salso *VE*: sine salso *Hum*
6. super fundes *E*   8. ?BALANVM *E*   9. balanum *E* | urticas *GiVo*
12. APICII *E* | TALASSALIBꟄ LIBER *V*: TALASSILIBVS LIBER *E* | NONVS *CGSG*: VIIII *VE*

9.10.11. **Another salt fish recipe**: pound cumin, pepper, *liquamen* and stir in a little *passum* or *caroenum* and plenty of pounded hazelnuts. Pound it all together. Pour out into a dish. Drizzle on a little oil and serve.

9.10.12. **Another recipe for salt fish**: **for salt fish**: take as much cumin as you can pick up in five fingers, half that amount of pepper, and one peeled clove of garlic; pound, pour on *liquamen* and drizzle on a little oil. This is an excellent remedy for a poorly stomach and restores the digestion.[1]

9.11. RELISH FROM BAIAE.

Relish from Baiae: put chopped oysters, mussels, and sea-urchins in a pan, add chopped roasted pine nuts, rue, celery, pepper, coriander, cumin, *passum*, *liquamen*, date and oil.

HERE ENDS BOOK NINE OF APICIUS, 'THE SEA'

---

[1] The title for this recipe is inappropriate, as it is a remedy and not a sauce or preparation for salted fish, let alone an alternative for it. It may have been included here on the basis of the title; alternatively, if as a recipe for a digestive remedy it found itself included at this point by chance, it is not inconceivable that the title was invented to try to make it fit. The recipe would be better placed in Book 1.

BOOK TEN

INCIPIT EIVSDEM ALIEVS LIBER
\<DECIMVS\>

I. in piscibus diuersis. II. in murenam. III. in anguillam.

I. IN PISCIBVS \<DIVERSIS\>

5   [10.1.1] **ius diabotanon in pisce frixo**: piscem quemlibet curas, lauas, friges. teres piper cuminum coriandri semen laseris radicem origanum rutam, fricabis; suffundes acetum, adicies careotam mel defritum oleum, liquamen temperabis; refundes in caccabum, facies ut ferueat; cum ferbuerit, piscem frictum perfundes, piper asperges et inferes.

10   [10.1.2] **ius in pisce elixo**: piper ligusticum cuminum cepulam origanum nucleos careotam mel acetum liquamen sinapi oleum modice. ius calidum. si uelis, uuam passam.

[10.1.3] **aliter in pisce elixo**: teres piper ligusticum coriandrum uiridem satureiam cepam, ouorum uitella cocta, passum acetum oleum et liquamen.

15   [10.1.4] **ius in pisce elixo**: piscem curabis diligenter; mittes in mortarium salem coriandri semen, conteres bene; uolues eum; adicies in patinam, cooperies, gipsabis. coques in furno. cum coctus fuerit, tolles, aceto acerrimo asparges et inferes.

[10.1.5] **aliter ius in pisce elixo**: cum curaueris piscem, adicies in sartaginem
20   \<piper liquamen coriandri \> semen aquam anetum uiridem et ipsum piscem. cum coctus fuerit, asperges aceto et inferes.

[10.1.6] **ius Alexandrinum in pisce asso**: piper cepam siccam ligusticum cuminum origanum apii semen, pruna damascena enucleata, mittis acetum liquamen defritum oleum, et coques.

25   [10.1.7] **aliter ius Alexandrinum in pisce asso**: piper ligusticum coriandrum uiridem, uuam passam enucleatam, uinum passum liquamen oleum, et coques.

1-2. ALIEVS LIBER \<DECIMVS\> *CGSG*: ALIE VESLIBVS *E*: ALIAE VESLIBVS *V*: HALIEVS LIBER \<X\> *Hum from list of books at start*   3. anguilla *E*   4. \<DIVERSIS\> *CGSG from section headings*   5. diabota non *VE* | lauas *André*: saluas *VE*: salsas *Gi* 7. defrictum *V*   8. cacabum *E* | feruuerit *V*   11. careotam *corr.* careatam *V* | callidum *V1*   15. ius *VE*: aliter ius *P*   17. asperges *E*   20. \<piper liquamen coriandri\> *CGSG*: *lacuna André* | semen *λ*: sem *VE*   23. mittis *E*: mus *V*: mustum *Mars*: mulsum *Gi*: mustaceum *Sch*   24. defrictum *V*

HERE BEGINS BOOK TEN OF THE SAME, 'THE FISHERMAN'

1. Sauces for various fish. 2. Sauces for moray eel. 3. Sauces for common eel.

10.1. SAUCES FOR VARIOUS FISH.
10.1.1. **Herb sauce for fried fish**: prepare, wash and fry whatever fish you like. Pound pepper, cumin, coriander seed, *laser* root, oregano, rue, pound again; pour on vinegar, add date, honey, *defrutum*, oil, flavour with *liquamen*. Put into a pan, bring it to heat; when it is simmering, pour it over the fried fish, sprinkle with pepper and serve.
10.1.2. **Sauce for boiled fish**: pepper, lovage, cumin, onion, oregano, pine nuts, date, honey, vinegar, *liquamen*, mustard, a little oil. Serve the sauce hot. If you want, add raisins.
10.1.3. **Another sauce for boiled fish**: pound pepper, lovage, green coriander, savory, onion, cooked egg yolk, *passum*, vinegar, oil and *liquamen*.
10.1.4. **A sauce for boiled fish**: carefully prepare the fish; put in a mortar salt and coriander seed, pound them well; coat the fish in this, put it in a dish, cover it up and seal it with gypsum. Cook in the oven. When it is cooked, take it out, sprinkle with very sharp vinegar and serve.
10.1.5. **Another sauce for boiled fish**: when you have prepared the fish, put in a frying-pan pepper, *liquamen*, coriander seed, water, green dill and the fish itself. When it is cooked, sprinkle with vinegar and serve.
10.1.6. **Alexandrian sauce for grilled fish**: pepper, dried onion, lovage, cumin, oregano, celery seed, stoned damsons, put in vinegar, *liquamen*, *defrutum*, oil and cook it.[1]
10.1.7. **Another Alexandrian sauce for grilled fish**: pepper, lovage, green coriander, de-seeded raisins, wine, *passum*, *liquamen*, oil and cook it.

---

[1] *E*'s reading *mittis* is surely correct here. The recipe concludes with the instruction *coques*, so an instruction to 'put in' half way through is not out of place. Wine is often required as a bulk liquid, but although *mulsum* is also well attested in recipes in this section of the book, it is not necessary here in a thick sauce.

[10.1.8] **aliter ius Alexandrinum in pisce asso**: piper ligusticum coriandrum uiridem cepam damascena enucleata passum liquamen acetum oleum, et coques.

[10.1.9] **ius in grongo assa**: piper ligusticum cuminum frictum origanum cepam siccam ouorum uitella cocta uinum mulsum acetum liquamen defritum, et coques.

[10.1.10] **ius in carnutam**: piper ligusticum origanum cepam uuam passam enucleatam uinum mel acetum liquamen oleum, et coques.

[10.1.11] **ius in mullos assos**: piper ligusticum rutam mel nucleos acetum uinum liquamen oleum modice; calefacies et perfundes.

[10.1.12] **aliter ius in mullos assos**: rutam mentam coriandrum feniculum, omnia uiridia; piper ligusticum mel liquamen et oleum modice.

[10.1.13] **ius in pelamide assa**: piper ligusticum origanum coriandrum uiridem cepam uuam passam enucleatam passum acetum liquamen defritum oleum, et coques. hoc ius conuenit et in elixa. si uis et mel addes.

[10.1.14] **ius in percam**: piper ligusticum cuminum frictum cepam pruna damascena enucleata uinum mulsum acetum oleum defritum, et coques.

[10.1.15] **ius in pisce rubellione**: piper ligusticum careum serpillum apii semen cepam siccam uinum passum acetum liquamen oleum. amulo obligas.

<II. IN MVRENAM>

[10.2.1] **ius in morena assa**: piper ligusticum satureiam crocomagna cepa, pruna damascena enucleata, uinum mulsum acetum liquamen defritum oleum, et coques.

[10.2.2] **aliter ius in morena assa**: piper ligusticum pruna damascena uinum mulsum acetum liquamen defritum oleum, et coques.

[10.2.3] **aliter ius in morena assa**: piper ligusticum nepetam montanam coriandri semen cepam nucleos pineos mel acetum liquamen oleum, et coques.

[10.2.4] **aliter ius in morena elixa**: piper ligusticum anetum apii semen rus Syriacum careotam mel acetum liquamen oleum sinape defritum.

1. alexandrum *E*   4. gongro *M2*: congro *Ven* | asso *Hum*   7. carnutam *VE*: cornutam *Hum*   8. enucleatam *T*: et nucleatam *VE*   14. enucleatam *Hum*: et nucleatam *VE* | passum *Hum*: passam *VE*   15. et in *E*: ex in *V* | addis *E*   16. fritum *E* 17. defrictum *V*   19. amolo *V1*   20. II *add. Milham* | IN MVRENAM *add. MO* 21. murena *λ* | croco magna *VE*: crocomagma *Sch*   22. enucleata *λ*: et nucleata VE 24. morena *E*: morenas *V*: murena *λ*   26. murena *λ*   28. murena *λ* | anetum *André*: acetum *VE*: anethum *Hum* | rhus *λ*   29. defritum *E1*: defrictum *E2*, *V*

10.1.8. Another Alexandrian sauce for grilled fish: pepper, lovage, green coriander, onion, stoned damsons, *passum*, *liquamen*, vinegar, oil, and cook it.

10.1.9. Sauce for grilled conger eel: pepper, lovage, roasted cumin, oregano, dried onion, cooked egg yolk, wine, *mulsum*, vinegar, *liquamen*, *defrutum*, and cook it.

10.1.10. Sauce for *cornuta*:[1] pepper, lovage, oregano, onion, de-seeded raisins, wine, honey, vinegar, *liquamen*, oil and cook it.

10.1.11. Sauce for grilled mullet: pepper, lovage, rue, honey, pine nuts, vinegar, wine, *liquamen*, a little oil; warm it through and pour it on.

10.1.12. Another sauce for grilled mullet: rue, mint, coriander, fennel, all of them green; pepper, lovage, honey, *liquamen*, and a little oil.

10.1.13. Sauce for grilled young tuna: pepper, lovage, oregano, green coriander, onion, de-seeded raisins, *passum*, vinegar, *liquamen*, *defrutum*, oil, and cook it. This sauce is also suitable for boiled fish. If you wish, add honey too.

10.1.14. Sauce for perch: pepper, lovage, roasted cumin, onion, stoned damsons, wine, *mulsum*, vinegar, oil, *defrutum*, and cook it.

10.1.15. Sauce for *rubellio* fish:[2] pepper, lovage, caraway, wild thyme, celery seed, dried onion, wine, *passum*, vinegar, *liquamen*. oil. Thicken with starch.

10.2. SAUCES FOR MORAY EEL.

10.2.1. Sauce for grilled moray: pepper, lovage, savory, saffron paste,[3] onion, stoned damsons, wine, *mulsum*, vinegar, *liquamen*, *defrutum*, oil, and cook it.

10.2.2. Another sauce for grilled moray: pepper, lovage, damsons, wine, *mulsum*, vinegar, *liquamen*, *defrutum*, oil, and cook it.

10.2.3. Another sauce for grilled moray: pepper, lovage, mountain catmint, coriander seed, onion, pine nuts, honey, vinegar, *liquamen*, oil, and cook it.

10.2.4. Another sauce for boiled moray: pepper, lovage, dill, celery seed, Syrian sumac, date, honey, vinegar, *liquamen*, oil, mustard, *defrutum*.

---

[1] An unknown fish. It may be a variant for *cornuda*, 'hammer-head shark'.

[2] Pliny, *HN*. 32.138. Probably the gurnard: Dalby, *Food in the Ancient World*, p. 170.

[3] The residue of saffron from the production of saffron oil: Pliny, *HN*. 21.139; Dalby, *Food in the Ancient World*, p. 290.

[10.2.5] **aliter ius in morena elixa**: piper ligusticum careum apii semen coriandrum mentam aridam nucleos pineos rutam mel acetum uinum liquamen oleum modice. calefacies et amulo obligas.

[10.2.6] **ius in morena elixa**: piper ligusticum careum cuminum nucleos careotam sinape mel acetum liquamen et oleum et defritum.

[10.2.7] **ius in lacertos elixos**: piper ligusticum cuminum rutam uiridem cepam mel acetum liquamen oleum modice. cum bullierit, amulo obligas.

[10.2.8] **ius in pisce elixo**: piper ligusticum petroselinum origanum cepam aridam mel acetum liquamen uinum oleum modice. cum bullierit, amulo obligas et in lance inferes.

[10.2.9] **ius in pisce asso**: piper ligusticum timum coriandrum uiridem mel acetum liquamen uinum oleum defritum. calefacies et agitabis rutae surculo et obligabis amulo.

[10.2.10] **ius in tinno**: piper cuminum timum coriandrum cepam uuam passam acetum mel uinum liquamen oleum. calefacies, amulo obligabis.

[10.2.11] **ius in tinno elixo**: piper ligusticum timum condimenta mortaria cepam careotam mel acetum liquamen et oleum et sinape.

[10.2.12] **ius in dentice asso**: piper ligusticum coriandrum mentam rutam aridam malum cidoneum coctum mel uinum liquamen oleum. calefacies, amulo obligabis.

[10.2.13] **<ius> in dentice elixo**: piper anetum cuminum timum mentam rutam uiridem mel acetum liquamen uinum oleum modice. calefacies et amulo obligabis.

[10.2.14] **ius in pisce aurata**: piper ligusticum careum origanum rutæ bacam mentam myrtæ bacam oui uitellum mel acetum oleum uinum liquamen. calefacies et sic uteris.

[10.2.15] **ius in pisce aurata assa**: piper coriandrum mentam aridam apii semen cepam uuam passam mel acetum uinum liquamen et oleum.

[10.2.16] **ius in scorpione elixo**: piper careum petroselinum careotam mel acetum liquamen sinape oleum defritum.

5

10

15

20

25

30

---

1. ius *VE*: aliter ius *P* | murena *λ*   4. murena *λ*   5. careotam *E1, V*: caroetam *E2* | sinapem *V* | defritum *corr.* defrictum *E*   11. *10.2.9. after 10.2.10 E, all in the same hand; start of each marked `/; illegible note in r/h margin*   12. agitabis *PJ*: zitabis *VE* | rute *E* 15. obligas *V*   16. mortaria *V*: mortarea *E*: moretaria *Hum* | cepa *V*   17. liquamen et oleum et sinape *V*: liquamen oleum sinape *E*   21. <ius> *CGSG*   24. rutę *V* 25. myrtæ bacam *E*: myrta ebacam *V* | ouitellum *V*   27. api *V*

10.2.5. **Another sauce for boiled moray**: pepper, lovage, caraway, celery seed, coriander, dried mint, pine nuts, rue, honey, vinegar, wine, *liquamen*, a little oil. Warm it through and thicken with starch.

10.2.6. **Sauce for boiled moray**: pepper, lovage, caraway, cumin, pine nuts, date, mustard, honey, vinegar, *liquamen*, and oil and *defrutum*.

10.2.7. **Sauce for boiled mackerel**: pepper, lovage, cumin, green rue, onion, honey, vinegar, *liquamen*, a little oil. When it has boiled, thicken with starch.

10.2.8. **Sauce for boiled fish**: pepper, lovage, parsley, oregano, dried onion, honey, vinegar, *liquamen*, wine, a little oil. When it has boiled, thicken with starch and serve on a dish.

10.2.9. **Sauce for grilled fish**: pepper, lovage, thyme, green coriander, honey, vinegar, *liquamen*, wine, oil, *defrutum*. Warm it through and stir it with a sprig of rue and thicken with starch.

10.2.10. **Sauce for tuna**: pepper, cumin, thyme, coriander, onion, raisins, vinegar, honey, wine, *liquamen*, oil. Warm it through, thicken with starch.

10.2.11. **Sauce for boiled tuna**: pepper, lovage, thyme, these are the mortar spices;[1] onion, date, honey, vinegar, *liquamen*, oil, mustard.

10.2.12. **Sauce for grilled dentex**: pepper, lovage, coriander, mint, dried rue, a cooked quince, honey, wine, *liquamen*, oil. Warm it through, thicken with starch.

10.2.13. **Sauce for boiled dentex**: pepper, dill, cumin, thyme, mint, green rue, honey, vinegar, *liquamen*, wine, a little oil. Warm it through and thicken with starch.

10.2.14. **Sauce for gilthead bream**: pepper, lovage, caraway, oregano, rue berries, mint, myrtle berries, egg yolk, honey, vinegar, oil, wine, *liquamen*. Warm it through and use it like this.

10.2.15. **Sauce for grilled gilthead bream**: pepper, coriander, dried mint, celery seed, onion, raisins, honey, vinegar, wine, *liquamen*, and oil.

10.2.16. **Sauce for boiled scorpion fish**:[2] pepper, caraway, parsley, date, honey, vinegar, *liquamen*, mustard, oil, *defrutum*.

[1] See the Glossary, *condimentum*, for a discussion of this term.
[2] For this fish, see Pliny, *HN*. 32.151; Dalby, *Food in the Ancient World*, p. 278, identifies it as the 'rascasse' nowadays used in bouillabaisse.

[10.2.17] **in pisce oenogarum**: teres piper rutam, mel commisces, passum liquamen caroenum et sic igni mollissimo calefacies.

[10.2.18] **in pisce oenogarum**: ut supra facies. cum bullierit amulo obligabis.

<III. IN ANGVILLAM.>

5 [10.3.1] **ius in anguilla**: piper ligusticum apii semen anetum rus Syriacum careotam mel acetum liquamen oleum sinape et defritum.

[10.3.2] **ius in anguillam**: piper ligusticum rus Syriacum mentam siccam rute bacas ouorum uitella cocta mulsum acetum liquamen oleum. coques.

EXPLICIT <APICI ALIEVS> LIBER

10 # DECIMVS

1. ruta *V* | cōmisces *V*   2. sic igni *CGSG*: signi *VE*: igni *ζ*   3. <aliter> in pisce *Hum* | obligas *E*   4. <III> *CGSG* | < IN ANGVILLAM> *Hum, from list at start of book*   5. rhus *λ*   7. <aliter> ius *GiVo* | rhus *λ*   7-8. rute bacas *E*: ruta ebacas *V*   9-10. EXPLICIT <APICI ALIEVS> LIBER DECIMVS *CGSG*: EXPLICIT LIBER X *V*: EXPLICIT FELICITER AMEN *E*

10.2.17. ***Oenogarum* for fish**: pound pepper, rue; stir in some honey, *passum*, *liquamen*, *caroenum* and warm it through over the gentlest of fires.

10.2.18. ***Oenogarum* for fish**: make as above. When it has come to the boil, thicken it with starch.

10.3. SAUCES FOR COMMON EEL.

10.3.1. **Sauce for eel**: pepper, lovage, celery seed, dill, Syrian sumac, date, honey, vinegar, *liquamen*, oil, mustard, and *defrutum*.

10.3.2. **Sauce for eel**: pepper, lovage, Syrian sumac, dried mint, rue berries, hard-boiled egg yolk, *mulsum*, vinegar, *liquamen*, oil. Cook it.

HERE ENDS BOOK TEN OF APICIUS, 'THE FISHERMAN'[1]

---

[1] We have emended the *explicit* to mirror that found in other books, but have every sympathy with the scribe of *E*, 'It ends happily, amen!'

THE EXTRACTS OF APICIUS

BY

VINIDARIUS

LATIN TEXT

&

ENGLISH TRANSLATION

SIGLA

and abbreviations for the *Excerpta Vinidarii*

A   Paris, Latinus 10318 (*codex Salmasianus*).

Sch   C. T. Schuch, Heidelberg, Winter, 1874 (2nd ed.).

GiVo   C. Giarratano, F. Vollmer, Leipzig, Teubner, 1922.

Ihm   Suggestions made in his commentary on a diplomatic transcript of the text by M. Ihm (*Archiv für lateinische Lexicographie und Grammatik* XV (1908), 63-73).

Bra2   E. Brandt, *Untersuchungen zum römischen Kochbuche, Philologus* Supplementband XIX, Heft III, Leipzig 1927.

Milham M. E. Milham, Leipzig, Teubner, 1969.

André   J. André, Paris, Belles Lettres, 1965 (1st ed.), 1974 (2nd ed.).

André 1961 J. André, *L'Alimentation et la cuisine à Rome* (Paris, 1961; revised ed. 1981).

CGSG   C. Grocock, S. Grainger (the present edition).

< . . .>   conjectural supplement.

[. . .]   conjectural deletion.

†. . . †   seat of corruption.

Note: in the apparatus we report others' conjectures and readings to a fuller extent than is usual. These are included to show how the text has been handled in previous editions, and how more difficult readings in the MSS have been addressed.

APICI EXCERPTA
A VINIDARIO VIRO INLVSTRI

III. BREVIS PIMENTORVM QUAE IN DOMO ESSE DEBEANT VT CONDIMENTIS NIHIL DESIT: crocu piper zingiber lasar foliu baca murte costu cariofilu spica Indica addena cardamomu spica nardi.

de seminibus hoc: papaber semen rude baca rute baca lauri semen aneti semen api semen feniculi semen ligustici semen eruce semen coriandri cuminu anesu petroselinu careu sisama.

de siccis hoc: lasaris radices menta nepeta saluia cuppressu origanum zyniperum cępa gentima [bacas] timmi coriandrum pirethru citri <folia> pastinaca cępa ascalonia radices iunci anet<um> puleiu ciperum aliu osprea samsucu innula silpium cardamomum.

de liquoribus hoc: mel defritu carinu piperiu passu.

de nucleis hoc: nuces maiores nucleos pinos amicdula aballana.

de pomis siccis hoc: damascena datilos uba passa granata. hęc omnia in loco sicco pone ne odorem et uirtutem perdant.

---

1. Title: *placed centrally in the page after* sisama, *l. 8 below, in A*   2. VIRO INLUSTRI *GiVo*: VIR INLVT. *A, with macron over both* N *and* V   4. crocum *Salmasius in Ihm*: crocu *A*: *NB. almost all superscript marks indicating the ending* –um *are missing from this section of the* breuis ciborum. *See Introduction, p. 115* | murte *André*: murre *A*: mirte *GiVo*: myrte *Milham* 6. semen rutae *Milham*   9. iuniperum *Milham*   10. bacas *del. CGSG* | <folia> *CGSG*: <folia> citri *André* | pastinaca *André*: fastinaca *A*   11. ascolonia *A1* | anetum *Milham*: anet *A*: anetu *André* | alia *Sch* | osprea *André*: ospera *A*   12. silpiū *A*: silpiu *Sch* | cardamomu *Sch*   13. piperiu *André*: apiperiu *A*: apyrinum *sugg. Sch*: piperatum *André* *1961*   14. nuclos *A*: nucleos *André* | amicdula *André*: acmidula *A*: amygdala *Milham* | abellana *André*   15. uba passa *A2*: uua passa *A1*: uuam passam *Milham*

---

[1] For Vinidarius see Introduction, pp. 32ff. The title in the Paris MS is located in the middle of the text, after the section on seeds.

[2] *pimentum* is not seen in *Apicius*; in classical Latin *pigmentum* refers to colour and in a transferred sense to rhetorical colouring. It is found in medicinal writers meaning 'drug' or 'ingredient' from

THE EXTRACTS OF APICIUS BY VINIDARIUS, *UIR INLUSTRIS.*[1]

III. A SUMMARY OF THE FLAVOURINGS[2] WHICH OUGHT TO BE IN THE HOME SO THAT NOTHING IS MISSING FROM THE SEASONINGS: saffron, pepper, ginger, *laser, folium*, myrtle berries, *costum*, clove, Indian nard, *addena*,[3] cardamom, spikenard.

Seeds as follows: poppy seed, green rue berries, bay berries, dill seed, celery seed, fennel seed, lovage seed, rocket seed, coriander seed, cumin, anise, parsley, caraway,sesame.

Dried condiments as follows: *laser* roots, mint, calamint, sage, turmeric,[4] oregano, juniper, onion, gentian, thyme,[5] coriander, Spanish camomile, citron leaves, parsnip, *ascalonian* onions, bullrush roots, dill, pennyroyal, sweet rush,[6] garlic, dried vegetables, *samsucum*,[7] elecampane, *siiphium*, cardamom.

Liquids as follows: honey, *defrutum, caroenum*, pepper sauce, *passum*.[8]

Nuts as follows: larger nuts,[9] pine nuts, almonds, hazelnuts.

Dried fruits as follows: damsons, dates, raisins, pomegranates. Put all these in a dry place so that they do not lose their fragrance and flavour.

---

the fourth century. It is also noteworthy that this first list has no title or introductory defining term, as the others have.

[3] This term is not known as a spice, but the word may be a corruption of *addenda*, referring to the two 'additional' spices which follow.

[4] See Miller, *Spice Trade of the Roman Empire*, pp. 77-9.

[5] *bacas timmi*: thyme 'berries' are othewise unattested and seem unlikely given the size of the seed produced by the plant; however, 'gentian berries' might refer to the larger seeds produced by this plant, whose corollas can be 2 inches across in the Alpine variety (so Grieve, *Modern Herbal*, p. 348). However, berries should be among the seeds above, and we therefore delete *bacas*.

[6] See note on *Apicius* 1.6.

[7] This is an unknown term, but just might be a corruption of *sambucum*, 'elderberries', which are readily dried: see *Apicius* 4.2.8.

[8] It is curious that oil, wine, vinegar and *liquamen* are missing.

[9] These 'larger nuts' might be walnuts.

BREVIS CYBORUM

I. caccabina minore. II. caccabina fusile. III. ofellas garatas. IIII. ofellas assas. V. aliter ofellas. VI. ofellas garaton. VII. pisces scorpiones rapulatus. VIII. pisces frixos cuiuscumque generis. VIIII. item pisces frixos. X. pisces assos.
5 XI. pisces inotogonon. XII. sardas. XIII. item pisces inotogonon. XIIII. mullos anetatos. XV. aliter mullos. XVI murenas et anguillas. XVII. lucustas et isquillas. XVIII. pisces elixos. XVIIII. patinas oborum. XX. porcello coriandratu. XXI. porcello inococtu. XXII. porcello eo iure. XXIII. porcello tymmo sparsu. XXIIII. porcellu exozome. XXV. porcellu lasaratu. XXVI. porcellu iuscellu. XXVII.
10 agnu simplice. XXVIII. hędu lasaratu. XXVIIII. turdos apontomenus. XXX. turtures. XXXI. ius in perdices.

I. cacabina minore: olera diuersa elixa compone et pullina inter se, si uolueris; condis liquamine et oleo et bulliat. teres piper modicum et folium et cum tritura conmisces ouum et tribulas.

15 **<Ia> alia tritura unde perfundes caccabina:** teres ergo folium quantum con-pedat cum cerifolio uno et quarta parte de lauri baca, et medium caulis elixi et folia coriandri, et solues de iuscello eius et uaborabis in cinere calido; et adornas antequam fundas in uasculo; perfundis conditum et sic ponis.

II. caccabina fusile: malbas porros betas siue coliclos elixatos turdos atque esicia
20 de pullu copadia porcina siue pullina et cetera que in presenti habere poteris conpones uariatim. teres piper lygisticum cum uini ueteris pondo duo, liquamen pondo I, mel pondo I, olei aliquantu. gustata, idem permixta et temperatam mittis in patinam et fac ut modice ferueat, et cum quoquitur adicies lactes sextario uno, oua dissoluta cum lacte; perfundes patinam; mox constrinxerit, inferes.

---

2. caccabinam minorem caccabinem fusilem *Milham*   3. garaton *André*: graton *A*
5. in otogonon *A*: oenoteganon *André*   7. ouorum *Milham*   8. inococtu *CGSG* :
inoc cuctu *A*: inocuctu *André*: oenococtum *Milham* | sparsu *CGSG*: crapsu *A*: sparsum *André,*
Milham   9. oxizomo *André*: oxyzomum *Milham*   10. agnus implice *A* | hędu
lasaratu *GiVo*: hędulas aratu *A*: haedum laseratum *Milham* | apontomenus *A*: a ponto menus *Sch*:
aponcomenos *André*: hapantamenos *Vo*   12. diuerse *Sch* | conpone *Sch* | pullinam *Sch* | interse
A: intersere *Sch*   14. commisces *Milham*   15. alia *CGSG*: alias *A* | caccabinam
GiVo   15-16. conpetat *Sch*   16. una *GiVo*   17. uaporabis *Sch* | adornas *CGSG*:
adora *A*: adorna *Sch*: ad horam *André*   18. conditam *Sch*   19. caccabinam fusilem *GiVo*
| maluas *Sch* | atque *Salmasius in Ihm*: adque *A*   19-20. esicia de pullu *CGSG*: esiciate pullu
A: isicia de pullo *Ihm*: esiciatum pullum *Sch*   22. iustata *Sch* | idem *CGSG*: id *A*: item *Vo*:
id. permixta et temperata *del. Sch*   23. sextario uno *CGSG*: ꝅ uno *A*: sextarium uno *Ihm*:
lactes in uno *Sch*: sextarium unum *GiVo*

SUMMARY OF FOODS

1. Simple *caccabina*. 2. *Caccabina* pudding. 3. *Ofellae* in *garum*. 4. Roasted *ofellae*. 5. Another recipe for *ofellae*. 6. *Ofellae* in *garum* sauce. 7. Scorpion fish with turnips. 8. Fried fish of any kind at all. 9. Another recipe for fried fish. 10. Grilled fish. 11. Fish *oenoteganon*. 12. Bonito. 13. Another fish recipe *oenoteganon*. 14. Mullet in dill sauce. 15. Another recipe for mullet. 16. Moray eels and eels. 17. Spiny lobster and prawns. 18. Boiled fish. 19. Egg *patinae*. 20. Piglet in coriander sauce. 21. Piglet cooked in wine. 22. Piglet in its own sauce. 23. Piglet sprinkled with thyme. 24. Piglet in a sour sauce. 25. Piglet in a *laser* sauce. 26. Piglet in a sauce. 27. A simple lamb recipe. 28. Kid in a *laser* sauce. 29. Stuffed thrushes. 30. Turtle doves. 31. Sauce for partridges.

1. Simple *caccabina*: arrange various boiled greens and, if you want, include layers of chicken meat among them: flavour with *liquamen* and oil and let it boil. Pound a little pepper and *folium*, and mix an egg with the pounded spices and beat.[1]

1(a). Another spice mix to flavour the *caccabina*: now pound as much *folium* as you need, with one clove and a quarter amount of bay berries, together with half a boiled cabbage and some coriander leaves which you mash in their own juices; then heat it up in the hot ashes. Prepare (the ingredients of the *caccabina*) before putting them in a vessel, pour on the seasoning and serve it like this.[2]

2. *Caccabina* pudding: place in layers mallows, leeks, beets or boiled cabbage, thrush meat, chicken forcemeat, morsels of pork or chicken and anything else you happen to have to hand. Pound pepper, lovage with 2 lb. of old wine, 1 lb. of *liquamen*, 1 lb. of honey, and a little oil.[3] Taste it, stir again and adjust the flavour then place in the dish and bring it gently to heat, and when it is cooking, add 1 pt. of milk, with eggs dissolved in it; pour this on the *patina*; as soon as it has set, serve it.

---

[1] This mixture is presumably poured on and the dish is cooked as if it were a *patina* (q.v. in Glossary).

[2] This *caccabina* appears to be egg-free and uses vegetable purée as an alternative.

[3] This recipe appears to have liquids such as *liquamen* weighed in pounds, See Introduction, 'Roman weights and measures' p. 85. It is possible that *pondus* has the same meaning as *libra* (= 12 fl. *uncia* = 1 *hemina* = ½ pt.).

III. ofellas garatas: ponis ofellas in sartagine, adices liquamen libra I, olei similiter, mellis aliquantum et sic frigis.

IIII. ofellas assas: exbromabis diligenter et in sartagine mittis. friges inogaru. postea simul cum ipsu inogaru inferes et piper aspargis.

5 **V. aliter ofellas:** [si] in liquamine frigantur et calide melle unguantur et sic inferantur.

VI. ofellas garaton: lasar zingiber cardamomum et uno acitabulo liquamen misces cum his omnibus tritis et ibi ofellas quoques.

VII. pisces scorpiones rapulatos: cocis in liquamen et oleo et cum mediauerint
10 coctura tolles. rapas elixas madidas et minutissime concisas manibus depressabis ut umorem non habeant et cum pisce obligas et bulliat cum oleo abunde. et cum bulliuerit teres ciminum lauri baca dimidia, addes propter colore crocu. amulabis de oridia propter spissitudinem. superfundes et tunc inferes. addes modicum acetu.

15 **VIII. pisces frixos cuiuscumque generis sic facies:** teres piper coriandri semen lasaris radices origanu ruta cariotam; suffundes acetum oleum liquamen, adicies defritum. hęc omnia temperabis et in caccabulo mittis et ferbeat. cum calefeciris eosdem pisces superfundes. asparso piper et inferes.

VIIII. item pisces frixos sic facies: teres piper ligusticu baca lauri coriandrum
20 mel liquamen uinu; passu uel carenu temperas. coques igni lentu, amulo orizie obligas et inferes.

X. pisces assos: teres piper ligisticum saturegia cipam siccam; suffundes acetu, adicies cariota anetu ouorum uitella mel acetum liquamen oleu defritu. hęc omnia in uno mixta perfundes.

---

1. adices *A*: adicies *Sch*: adicis *GiVo* | libram *GiVo* 3. sartaginem *Sch* | mittes *GiVo* | oenogaro *Sch* 4. ipso oenogaro *Sch* 5. si *del. Sch* | calidae *Sch* 7. garatas *GiVo*: NB graton *in contents list* | lasaratas *Sch* | gingiber *Sch* | uno acetabulo *Sch*: unum acetabulum *GiVo* | liquamen *CGSG, cf. III*: liq *A*: liquaminis *Sch* 8. misces cominum his *Sch* 9. coquis *Sch* | liquamine *Sch* | mediauerit *Ihm* | cum in mediam uenerint cocturam *Sch* 11. et cum *Sch*: etiam *A*: et iam *Ihm* 12. bulliuerit *CGSG*: bulliuit *A*: bullierit *Sch* | cuminum *GiVo* | bacam dimidiam *Sch* | colorem crocum *Sch* 13. amolabis *Sch* | oryza *GiVo* 14. acetum *Sch* 16. radicem *Sch* | origanum *Sch* | rutam *Sch* | liquamen *Sch*: liq; *A* | adicies *Sch, cf. XIII*: adices *A*: adicis *GiVo* 17. defrictum *Sch* | ferueat *Sch* | calefeceris *Sch* 18. eodem *GiVo* | asperso *André* | pipere *Sch* | et *om. GiVo* 19. ligisticum *Sch* | bacam *Sch* 20. mel liquamen *GiVo*: mel liq; *A*: mellique *Sch* | uinum passum uel carenum *GiVo* | lento *Sch* | oridiae *Sch*: oryzae *GiVo* 22. ligusticum *GiVo* | satureiam *Sch* | cepam *Sch* | acetum *Sch* 23. cariotam anethum *Sch* | oleum *Sch* | defrictum *Sch*: defritum *GiVo* 24. in uino *André*

3. *Ofellae* in *garum*: put the *ofellae* in a frying-pan, add ½ pt. of *liquamen*, a similar amount of oil, a lesser amount of honey, and fry them in it.[1]

4. Roasted *ofellae*: bring the *ofellae* carefully to the boil, drain them and put them in a frying-pan; fry them in *oenogarum*. Afterwards serve them with the same *oenogarum*, and sprinkle with pepper.

5. Another recipe for *ofellae*: they are fried in *liquamen*, and they are brushed with honey while hot, and served like this.

6. *Ofellae* in *garum* sauce: take *laser*, ginger, and cardamom, and mix all these pounded spices with a cupful of *liquamen*. Cook the *ofellae* in this.

7. Scorpion fish with turnips: cook (the fish) in *liquamen* and oil, and when it is half-cooked take it out. Boil turnips until they are really soft, cut them up into very small pieces and squeeze them in the hands so that they are free of moisture, and then blend them with the fish[2] and let it boil with plenty of oil. When it has boiled, pound cumin, half the quantity of bay berries, add saffron to give it colour. Thicken with rice starch to give it body. Pour it over the fish, then serve. Add a little vinegar.[3]

8. You make fried fish of whatever kind at all like this: pound pepper, coriander seed, *laser* roots, oregano, rue, date; pour on vinegar, oil, *liquamen*; add *defrutum*; blend all these and put in a pan and bring it to heat.[4] When you have heated it up, pour it over the fish. Serve sprinkled with pepper.

9. You can also make fried fish like this: pound pepper, lovage, bay berries, coriander, honey, *liquamen*, wine, flavour with *passum* or *caroenum*. Cook over a slow fire, thicken with rice starch, and serve.

10. Grilled fish: pound pepper, lovage, savory, dried onion; pour on vinegar; add date, dill, egg yolks, honey, vinegar, *liquamen*, oil, *defrutum*. Mix all these into one and pour on.

---

[1] Technically (and in the modern sense of the word) 'frying' requires an oil of some sort, but in ancient recipes the term has a more general sense of 'seethe' or 'boil rapidly in a small amount of liquid' so that it reduces.

[2] *obligas* can hardly have its normal sense of 'thicken' here. This extended meaning is not found in *Apicius*.

[3] There are liquids missing from this recipe: the saffron sauce would need wine before it could be thickened.

[4] *hęc omnia temperabis*: we would normally translate *temperabis* as 'flavour' or 'balance the flavour', but here the context makes it necessary to render it as 'blend'. The extended meaning of 'taste' and 'adjust the flavour' is always understood in this term, wherever it is found.

XI. pisces inotocano: friges pisces; teres piper ligisticum rutam condimenta uiridia cepa sicca. adicies oleo <uinum> liquamen et inferes.

XII. sardas sic facies: teres piper ligustici semen origanu cępam siccam ouorum cottorum uitella acetu oleum. hęc in unum temperas et perfundes.

5   **XIII. pisces inotogono:** a crudo pisces quos uolueris labas, conponis in patinam; mittis oleum liquamen uinum fasciculos porri et coriandri; coquitur. teres piper origanu ligisticum et fasciculos quos elixasti teres et suffundes inpesa de patina. facis ut obliget. cum bene tenuerit, piper asparso inferebis.

XIIII. mullos anetatos sic facies: rades pisces, lababis, in patinam conponis;
10   adicies oleum liquamen uinu fasciculos porri et coriandri; mittes ut coquatur. adicies piper <anethi semen> in mortario, fricabis; adicies oleum et parte aceti; uino passo temperauis. traicies in caccabo, ponis ut ferueat. amolo obligabis et patinam piscium perfundis. insuper piper aspargis.

XV. aliter mullos: rades, labas, conponis in patinam. adicies oleo liquamen
15   uinu, in coctura fasciculum porri et coriandri. inponis ut coquatur. teres piper ligisticum origanum, adicies de iure suo – hec de patella – uino passo temperas; mittis in caccabo, ponis ut ferueat; amulo obligabis et patella postea perfundes. piper aspargis et inferes.

---

1. in eleogaro *Sch*: oenoteganon *Ihm*: inotegano *André* | ligusticum *GiVo*   2. cepam siccam *Sch* | adicies *Sch*: adices *A*: adicis *GiVo* | ex oleo *Sch*: oleum *GiVo* | <uinum> *GiVo* 3. origanum *Sch* | cepam *Sch*   4. coctorum *Sch* | acetum *Sch*   5. item pisces *Sch* | in eleogaro *Sch*: oenoteganon *Ihm*: inotegano *André* | lauas *Sch* | patina *Sch* 7. origanum *Sch* | ligusticum *GiVo* | inpensam *Sch*: impensam *Milham*   8. pipere *Sch* 9. anecatos *Sch*: anethatos *GiVo* | lauabis *Sch* | conpones *Sch*: componis *Milham*   10. uinum *Sch*   11. <anethi semen> *CGSG* | fricabis *Sch* | partem *GiVo*   12. temperabis *Sch* | caccabo *Ihm*: cabo *A*: caccabum *Sch* | amulo *GiVo*   14. lauas *Sch* | componis *Milham* | patinam *André*: ?patinam or patiniim *corr.* patinim *A*: patina *Sch* | adicies *Sch*: adices *A*: adicis *GiVo* | oleum *Sch* | liquamen *Sch*: liq; *A*   15. uinum *Sch* | fasciculum *Sch*: fasculum *A*: fasciculos *André* | imponis *Milham*   16. ligusticum *GiVo* | hec de patella *del. Sch, reading* hoc | 17. caccabum *Sch* | amolo *Sch* | patellam *Sch*   18. inferes *Sch*: inferis *A*

---

[1] The MS reading *inotocano* seems to be a clumsy spelling of *oenoteganon*, as Ihm suggested. See *EV* 29, where we interprete *cum inogaru* as 'with oenogarum', the *ino* clearly referring to *oeno* 'wine'. The term is formed after the pattern of *zomoteganon*, at *Apicius* 4.2.27. *zomos* is the Greek for 'broth' or 'sauce', and *teganon* is Greek for 'frying-pan'. The *teganon* need not be made of metal, however. The standard frying-pan form is in fact ceramic rather than metal in Athens during the first and second centuries AD. See Riley, 'The Coarse Pottery', forms 464 and 463 (see the Introduction, p. 79 n. 4).

11. Fish in *oenoteganon*: fry the fish; pound pepper, lovage, rue, green herbs, dried onion; add oil, wine and *liquamen*, and serve.[1]

12. You make (a sauce for) bonito like this: pound pepper, lovage seed, oregano, dried onion, hard-boiled egg yolks, vinegar and oil. Blend all these into one and pour on.

13. Fish in *oenoteganon*:[2] wash a raw piece of fish of your choice, arrange in a dish; add oil, *liquamen*, wine, and bundles of leek and coriander; cook it. Pound pepper, oregano, lovage, and pound the bundles which you have boiled, and pour on some of the cooking liquor from the *patina*.[3] Thicken it. When it has thoroughly set, sprinkle with pepper and serve.

14. You make mullet in dill sauce like this: scale the fish, wash it, and arrange in a dish, add oil, *liquamen*, wine, a bundle of leek and coriander; put it to cook. Put in a mortar pepper and dill seed,[4] pound it; add oil and a lesser amount of vinegar;[5] flavour with wine and *passum*. Transfer to a pan, bring it to heat, thicken with starch, and pour it over the *patina* of fish. Sprinkle pepper over it.

15. Another recipe for mullet: scale, wash and arrange (the fish) in a dish; add oil, *liquamen*, wine; put a bundle of leek and coriander for it to cook with. Put it to cook. Pound pepper, lovage, oregano; add some cooking liquor - this comes from the dish – flavour with wine and *passum*. Put it in a pan, bring it to heat, thicken with starch and afterwards pour it on the dish,[6] sprinkle with pepper and serve.

---

[2] The MS reads *inotogono*, another very awkward rendering of *oenoteganon*, and we translate as above at *EV* 11.

[3] The recipe is very abrupt towards the end but, as we have seen with many different *patinae*, eggs are added to the sauce, which is then poured back over the fish and the dish cooked in the embers until set.

[4] *Anetatos* implies a dill sauce, yet dill is missing – hence our adding it. It is likely that the *fasciculum* of leek and coriander was also used in the sauce, and that a substantial part of the recipe is actually missing.

[5] *partem* is odd way of expressing a quantity; it must refer to a smaller, part-volume of the amount of oil used.

[6] *Patina* and *patella* seem to be interchangeable here. They have the same meaning, i.e. a round, shallow, flat-bottomed ceramic or metallic dish. See the Glossary.

XVI. murenas aut anguilas uel mullos sic facies: purgabis, conponis in patinam diligenter. adicies in mortario piper legisticum origanum menta cępam
arida, effundes uini acetabulum, liquaminis dimidium, mellis tertiam partem,
modice defritu ad cucliare. debent autem hoc iure coperiri, ut super cotturam
5   supersit aliquid iuris.

XVII. locustas <et isquillas>: teres piper ligisticum api semen, effundes acetum
liquamen ouorum uitella et mixta in unum perfundis et inferes.

XVIII. in piscibus elexis: teres piper ligisticum appi semen origanum; suffundes
acetum, adicies nucleos pineus, gariota quod satis sit, mel acetu liquamen
10   sinapem. temperabis et uteris.

XIX. patina soliarum ex obis: rades, purgas, conponis in patinam; adicies
liquamen oleum uinum fasciculum porri et coriandri [semen]; mittis ut quoquatur. teres piper modicum origanum, suffundis iux suo sibi; adicies iuri dicem
cruda oua; dissoluis et in unum corpus facies. traicies in patinam super solias.
15   ad ignem lentum pones ut decoquat, et cum duxerit piper adspargis.

XX. porcellum coriandratum: assas porcellum diligenter; facies mortarium
sic in quo teres piper anetu origanum coriandrum uiride; admisces mel uinum
liquamen oleum acetum defritum. hec omnia calefacta perfundes et aspargis uua
passa nucleos pineos et cepam concisam, et sic inferes.

1. murenas *CGSG, cf. list at start*: murena *A*: murenam *GiVo* | anguillas *Sch* | conpones *Sch*:
componis *Milham*   1-2. patina *Sch*   2. mortarium *Sch* | ligisticum *Sch*: ligusticum
GiVo | mentam *Sch*   3.aridam *Sch* | et fundes *Sch*: infundes *GiVo* | uini *Sch*: uinu *A*:
uinum *GiVo* | acetabulum *Sch*: acetabuli *A*   4. defrictum *Sch*: defritum *GiVo* | cucliare
André: clucliare *A*: cocleare *GiVo*: cocliare *Ihm*: ad dulcorem *or* glucliare *sugg. Sch* | coperiri *Ihm*:
coperi *A*: cooperiri *sugg. Sch* | cocturam *Sch* | superset *A1*   6. locustas *CGSG*: locusta
A: locustam *GiVo* | <et isquillas> *CGSG, cf.index*: <et squillas> *Sch*: <et isquilla> *André*: <et
scillas> *Sch* | ligusticum *GiVo* | et fundes *Sch*: infundes *GiVo*   7. liquamen *Sch*: lique
A | ouorum *Sch*: ouoram *A*   8. in *om. Sch* | pisces elixos *Sch* | elixis *GiVo* | ligusticum
GiVo | api *Sch*   9. pineos *Sch* | cariotam *Sch*: cariota *Ihm*: caryotam *Milham*: caryotae
GiVo | acetum *Sch* | liquamen *Sch*: liq; *A*   10. sinape *Sch*   11. patina soliarum
André: patinas oliarum *A*: patina solearum *Sch* | ouis *Sch* | componis *Milham* | patina *Sch*
12. oleum *Sch*: olei *A* | semen *del. CGSG*   12-13. coquatur *Sch*   13. ius de suo sibi
Sch | iuri *A*: uinum *Sch* | decem *Sch*   14. dissolues *Sch* | soleas *Sch*   15. decoquat
Sch: dequocat *A* | aspargis *Sch*   16. moretarium *Vo*   17. siccum *Sch* | in quod *Vo*
| anethum *Sch*   18. liquamen *Sch*: liq; *A* | acetum *Sch*: anetum *A*: acetu *André* | defrictum
Sch   18-19. unam passam *Sch*   19. et siccum *Sch*

16. You make moray eels, eels and mullet like this: clean (the fish) and arrange carefully in a dish. Put in a mortar pepper, lovage, oregano, mint, dried onion; pour on a cup of wine, ½ cup of *liquamen*, ⅓ cup of honey, and just a spoonful of *defrutum*. (The fish) should be covered with this sauce so that the level of the sauce remains above the fish during cooking.

17. Spiny lobster and prawns: pound pepper, lovage, celery seed; pour on vinegar, *liquamen*, egg yolks; blend into one, pour on and serve.

18. Sauce for boiled fish: pound pepper, lovage, celery seed, oregano; pour on vinegar, add pine nuts, as much date as you need, honey, vinegar, *liquamen*, mustard. Balance the flavours and use.

19. *Patina* of soles with egg: scale, clean and arrange (the fish) in a dish; add *liquamen*, oil, wine, a bundle of leek and coriander;[1] put it to cook. Pound pepper, a little oregano; pour on some of the cooking liquor; add to the sauce 10 raw eggs; beat into a smooth emulsion. Transfer to the dish on top of the soles. Place on a gentle fire so that it cooks through and, when it has set, sprinkle with pepper.

20. Piglet in coriander sauce: roast the piglet carefully; prepare the mortar spices by pounding pepper, dill, oregano, green coriander; mix in honey, wine, *liquamen*, oil, vinegar, *defrutum*. Bring all these to heat and pour over the piglet, and sprinkle over raisins, pine nuts and chopped onion, and so serve.

---

[1] *Semen* makes no sense here. Each *fasciculum* has leek and green coriander as a matter of course, both here and in the body of *Apicius*. We suspect that 'seed' has been added by someone unfamiliar with the recipes, though at what stage in the transmission of the text is not clear.

XXI. porcello unococto: porcellum accipies, ornauis, quoque in oleo et liquamen. cum quoquitur adicies in mortario piper ruta baca lauri liquamen, passu siue carenu, uino uetus; simul omnia teres. temperas et traicies in patinam heneam. mittis eum [XXII] porcellum eo iure, perquoque; cum autem leuas,

5 amulo oblicabis et sic in uas transferes et inferes.

XXIII. porcellum timo sparsum: porcellum lactentem pridie occisum elixas sale et anetu, et in aqua frigida adsidue intingis ut candorem habeat. deinde condimenta uiridia timmum polleium modicum oba dura ciba concisa minuta; ea omnia superspargis, et condis liquamen emina una olei pondo uno passo pondo

10 uno et sic ministras.

XXIIII. porcello exodiomum: porcellum accuratum ornauis et mittis in iuscellum sic condito: aicies in mortario piper grana L, mellis quantum conpedat, cepas siccas III coriandri uiridis siue sicci modicum, liquaminis emina, olei sextarium I, aque emina I; simul temperas in caccabulo. mittis in eo porcellum.

15 dum bullire cęperit, sępius agitauis ut spissum fiat. si aliquid minus iuris facere ceperit, tunc adicies emina I aque. sic perquoque et sic porcellum inferes.

XXV. porcellum laseratum: teres in mortario piper ligisticum careum; misces ciminum paululum, lasar uiuum lasaris radicem; suffundis acetum, addis nucleos pineos cariotam mel acetum liquamen senape factu. oleo omnia temperas et

20 perfundis.

1. porcellum *Sch* | aeno coctum *Sch*: oenococtum *Ihm*: inococto *André* | ornabis *Sch* | coques *Sch*: coque *GiVo*   2. liquamen[1] *CGSG*: liq; *A*: liquamine *Sch* | coquitur *Sch* | mortarium *Sch* | rutam bacam *Sch* | liquamen[2] *Sch*: liq; *A*   3. passum siue caroenum *Sch* | uinum *Sch*   4. aeneam *Sch*: eneam *André* | XXII *del. André, running XXI and XXII into one recipe* | ex suo iure *Ihm* | percoques *Sch*   5. amolo *Sch* | obligabis *Sch*   6. thymo *GiVo* | sparsum *Sch*: crapsum *A*   7. aneto *Sch*: anetho *GiVo*   8. timum *Sch*: thymum *GiVo* | puleium *Sch* | oua *Sch* | ciba *A*: cepam *Sch* | concisam *Sch* | minutatim *Sch*   9. passi *Sch*: passum *Milham*   11. porcellum *GiVo* | oxizomum *Sch*: oxyzomum *GiVo*: oxidiomum *André* | ornabis *Sch*   12. conditum *Sch* | adicies *Sch* | mortarium *Sch* | piperis *Sch* | quantum *Sch*: quan *A* | conpetat *Sch*   13. liquaminis *Sch*: liq; *A* | eminam *Sch*: heminam *GiVo*   14. eminam *Sch*: heminam *GiVo*   15. sępius] cepa ius *Sch* | agitabis *GiVo*   16. eminam *Sch*: heminam *GiVo* | percoques *Sch*: perquoq(ues) *Ihm*: percoque *GiVo*   17. ligusticum *GiVo*   18. cuminum *GiVo*: cyminum *Milham* | lasaris radicem *del. Sch*   19. sinape *GiVo* | factum *Sch*

21. Piglet *oenococtum*:[1] take the piglet, dress it, and cook in oil and *liquamen*. While it is cooking, pound in a mortar pepper, rue, bay berries, *liquamen*, *passum* or *caroenum*, old wine; pound everything together. Balance the flavours, transfer to a bronze dish. Put the [22] piglet into the sauce and finish cooking it. When you lift it out, thicken (the sauce) with starch, transfer to a bowl and serve it like this.[2]

23. Piglet sprinkled with thyme: boil a suckling pig killed the day before with salt and dill, and then plunge it repeatedly in cold water to take the heat away.[3] Then take green herbs, thyme and a little pennyroyal, hard boiled eggs, finely-chopped onion; sprinkle all these over and then make a dressing of ½ pt. *liquamen*, 1 lb. oil and 1 lb. *passum*, and serve it with this.

24. Piglet in *oxyzomo*:[4] carefully dress a piglet and put it in a sauce flavoured with these spices: put in a mortar 50 peppercorns, as much honey as necessary, 3 dried onions, a little green or dry coriander, ½ pt. *liquamen*, 1 pt. oil, ½ pt. water; blend all these in a pan. Put the piglet in this; when it has begun to boil, stir it quite often to keep it boiling.[5] If the sauce begins to reduce too much, add ½ pt. water. Finish cooking it and so serve the piglet.

25. Piglet in *laser* sauce: pound in a mortar pepper, lovage, caraway; mix in a little cumin, fresh *laser*, *laser* root;[6] pour on vinegar, add pine nuts, date, honey, vinegar, *liquamen*, prepared mustard. Blend all these with oil and pour on.

---

[1] We prefer to interpret the MS reading *unococto* as *oenococtum*, on the grounds that the recipe contains *passum* or *caroenum* and old wine. Schuch's suggestion *aeno coctum* is based on the instruction to use a bronze pan., but it is hard to see what difference this makes in culinary terms. It is still possible, as Andrew Dalby has pointed out, that an original technique of cooking in metal rather than ceramic lies behind it, but see above p. 318 n. 1.

[2] We have combined this and the next recipe into one, agreeing with André, 1974. For clarity we retain the recipe numbers found in the MS. The *vas* is a bowl for the dipping sauce, which is served separately.

[3] *ut candorem habeat* must surely refer to the water cooling the piglet down, rather than to giving a white appearance to the piglet, though the usage of *candor* in this way is rare. In any case, a freshly-boiled piglet would already be white.

[4] The Greek for a 'sour sauce'.

[5] *Spissare* usually means 'thicken', which would be the normal culinary interpretation, but stirring a sauce does not make it thicken *per se*. However, it would make it boil more rapidly, leading to reduction, which is referred to in the next sentence. Cf. Petronius *Sat.* 1.40, *spissare officium*, 'keep the service coming'. As there, the sense here is 'keep it on the boil'.

[6] See the Glossary, *laser*, for the distinction between fresh and root *laser*.

XXVI. porcellu iuscellatu: mittis in mortario piper ligisticum aut anesum coriandrum ruta baca lauri, fricauis; suffundis liquamen, porro, passi siue mellis modicum, uinum modicum olei aliquantum. cum coxeris amulo oblicauis.

XXVII. agnu simplice: de agno decoriato facies cupadiola, lababis diligenter, mittes in cacabo. adicies oleum liquamen uinum porrum coriandrum cultro concisum. cum bullire cęperit, sepius agitabis et inferes.

XXVIII. ędum lasaratum: edi intestinas bene purgatas imples piper liquamen lasar oleum et intra ędum mittes et bene consues et cum ędo simul cocuuntur; et cum decoxerit, adicies in mortario ruta baca lauri, et lebato ędo adque exugato ipso iure perfundis et sic ponis.

XXIIII. turdos apantomoenos: teres piper lasar baca lauri, admisces cum inogaro, et sic turdos per guttor imples et filo ligauis; et facies ei impesa in qua decocantur, quę habeat oleum sales aqua anetu et capita porrorum.

XXX. turtures: aperies, ornauis diligenter; teres piper lasar liquamen modicum; infundis ipsas turtures ut conbibant siui et sic assas.

XXXI. ius in perdices: teres in mortario piper apio menta et rutam; suffundis acetum, addis cariotam mel acetum liquamen oleum. simul coques et inferes.

EXPLICIT BREVIS CIBORVM

1. porcellum iuscellatum *Sch* | mortarium *Sch* | ligusticum *GiVo* | anetum *Sch* 2. rutam bacam *Sch* | fricabis *Sch* | porrum *Sch*   3. amolo *Sch* | obligauis *André*: obligabis *Sch*   4. agnum *Sch* | copadia *Sch*: copadiola *GiVo* | lauabis *Sch*   5. caccabum *Sch*: caccabo *GiVo*   6. cepa ius agitabis *Sch*   7. aedum *Sch*: haedum *GiVo* | aedi *Sch*: haedi *GiVo* | intestinis *Sch* | purgatis *Sch* | inples *Sch*   8. edum *Sch*: haedum *GiVo* 9. mortarium *Sch* | rutam bacam *Sch* | leuato *Sch*: leuatum *GiVo* | ędo *CGSG*: ędi *A*: aedo *Sch*: haedum *GiVo* | adque exiccato *Sch*: atque exsucatum *GiVo*: atque exsucato *Milham* 10. aedo ipso iure *Sch*   11. apontomoenos *Sch*: hapantamynos *GiVo*: aponcomenos *André* | bacam *Sch*   11-12. cum inogaru *André*: cumino garu *A*: comino garum *Sch*: cumino garum *GiVo*: cum inogaro *Bra2*: cuminum garum *Milham*   12. turdos *Sch*: turdo *A*: turdum *GiVo* | guttur *Sch* | ligabis *Sch* | eis *Sch* | inpensam *Sch*: impensam *GiVo* | in quo *Milham* 13. decoquantur *Sch* | aquam *Sch* | anetum *Sch*: anethum *GiVo*   14. onerabis *Sch*: ornabis *GiVo*   15. ipsos *Sch* | combibant *André* | sic] sicci *Sch*: sibi *Ihm*   16. apium mentam et rutam *Sch*   17. acoetum *Sch*

26. Piglet in a sauce: put in a mortar pepper, lovage or anise,[1] coriander, rue, bay berries; pound; pour on *liquamen*, leek, a little *passum* or honey, a little wine, and some oil. When it has cooked, thicken with starch.

27. A simple lamb recipe: cut little chunks from a skinned lamb, wash carefully and put in a pan. Add oil, *liquamen*, wine, leek and coriander chopped with a knife. When it has begun to boil, stir it quite often and serve.

28. Kid in *laser* sauce: clean the kid's intestines well and fill them with pepper, *liquamen*, *laser*, oil and put them back into the kid and sew it up well so that they are cooked along with the kid. And when it has finished cooking, put in a mortar rue and bay berries. Take the kid[2] and strain its own juices (into the mortar) and then pour the sauce on and so serve.[3]

29. Stuffed thrushes:[4] pound pepper, *laser*, bay berries; mix with *oenogarum*,[5] and fill the thrushes from the neck end and tie with string, and then make a cooking liquor for them containing oil, salt, water, dill and leek.

30. Turtle doves: open them up and dress them carefully; pound pepper, *laser*, a little *liquamen*; pour it into the doves so that they marinade and so roast them.

31. Sauce for partridges: pound in a mortar pepper, celery (seed), mint and rue; pour on vinegar, add date, honey, vinegar, *liquamen*, oil. Cook them together and serve.

HERE ENDS THE SUMMARY OF FOODS

[1] Pliny (*HN.* 20.187) recognizes that lovage and anise are interchangeable.

[2] The kid is either boiled or roasted, after which it appears its juices are drained out into the mortar. The juices are more likely to be concentrated and worth using if roasted (as is this case with any gravy), while a boiled kid would probably make more of a watery juice, at least initially. It is also possible that oil, wine, *liquamen* are also meant to go into the mortar.

[3] This recipe recalls *Apicius* 8.6.6 and 8.6.11; see also Macrobius 3.13.13 for the 'Trojan boar' which appears to have other kinds of meat or fowl as stuffing.

[4] *aponcomenos*: perhaps from Greek *apokoō*, 'fill', 'stuff' (so André: cf. Porphyry, *De Abs.* 2. 30), or *apokoptomenous*, 'cut off' (Schuch). Ihm comments 'I know no plausible explanation' (*Apicius-Exzerpte*, p.72).

[5] The MS reads *cumino garu*: 'with cumin and *garum*'. This would be a rare reference to garum and, given the position of the phrase in the text after the spices, we are inclined to reject the cumin. It is far more likely to be *cum inogaru*, referring to the ubiquitous *oenogarum*; see *EV* 11 and 13, where *inotocano/inotogono* is interpreted as *oenogarum*.

APPENDICES

1. A GLOSSARY TO *APICIUS*.

2. ORIGINAL SOURCES ON APICIUS, COOKING AND LUXURY DINING.

3. NAMED RECIPES IN *APICIUS*.

4. EXCURSUS ON *GARUM* AND *LIQUAMEN*.

5. CONCORDANCE OF RECIPES WITH EARLIER EDITIONS.

1.   A GLOSSARY TO *APICIUS*.

Alica is the Latin term for a form of emmer groat that, in its finest form, is very similar to semolina in texture. It apparently came in many different grades, ranging from a coarse cleaned cracked wheat to a very fine grain:

> Alica *is made from* zea, *which we have called a seed. Its grain is pounded in a wooden mortar, lest the hardness of a stone one grind it down, and as is well known the motion of the pestle is the punishment work of men in chains; it has an iron cap on its tip. Once the outer coat has been removed, the naked kernel is broken up with the same tool. In this way three kinds of* alica *are produced: very small and middling, while they call the very largest* aphairema *or 'that which is removed.'* Pliny, *HN.* 18.112.

In *Apicius*, *alica* is used in its relatively coarse form, i.e. the middling variety. It is either soaked or cooked, as the equivalent of rusk in sausages, as the basis for a sweet porridge, and to bulk up all manner of forcemeat. In a finer form it is used to make the sheets of *tracta* which are then dried and ultimately crumbled into liquid as a thickener. For *tracta* in the cake called *placenta*, see Cato, *De Agricultura* 76, and also *tracta* below. *Alica* is often rendered as 'spelt grits' or 'groats' in other translations. The Greek term *alikos* survives in the work on baking by Chrysippus, but here it has the meaning of a rice groat rather then emmer wheat.[1]

Allec This by-product of fish sauce production was used as a fish paste in its own right. During the process of fermenting *garum* or *liquamen,* the fish particles sink to the bottom and form a layer that was used as a fish paste, very similar to anchovy paste in appearance. Its quality rather depended on the quality of the fish used to make the fish sauce. Cato gave his farm slaves *allec* as part of their ration; this was likely to be a low-grade fish sauce by-product that would have added protein to their diet.[2] According to Pliny, *HN.* 31.95, *allec* began

---

[1] Athenaeus 647d.

[2] Cato, *De agricultura* 54.

to be made in its own right from *apua*: any kind of small fry. This product would have resembled anchovy paste even more closely.

Allec could also be made as a designated fish product from specific ingredients such as mullet livers, oysters and sea urchins. These designated products were much more expensive. In *Apicius*, *allec* appears on only three occasions, while the fish sauce known as *liquamen* is almost universal. At 7.2.2 sow's udder is eaten with *allec* and mustard, with the implication that the diner controls the application of the allec. At 7.6.14, an *allecatum* (a sauce made with strained *allec*) is served with meat, and at 9.10.1 sardines stuffed and baked in papyrus are then flavoured with oil, *caroenum* and *allec* as a final dressing. Anchovy paste is a suitable substitute if you wish to use it.

Ammi This spice has the Indian name of ajowan/ajwain today and can often be found in Indian supermarkets under the name of 'lovage seed'. However, this is misleading as it is not lovage seed. In appearance it looks a little like celery seed, though slightly larger, and it has a flavour similar to thyme. Ajwain was also called 'Ethiopian cumin' in ancient times, though the name is more often used for *Nigella sativa*, which has many names including black cumin, kalonja and onion seed. As is apparent from this, spice identification can sometimes be very confusing. *Ammi* appears only a few times in *Apicius*, as a spice in digestives (1.27, 1.32).

Amylum A form of starch made from soaked whole grains of wheat. When the grains have softened and starch has been released into the liquid, it is strained, and the liquor is allowed to thicken and ferment slightly into a dry paste with the aid of the sun and a leaven. At its best, its appearance is light, smooth and fresh. See Pliny, *HN*. 18.76, where he tells us that the name is Greek and means 'made without milling', and also that the best kind comes from Chios. In *Apicius*, *amylum* is used as a light thickener and has the same properties as cornflour or arrowroot, both of which are more than adequate substitutes. *Amylum* seems to be a fairly high-status product, despite its simplicity. Cato *De Agricultura* 87 gives a similar method to Pliny for its production, but cooks it in milk to make a thick smooth sauce or pudding. In this form it was a potential dish in its own right in a high-status meal, according to Macrobius, who records the menu of a feast held in the mid-first century BC which had *amylum* and *panes Picentes* as the starch components of the second tables.[1]

Asafoetida – *Parthian* laser *Ferula asafoetida*, family *umbelliferae*. Also known as 'hing', 'devil's dung' and 'food of the gods': the resin or gum obtained from the root of a plant native to Afghanistan. It is available in the UK, imported from India as a powder. The resin is ground and mixed with bean meal or flour; it is weaker in flavour and has a shorter life than the pure resin (which is less readily available here). In *Apicius*, *laser* is either from Cyrenaica in North Africa or from Parthia (Iran/Afghanistan/Iraq/Armenia). African *laser* was known as *silphium* (q.v. below) but, confusingly, writers also called the other types of resin from Parthia *silphium*. When *silphium* became extinct in the mid-first century AD, products from the plant from Parthia replaced it: there are recipes in *Apicius* which give the reader a choice, but the majority of recipes give no indication as to whether Parthian or African *laser* was intended. Both types of *laser* may well have been available for some time before the latter died out.[2]

In the countries of origin the stalk, leaf, resin (*opos* in Greek) and the root were consumed. The root and resin are likely to be the only products that travelled to Rome. In *Apicius* various terms are used to indicate this plant and we cannot be certain of their meaning or derivation. *Laser* is often qualified by other words which we are unable to define precisely. It seems clear that *silphium* was the name of the plant in Greek, but it was also the word used for the root. Galen tells us that 'people call the root of *silphium* by the same name as the whole plant'.[3] In Latin *sirpe*, *laser* and *laserpicium* are all terms for the resin. In *Apicius* the resin can be *uiuum* – 'living' – which we interpret as the fresh resin, which is moist and still in the process of drying out. It would have been unadulterated and unground, and liable to decay: it

---

[1] Macrobius 3.13.13. Later medieval recipes for *frumenty* are similar, though made with cracked wheat. They serve as accompaniments to meat dishes in the same way as *amylum*.

[2] See *silphium* below. See Theophrastus, *Enquiry into Plants,* 6.3.7 for the recognition of Syrian 'silphium' in 310 BC.

[3] Galen, Commentary on 'Diet in Acute Diseases' 15.877-8, a 'Hippocratic' text of the late fifth century. See particularly Andrew Dalby, 'Silphium and Asafoetida: evidence from Greek and Roman writers', in *Spicing up the Palate: Proceedings of the Oxford Symposium on Food and Cookery 1992* (Totnes, 1993), pp. 67-72.

was apparently unstable and did not travel, according to Pliny.[1] This is in contrast to a fully dried resin, which had been shaken with bean meal to 'fix' it for travel. Both these kinds of *laser* were dissolved in warm water, though the dried variety takes some time, as our own experiments have confirmed.[2] *Laser uiuum* must surely have been the most expensive variety, followed by the pure resin, unground. The resin could also be pre-ground before sale, as Pliny suggests when he says that Parthian *laser* was often adulterated and of a much inferior quality. It is likely that the variety of *laser* most readily available then, as today, would have been a pounded resin mixed with flour or bean meal in various quantities depending on quality. This is almost certainly the *laser* of the recipes.

In *Apicius* the recipes often talk of *laseris radix,* 'laser root', which is equated with *silphium* in 3.4.1. It is our belief that the dried root and resin reached Rome and were both used in cooking. One of Columella's recipes confirms this. He lists the ingredients for an *oxyporium* which include *seminis unciae duae laseris radicis quod silphium Graeci vocant* (1½ oz of *laser* root which the Greeks call *silphium*).[3] He then lists an alternative kind of digestive, which he suggests is made more valuable if mixed with the previous one, 'but if you have Syrian *laser* rather than *silphium* you will do better to add ½ oz of it.' We think that Syrian *laser* is the resin and that it is being suggested as an alternative to the root.[4] The resin has a powerful, pungent flavour and would be used in far smaller quantities than the root, hence the need to reduce the quantity. We cannot be certain about these products, but suspect that the root was a far more common item of commerce than the resin, and that the statement *silfi id est laseris radicem* found at 3.4.1 in *Apicius* should be taken literally: when *silphium* appears in (some) of the recipes it does mean the

---

[1] Pliny, *HN.* 19. 44. It is not clear whether 'living' resin travelled to Rome or stayed local to the Greek colony. If it did not travel then the recipes that call for it are necessarily early Greek in origin.

[2] 6.8.3. We are able to confirm that even 'old' resin does dissolve in warm water eventually.

[3] Columella 12.59.4.

[4] Theophrastus, *Enquiry Into Plants,* 6.3.7, says it is less pungent. Pliny, *HN.* 19.46, largely copies Theophrastus' detailed account of its cultivation in Cyrenaica, though he is talking of the inferior Middle Eastern variety that was adulterated with bean meal etc. This implies that virtually all the resin that was available in *c.*.AD 60–70 was ground up into a powder, and may well indicate that any recipe that requires the whole resin may be very early in date.

root as distinct from the resin. As we have seen, Galen believed the root was given the same name as the whole plant.[1] However the issue must remain unresolved: recipes that date from an earlier Greek period could well refer to the resin when they have *silfi/silfium* in the text.

In Vinidarius' excerpts, the situation in relation to *laser* is confused. In the commodity lists at the beginning of the text, *laser* appears among the uncategorized (but, we think) more expensive items, and *laser* root and *silphium* are among the dried items (*laser uiuum* does not appear in this list but is in a recipe).[2] Recipe 25 in the *Excerpta Vinidarii* is for a *laser* sauce for piglets. Among the ingredients are *laser uiuum* and *laser radix*. It would seem that the resin and the root had distinct characteristics. See the section on the *Excerpta Vinidarii* in the Introduction for a wider discussion of the list and text.

Asafoetida has a unique sulphurous smell, identified with rotten onion or garlic, which is an acquired taste. But like those two vegetables its pungency is tamed when cooked, and it becomes very palatable. The Romans used it particularly as a digestive, recognizing that it was effective in easing colic (and constipation, in larger doses). It was also used as a popular ingredient in sauces of all kinds, though it was considered very expensive, costing its own weight in silver *denarii*. Parthian *laser* was also known for its meat-tenderizing properties. Strabo records that it was originally discovered by Alexander's men in *Media* (Iran) on their return from India. They were without wood for cooking and had to eat horsemeat raw, but with the Median *silphion* the meat was made palatable.[3] We can confirm from repeated use that asafoetida does have a remarkable tenderizing effect on meat.

For the purposes of reconstructing the recipes, whether they call for *silphium* or *laser* or *laser radix* or *laser uiuum*, the cook has little choice but to use the resin sold as 'asafoetida mass' from Indian shops or the resin which is pounded and mixed with bean meal and turmeric and known as hing. This is

---

[1] At Cato, *De agricultura* 157.7 *silphium* is grated, an action not suited to resin but ideally suited to the root. See also p. 331 n. 3 above.

[2] Vinidarius did not take his list of commodities from the recipes he excerpted. Only a fraction of the items in the list are actually used in the body of the text. The general inadequacy of the list may imply that he did not know a great deal about food.

[3] Strabo, *Geography* 11.13.7, 15.2.10.

precisely what the Romans of the first century AD did too.[1] Alternatively, any acquaintance you may have who travels to the Middle East or India should be cultivated. Whichever form of the spice is available to you, care must be taken, as the spice can ruin a dish if used to excess.

Boletaria A form of serving dish or bowl, which may have been mushroom-shaped. It occurs in the text as a vessel for peas or lentils, and also for various kinds of meat in sauce and a pudding made with *alica* which resembles semolina pudding. We see the *boletaria* in a fresh light through Martial (14.101):

Boletaria
Although mushrooms have given me such a noble name, I am the servant of early-cut cabbage sprouts, the shame of it!

Bulbi The Greeks and Romans ate certain flower bulbs as well as the more obvious *allia*. Pliny *HN.* 19.93ff. appears to tell us that bulbs such as the lily and squill were eaten as well as used as medicine and lists many different named varieties which we cannot identify. Many flower bulbs are poisonous and should not be consumed today. However, the hyacinth bulb was the most popular, safe to eat and is still eaten in the modern world: the bulb of the grape hyacinth, known as *volvi* in Greek, is a delicacy in the Mediterranean. It is somewhat bitter and needs boiling for some time. In *Apicius* bulbs (probably grape hyacinth) are deemed a luxury food and recommended as an aphrodisiac (7.12.3).

Caroenum The identification of this product is difficult. It may have been a cooked wine syrup rather than a syrup made from fresh grape juice or must, although Palladius thought that all these syrups were made from must.[2] The term has been associated with the Greek for wine, *oinos*. Patrick Fass has suggested that if made from wine rather than must, the resulting syrup might not be so sweet.[3] However, an alternative origin is the Greek *karyinos*,

---

[1] At the time of writing we have not been able to locate asafoetida root but have high hopes of finding some one day.

[2] Palladius 11.18 ff.

[3] P. Fass, *Around the Roman Table* (trans. S. Whiteside, London, 2003), p. 148.

tentatively defined as a very sweet wine by Andrew Dalby, though how this differs from *passum* is hard to determine.[1] Palladius tells us that it was boiled down by one third of its volume, leaving two thirds behind. As we discuss with relation to *defrutum* below, the sweetness of the wine or must used determines how thick it will be in relation to the volume lost after reduction. If a must taken from grapes that would be used to make *passum* is used to make the *caroenum*, the two thirds remaining would result in good flavour but without the thickness, excessive sweetness, or the colour normally associated with *defrutum*.[2] It is quite possible that *caroenum*, though reduced, is still technically a wine rather than a syrup, as it may have been allowed to ferment after cooking. All these products may in fact have continued to ferment during storage. In *Apicius* it is used as an alternative to wine and is often the only form of liquid in an *oenogarum* sauce, which reaffirms its nature as a thin, flavoursome liquor that was used in larger quantites, in contrast to *defrutum*. The cook seems to have had the opportunity to create a wide variety of sauces by the subtle use of these syrups. Diocletian's Price Edict records *caroeni Maeoni* which suggests that though a common product in Roman food, it was also a Greek and specifically Lydian commodity, and was sold at the same price per *sextarius* as the best Falernian wine.

Cepa Various forms of onions appear quite regularly in the recipes. It is not possible to be exact about which Latin term corresponds with a given modern variety of *allium*. The most frequent term is *cepa*, which is simply an 'onion'. Many recipes also have *cepulla* as the regular term. This does not appear to be a specific type of onion but a late-Latin use of a diminutive for the normal word.[3] Consequently we simply translate it too as 'onion'. When *cepam*

[1] Verbal discussion with Andrew Dalby.

[2] Considerable confusion is generated by trying to define these syrups in terms of the level of reduction, as other commentators and ancient writers have tried to do. See *defrutum* below.

[3] It has been suggested by Dalby and others that a type of onion similar to the *welsh* onion was available to the ancients. The *welsh* onion is small and hollow-leaved, with subdivided yet small indistinct bulbs, and is used for its leaf. It is also known as the 'Japanese bunching onion' and by the name '*ciboule*', which is derived from *cepulla*. This particular onion comes from the Far East and did not appear in Europe until the late Middle Ages, when it was linked with *cepulla* and given its foreign name from its nature. (*Welsh* is a corruption of the Old German *welcsh* meaning 'foreign'.) The descriptions of onions found in ancient sources are not clear enough to permit certain identification.

aridam appears in the text we had first thought that it should be translated simply as 'onion' in the belief that the bulb would be dried on the outside, as happens today, and not cut up and fully desiccated. However, dried onions in Diocletian's Price Edict were sold by volume rather than by weight, suggesting that the onions were either quite small (which is a possibility) or that they were in fact cut up before being dried.[1] We have therefore retained the qualification 'dried' in the translation, but do not recommend that modern dried onion flakes are used, as we believe that they would be both too small and too dry. For the purposes of reconstructing the recipes, conventional onions should be used.

With *cepa ascalonia* we are on less sure ground. According to Pliny, this was an onion with a head or bulb that was grown from seed in one season. Theophrastus tells us that it was unusual in that it did not divide either from the root or through the plant. It was planted late and taken early, which implies that it was rather like a large spring onion when taken.[2] We must not assume because *ascalonia* is the origin of the word shallot that they are the same. In fact 'scallions', a fairly modern term for spring onions, also has its origins in the word *ascalonia*. Divided onions do occur in ancient sources, but not it seems in *Apicius*.[3] As this onion is apparently a conventional one rather than a shallot, and though it could be harvested early enough to resemble a spring onion, we have left the term itself un-translated and would recommend, for the purposes of reconstruction, either that plain onions or large spring onions of the kind seen in French markets are used.

Pliny contrasts *ascalonian* onions with an onion called *pallacana,* which we also find in the recipes. It was considered an onion but was said to run to leaf and to have hardly any bulb at all. The *pallacana* onion had hollow leaves and is identified with the Greek *getion* leek (see *Porrum*). It is described by Pliny as a type of 'cut and come again' onion that was used specifically for seasoning rather than as a vegetable. It is compared with the *porrum sectiuum* which was also cut for its leaf.[4] This so-called onion could be identified with

---

[1] Diocletian's Price Edict, 6.20 (ed. Laufer, p. 111). They sold at nearly 2 *denarii* per Italian pint, while first quality green onions were 4 *denarii* for 25.

[2] *Ascalonia* is linked to an area in Palestine rich in onions. Theophrastus, *Enquiry Into Plants* 7.2.3, 7.4.7-10; Pliny, *HN*. 19.101-7, 20.39-43.

[3] They are known as *schista*: see Pliny, *HN*. 19.101-7.

[4] Pliny, *HN*. 19.105 ff.

'chive' because of its seasoning quality and its cut nature. However a reference to *cepa pallacana* in *Apicius* contradicts this description. At 4.2.25 they are peeled and the green part is thrown away. This appears to suggest that they are a distinct type of onion rather than the chive, and the complete opposite to the account of this onion in Pliny.[1] It is quite possible that the *Apicius* recipe above is incorrect and that an *ascalonia* onion was intended, in which case *pallacana* may be identified as a form of chive. In view of the difficulty over precise identification we have, as with *cepa ascalonia,* left the term un-translated, as we feel that no single word would be sufficiently accurate. We recommend either using the tops of spring onions or fully grown chives, though neither term is adequate enough to be used in the translation.

Citrium – Citrus medica The citron is a large coarse citrus fruit native to north-east India. It has the familiar citrus flavour though it has a thick pithy skin and very little juice. It was known and used in the ancient world for its aromatic skin. Theophrastus tells us that it had fragrant leaves, and in *Apicius* the leaves are used to imitate the flavour of rose wine.[2] In Diocletian's Price Edict, *citrium maximum* and *sequens* (second quality?) appear. They are very expensive relative to the other fruits listed, but as we are not given the quantity against the price the actual value is unknown. It is possible that the *citrium* gourd is meant here (see below).

***Citrium* – gourd** *Citrium* appears in *Apicius* in two further recipes, yet it is doubtful that the citron fruit is meant. In the book on vegetables, at 3.5, a recipe for a sauce for *citrium* is given. Citron is unlikely to have been eaten as a vegetable. At 4.3.5, a recipe for *minutal dulce ex citriis* contains a vegetable or fruit that has been peeled, deseeded, diced and boiled. This *citrium* cannot be the citron above, as such preparation is impossible with a citrus fruit. It rather suggests a gourd of some sort, and the most likely example is the citron melon, *Citrullus vulgaris citroides.*

Clibanus/Testum A type of portable oven used for small-scale cooking. It was dome-shaped and sometimes had a flange to enable coals to be placed on top. The *clibanus* is Greek in origin and was equated with the Latin *testum,* which

---

[1] The botanical Latin name for 'chive' is *Allium schoenoprasum,* which means 'rush leek.'

[2] Theophrastus, *Enquiry Into Plants* 4.4.2; *Apicius* 1.4.

was almost certainly the same kind of oven.[1] The only distinction that can be identified is that a *clibanus* could be made of metal as well as ceramic: in all other respects the *modus operandi* is the same. The charcoal or wood embers direct heat through the fabric into the air inside the dome and so create a small yet fiercely hot oven space, perfect for bread and cakes and also for roasting meat. In *Apicius*, the *clibanus* is used to roast dormice, kidneys, a neck joint and a whole roasted kid, indicating that they varied in size considerably; this is confirmed from the remains of *testa* found in Italy.[2] The use of *clibanus* in *Apicius* reflects the use of Greek as the fashionable culinary language of the time: cf. *thermospodium,* 'hot embers', and *exbromare,* 'boil and discard the first water'. See figs. 6, 7 and 8 for an illustration of these ovens.

Colocasia This root vegetable is more commonly known as taro, and also as dasheen. It is called by Pliny 'the arum of the Egyptians', though it is not to be mistaken for the lotus root.[3] The corm is used as a vegetable and to bulk out meat or fowl dishes in *Apicius*. It does not seem to have been a major element of the diet of ordinary Romans, in contrast to modern Africa and the West Indies where it is a staple. Martial reveals the inner texture of the vegetable:[4]

Colocasia:
you will laugh at the vegetable from the Nile and its clinging fibres, when you pull at its naughty threads with mouth and fingers.

Coloefium This term occurs just once in *Apicius*, but has caused much confusion. It is a Latinized version of the Greek *cōluphion,* a diminutive of *cōlē,* which is either a 'leg of ham' or just 'ham'. In Plautus it refers to what can only be described as a form of ham sandwich: the meat is clearly off the bone.[5] The term occurs in the *Satyricon* of Petronius, where various forms of pork on

---

[1] See the discussion on cooking techniques on p. 82 above for a description of these ovens.

[2] See A.L. Cubberley *et al., 'Testa* and *clibani:* The Baking Covers of Classical Italy', in *Papers of the British School at Rome* 61 (1988), 98-119; J. Frayn, 'Home baking in Roman Italy', *Antiquity* 52 (1978), 57-157.

[3] Pliny, *HN.* 21.174.

[4] Martial 13.57.

[5] Plautus, *Persa* 92-3, 'make the *colyphia* nice and moist for the *collyra*' (a kind of bread roll).

the bone are carved to resemble other animals by the cook.[1] It also occurs at Martial 11.52.13 as a 'joint of meat'. In these instances, the bone is an essential element, but a considerable amount of meat is also necessary. In Vegetius' veterinarian treatise, *coloephium* occurs in remedy 85.1 as a cooked ham which is then boned. Vegetius defines the term *acrocoloefium* anatomically as the 'top ball of the joint above the knee' in a horse or ruminant. In a culinary sense, the most common meaning is a joint of ham and probably from the same part of the carcass, i.e. from the hip rather than the lower leg, and therefore a substantial piece of meat. In *Apicius* the term occurs at 4.4.2 and the recipe is repeated at 5.5.1. The recipes are for a *tisana*, which is a nourishing barley infusion intended as a convalescent soup. The *coleofium* is cooked *propter sucum*, on account of its liquor, i.e. for flavour. The term cannot in this case mean a whole or even small ham as the meat is not needed or served in a *tisana*. In each case the cooked barley is strained out and the smooth mixture is poured back *supra acronem coleofium*, over the top of the ham bone; but compare *acro–* with Vegetius' use of the word. He uses it of the large ball end of the leg bone. The ham bone is left in the *tisana* all the way through the cooking in order to continue flavouring the mixture. This has led previous editors to see a ham *joint* as fundamental to the recipe rather than simply a means of flavouring. Within this recipe a number of phrases stand out in the Latin because they appear to suggest that a much earlier compiler may have been similarly confused by the meaning of *coloefium*. These are the instruction *ut bene tegatur*, 'so it is well covered', and the second reference to *coloefium acronem*, which we believe was added in order to make the recipe fit the picture of a joint of meat (albeit a partly smoked and salted ham) being cooked in a *tisana*. We think the original recipe simply had one *supra acronem coloefium* to indicate that the bone should be transferred from the first pot to the second.

Conchicla There is some confusion about the meaning of this term. Its usual meaning of 'bean with its pod', from *conchis*, is unlikely in *Apicius*, as most of the recipes with this title involve peas. *FR* believed the term referred to the dish the beans or peas were served in, rather than to the food itself. This would have been a shell-shaped serving dish, from *concha*. Originally in

---

[1] Petronius, *Satyricon* 70.2.

Latin, *conchicla* were a 'poor man's bean' according to Juvenal, and Martial describes them as 'pale'.[1] The poets may have had a particular variety of bean in mind, but in Greek the the term is quite clearly associated with the pea. Andrew Dalby has identified the the term *konkhos* with 'pea soup' and we must therefore define the *conchicla* as a predominantly pea-based dish too.[2]

Condimentum/condimenta This term provided us with the most difficulty when interpreting individual recipes. The confusion found in the recipes highlights the possibility that numerous cooks created the recipes in *Apicius* and that they used technical terms without precision or consistency. *Conditura* refers to 'seasonings' that are completed spice mixtures. *Condimentum* just has the meaning of 'seasoning' and occurs alone at 7.4.3; as the recipe is talking about when to add the seasonings to *ofellae*, it should be taken as a general term. It also appears in this general sense at 8.8.4 where a *globus condimentorum*, a 'ball of seasonings' made up of seeds and egg yolk, is used to make a sauce. The term seems specifically to mean 'spice' when it appears at 7.5.2, where we have interpreted *condimenti lauri bacas <scripulos> quinque* as '5 scruples of bay berry spice'.[3] At 8.3.2 a sauce for venison begins 'pepper, *condimentum,* rue, onion', then continues with the liquids. The next recipe repeats the formula, with parsley, oregano and rue before the liquids. It is not clear what is meant: it seems we are to add our choice of spices.

At 6.2.11 in a sauce for fowl we have pepper, caraway, celery seed, parsley, then *condimenta mortaria*, followed by date syrup and the usual liquids. *FR* assumed that the mixture known as *mortaria* found at 1.35 is meant here: in that recipe fresh mint, rue, coriander and fennel are ground with pepper, lovage, honey, liquamen and vinegar. These mixtures are in essence 'something made in a mortar', a simple paste or relish for bread according to the Pseudo-Virgilian poem *Moretum*, but at 1.35 the recipe seems to be a

---

[1] Juvenal 3.293, 14.131; Martial 13.7.

[2] Andrew Dalby, *Food in the Ancient World*, p. 252; Aristophanes, *Knights* 1171; Scribonius Largus, 233.

[3] The use of *condimentum* with bay berries also occurs in the recipe for *lucanicae* at 2.4 and suggests that the spice could be sold pre-ground. See the note on that recipe.

pre-made seasoning not unlike a modern-day spice paste.[1] We do not think the ingredients of these *mortaria* would be so well known that such a phrase need always mean the same paste, or that the cooks are specifically referring to such a specific paste when they use the term *condimenta mortaria*. At 8.1.1 we find *condimentum aprunum*, which suggests that you can buy a mixture already made up and labelled 'wild boar seasonings.' This mixture may have both spices and herbs in it and the ingredients will vary according to the person who mixed it to sell.[2] The recipes that use *condimenta mortaria* (the phrase occurs at 10.2.11 as well) do not contain any fresh herbs: are we being told just to add those?[3] There are plenty of recipes without any green herbs at all and, when they are required, the form of words seems clear: *condimenta uiridia*, 'green seasonings', i.e. herbs.[4] This is the case at 3.4.8, where a list of ingredients, with no indication of method or what the specific dish was, runs as follows: 'hard peaches, truffles, pepper, caraway, cumin, silphium, *condimenta uiridia*, mint, celery, coriander, pennyroyal, dates' and the usual liquids. The term here clearly refers to the list which follows, and not to another ingredient. Our interpretation of *condimenta mortaria* is that the ingredients before the phrase are defined by it, i.e. 'these are the mortar spices'. At 9.4.1 we read *condimenta coctiua* after a list of seeds and liquors. The meaning here is also unclear: either the term refers to unspecified 'cooking herbs', or (as we prefer) to the ingredients that have been listed before it, i.e. 'these are the cooking spices'. It seems that *condimentum* can be a very flexible term, depending on the cook, the recipe and the interpreter.

[1] For *mortaria* used alone, see 1.35 and note ad loc.; on *moretum*, see Ovid, *Fasti* 4.367; Columella 12.59.1-4; C. Grocock, S. Grainger, 'Moretum: a peasant lunch revisited', *The Meal. Proceedings of the Oxford Symposium on Food and Cookery 2001* (Totnes, 2002), pp. 95-103; A. Dalby, *Food in the Ancient World*, ad loc.

[2] A combination of particular spices (mustard, dill seed, fennel seed, coriander seed, black cumin) was found at a dig at No. 1 Poultry in the City of London. The building, identified as a warehouse, was burnt during the Boudicca revolt and contained a number of comestibles. The seeds were in sufficient quantity to suggest a pre-mixed *condimentum*. Small wooden spoons were found among the charred remains: see P. Rowsome, *Heart of the City* (English Heritage/Museum of London Archaeological Service, 2000), p. 22.

[3] Diocletian's Price Edict records, at the end of the fresh vegetables section (5.48, ed. Laufer p. 114), *condimen[torum] praemisquorum*, in bundles (8 for 4 *denarii*). We take these to be bundles of 'assorted herbs'.

[4] *Condimenta uiridia*: 3.4.8 and 6.2.17.

Conditum/Conditura/condimentum These words derive from two separate verbs, *condo* 'to put aside' or 'gather together', and *condio* (1) 'to preserve' as in fruit in vinegar, etc.; and (2) 'to season' or 'to make flavoursome'(so *LS*). The cooks and creators of the recipes often do not distinguish between them and can sometimes use them in an idiosyncratic manner which leads to confusion when translating.

Conditum This works simply as a term for general seasoning or flavour. At *Apicius* 3.10.4 we find *fabe nondum condite,* 'beans not yet seasoned'. In the *Excerpta Vinidarii* 24, a *iuscellum sic conditum* 'a sauce flavoured this way' continues with the usual list of ingredients. *Conditum* means 'a having-been-flavoured thing' and, with *uinum* assumed, we find *conditum paradoxum*, a spiced wine (*Apicius* 1.1). This term generally refers to a wine which has been flavoured in some way with herbs and spices as well as honey. In *Apicius* it is also used in sauces for meat in the same way as *defrutum* or *caroenum*. [1]

Conditura A noun deriving from a future active participle, meaning 'that which will season or flavour', it occurs frequently in place of *ius*, meaning 'sauce' or 'pre-prepared seasonings'. At *Apicius* 3.10.4, beans that have not been seasoned are stirred with leeks into a *conditure in qua eos manducaturus es*, 'the sauce you are going to eat them with'. At 6.8.3 a simple *oenogarum* is listed and then, *condituram super pullum facies*, 'make the sauce (to go) over the chicken'. *Conditura* can also refer to mixtures of spices that have not yet become a sauce: cf. 8.8.8, *leporem esiciatum: eadem conditura condies pulpam,* 'Hare forcemeat: flavour the meat with the same seasonings'.[2]

Copadia/ cupadia/ coppadia A general term for morsel, titbit or dainty delicacy. The word derives from the verb *cupio*, 'to desire'. We even find reference to a *forum cupedinis*, 'a market selling desirable (*scil.* expensive) foods'.[3] It appears to be a non-specific word that could be attached to any number of

---

[1] *Conditum* as spiced wine: *Apicius* 7.6.4; 8.7.13; 8.8.3. A tenth-century gloss to *Querolus* act 2 sc. 1 comments *conditum id est saporem*, 'conditum that is flavour'.

[2] In this case an *oenogarum* is the only possible *conditura* in the previous recipe. An *oenogarum* would not normally be used to flavour meat but to be served with it. The hare *isicia* recipe may have been taken from another section where a recipe with suitable spices would have preceded it.

[3] Varro, *LL.* 5.146.

different foods. In *Apicius* the term seems to have a more precise meaning. In the book called *Polyteles,* 'Luxury dishes', in the meat section (7.6), we find *in elixam et copadia* '(sauces) for boiled (meat) and morsels'. The contrast with *in elixam* suggests meat cooked other than by boiling, but the meat in question has to be different from the *ofellae* (see below) in an earlier section, which are roasted and/or grilled, and also different from the sauces offered for whole joints of roasted meat. The only remaining variety of meat to which *copadia* could refer in *Apicius* is the already-cooked 'leftovers', and in this case small chunks cut from whole roasted joints that were served for the spectacle, but intended to provide food for many evenings.

Cucumeres The sweet salad variety of cucumber was little known in the ancient world. This cucumber is most likely to be the 'chat melon', *Cucumis melo*, an elongated gourd that was probably quite bitter and certainly needed cooking, as in 3.4.1–3. It is quite possible that the true cucumber *Cucumis sativus* arrived in the Mediterranean region during the classical period, but there is no archaeological or literary evidence to confirm it. One recipe in *Apicius*, the *sala cattabia* at 4.1.1, includes uncooked cucumber in a salad which just might be a reference to a modern cucumber. Diocletian's Price Edict records just one type of *cucumis* in two standards, sold at 4 *denarii* for 20.

Cucurbitae In the Roman world, gourds were used both as food and as various kinds of vessel for wine and water. They resembled the marrow of the New World in use and in appearance, but were in fact unrelated. In *Apicius*, an elongated gourd is stuffed and treated just as we stuff marrow today. These gourds were sold at the same price as *cucumeres*, according to Diocletian's Price Edict. See also Pliny, *HN.* 19.69ff., where he describes their cultivation and tells us that 'the longer and thinner gourds are, the more agreeable they are as food'.

Cymae/coliculi Cabbage was a 'common man's food' and as a result less popular with the wealthy. Pliny recounts that Tiberius' son Drusus rejected *cymae* on the advice of Apicius.[1] In its basic form, a headed cabbage was known as *holus*. In *Apicius*, a seasonal and more expensive form of cabbage known

---

[1] Pliny, *HN.* 19.137.

as *coliculi* and *cymae* is referred to. Diocletian's Price Edict reckoned that 5 *coliculi optimi* should cost 4 *denarii*, and 10 of the next quality the same price.[1] *Caulis*, which actually means 'stalk', seems to refer to an open cabbage stalk with some green attached , so the diminutive term *coliculus* should therefore refer to a small tender stalk with its leaf.[2] However, *coliculus*, according to the Edict, was sold as an item, and it is also a solid mass in *Apicius* 3.9.2, as one is cut in half. *Cyma* on the other hand is normally translated as 'cabbage sprout'; however in the Price Edict they are priced as bundles for the same price as 5 *coliculi optimi*. *Cyma* is described by Pliny as a delicate and tender spring cabbage. The term *cima* is still used in Italy for forms of spring greens associated with cabbage and broccoli. It has been translated as 'sprouts' in the Loeb translation of Pliny, but is not to be associated with Brussels sprouts, which are a medieval development.[3] Pliny goes on to say that this kind of cabbage is a 'cut and come again' variety that sends out many young tender stalks. If a cabbage head is required, then the seedling is planted in the spring and produces a loosely gathered head, which is what we think *coliculus* refers to. The evidence for the various kinds of cabbage is rather contradictory and any precise identification of either *cymae* or *coliculi* with a modern variety is difficult. We have translated *cyma* as 'spring greens' and *coliculus* as 'cabbage'.

Cyperus A herbaceous sweet sedge, native to India as well as the Mediterranean region, with edible rhizomes and root. It could be either *Acorus calamus* or *C. esculentus* – the little rhizomes of which are known as *amande de terre* in French. The terms may refer to the imported Indian spice, rather than to the native, which was used in perfume and medicine. Galingale, papyrus and turmeric are all from the same genus.[4] This spice is included in the list of foods at the beginning of the *Excerpta Vinidarii* and is also used to flavour Liburnian oil in *Apicius* 1.4.

---

[1] Diocletian's Price Edict 6.9,10 (ed. Laufer, p.111).

[2] The diminutive form of a word does not necessarily imply smaller size. In everyday Latin diminutives were often used as the standard term: cf. *cepulla* for *cepa*.

[3] Pliny, *HN*. 19.137f.

[4] See Pliny, *HN*. 21.117-18; M. Grieve (ed. C. F. Leyel), *A Modern Herbal* (London, 1973), p. 726; Miller, *Spice Trade of the Roman Empire*, p. 78.

Defrutum/sapa *Defrutum* is the most common form of cooked syrup in *Apicius*. It seems that ancient writers attempted to define these syrups by referring to the amount of reduction which is involved in each, as do modern writers. Then, as now, they could not agree as to the precise amount of 'boiling off' that was required. We believe that these problems would be greatly reduced if the issue of the amount of reduction was put to one side and other issues considered. A statement in Columella may resolve the situation: if we translate *sapa*, found in the passage which follows, as the general term for an unflavoured boiled syrup of whatever reduction, it not only eliminates the term from the debate altogether, but more importantly explains why it does not appear in the *Apicius* recipes as a cooking ingredient but does appear amongst the preserving recipes in Book 1:

Quidam partem quartam eius musti, quod in uasa plumbea coniecerunt, nonnulli tertiam decoquunt. Nec dubium, quin ad dimidium si quis excoxerit, meliorem sapam facturus sit, eoque usibus utiliorem, adeo quidem, ut etiam vice defruti sapae, mustum, quod est ex ueteribus uineis, condire possit.

(Some boil off a quarter volume of the must, which they have put in lead vessels, others boil off a third. There is no doubt that if anyone cooks it down to half its volume he will make a better syrup and on that account a more useful one in practice to the point where it can preserve the must from old vineyards, in place of *defrutum* syrup.)[1]

If one considers that the different batches of grape juice employed for this purpose could have had a considerable variation in sugar content, it is not surprising that the *consistency* was more important than how much is boiled off. A very sweet must will be very thick very quickly, while a sour juice will never get thick at all. At 12.21, Columella says that 'must of the sweetest possible flavour will be boiled down to a third and when boiled down as I said above is called *defrutum*'. The definition is not related to the level of reduction but to its 'boiled down' nature. Columella suggests that the thicker

---

[1] Columella 12.19ff. *Defruti sapae* seems to confirm that *defrutum* is a form of *sapa*. *Sapa* appears once in *Apicius* at 1.22 where it is a 'syrup used to preserve blackberries'.

and richer the *defrutum* is, the better it is (20.3), implying that the name is the same whether a half, third or a quarter is left. The people referred to as 'some' at the beginning of the quotation above were trying to save money by cutting back on the amount of reduction they allowed for their syrup-making, which Columella suggests did not save money in the long run as it was less effective. In wine-making, *defrutum* was used as a seasoning (*conditura*) or preservative. Columella tells us that *defrutum* should always be boiled with either quinces or some other form of flavouring, and it is this flavouring along with the thickness that should define *defrutum*. Further spices were also added to a *defrutum* before it was used to preserve wine.[1]

In *Apicius* 2.2.8 a *defrutum* flavoured with quinces that has been exposed to the sun until the consistency of honey is achieved is added to a sauce for forcemeat. In the same recipe an alternative *defrutum*, said to be known as *color*, 'colouring', by the Romans, is made from dried figs that were apparently cooked in must. *Defrutum* was therefore a specific form of syrup identified by its thickness, richness and fruit flavourings, in contrast to *sapa*, which was just syrup with no additives.[2] Using this manner of definition the level of reduction was less important than the consistency and flavourings.[3] *Defrutum* is used in *Apicius* to add depth and richness and colour to sauces throughout the book. It is used as a flavouring, not as a bulk liquid as is the case with *caroenum*. Modern substitutes require some effort: cartons of grape juice have none of the freshness of must, but will suffice with a few quinces or figs added for flavour and reduced to a third. Do this in the winter when wasps are not about and in sufficient quantity for a year at least.

Folium (see also ***malabathrum***) *Folium*, which simply means 'leaf' in Latin, occurs frequently in *Apicius* and in other ancient culinary writings in a way

---

[1] Sweet rush, iris, fenugreek: see Columella 12.20.2.

[2] In Italy today, wine syrups known as *saba* are still used. These syrups are the origin of balsamic vinegar, which was developed when the liquors were allowed to re-ferment in their oak barrels.

[3] However, Pliny *HN.* 14.80 and Palladius 11.18 stress the level of reduction as the key issue in defining *defrutum*. It clearly was important, but only in combination with the other factors such as thickness and flavourings. Columella may have had more first-hand experience of farming than a theoretical knowledge, and also gives the clearest information. Pliny loc.cit. gives the Greek terms *siraeum* and *hepsema* as well as the Latin *sapa*. They all appear to be types of syrup.

which clearly indicates that ancient cooks were using the word to refer to a specific leaf rather than a general one. However, what that leaf was is obscure. It is unlikely to be another term for 'bay leaf,' as this appears quite unambiguously throughout the text as *folium lauri*. Andrew Dalby believes that the term is another word for *malabathrum*,[1] but this does not always accord with its use in *Apicius*. At 9.1.3 we are told to add '*folium* and *malabathrum* if you like': the *et* is the reading of both MSS. At 1.29 we have 'pepper, lovage, parsley, dried mint, *folium(,) malabathrum,* plenty of cumin etc.' The same formula is found in recipe 30. We might have expected a genitive here (even in *Apicius*: cf. *folium lauri* noted above) if the leaf is to be linked grammatically with the *malabathrum*. Pliny recounts that *malabathrum* was used to flavour wine, and the first recipe in *Apicius* is for a spiced wine flavoured with *folium*, which indicates some kind of similarity between the two. The term *malabathrum* does not appear in the *Excerpta Vinidarii* at all, but *folium* does.[2]

Garum/liquamen/muria   See Appendix 4, which contains a detailed excursus on these fish sauces.

Hydrogarum   This sauce is rather more complex than its name implies. In *Apicius* Book 2, many kinds of *isicia* are cooked in *hydrogarum*, a water-based cooking liquor and also a sauce for serving with meat dishes. At 2.2.2, pepper, lovage, pyrethrum, *liquamen* and water are heated and the *isicia* are heated up in this. At 2.2.5, seven parts of water to one of *liquamen*, celery leaf and pepper form the cooking liquor for *isicia*. These sauces can be served with the *isicia* and are also served separately as a digestive that can be drunk.

Isicia   This term can be interpreted in many ways, depending on the context. In Diocletian's Price Edict, *isicia* simply refers to minced or chopped meat, either of beef or pork.[3] Thus defined, it is raw and formless. When *isicia*

---

[1] A. Dalby, *Food In the Ancient World*, p. 206.

[2] In the *Alphita*, a fourteenth-century medieval glossary of Latin herbs and spices, we are told that 'When folium is found on its own it means the leaf of clove.' Sadly, such certainty is not found in the ancient sources. Clove leaf is very aromatic, but is unattested in ancient trade and plays no part in modern commerce in the spice.

[3] Diocletian's Price Edict 4.14 (ed. Laufer p.104).

occurs in *Apicius* it never means simply 'minced meat', but has the meaning of 'flavoured forcemeat' which seems in addition to have a specific shape which we assume is round: therefore 'meat ball' is the basic concept indicated by the term. These could just as easily be flat and the concept becomes a burger. These forcemeat shapes can be wrapped in caul fat (*omentum*) from which they are named (2.1.4, 6,7). We translate these as 'faggots', which have also traditionally been wrapped in caul. *Isicia* can also refer to formless forcemeat which may or may not subsequently be given a specific shape; for example it may be used as stuffing. In the recipes for *minutal*, which we define as a stew made of various components but invariably flavoured with *isicia* and other kinds of chopped meat, we find the words *isicia minuta* (4.3.4), *isiciola minuta* (4.3.5), *isiciola ualde minuta* (4.3.2). The question is, are these small (and very small!) meatballs, following the model from Book 2; or are they made into meatballs of a normal size, cooked and then chopped small; or (as we think) is the forcemeat very finely reduced or ground into a paste, not unlike a smooth pâté, which flavours and to some extent thickens the sauce? If the forcemeat is uncooked when it used, as appears to be the case, then the latter theory seems the most likely. The name *minutal* seems to corroborate this, and suggests that the dish should be regarded as a minced- or chopped-meat stew. However, when we find *isicia* in Book 8 they seem to have a particular shape. Recipe 8.7.14 for a stuffed and roasted piglet has among the ingredients for the stuffing *pullus isiciatus particulatim concisus,* 'chicken forcemeat cut into pieces', which suggests either that chicken forcemeat balls have already been formed and cooked, or (as seems more likely) that *particulatim concisus* stresses the finely chopped and loose texture which is required. The term is not found in early Greek texts, though it does appear in Athenaeus: the origin and meaning of the word is discussed and Paxamus is given as the source.[1] The Athenaeus text suggests that *isicia* were popular in the early second century AD as they were used in a dish served to the *Deipnosophists*. However, the speaker is the cook and he specifically makes mention of the term being non-Attic and one he should shun, i.e. a commonplace Greek term. The only interpretation is that *isicia*, meaning minced meat, is (as with so much of Roman food) a Greek concept before it was Roman.

[1] Athenaeus 376d.

Laganum Current thinking is that *laganum* is the first instance of lasagne pasta in food history.[1] However our earliest reference to this term suggests that it originally meant a 'layer' or 'sheet' which could be made of various different ingredients including honey, dried fruits and nuts as well as flour, oil, etc.[2] *Lagana* is a regional word for 'pasta' in Italy today, but it did not necessarily indicate a boiled pasta in Roman times: Horace ate *lagana* with leeks and chickpeas as a light lunch in *Sat.* 1.6.115, but there is no evidence that these *lagana* were boiled. In Leviticus 2.4 and 7.12, the unleavened bread offered with oil at the temple was translated as *lagana* by Jerome, and it is likely that Horace's *lagana* were a similar kind of bread. Pliny also refers to *artolagani* in his section on different types of bread.[3] Chupatti and paratha spring to mind as familiar equivalents. Oribasius talks of *lagana* in terms of *itria*: 'there are two types of *itria*; the better kind is called *rhyemata* (flowed-out) and the inferior *lagana*.'[4] At 9.1 he quotes from Athenaeus that *lagana* are thin and insipid, being light and easily digested.

The sheet of dough, either made simply from flour and water or, according to Athenaeus, with the addition of wine, pepper, milk and oil, could be fried as a pancake or baked quite dry as bread.[5] The products *lagana*, *tracta* (q.v.) and the Greek *itria* seem to be very similar in form.[6] A recent article by Susan Weingarten on the evidence from Jewish sources for these products has pointed out that they can be seen as identical in certain circumstances.[7] The distinction between *tracta* and *lagana* seems to be related to the way in which they are

---

[1] Bober, *Art, Culture and Cuisine,* p. 156.

[2] See Athenaeus 648a for the sweetmeat known as *gastris*, which was made with *lagana*: layers of boiled honey and sesame seed which we might term *rhyemata* = 'flowed-out', referred to as 'superior' by Oribasius. See below, n. 4.

[3] Pliny, *HN.* 18.105.

[4] Oribasius *CM* 1.7.3. *Itria* are not mentioned in *Apicius* and so their definition is not considered here, though we think 'biscuit' is a good interpretation. See Athenaeus 646d, where they are made with honey and sesame.

[5] Athenaeus 113d. For more information on pasta, see C. Perry, 'The Oldest Mediterranean Noodle: a Cautionary Tale', *Petits Propos Culinaires* 9 (1981) pp. 42-5, and Dalby, *Food in the Ancient World*, art. 'Pasta'.

[6] *lagana* can function like *tracta* and when crumbled be used to thicken sauces: cf. Athenaeus 663e.

[7] Susan Weingarten, 'The debate about ancient *tracta:* evidence from the Talmud', *Food and History,* Institut Européen d'Histoire de l'Alimentation, Vol. 2 No. 1 (2004), 21-39.

cooked: *tracta* were formed from a dough of wheat products and water and then dried naturally in the sun or at a distance from the fire. They were not cooked until crumbled into sauces as a thickener or enveloped in a cake and baked. *Lagana* on the other hand were formed from a wheat dough that was properly baked, or fried, and may be therefore defined as bread or possibly pancake.

The variety of shapes for *lagana* was pretty much endless. However, if they were to be used as a kind of bread scoop, as Grant suggests, then a rounded shape is the likeliest possibility and would have been the easiest to manufacture. In *Apicius* these *lagana* are used to separate meat in sauce in a dish known as a *patina Apiciana* at 4.2.14. This dish has been interpreted as a lasagne in the past, but we now visualize it more as a tower of folded or flat tacos or chupattis. The dish may have been served in wedges, but we suspect that each layer was a separate portion and the reed provided the means of service. The *patina Apiciana* cannot be returned to the oven, as the finished dish is turned out on to a platter and decorated with the reed ready to be served. It is finished at this point, and this must mean that the *lagana* were cooked before they were used. Given that boiled sheets of pastry are simply not attested in the ancient recipes at this point, we must reject the proto-pasta identification for *lagana* in *Apicius* and interpret them as cooked flat, unleavened bread.

Laser See under asafoetida and *silphium*.

Malabathrum This dried aromatic leaf was highly prized in Rome. Current thinking is that it was the leaf of cinnamon or, to be more precise, of *Cinnamomum tamala* which is in fact cassia, the so-called 'inferior cinnamon'.[1] This is known today as *tejpat* in the region of the Himalayas where it grows; the ancient name is apparently derived from the Sanskrit *tamālapattra*, which means 'dark leaf'.

Pliny does not equate cassia with *malabathrum,* and gives no clues to an identification. He tells us that oil was extracted from the leaf, which was

[1] Cassia is native to China and is grown now in India, where the leaf is known as the 'Indian bay leaf' and is used in a similar way. Cassia makes up the majority of 'cinnamon' imported into the UK. See Dalby, *Food in the Ancient World*, p. 206.

used in cosmetics, that it should taste like nard, and that the scent of the leaf in warmed wine surpassed all others. He also says that the leaf was used as a breath freshener as well as to perfume clothes. *Malabathrum* appears three times in the recipes, two for fish and one for a sauce without designation. There is no hint as to what form it took.[1] Whether the leaf was crushed and used as a spice or the medicinal oil was used in food is not clear. As we cannot be sure of its identification, substitutes are difficult. Bay leaf or cinnamon (or even both) could be used depending on your taste, though neither is really adequate. There are a further 12 occasions where the term *folium* is used in recipes, and current thinking also identifies this with *malabathrum* (see under *folium*).

Mortarium   The mortar of the Roman kitchen is a very versatile piece of equipment, so ubiquitous on Roman sites throughout the empire that one cannot picture a scene of food preparation in the Roman world without one. They vary in size and profile, but the basic structure is always the same: a round, shallow bowl with a wide overhanging rim. The base is relatively small with gentle sloping sides. A pouring spout is formed in the rim, and the whole body has a very rough surface; this is achieved with coarse sand in the clay as well as larger grits embedded in the upper surface of the bowl to facilitate grinding. The *mortarium* functioned as an all-purpose mixing bowl for grinding spices, making sauces, pounding meat and making bread and cakes. It was even used as a makeshift lid for pots and pans.

Mulsum   This is simply a mixture of wine and honey that is served as a drink. When wine, honey and spices such as pepper are mixed together, the drink is then called *conditum*, i.e. spiced wine. *Mulsum* is not 'mead' as the honey is mixed at or just before drinking and not at the time of pressing or fermentation. *Mulsum* was served at the beginning of the meal as a kind of aperitif. We find in Book 1.2 a recipe for *conditum melizomum uiatorum*, 'travellers' spiced honey wine', which is made as a cordial which you dilute as required rather than mixed in advance.[2]

---

[1] *Malabathrum* 1.15; 1.16; 9.1.3 repeated at 9.7.1 Pliny, *HN.* 12.53, 129; 12.93.
[2] *Melizomum* is a Greek term for honey sauce, used here for a drink.

Nardostachyum (spikenard, Indian nard) This is an aromatic plant native to the Himalayas which was highly valued as a perfume as well as a medicine in ancient times. The ancient variety is now known as *Nardostachys jatamansi*, a member of the valerian family noted for its sedative effects on the body. It is used a great deal in incense sticks today. The root, leaf and spike (root bud) as well as an oil extracted from one or other of these were all used commercially, and distinguishing them in relation to the spices used in *Apicius* is not easy. The oil and an ointment made from it are likely to have been normally used for perfume or medicine, which leaves the dried 'spike' as the culinary spice along with the leaf. This plant occurs in the text in two forms: we find *spicam Indicam* at 1.16.2, 6.5.4, and 9.8.2, and *nardostachyum* at 7.6.8 and 8.2.7. It is of interest that *costus* (another spice now only used as a perfume), *malabathrum* and *folium* are also in these recipes too. This combination of spices seems to indicate a late date for these recipes: Anthimus in *c.* AD 510 advocated using *spikenard* with *costus* and clove – which is virtually a medieval spice-mix – in his first recipe.

Nuces/nuts The identification of the various nuts in *Apicius* is tricky; the dilemma revolves around whether the cooks had specific nuts in mind when they used the term *nuces* or whether they used the term generally. It is not clear whether Latin had a general term for nuts and if one assumes that, like French, Latin did not, then the interpretation of Latin *nuces* becomes crucial. Pliny discusses nuts in some detail, and appears to use *nuces* as a general term for nuts. He contrasts *nuces* with the lesser acorn class of fruits.[1] The *Etymologiae* of Isidore of Seville is given little credit because of the many false derivations found there, but does give a very precise description of the whole family of nuts which may be of use as it distinguishes between *iuglandes* (walnuts) and *nuces* (nuts generally):[2]

Nux *is so called because the shade or dew from its leaves harm neighbouring trees. Latins call it by another name, the* iuglandes *(walnut), as if the 'glands of Jove'…However all fruits covered in a fairly hard shell are called* nuces *as pine nuts, hazelnuts, acorns, chestnuts, almonds.*

---

[1] Pliny, *HN.* 15.92
[2] Isidore of Seville, *Etymologiae* 17.7.21-2.

It appears that the singular form *nux* refers to the walnut tree and its fruit. The walnut is also called the *iuglandes*. The term *nuces* is the nominative plural of *nux* and therefore can mean walnuts. However, *nuces* can also refer to the whole idea of nuts, whatever their name. The recipes use the single term *nuces* more than any other, and we must decide between 'nuts', 'hazelnuts' or 'walnuts'. The last is the interpretation we have received from Andrew Dalby, but we think that individual cooks have used these terms independently and without precision, and that it is no longer possible to be sure which nuts they mean. It is quite possible that the cooks actually intended that the term be ambiguous and dependant on what was available. In *Apicius*, almonds (*amygdala*) and pine nuts (*nucleos pineos* or just *pineos*) are clearly identifiable, but when it comes to hazelnuts and walnuts we are on less sure ground. There is a wild hazelnut in Italy, but the Asian cultivated variety was more desirable and specifically named. We may also assume that hazelnuts were the most common and readily available nut in Italy. In *Apicius* we find *pontica* and also *abellana*, which we think may be used to mean these imported hazelnuts. Pliny confirms the use of both names, and we might equate these varieties with the filbert and cob nut, which are in fact varieties of hazelnut.[1] He also recognizes the 'smooth nut' (*calva*), which seems to be another form of hazelnut. We find *calva* in *Apicius* at 6.2.19 and 9.10.7, and translate it as 'smooth nut.' Walnuts were popular, according to Pliny, and were thrown at weddings because they made a satisfying noise.[2] The walnut has a distinctively strong flavour which can dominate in cooking and (in the view of SG), is less likely to be the typical 'nut' found in the recipes. When *nuces* appear they seem to act largely as a thickening agent in Roman sauces. Walnuts defined as *nuces iuglandes* or just *iuglandes* are not mentioned in *Apicius*, though acorns (*glandes*) are found at 8.8.3, where a stuffing for hare has *nucleos integros, amygdala, nuces siue glandes concisas*, which we translate as 'whole pine nuts, chopped almonds, hazelnuts or acorns'. Acorns were a traditional rustic food for the poor, and we might consider them out of place here and take the word to be *iuglandes* and therefore walnuts.[3] In such a case the *nuces* must mean hazelnuts. At 6.2.16, in a white sauce for birds,

---

[1] Pliny, *HN*. 15.88f.

[2] Pliny, *HN*. 15.86.

[3] See S. Mason, 'Acornutopia? Determining the Role of Acorns in Past Human Subsistence', in *Food in Antiquity*, pp. 12-24.

we find *ponticam uel amygdala tostam uel nuces depilatas*, which we have rendered as 'roasted hazelnuts or almonds or (any) skinned nut'. It would be unlikely that a walnut would be intended here for numerous reasons: the sauce is white and would be discoloured by walnuts; it would be virtually impossible to skin them; and the term cannot mean shelled: that would surely be taken for granted. As a rule we have translated *nuces* as 'nuts' rather than refer to any specific variety, and suggest that the cook experiments. [1]

Ofellae *Ofella* is the diminutive of *offa,* a 'bit' or 'morsel' of food, and more specifically a pellet of flour and water, possibly used as food for weaning a baby.[2] In a more specific sense, *ofellae* can mean 'lumps of meat', generally small enough to be eaten with the fingers. We also find *offula,* which has the similar meaning of a 'bit' or 'piece', though less often specifically referring to meat. We might define it more as 'little snack'.[3] Cato *De agricultura* 162 mentions *ofellae Puteolanae,* which seem to be large pieces of pork salted in barrels. A further indication that *ofellae* may be preserved in some way is found in *Excerpta Vinidarii* 4, where the meat is brought to the boil in water, which is then discarded.[4] Such a process indicates that the salt used to preserve the meat is reduced. In *Apicius, ofellae* are more elaborate and appetizing. They are made of pork rib or belly that has been boned but left in one piece, scored through the meat but left on the skin, marinated for 3 days, roasted and then pulled off the fat and skin. They are then mouth-sized portions that a reclining diner could easily reach and consume with as little mess as possible, and they are intensely flavoured. In the recipe at 7.4.1, the meat is tied up in what seems to be a square that allows the meat side to be exposed to the heat while the fat is enclosed, keeping the whole joint moist. Martial's Saturnalia gifts once again provide a detailed parallel that brings the recipes to life:[5]

A gridiron with skewers
Let the wide-spaced gridiron sweat with the curving ofellae for you, let the foaming boar smoke on the long blades.

---

[1] The popularity of walnuts in later medieval cookery must be acknowledged.
[2] Pliny, *HN.* 18.84.   [3] Cf. Suetonius, *Claudius* 40.1.
[4] Just as a bacon or ham joint is treated today. See the Introduction, p. 92, for a discussion on the term *exbromare.*   [5] Martial 14. 221.

Oenogarum A compound sauce made with a base mixture of wine and *liquamen* with simple or more complex seasonings and wine flavourings. There are 14 separate occasions where a sauce identified as an *oenogarum* is defined precisely. At 4.5.1 a vegetable and meat *patina* recipe has the instruction 'make an *oenogarum* for it like this', and pepper is then pounded with lovage, wine, *passum* or sweet wine, and oil, and it is heated and thickened with *amylum*. At 4.2.31 a sauce of pepper, *liquamen*, wine, and oil is again defined as an *oenogarum*.[1] The ingredients of the sauces vary quite a lot but the basic formula is quite clear: *liquamen* and a variety of wines and syrups are found in every identified *oenogarum,* together with pepper; coriander, rue and lovage also regularly appear. Over half of the recipes include oil, and a similar number are thickened with *amylum*.

    Oenogarum is served with *isicia,* vegetables, fish, seafood, complex dishes such as *patinae* and all manner of meat cuts. It appears to have been the standard sauce of choice for ancient cooks – the gravy of Roman cuisine. The evidence for this sauce is so secure within the text of *Apicius* that when apparent contradictions are seen they may well reveal a hand other than the recipe's creator at work. At 4.2.5 a recipe for a simple asparagus *patina* contains the instruction to pound pepper with *liquamen*, adding wine, *passum* and oil, then to heat it and to 'grease a dish, in it mix 6 eggs with the *oenogarum*'; the *patina* dish is then put in the hot ashes. At this point we are told to 'put in the sauce written above'; this has obviously gone in already, with the eggs; the ingredients listed are those of a standard *oenogarum*. The fact that the superfluous line comes after the instruction to put the dish in the hot ashes is also an indication that someone has misunderstood the preceding instructions.[2] Perhaps a scribe or compiler, who does not realize that the *oenogarum* is the 'the sauce written above', has attempted to correct what he saw as a confusing or incomplete recipe. It is likely that the phrase 'put in the sauce written above' has been lifted directly from recipe 9 in this section, where, in context, it makes perfect sense. Sauces similar to *oenogarum*, but with different seasonings, are found described in the satires of Horace:[3]

---

[1] *Oenogarum* is also defined specifically at 4.5.3, 7.12.2, 8.8.7, 10.3.11, 12.

[2] It would be sensible to put the dish in the ashes first to warm it up before adding the mixture as occurs in recipe 9 above so that the contrast in temperature did not break the vessel.

[3] Horace, *Sat.* 2.4.63-9.

It is worth the effort to get to know thoroughly the nature of the double sauce. Simple sauce is made from pure olive oil which is worthy of being blended with fragrant pure wine and muria, *provided the latter comes with a powerful whiff from a Byzantine jar. When this is blended with chopped herbs and has come to the boil and has stood (it is) sprinkled with saffron from Parnassus. You will add the oil which the prized berry of the Venafran olive produces.*

The 'double sauce' here may be the same as the 'simple' but with the addition of *amylum* to thicken it. In *Apicius* at 3.4.5 an *oenogarum simplex* is served with marrow. The term occurs on three other occasions.[1] Another sauce mentioned in Horace *Sat.* 2.8 contains similar ingredients but very different spices from those in *Apicius*: Venafran oil, Spanish *garum*, foreign wine five years old, white pepper, vinegar from Methymnian grapes, rocket, bitter elecampane. These elevated sauces, described in satire, may have little to do with real culinary practice as it occurred in a Roman kitchen. There may be all kinds of subtle humour in the choice of ingredients that are beyond our understanding. However, the choice of ingredients nonetheless reflects another level of culinary perfection way above the ordinary sauces of *Apicius*. See also Appendix 4.

Oxygarum *Oxygarum* is another compound sauce, similar to *oenogarum*. It contains fish sauce and vinegar instead of (or as well as) wine, but with similar seasonings. We find reference to it in Horace, *Sat.* 2.8 (cited above), where vinegar from Methymnian grapes is used to make an exclusive sauce for a gourmet. At 1.34 a compound spice mix is added to *liquamen*, vinegar and honey to make a medicinal *oxygarum* for the digestion.

Passum This was a raisin wine made with grapes that had been allowed to dry in the sun on a raised platform, making them very sweet. The resulting raisins were then mixed with must and allowed to become soft again. They were then pressed, and the 'first' *passum* was fermented and stored. The remaining skins were then trodden with more must pressed from grapes that had dried for a shorter time, to make a 'second pressing' *passum*. Cheaper varieties

[1] Also 3.20.1, 4.2.20, 4.2.26.

could be made using water for the second quality. There are many different modern varieties of raisin wine; each region of the Mediterranean has its own special blend. A '*vin doux*' or muscat wine is a suitable equivalent. See also *caroenum*.

Patina In its simplest manifestation this term refers to a round shallow vessel made of terracotta used to cook and serve food. On occasion *patinae* were also made from bronze or other metals. When the term is used in *Apicius* to mean the vessel rather than the finished dish known as *patina*, we translate it as 'dish'. They vary in diameter and can be flat with low straight sides, or slope deeply inwards towards a small base, making them unstable on a flat surface. This latter shape is a common late Hellenistic form, and was used in a cooking technique involving hot embers: see Introduction, p. 79, for a discussion. We hear of a giant *patina* ordered to be made by Vitellius at a cost of 100,000 *sestertii*; according to Suetonius, this *patina* was called the 'Shield of Minerva,' and contained 'liver of pike; brains of pheasants and peacock; tongues of flamingos and the "blood" of lamprey'.[1] A mixture such as this seems entirely unappealing to us and we suspect it was equally so to the guests who had to eat it. The term *patina* and its diminutive *patella,* which was almost certainly the same kind of vessel and dish, eventually mutated into 'paella'.

   A *patina* was also a particular kind of food cooked in the dish. The vast majority of these *patinae* are cooked and set with eggs; there are a number of recipes where eggs are not used but the finished dish still has the name *patina*.[2] The cooked dish *patina* was a mixture of various kinds of fish, meat or vegetables (or combinations of all three) bound with egg or with a sauce and allowed to set or cook over a charcoal fire. Sometimes the dish was not stirred when egg was used, and the finished *patina* resembled a savoury custard. On other occasions it is clear that the *patina* had to be stirred and that the finished dish was not unlike scrambled egg. The ratio of egg to liquid is quite high, and this results in a firm mixture that can easily be eaten with the hands as long as it is not overcooked. For the specific cooking method employed, and illustrations, see the Introduction, p. 78, and also *thermospodium/cinerem calidem* below.

[1] Pliny, *HN.* 35. 165; Suetonius, *Vitellius* 13.
[2] 4.2.11, 19, 21, 22, 23, 24, 25, 29, 30, 32, 34, 37; 12 out of 37 *patinae* do not use, or omit, egg.

In the *Excerpta Vinidarii* a cooked dish of a very similar type – eggs and vegetables and meat all set together in a *patina* dish – is called a *caccabina*. This term seems to be related to the word *caccabus*, which is normally interpreted as a 'general cooking pot'. This change in terminology hints at some development in Roman food between the time and style of the *Apicius* recipes and those available to be collected at the time of Vinidarius.[1] There are a great many different kinds of *patina* in *Apicius*: some appear so simple, in fact no more than a Spanish omelette in form, that without the more expensive spices one might imagine all types of Romans eating them, while some are very complex, with numerous ingredients and an elaborate layered structure. We do not very often hear of *patinae* being specifically included in high-status menus. The vast majority of recorded menus include food items such as roast boar or a particular fish, but named compound dishes such as these are lacking. A menu recorded in Macrobius lists amongst many things oyster *patina*, fish *patina* and sow's udder *patina*.[2] The date for this feast is *c.* 50 BC, suggesting that these dishes were early components of Roman cuisine and almost certainly part of the Greek influence on Roman food: the terms *patina/patella* stem from the rare Greek *patanē/batanē*, meaning 'general dish' or 'vessel'.[3] The recipe at 4.2.17 is a Greek dish known as a *patella thirotarricam*, 'cheese and salt fish *patella*'.[4] It is exactly the same kind of dish as the other *patinae/patellae*, i.e. fish and cheese in a sauce that is set with egg, a fairly common ordinary meal according to Cicero.[5]

Picentine bread This particular bread is found in the text just once, at 4.1.2, where it is used to line a mould for salad ingredients. The detailed method for this bread is found in Pliny at *HN.* 18.106, where he tells us that *alica* is soaked (probably in fresh grape juice which would act as a very effective leaven) for nine days and then formed into dough with more flour in the manner of *tracta*, i.e. using just enough flour to absorb the moisture. The *alica* (see above) was a fine wheat groat, very similar to semolina, which

---

[1] See Introduction, pp. 32ff., for a discussion on the dating of the *Excerpta Vinidarii*.
[2] Macrobius 3.13.12. The feast was in honour of the inauguration of Lentulus as the priest of Mars; Caesar, as *rex sacrorum,* was among the guests.
[3] Athenaeus 169e-f; *patanē* became *patina*, deriving from the same root as 'pan' in English.
[4] From *tyro,* 'cheese', and *tarichos,* 'salt fish'.
[5] Cicero, *Ad fam.* 9.16.9.

had lost its bran and husk and, according to Pliny, had been whitened even more with chalk. The resulting dough would have risen easily without the limitations of a whole-wheat dough, producing a light, aerated bread. It was then baked in individual pots, apparently until they broke. The nature of the finished bread seems to have been dry but, as both Pliny and Martial indicate,[1] it was always soaked in honey-water:

Bread from Picenum
Ceres from Picenum grows thus with a snow-white nectar, just as a light dough swells out when water is added.

Porrum Pliny identifies two types of leek and we see both in *Apicius, porrum sectiuum* and *porrum capitatum*.[2] The Greek term *prason* is not found in *Apicius*. *Porrum capitatum* is now recognized as a particular Middle-Eastern variety known as *A. kurrat*. It is a leek that produces both the compact layers of leaf as well as a distinct bulb or head if allowed to. Pliny appears to suggest at one point that *capitatum* and *sectiuum* were in fact the same plant, the latter being a young version of the former. In the *sectiuum* bed 'it is cut until it gives out, and it is always manured if it is grown for its head, before being cut'. This cut variety of leek may be equated with chive.[3] When it had grown fully it was transferred to a new bed with the tops of the leaves lightly cut back from the heart and with the outer layers of the bulb peeled off. Modern leeks are not cut like this, but if they were sown thickly and cut regularly they would no doubt continue to force leaves. Pliny suggests that after they were transferred and cut back, the bulb was forced to enlarge with tiles or stones placed on the top.[4] The Greek '*getion* leek', sometimes translated as 'horn onion' and equated with spring onions and the *palachanan* onion, has something in common with these dual forms of leeks. As young plants they are considered as bulbless onions that are grown to cut and come again, but if left to mature they can have heads or bulbs as big as turnips according to

[1] Pliny, *HN.* 18.106, Martial 13.47.
[2] Pliny, *HN.* 19.108 ff.
[3] See *cepa* above. The German for this cut leek is *schnittlauch*, which is also the modern term for chive.
[4] It should be noted that when the ancients talk of 'heads' in relation to onions or leeks they always mean the bulb and not the green tops.

Polemon the Geographer.[1] We have translated all references to both *capitatum* and *sectiuum* as 'leek'. It is very difficult if not impossible to get the *A. kurrat* leek that produces both head and leaf in Britain. We are unable to identify these *allium* varieties with any precision and, in fact, cannot with certainty distinguish between onions and leeks in some circumstances. Martial gives a tantalizing glimpse into the issue:[2]

Porri Sectiui
Whenever you have eaten heavily-flavoured strips of leek from Tarentum,
kiss with your mouth shut!

Porri Capitati
Wooded Aricia sends superb leeks: look at the green tops on the snow
white stems.

Seafood A number of types of cephalophods and crustacea are listed in *Apicius*. While identification is difficult, we have translated the different types as follows:[3]

  cammarus – fresh water crayfish, not unlike a large prawn;
  marina de cammaris (2.1.1) – also prawns;
  squilla – prawn/shrimp;
  astacus – lobster;
  lolligo – squid;
  sepia – cuttlefish;
  locusta – a salt-water crawfish, also known as a spiny lobster, *langouste*
  or scampi.

Silphium Also known as *laserpicium, laser, sirpe*. See *asafoetida*. The miraculous spice of legend, uniquely grown in Cyrenaica in northern Libya, it was said to have great healing powers, to be an aphrodisiac and digestive. According to Pliny, it was never properly cultivated and eventually died out through over-cropping. He also tells us that, within his memory, the last stalk was

---

[1] Athenaeus 732b.
[2] Martial 13.18,19.
[3] Cf. Dalby, *Food In The Ancient World*, articles 'Crayfish', 'Cuttlefish', 'Lobster', 'Shrimp', 'Squid'; see also A. Davidson, *Mediterranean Seafood* (London, 1981).

delivered to Nero, suggesting a date of AD 41–68 for its extinction.[1] In the time
of Alexander (*c.* 328/7 BC), the asafoetida that eventually replaced *silphium*
in the kitchen had been identified in Afghanistan and used as a tenderizer for
meat by his soldiers.[2] Given this early date for the recognition of asafoetida as
a substitute, it is not impossible that both varieties of the spice were available
in Rome together for some time before *silphium* proper died out.

Tracta This raw pastry product has also been likened to pasta in recent times
but it is a different concept from pasta, despite having some similarities.[3] In
Apicius, discs (*orbiculi*) of *tracta* are crumbled into various kinds of stew
that are known as *minutalia*.[4] In its fine, crumbled state we can confirm that
tracta thickens stews very effectively, and produces a more robust and stable
emulsion than the other thickener employed in Roman food, *amylum* or wheat
starch. In the recipe for *placenta* in Cato *De Agricultura* 76 we are told how
to make *tracta*: 2 lb. of *alica* (that is, a fine semolina made from a durum
wheat used today for pasta) is soaked in water, drained and then kneaded into
a dough with twice as much flour. The *tracta* are then formed and allowed
to dry, either through indirect heat from a fire or simply by leaving them in
the sun. They are not cooked and we are not told into what shape they are
formed. Evidence from other sources suggests that Picentine bread, made with
alica, was kneaded *ad speciem tractae*.[5] This is not, as has been suggested, a
comment on the appearance of the Picentine bread, which is obvious from the
fact that it was baked in little pots, but is much more likely to be a comment
on the method.[6] The *alica* in Picentine bread was soaked for nine days in
grape juice and then formed into a dough with more flour in precisely the same
way as the dough for *tracta* is made in Cato. The cake referred to by Cato
only functions with sheets of pastry, as anything thicker would fail to cook
inside the cake and, as we have seen in the recipes, *orbiculi* – discs – were

[1] Pliny, *HN.* 19.35-38, 22.100-6; Theophrastus, *History of Plants* 6.3, 9.1.7; see also Dalby, *Food in the Ancient World*, pp. 303-4.

[2] See p. 333 n. 3 above; Dalby, *Food in the Ancient World*, p. 20.

[3] C. Perry, 'The Oldest Mediterranean Noodle: a Cautionary Tale,' *Petits Propos Culinaires* 9 (1981), pp. 42-5.

[4] 4.3.1-8.

[5] Pliny *HN.* 18.106.

[6] *ad speciem* can mean 'in the manner of' as well as 'with the appearance of' (*LS*).

the normal shape for *tractae*. It has been suggested that a ball of dough, or even an indistinct lump, was the form of the *tracta* used in *Apicius*, but such a ball would not crumble at all, as directed by the recipe, without great force, and would not dry in the centre.[1]

Experiments using a fine semolina and rolling/pulling the *tractae* as thin as possible – there is a limit to how thin these sheets can be – have proved successful. Drying times have been relatively short in a warm kitchen. In a fully dry state these sheets of raw pastry crumble with ease into a fine groat which, when added to sauces, successfully fulfils the function given to them in the recipes. One may ask, why not simply add the semolina? Experiments have demonstrated that *tractae* are able to exude a slow release of starch in their soaked, moulded and dried state, while raw semolina would simply go lumpy. It should also be noted that if the *tractae* are encouraged to dry with too much heat and, as a result, are – at least in part – cooked, they do not release their starch and fail to thicken as directed in the recipe.[2]

Thermospodium/cinis calidus These terms occur mainly in Book 4, among the recipes for *patinae*. *Cinis calidus* is a direct rendering into Latin of the Greek *thermospodium* and simply means 'hot embers'. There is no evidence that the term refers to any kind of cooking or baking equipment, as has been suggested.[3] In fact the two terms seem to be interchangeable, so that particular cooks will have used one or the other out of habit. At 4.2.9 both terms are used in the same recipe, almost as if the writer wants particularly to ensure that the reader understands. See *patina* above and the Introduction, p. 79, for the cooking technique.[4]

---

[1] This interpretation assumes that the *alica* is a coarser cracked unsifted wheat product that would form loosely bound and therefore more crumbly lumps not unlike the product known as *trahanas* still used in Greece and Turkey today. Cf. C. Perry, 'Oldest Mediterranean Noodle', and 'What was *tracta*?', *PPC* 12 (1982), ' Notes and Queries: *tracta/trachanas/kishk*', *PPC* 14 (1983), 'Trakhanas revisited', *PPC* 55 (1997).

[2] For a more thorough treatment see S. Grainger, 'Cato's Roman Cheesecakes', in *Milk: Beyond the Dairy: Proceedings of the Oxford Symposium on Food and Cookery 1999* (Totnes, 2000), pp. 168-77.

[3] See Cubberley, *'Testa* and *clibani'*, 98; Frayn, 'Home baking in Roman Italy'.

[4] *Thermospodium* occurs at 4.2.4 without an alternative, and there is a similar single use of *cineri calido* at 4.2.5. At 4.2.33, *thermospodium* occurs twice in a sentence and at 4.2.36 there is a single *cinerem calidam*.

2. ORIGINAL SOURCES ON APICIUS.

COOKING AND LUXURY DINING.

1. Tertullian, *De anima* 33–4 AD 160–240

Si ita iudicabitur, nonne illa anima plus solacii quam supplicii relatura est, quod funus inter cocos pretiosissimos inuenit, quod condimentis Apicianis et Lurconianis humatur, quod mensis Ciceronianis infertur, quod lancibus splendidissimis Sullanis effertur, quod exsequias conuiuium patitur, quod a coaequalibus deuoratur potius quam a miluis et lupis.[1]

(Tertullian is refuting the doctrine of metempsychosis, and wonders whether a glutton transformed into a beast destined for consumption might not actually enjoy the idea of bringing pleasure.)

'If the matter is judged in this way, then surely that soul (i.e. of a glutton) will receive more pleasure than punishment, because it finds its death among the most expensive cooks, because it is interred in Apician and Lurconian spices, because it is served at Ciceronian tables, because it is carried in the most beautiful Sullan dishes, because it endures the obsequies of fellow-diners, because it is devoured by its co-equals rather than by birds of prey and wolves.'

2. Tertullian, *De ieiunio* 12

Quod ergo cessatis paracletum, quem in Montano negatis, in Apicio credere?[2]

'What stops you trusting the Spirit in Apicius when you deny him in Montanus?'

[1] Ed. J. Waszink, in *Tertulliani Opera II: Opera Montanistica, CSEL Series Lat.* II (Turnhout, 1954); see also Waszink's commentary in his edition of the *De Anima with Introduction and Commentary* (Amsterdam, 1947).

[2] Ed. A. Rifferscheid, G. Wissowa, in *Tertulliani Opera II: Opera Montanistica, CSEL Series Lat.* II (Turnhout, 1954).

3. Tertullian, *De pallio* 5.7

Taceo Nerones et Apicios, Rufos.[1]

'I say nothing about Neros and Apiciuses, Rufuses.'

4. Tertullian, *Apologeticum* 3.6

Aeque medici ab Erasistrato (sc.nuncupantur) et grammatici ab Aristarcho, coqui etiam ab Apicio?[2]

'In the same way are not doctors named after Erasistratus, and grammar-teachers after Aristarchus, and cooks also after Apicius?'

5. Jerome, *Epistulae* 29.1, *Ad Marcellam*   before *c.* AD 420

Non sunt suaues epulae, quae non et placentam redoleant, quas non condit Apicius, in quibus nihil de magistrorum huius temporis iure suffumat.[3]

'Those feasts are not sweet which do not reek of *placenta*, which Apicius does not flavour, in which there is no trace of the sauce of the masters of this age.'

6. Jerome, *Aduersus Iouinianum* 1.40

Nam cum monachum esse se iactitet, et post sordidam tunicam, et nudos pedes, et cibarium panem, et aquae potum, ad candidas vestes, et nitidam cutem, ad mulsum et elaboratas carnes, ad iura Apicii et Paxami, ad balneas quoque ac frictulas et popinas se conferat.[4]

'Now when he (sc. Iouinianus) boasts that he is a monk, and after a shabby tunic, and bare feet, and coarse bread, and water to drink, he takes himself off to bright clothing, and a polished skin, to *mulsum* and fancy meat-dishes, to the sauces of Apicius and Paxamus, and also to the baths and massage-parlours and bars.'

---

[1] Ed. A. Gerlo, in *Tertulliani Opera II: Opera Montanistica, CSEL Series Lat.* II (Turnhout, 1954). Earlier editions (and the majority of MSS) read *et Rufos*. The term *Rufus* here must mean something like 'hot-head'.

[2] Ed. E. Dekkers, in *Tertulliani Opera: CSEL Series Lat.* II (Turnhout, 1954).

[3] Ed. I. Holberg, in *Hieronymi Opera Sect. I Pars I: CSEL* LIV (Vienna, Leipzig, 1910).

[4] Ed. J-P. Migne, *Patrologia Latina* XXIII (Paris, 1883).

7. Scriptores Historiae Augustae, Aelius Lampridius, *Heliogabalus* 18.4

end of the 4th century AD

cum ipse privatus diceret se Apicium, imperatorem uero <Neronem>, Othonem et Vitellium imitari.[1]

'Since he himself said as a private citizen that he imitated Apicius, but as emperor he imitated Nero, Otho and Vitellius.'

8. Scriptores Historiae Augustae, Aelius Lampridius, *Heliogabalus* 20.5

Comedit saepius ad imitationem Apicii calcanea camelorum et cristas uiuis gallicaneis demptas, linguas pauonum et lusciniarum, quod qui ederet a pestilentia tutus diceretur.

'He quite often ate camel hooves, cockscombs taken from living birds, and the tongues of peacocks and nightingales in imitation of Apicius, because a person who ate them was said to be safe from the plague.'

9. *Querolus* Act 2 Sc. 1 (Budé § 42)

?after AD 410

Cedant iuris conditores, cedant omnia cocorum ingenia, cedant Apici fercula.[2]

'Away with the seasoners of sauce, away with all the wiles of cooks, away with the dishes of Apicius.'

10. Sidonius, *Epistulae* 4.7.2

d. AD 488

Illic ea comitate retractabitur ac si inter Apicios epulones et Byzantinos chironomuntas hucusque ructaverit.[3]

'There he will be treated with such comradeship as if up to this point he had belched among Apician feasters and Byzantine master-carvers.'

[1] Latin text of 7 and 8 ed. E. Hohl (Leipzig, Teubner, 1971).

[2] Ed. C. Jaquenard-le-Saos (Budé series, Paris, 1994).

[3] Latin text of 10 and 11 from B. Anderson, *Sidonius: Poems and Letters* (2 vols., Cambridge, Mass., and London, 1936, 1965).

11. Sidonius, *Epistulae* 4.25.2

Hic per fragores parasiticos culinarum suffragio comparatos Apicianis plausibus ingerebatur.

'Through the clamour of parasites won with the help of his kitchens, he was being proposed with Apician acclaim.'

12. Venantius Fortunatus, *Carmina* 7.2.1–4   before *c.* AD 600
Item ad eundem cum rogaretur ad cenam

Nectar, uina, cibus, vestis, doctrina, facultas –
   Muneribus largis tu mihi, Gogo, sat es.
Tu refluus Cicero, tu noster Apicius extas:
   hinc satias verbis, pascis et inde cibis.[1]

'Another poem to Gogo, when he was invited to dinner.

Nectar, wines, food, clothing, learning and wit – with generous gifts you supply my every need, Gogo. You are pre-eminent as Cicero come back to us, as our own Apicius: from one you are readily supplied with words, from the other you are fed on foodstuffs.'

13. Isidore of Seville, *Etymologiae* 20.1.1   before AD 636
DE MENSIS. Primus Daedalus mensam et sellam fectit. Coquinae apparatum Apicius quidam primus conposuit, qui in eo absumptis bonis morte voluntaria periit; et merito, quia is, qui gulae atque edacitati seruit, et animam et corpus interfecit.[2]

'ON DINING. Daedalus was the first to make a table and chair. A fellow called Apicius was first to lay out the apparatus of the kitchen, and when all his goods had been used up he took his own life there; and deservedly so, because a man who is a slave to his belly and to gluttony kills both body and soul.'

---

[1] Ed. M. Reydallet (Paris, 1998).
[2] Ed. W. M. Lindsay (Oxford, 1912).

REFERENCES TO AN APICIAN TEXT

14. Scriptores Historiae Augustae, *Aelius* 5.9

Atque idem Apicii ab aliis relata idem Ouidii libros amorum in lecto[s] semper habuisse, idem Martialem, epigrammaticum poetam, Vergilium suum dixisse.[1]

'And he also is said to have had (things reported by others) about Apicius and the books of *Amores* of Ovid always by his bed, and to have said that Martial, the poet of epigrams, was his Vergil.'

15. Jerome, *Epistulae* 33.3

Paxamus et Apicius semper in manibus.[2]

'Paxamus and Apicius always to hand.'

16. *Scholia* on Juvenal 4.23   after *c.* 4th century AD

Apicius auctor praecipiendarum cenarum, qui scripsit de iuscellis: fuit nam exemplum gulae.[3]

'Apicius was the author of how to arrange dinners, who wrote about sauces: for he was the exemplar of a glutton.'

17. Mythographi Vaticani 2.269 (Mai ed. 225)   ?5th century AD

De Apicio

Apicius quidam uoracissimus fuit qui de condituris multa scripsit. Postquam ergo omne patrimonium dilapidauit, tandem cum egere cepisset, non ferens pudorem ueneno periit.[4]

'Apicius

'Apicius was a very greedy fellow who wrote much about seasonings/ sauces. So, after he had ruined all his inheritance, when he finally began to be in want, unable to bear the shame he died by poison.'

---

[1] Latin text from E. Hohl's Teubner edition (Leipzig, 1971).

[2] Ed. I. Holberg, in *Hieronymi Opera Sect. I Pars I: CSEL* LIV (Vienna, Leipzig, 1910).

[3] Latin text ed. P. Wessner (Teubner, Stuttgart, 1967).

[4] Latin text ed. P. Kulcsár (*CSEL Series Lat.* 91c, Turnhout, 1987).

18. Gloss on *Querolus*, Act 2 Sc. 1, in MS Paris 8121A   10th century

Apicius proprium nomen glutonis qui primus coquinae usum inuenit et de
condituris multa scripsit consumptoque omni patrimonio pudore egestatis
uenenum hausit. cuius et Iuuenalis in primo libro meminit.[1]

'Apicius is the proper name for a glutton; he was the first to discover/
devise the use of the kitchen and wrote much about seasonings, and
having used up all his inheritance he drank poison because of his shame
of poverty. Juvenal also mentions him in his first book.'

---

[1] Cited by R. Peiper in his Teubner edition (Leipzig, 1875).

3. NAMED RECIPES IN *APICIUS*.

A number of recipes in *Apicius* are named after specific individuals.[1] The most common epithet based on a name is, unsurprisingly, the adjective *Apicianus, -a, -um*, which occurs in 7 recipes: 4.1.2 *sala cattabia Apiciana*; 4.2.14 *patinam Apicianam*; 4.3.3 *minutal Apicianum*; 5.4.2 *conciclam Apicianam*; 6.7 *anserem elixum calidum ex iure frigido Apiciano*; 7.4.2 *ofellas Apicianas;* 8.7.6 *porcellum lacte pastum elixum calidum iure frigido crudo Apiciano*. These clearly refer back to the 'Apician' tradition discussed in the Introduction. Other recipes appear to indicate a traditional origin with other historical figures, though it is frequently impossible to say precisely which of the several persons often suggested by a given name is intended.[2] There is no mention of any 'Apicius' in *Pros. I* , *II* or *III*.

As an indication of the difficulty in assigning the named recipes precisely, there are a number of individuals listed in *Pros. I* which might be linked with the *porcellum Celsinianum* in 8.7.12. 'Celsinus 1' was a *consiliaris* (?of Diocletian) dated to 284/305; 'Celsinus 3' was ?vicar of an unknown diocese before 388 who lived in Berytus; 'Aurelius Celsinus 4' was proconsul of Africa 338–9 and prefect of the city of Rome in 341; 'Clodius Celsinus 5' was a *uir egregius* (of Caria?) in the late third century; 'Clodius Celsinus 6' (*signo Adelphius*) was prefect of the city of Rome in 353, proconsul before 351 (possibly of Africa) and may have been the same man as 'Clodius Celsinus 7', a *uir clarissimus consularis* of Numidia 333/7. We can probably safely discount 'Celsianus 2', a Cappadocian philosopher dated to *c.* the early or middle fourth century AD.

---

[1] The first study of these named recipes was done by Brandt, *Untersuchungen*, pp. 91-5. We differ from his conclusions on a number of points.

[2] In the discussion which follows, we refer to entries in the three volumes of *The Prosopography of the Later Roman Empire* (Vol. I, *AD 260–395*, ed. A. H. M. Jones, J. R.Martindale & J. Morris, Cambridge 1971; vol. II, *AD 395–527*, ed. J. R. Martindale, Cambridge 1980; vol. III, *AD 527–641*, ed. J. R. Martindale, Cambridge 1992) using the abbreviations *Pros.I*, *Pros. II*, *Pros. III*. Given the likely date of the compilation of *Apicius* as we have it, individuals mentioned in *Pros. III* are perhaps unlikely to have been the origins of any named recipes, but they are included for completeness. On the other hand, the attribution of excerpts of an *Apicius* collection to the otherwise-unattested 'Vinidarius' may suggest a late date for the compilation of the *Apicius* which survives. Reference is also made to the *Oxford Classical Dictionary* (*OCD*), 3rd ed. rev. S. Hornblower, A. Spawforth (Oxford, 2003).

In the case of *porcellum Flaccianum* at 8.7.8, *OCD* has 9 entries under 'Flaccus' from *c.* 237 BC to *c.* AD 38. The eighth of these is a scholar-freedman of some repute, one 'Verrius Flaccus'. The recipe might equally be linked to the 'Valerius Flaccus' who wrote the *Argonautica, c.* 70–95 AD, or to two individuals in *Pros. I*, 'Flaccianus' the *uir clarissimus* and proconsul of Africa in 393, and 'Flaccus' *rationalis summae* 286/93.

Brandt linked the 'Fronto' of *Frontonianum porcellum*, 6.8.12 and 8.7.10, with the land-surveyor mentioned in *Geoponica* 7.12;[1] the recipe can be precisely dated if this is the same man as the 'Sextus Iulius Frontinus' who was *praetor urbanus* in 70 AD, *consul suffectus* in 74 and again in 98, governor of Britain 74–8, and *ordinarius* in 100. *OCD* provides another possible link in 'Marcus Cornelius Fronto' of *c.* 100–166 AD, a contemporary of Marcus Aurelius and the foremost Roman orator of his day. In addition, the term *Frontoniani* also appears in Sidonius Appolinaris *Epistles* 1.1.2 as 'followers of Fronto', while *Pros. I* lists a *palatinus* of the East in the early fourth century, *Pros. II* a *comes* in the West from 452–455, and *Pros. III* has two entries, the first for an advocate of the ?sixth century, the second a *comes*, proconsul (possibly of Asia) and *pater ciuitatis* (at Side in Pamphylia), again possibly in the sixth century.

The obvious individual with whom *patellam Lucretianam* at 4.2.25 could be linked is the poet Lucretius, *c.* 94–55 BC, though we might question whether his Epicurean philosophy would sit well with the luxury living represented by the recipe. *Pros. I* mentions a 'Lucretius Paternus', ?governor 329, and a 'Fl. Lucretius Florentinus (Ru)sticus' who was *uir perfectissimus* and *praeses* (of Tripoli) in the fourth century. *Pros. II* mentions a 'Lucretius' who was a friend of Caelius Aurelianus.

We are on firmer ground with *minutal Matianum* at 4.3.4. The recipe is probably called after the apples, rather than referring directly to the Matius who was the friend of Cicero.[2] These are referred to in Pliny, *HN.* 12.13.4, 15.49, in Athenaeus 82c, and in Diocletian's Price Edict, 65 (*mala optima Mattiana*). According to *OCD*, the friend and assistant of Augustus who went by the name Gaius Matius and was an expert in gastronomy and arboriculture has been identified with Cicero's friend, but seems to be a part of the subsequent generation (a son, perhaps).

---

[1] Brandt, *Untersuchungen,* p. 92.
[2] See Introduction, p. 53.

Of the person behind *leporem Passienum* at 8.8.7, Brandt comments 'wissen wir nichts.'[1] The only name which comes near to it is the 'Passenus Paulus' mentioned in *OCD* as a contemporary *eques* whom the Younger Pliny praises for the quality of his elegiac verses comparable to those of his ancestor Propertius.

The recipe for *hedum siue agnum Tarpeianum*, 8.6.9, can hardly derive from the mythological Tarpeia or the rock used for executions at Rome which was named after her. *Pros. I* mentions a 'Tarpeius' who was a *uir clarissimus* and procurator of Q. Clodius Hermogenianus Olybrius in 384.[2]

Far more possibilities present themselves with the 'Terentius' or 'Terentia' who lies behind the various recipes linked with that name: *minutal Terentinum* and *esicium Terentinum* (4.3.2), *ex iure Terentino* (4.2.13), *impensam Terentinam* (8.7.1). Brandt linked these to the 'Terentius' mentioned in Athenaeus 647c, or perhaps to a 'Tarantinos' mentioned in the *Geoponica*.[3] It might conceivably be linked to the fabulously wealthy Terentia with a connection to the Fabii who was married to Cicero; divorced in 48 BC, she lived to the great age of 103. There are also a number of possibilities from a later period. *Pros. I* lists three: first, a baker of humble origins who acquired office through a successful prosecution and was *corrector Tuscae c.* 364–5, but executed in 374 when found guilty of forgery.[4] Here at least there is some sort of culinary link. The second is *comes et dux* of Armenia *c.* 369–74. Reference is also made of a 'Terentius Marcianus' who was *vir perfectissimus* and *praeses* of Lycia and Pamphylia in the late third or early fourth centuries. *Pros. II* recalls that Zosimus calls the British *magister utriusque militiae* of Constantine III from 407–9, Gerontius, by the name 'Terentos'.[5] He however is as unlikely to be the source of this recipe as is the infantry commander in Africa, 533–36, in *Pros. III*.

We can speak with more confidence regarding *betacios Varrones* at 3.2.4, and *Varro* at 7.14.4. These recipes may well derive from comments in the Menippean satires written by M. Terentius Varro, also the author of the extant *De Re Rustica*.[6] None of the volumes of the *Prosopography of the Later Roman*

---

[1] *Untersuchungen*, p. 93; he brackets *Flaccus, Lucretius* and *Tarpeius* in the same sentence.

[2] Symmachus, *Relationes* 28; he was Olybrius' legal representative.

[3] *Untersuchungen*, pp. 92-3.

[4] Ammianus Marcellinus 27.32.

[5] Zosimus 6.4.2.

[6] So Brandt, *Untersuchungen*, p. 93.

Empire list a 'Varro'. In similar vein they make no mention of a 'Vitellius', and the origin of the three recipes *pisam Vitellianam* (5.3.5), *pisam siue fabam Vitellianam* (5.3.9), and *porcellum Vitellianum* (8.7.7) must surely be the short-lived emperor Vitellius (AD 15–69) whose gross eating habits were gleefully recorded by Suetonius, and in less macabre detail by Tacitus. He was evidently interested in more 'serious' aspects of food: Pliny the Elder noted that he was renowned for introducing pistachio nuts into Italy.[1]

Porcellum Traianum in 8.7.16 is much less easy to assign to an individual. The 'obvious' choice is the emperor Trajan (AD 98–117), though Brandt notes that he was better known as a drinker than an eater.[2] There are other less likely candidates. *Pros. I* lists three men under the name: the first a *praefectus (militum)* of Egypt in 357, the second a *magister peditum* in Thrace, 377–8, the third a *praepositus (militum)* in the Thebaid 367/75. It also records a *vir ducenarius* called 'Traianus Mucianus' in the late third century. There are no references in *Pros. II*, but five in *Pros. III*: a *vir consularis et spectabilis* at Rome in 533; an officer of Belisarius' bodyguard, 537–41; one 'Patricius Traianus', *quaestor sacri palatii* and envoy to Persia, dated to 575; and two figures dating from the sixth or seventh centuries, the first an honorary consul, the second a *tribunus* in Africa.

The choice is more limited in the case of *concicla Commodiana* at 5.4.4. Commodus, son of Marcus Aurelius and sole emperor AD 180–192, had a reputation for gluttony,[3] and there is only one reference, in *Pros. III*, to a 'Commodus' who was *comes Italiae* in 587 and who is unlikely to be the origin of the recipe.

For *pultes Iulianae* the choice is wider: Brandt suggested that the recipe could have originated with Didius Severus Iulianus, chosen by the praetorians after a mock auction to succeed Pertinax in AD 193, but the possibility that Julian the Apostate (332–63) is referred to cannot be ruled out.[4] However, the adjectival form might derive either from 'Iulianus', an extremely well-attested name (40 entries in *Pros. I*, 24 in *Pros. II*, 41 in *Pros. III*), or from any 'Iulius' or 'Iulia' so that, as with almost all of the named recipes in *Apicius*, definite attribution is impossible.

---

[1] Suetonius, *Vitellius* 13; Tacitus, *Hist.* 2.62; Pliny, *HN.* 15.29.

[2] *Untersuchungen*, p. 93, citing Pseudo Aurelius Victor, *Epit.* 13.4.

[3] Brandt, *Untersuchungen*, p. 93; cf. Aelius Lampridius, *Vita Commodi* 2.7, 10.1.

[4] Brandt, *Untersuchungen*, p. 93, citing Aelius Spartianus, *Didius* 3.8.9, who reproaches Didius with gluttony, and Ammianus Marcellinus 22.4.10.

4. EXCURSUS ON *GARUM* AND *LIQUAMEN*.

The debate about fish sauce is ongoing and the issue remains controversial. How we interpret these sauces is integral to understanding Roman food, particularly so in the case of the recipes in *Apicius*.[1] There are some very basic facts about fish sauce that are often forgotten by commentators and there are also contradictions in the evidence that are confusing and therefore frequently overlooked.

It is evident from the archaeological record that fish sauce production formed a substantial part of both economic production and commerce for the whole period to which our *Apicius* refers.

In the beginning, *garos* was the term for a Greek fish sauce of some kind, probably developed in the Aegean islands from around the fifth century BC. We have no early Greek evidence for how it was made and though there are a few references in Athenaeus, they do no more than confirm that it was smelly, considered rotten, and made from fish and salt.[2]

Pliny the Elder, writing in the mid-first century AD, says that *garum* was made from *intestinis piscium ceterisque quae abicienda sint sale maceratis*, 'from the innards of fish and the refuse that would otherwise be thrown away, mixed with salt'.[3] He then contrasts this kind of sauce with one that used to be made from a fish called *garos* by the Greeks. The idea that this most precious of Roman sauces was being made from the most useless and apparently disgusting things is corroborated by Martial's Saturnalia gift of *garum sociorum* 'made from the first blood of a still-breathing mackerel', *expirantis adhuc scombri de sanguine primo*.[4] A sauce made this way would be quite a dark, pungent liquor.

---

[1] In what follows we are greatly indebted to the in-depth study of R. I. Curtis, *Garum and Salsamenta: Production and Commerce in Materia Medica* (Leiden, 1991). The conclusions here are a development of the paper by Sally Grainger, 'Towards an authentic Roman sauce: or, can we truly know what *liquamen* was?', in *Authenticity in the Kitchen: Proceedings of the Oxford Food Symposium on Food and Cookery 2005* (Totnes, 2006).

[2] Athenaeus 67c, quoting from Sophocles' *Triptolemus*.

[3] Pliny, *HN*. 31.93. Pliny also mentions that mackerel was used for the most exclusive product.

[4] Martial 13.102.

We shall see that, according to Manilius, a separate sauce seems to have been made from the empty mackerel bodies. Are we to think of this as *garum* too? Was the original Greek sauce made of fish blood, or was a blood sauce a later Roman development?

Martial tells us in his list of Saturnalia presents that *muria* was another form of fish sauce made from tuna, that seems to be relatively inferior to mackerel blood *garum*.[1] It is not clear whether *muria* was made from the viscera of tuna or from the flesh of the fish or both. Tuna is a large fish producing a substantial quantity of intestines and also flesh. A sauce made from tuna would be more plentiful, less exclusive and therefore not so suitable as a gift for a member of the élite, it seems. We find in the *Geoponica*, a tenth-century AD Greek manual (part of which dates from the sixth century), that the most expensive form of *garum* was now made from the intestines, gills, juice and blood of tuna, and was called *haimation*, 'bloody'.[2] However, *muria* is also the Latin for 'brine', and was the term for a fish brine: when cleaned fish was salted for the market, water was drawn out of the fish by the salt. This liquor was drained off and used as a different kind of fish sauce under the title *muria salsamenti*, 'brine of salted fish'.[3] This kind of sauce would be quite pale in colour and also very clear and free flowing. A fish sauce called *muria* made its way to the Roman fort of Vindolanda on Hadrian's Wall, and is recorded on the little wooden tablets that preserve the mess bills of middle-ranking officers in a late-first-century AD auxiliary unit.[4]

In some of the Latin sources we find reference to another kind of fish sauce called *liquamen*, and of course *liquamen* is the term used in *Apicius*. A definition of this is found in a late and often unreliable source, Isidore of Seville's *Etymologiae*. Isidore wrote in the sixth century AD about the origin of familar words, but his reasoning on the derivations and origins of words is doubtful on many occasions. He quotes Pliny the Elder on the origins of *garon* in Greek, then talks about *liquamen*:

[1] Martial 13.103.

[2] *Geoponica* 20.46.1-6. We even find a sixteenth-century source that describes *garum* being made with blood by individual fishmongers in Constantinople. See A. Dalby, *Flavours of Byzantium* (Totnes, 2003), p. 68.

[3] Gargilius Martialis, *Curae boum ex corpore* 4 (*muriam salsamenti optimam*); cf. Galen, *De simplicium medicamentorum temperamentis ac facultatibus*, 12.377k.

[4] A. Birley, *Garrison life at Vindolanda, A Band of Brothers* (Stroud, 2002), p.121.

liquamen dictum eo quod soluti in salsamento pisciculi eundem humorem liquant. cuius liquor appelatur salsugo uel muria. proprie autem muria dicitur aqua sale commixta.

Liquamen is so called because little fish dissolved during salting produce the liquid of that name. Its liquor is called *salsugo* or *muria*. Now strictly speaking, *muria* is the name of water mixed with salt.[1]

Here we have a third kind of fish sauce where little fish are dissolved completely with salt into a liquor that is very reminiscent of modern-day Thai fish sauce. These modern sauces can vary in colour, but the ancient version would certainly appear darker than *muria*, and yet probably paler than *garum*.

It has generally been accepted that *garum* and *liquamen* were the same thing: a form of fermented fish sauce used in Roman cooking. This is accurate as far as it goes, but the wider issue of precisely what *liquamen* was in relation to *garum* has not been considered fully or understood.[2] In Diocletian's Price Edict of AD 301, written in Latin and Greek, the Latin term *liquamen* is rendered in Greek as *garon*.[3] As we shall see, this does not necessarily mean that Latin *garum* was also the same as Greek *garon*. The main recipe in the *Geoponica* for fish sauce states that fish blood and entrails as well as small fish such as sprat, smelt, mullet were all salted and shaken and fermented in the sun. This product is identified as *liquamen* at the beginning of the recipe, *garum* in the middle, and when the basket is placed over the vessel it is *liquamen* once more.

This problem over terminology is reflected in gourmet writing of the middle to late Imperial period too. One important point to bear in mind is that this 'composite' sauce, combining both blood and fish, may have been a late development and not in common use in the first century AD.

The *Geoponica* also tells us that the Bithynians, in north-west Asia Minor, made their *garum* from different kinds of small fish (sometimes with the addition of *allec*) as well as salt. Crucially, an area associated with Greek culture makes fish sauce from whole small fish and no blood. A fish sauce recipe found in a work by Gargilius Martialis, dated to the third century AD, but suspected to

---

[1] Isidore of Seville, *Etymologiae,* 20.3.20. The term *liquamen* is cognate with *liquere/liquescere*, meaning 'to be liquid' and 'liquefy'.

[2] Curtis, *Garum and Salsamenta,* pp. 6-26.

[3] Diocletian's Price Edict, 3.6-7.

contain much later material, contains many aromatic herbs and small whole fish, as well as salt, layered in a barrel. It was only left for about 30 days in total, as opposed to the sauces in the *Geoponica*, which were left for up to three months or more. The resulting so-called liquid will be viscous and more like a paste after 30 days, but will separate and clear if left for long enough.[1] This particular recipe in Martialis is of note as it is entitled *Confectio liquaminis quod oenogarum vocant*, 'a sauce made with *liquamen* which is called *oenogarum*'. We will return to these compound sauces later, though it is of interest to note that the herbs and spices listed to make the sauce include costus, clove and cinnamon, spices that are typical of early medieval food rather than the food in *Apicius*.[2] We can also see that some form of fish sauce could be made by simply cooking down fish matter in water and wine until it was reduced, then straining it.[3] These recipes refer to the mixture as *garum* even though they are remote in character from the blood *garum* of Pliny the Elder.

A key piece of evidence that these sauces were different comes from a gourmet's letter. In *c.* AD 390, Ausonius wrote from Bordeaux to his former pupil Paulinus, thanking him for a gift of *muria*:[4]

> *Veritus displicuisse oleum, quod miseras, munus iterasti, addito etiam Barcinonensis muriae condimento cumulatius praestitisti. scis autem me id nomen muriae, quod in usu uulgi est, nec solere nec posse dicere, cum scientissimi ueterum et Graeca uocabula fastidientes Latinum in gari appellatione non habeant. sed ego, quocumque nomine liquor iste sociorum uocatur, 'iam patinas implebo meas'...*

> 'Fearing that the oil which you had sent was not pleasing, you repeated your gift and distinguished yourself more fully by adding in addition a *condimentum* of *muria* from Barcelona. But you know that I have neither the custom nor the ability to say that word *muria*, which is in the use of the

---

[1] Ps-Gargilius Martialis 62. *Garum* is sometimes advertised as 'aged', which would allow this product to separate in its vessel; cf. Curtis, *Garum and Salsamenta*, Appendix II.

[2] The fish sauce recipe also uses herring, which was unknown until the medieval period: see Curtis, *Garum and Salsamenta*, p. 12, n. 22. See Glossary, *oenogarum*, and Introduction, p. 34 n. 2.

[3] Ps-Rufus Festus, *Breviarium* (Förster, p. 23, cited by Curtis, *Garum and Salsamenta*, Appendix I.4).

[4] Ausonius, *Ep.* 21, from Prete's Teubner ed. (Leipzig, 1978); no. 19 in R. P. H. Green's edition (Oxford, 1999).

common folk, although the most learned of our ancestors and those who
shun Greek expressions do not have a Latin expression for the appellation
garum. But I, by whatever name that liquor of our allies is called, "will
soon fill my *patinas*"…'

Ausonius states that the Latin language does not have a term for *garum*, and if
you shunned Hellenistic things there was no corresponding word you could use.
For Ausonius at least, *liquamen* is not *garum*. It is difficult to know which kind
of sauce he had received. It is initially referred to as *muria*, which as we have
seen may have been a blood or a fish sauce. He has an obvious interest in the
details of these fish sauces and we would expect him to have the best products
and to understand the complexities of designation and definition, yet he hints at
a recognized confusion among the cognoscenti as to the names of these sauces.
Given that the sauce in question is referred to as *sociorum*, and that Ausonius
appears to be a gourmet, we would expect a blood sauce rather than a fish sauce,
but this is not certain.[1] We will have to consider whether *garum* and *liquamen*
and *muria* were used in different ways. One might consider that a blood sauce
and a fish sauce would be sufficiently different to warrant different methods of
use and different ratios with other ingredients.

The *Astronomica*, a poem by Manilius, provides considerable detail (albeit
cast in poetic form) about fish sauce production that may shed light on the issue.
It describes activity on a beach where fish are landed and prepared, and as a
consequence is worth citing in full:

> *nec cepisse sat est: luctantur corpora nodis*
> *exspectantque nouas acies ferroque necantur,*
> *inficiturque suo permixtus sanguine pontus.*
> *tum quoque, cum toto iacuerunt litore praedae*
> *altera fit caedis caedes: scinduntur in artus,*
> *corpore et ex uno uarius discribitur usus.*
> *illa datis melior, sucis pars illa retentis.*

[1] A suggestion from Andrew Dalby that the quotation may contain a gloss seems the more
believable as we should expect a blood sauce here. Ausonius says he does not want to mention
muria yet he has already done so at *Barcinonensis* (*muriae*) *condimento*. This seems odd especially
as the phrase works without the additional *muria*. This letter, along with the tuna blood sauce in
the *Geoponica*, is the only evidence to suggest that *muria* could be associated with a blood sauce.
If the sauce received by Ausonius was a blood *garum*, then *muria* is firmly defined as a brine or
salted fish brine.

hinc sanies pretiosa fluit floremque cruoris
euomit et mixto gustum sale temperat oris.
                            (Manilius 5.664-72)

'Nor is it enough to have caught them: their bodies struggle against the net and they await fresh battles and are put to the sword [i.e. cut up with a knife]: the sea is stained, mixed with their blood. Then again, when the catch lies all along the shore [or perhaps brought ashore whole, with transferred epithet: see the phrases following], a second slaughter is made of the slaughter: they are jointed [lit: cut into their limbs] and from the one body different purposes are allotted: one part is better with its juices drained, another with them kept in. From some a precious fluid flows out, pouring out [lit. vomiting up] the flower of the gore, and mixed with salt, balances taste in the mouth.'

This is the blood drained to make *garum*: we appear to have confirmation that blood alone was used. The choice of words here suggest that the consumer has some role in making the balance of taste in the mouth happen rather than the cook, especially when contrasted with the 'juice for food' mentioned below. The text continues (vv. 673-5):

illa putris turbae strages confunditur omnis
permiscetque suas alterna in damna figuras
communemque cibis usum sucumque ministrat.

'The whole of the remainder – a mass of decaying slaughter [i.e. the drained carcasses] sinks to the bottom and mingles its shapes in a second demise, serving up a common condiment and a juice for food.'

There seems to be a separation of solid and liquid matter here; the solid will clearly become *allec*, the fish paste, and the implication is that it was a table condiment. The *sucus* (juice) above this paste is another fish sauce, but which kind – *muria* or *liquamen*? The *tituli picti* labels that are attached to amphorae identify all the types of fish sauce, but one in particular is worded *liquamen*

378

optimum scombri, 'best *liquamen* of mackerel'.[1] It appears that *liquamen* need not be made from whole small fish, but also pieces of larger fish. However, the issue is complicated by what seems to us to be a description of a different operation which immediately follows upon the last one in the text of Manilius, and is marked as such by the initial *aut* in an emphatic position:

> *aut, cum caeruleo stetit ipsa simillima ponto*
> *squamigerum nubes turbaque immobilis haeret,*
> *excipitur uasta circum uallata sagena*
> *ingentique lacus et Bacchi dolia complet*
> *umorisque uomit socias per mutua dotes*
> *et fluit in liquidam tabem resoluta medullas.*
>   (Manilius, 5.676-81)

'Or, when a cloud of scaly creatures comes to a halt and sticks fast in an unmoving shoal, closely resembling the blue-green sea itself, it is hauled out, hemmed in all around by a vast net, and fills huge tanks and wine-jars, and it exudes the shared wealth of its fluid over itself, and dissolving from the inside it flows out into liquid gore.'

We have a detailed description of a sauce made from whole small fish which we have been told is *liquamen*. There seems to be little doubt at this point that originally *garum* and *liquamen* were made by different processes. There has been a general assumption that because *garum* and *liquamen* appear to mean the same things in the late empire, they always did.

Cooks, expressing themselves in the Apician recipe text, always contradicted this generality, though it has seldom been acknowledged. *Garum* (with rare exceptions) only appears in references to the early Greek compound sauces such as *oenogarum,* while the standard term in the text for fish sauce is *liquamen*. In fact, as we have seen with Gargilius, quoted above, and throughout *Apicius*, when an *oenogarum* is described, it always contains *liquamen*. If *garum* was such an important and potentially exclusive ingredient in Roman cooking, why don't we find *garum* referred to in these high-status recipes? It has been assumed in the past that the recipe collection was compiled in the late empire by gourmets

---

[1] Curtis, *Garum and Salsamenta*, Appendix II.

from the literary élite, who used the term *liquamen* rather than *garum* because it was, at that time, the standard term for the basic kind of fish sauce available. The *Geoponica* and Diocletian's Price Edict seem to confirm this theory. However, in our opinion, the recipes are clearly the product of cooks, compiled over many decades, even centuries, rather than being composed by gourmets at a fixed period in time, and it is clear that the nature of fish sauce is considerably more complex than this simple theory allows.

Garum is found in all kinds of late imperial literature, so this cannot explain its omission from *Apicius*, but, crucially, *liquamen* is not found in any early literature.[1] Our explanation for this strange circumstance is that the product termed *garum* in Latin, made from blood and fish viscera and as defined by Pliny the Elder, was a later development through Roman influence and used largely but not exclusively by the consumer after the food was served: it was primarily a table condiment that could also be used in the kitchen. It was relatively expensive and, when made with especially selected ingredients, exclusive to an élite market and so would feature in culinary literature writen by the élite. This particular sauce is not included in Diocletian's Price Edict. However, Greek *garon*/Latin *liquamen*, as recorded in Diocletian, was made with small whole fish or pieces of fish dissolved into a sauce and was primarily the product used by cooks in the kitchen. As a result it might be rarely encountered by gourmets and therefore rarely mentioned in Latin literature written by them, but would feature strongly in recipe collections writen by cooks. *Muria* would then be the less exclusive fish sauce used by the majority as a salt substitute, pale, weak and inferior, as Martial and Ausonius suggest. It is difficult to comprehend how this confusion over terminology may have occurred. We suspect that when the Romans embraced Greek cooking in the second and first centuries BC, the Greek term was transferred to the blood sauce for reasons of marketing and exclusivity: the Greek term was simply more fashionable. The confusion stems from the confusion of some of the gourmets who wrote about food, but the cooks responsible for the recipes in *Apicius* did not share their muddle. We ought to trust them to use the terminology accurately, more so in fact than any other writer.

We can now see that the composite sauce in the *Geoponica* is made from a combination of both earlier types of fish sauce, i.e. small and medium whole

---

[1] *Liquamen* appears in Latin for the first time at Columella 9.14.3 and only exists in Greek in the *Geoponica*.

fish and intestines from larger fish cleaned for immediate sale or for salting. This composite sauce may have been a late development or it may be that such sauces coexisted with separate blood and whole fish varieties. However, we believe that the high-status cook would still demand the original distinct varieties of fish sauce. An alternative explanation may be that the addition of blood and intestines to other fish matter speeded up the dissolving process, accelerating production.[1] It is possible that the Roman gourmet developed a liking for this blood-rich sauce, and that from this point a pure blood sauce was developed to cater to this market, though it appears that the Greek name latinized as *garum* was applied to the more exclusive product, and a new term, *liquamen*, had to be coined for the whole fish sauce.

The freshness of the fish (or as Martial puts it, using fish that was 'still-breathing' when it was drained) seems to be crucial. The account of fish sauce production in Manilius' *Astronomica* quoted above, suggests that the fish were very recently caught when they encountered the salt; the fish or entrails were broken down as a result of enzyme action rather than through bacterial decay because of the level of salt. Experiments Sally Grainger has conducted with extremely fresh whole fish and fish entrails also lead us to think that these sauces did not smell excessively, either. The amount of salt used, the length of time the product was left to ferment and the heat levels may also have been determining factors in defining these sauces. Whatever the combination of fish and fish matter, the mixture takes a few months to dissolve, ferment and clear: the fluid at the top is the fine, free-flowing liquid variously called *garum/liquamen/muria*. Pliny says that some varieties at least had the appearance of aged honey wine;[2] in sum, it was therefore a dark, pungent, free-flowing salty liquor. The paste at the bottom was the *allec* and was also a table condiment, a true pickle in appearance and the precursor to anchovy paste (though the latter is unfermented). Pliny says that *allec* was also made independently of *garum*, from such things as oysters, sea urchins and sea anemones as well as very small fish. These pastes have a stronger link to modern anchovy pastes as they were probably not fermented but simply dissolved. A modern practice in fish sauce production involves diluting the residue with sea water and allowing a second quality fish sauce to form. We

---

[1] The enzymes which dissolve the fish flesh are present in the viscera. If these enzymes were present on the inside *and* on the outside of the pieces of fish, then the dissolving process woud be that much quicker.

[2] Pliny, *HN*. 31.95.

find a second quality *liquamen* and *garum* in Diocletian's Price Edict, and so it is quite possible that such practices occured in the ancient world too. [1]

Considerable evidence of manufacture comes from Pompeii, originally a Greek colony, where *garum, liquamen, muria* and *allec* were all made and sold separately. Amphora labels, from the area and further afield, describe *gari flos* (flower of *garum*), *liq. flos* (flower of *liquamen*), and *muria flos* (flower of *muria*) among many other catagories of wording such as *optimum, excellens*, and *primum*.[2] Despite the fact that *gari flos*, made from mackerel, was supposed to be the most expensive of the fish sauces, it is the most common label and is often found in relatively modest houses and *popinae*.[3] Fish sauce amphora finds elsewhere in Italy do not contradict these findings. Grant's conclusion that fish sauce was a product only used by an élite is unlikely.[4] In Pompeii at least, fish sauce was in widespread use: whether a *pure blood* sauce was in common use is the question to ask. The culture of élitism (and economic reality) within high-status dining circles meant that rare items were expensive and desirable. The more difficult a product was to obtain, the costlier it would become, and a fish sauce made from the blood of a designated fish would be a great luxury. The degree of desirability would be reduced if the blood came from less select fish such as tuna, and a blood fish sauce made with any and assorted fish would be the cheapest. It is not unthinkable to imagine that many people were sold a fish sauce that was not quite what it said on the *tituli picti* label. A high-status Roman would want to know that his *garum* was of the correct kind, and it seems that the

---

[1] Diocletian's Price Edict 3.7 (ed. Laufer p. 104); Curtis, *Garum and Salsamenta*, Appendix II.

[2] Curtis, *Garum and Salsamenta*, p. 195.

[3] *Muria* and *liquamen* are also well attested.

[4] Grant argues (*Roman Cookery*, London, 1999, p. 19) that fish sauce usage was limited to high-status groups. His argument is based on a selective use of recipes from literary sources which do not make use of fish sauce, either from admitted prejudice or because the majority of them are wheat-based bread and cake recipes where fish sauce has no place. He also identifies the recipes he uses as having a lower status because they are not Apician, rather than seeing them as part of a continuum of recipes. Moreover, writers such as Cato, Columella, Galen, Oribasius *et al.*, whose works span 500 years, scarcely reflect common cuisine in contrast to *Apicius*, which Grant regards as representing the sole high-status source for food. It remains to point out that all *literature* is to some degree high-status (although other surviving written texts such as graffiti, labels and so forth, may not be), and that the voice or taste of the 'ordinary Roman' is consequently difficult to identify clearly in it. It is quite likely (for example) that subsistence farmers did not use fish sauce very much, but this was probably due to lack of funds, not preference, given its ubiquity. Note Cato's custom of giving *allec* to the slaves on his farm, *De agricultura* 54.

tituli picti or labels attached to amphora are specifically intended to distinguish the different grades, though they have as yet not revealed their secrets. The answer is undoubtedly hidden within the labels, though no detailed study has yet been done.

Doctors and vets used all the kinds of fish sauce in their remedies, and a brief examination of their texts seems to show that Greek *garon* is distinguished from Roman *garum*. This is not the place for a detailed analysis of the material: however, the veterinary writers Pelagonius and Vegetius, writing in the fourth century AD, used both *garum* and *liquamen* in their remedies.[1] They may have simply copied remedies from Greek and Latin sources that they used without altering the usage, but the simplest explanation, as we have seen, is that the sauces were sufficiently different to warrant including both. Galen rarely uses any term but *garon* in his extensive medical treatises and we would maintain that he means a whole-fish sauce rather than a blood sauce. It is mainly used in combination with oil and vinegar to improve the flavour of various dishes. However we do find reference in Galen to a *garos melan*, 'black *garum*', which seems to indicate a blood sauce.[2] It has been interpreted as a reference to the best *garum* or *garum sociorum*, the trade name for an expensive form of fish sauce from southern Spain which according to Martial was made with mackerel blood.[3] It is rare to find an epithet attached to *garon* in Greek sources, and *liquamen* is limited to one reference: it only appears in Greek in the *Geoponica*. This absence of *liquamen* in the Greek sources is significant: in addition to Galen's *garos melan,* a sixth-century papyrus has a reference to *garo 'u' haimatitou*, 'bloody *garon*', and we find the same designation in the similarly-dated *Geoponica*: *garos haimation*.[4] These are likely to be references in Greek to Roman *garum* made with blood, and as such they need an additional epithet to distinguish then from *garon*, the plain fish sauce.

There may be evidence of the transition between the individual fish sauces and the composite sauce in the *Geoponica* reflected in *Apicius*. We find a qualifying epithet attached to *liquamen* at 2.5.3, where in a sausage recipe we find the instruction *alicam purgas et cum liquamine intestini et albamine porri concisi*

---

[1] Pelagonius: *liquamen*, 9; 11.2; 13; 98; 455; 457; *garum*, 428; 213. Vegetius: *liquamen*, 1.10.1; 1.17.10,16; 11.91.2; 11.108.2; 11.132.4 1V.6.1; *garum*, 11.28.8; 111.28.10.

[2] Galen, *De Compositione Medicamentorum secundum locus* 3 (=12.637k).

[3] Martial 13.103; Curtis, *Garum and Salsamenta*, p. 8 n.11.

[4] P. Amst. inv. no. 44; *Geoponica* 20.46.6.

minutatim simul elixas. This mixture is later added to meat and stuffed into an *intestinum*, 'sausage skin'. Reading *intestini* after *liquamine* might be thought a corruption through dittography, but *intestinum* is a general term for 'viscera' or 'intestines' as well as the individual 'tubes' that become sausage skins. We have been discussing blood up until now because the internal organs of most freshly-caught fish are blood red and quite liquid when opened, but if we think of them as viscera and translate the sentence 'soak *alica* and boil it together with blood *liquamen* and finely chopped white of leek', we may have a later addition to the collection of recipes written at a time when *liquamen* was evolving from an entirely whole-fish sauce to a general fish sauce made with both fish and blood.

We should not be surprised to find that the references to fish sauces are confused. In literature, particularly satire, we find references to *garum* and even *muria* as exclusive ingrendients in sauces which the gourmet is able to discuss and describe while at table. It is worth quoting in full the passage from Horace *Satire* 2.4 again, as it is crucial in identifying these sauces.[1]

> It is worth the effort to get to know thoroughly the nature of the double sauce. Simple sauce is made from pure olive oil which is worthy of being blended with fragrant pure wine and *muria*, provided the latter comes with a powerful whiff from a Byzantine jar. When this is blended with chopped herbs and has come to the boil and has stood (it is) sprinkled with saffron from Parnassus.
>
> You will add the oil which the prized berry of the Venafran olive produces.

Is Horace being ironic in using *muria* here? Is his gourmet not quite as knowledgeable as he thinks? Another sauce mentioned in Horace *Sat.* 2.8 contains similar ingredients, with *garum* instead of *muria* and unusual spices not found in *Apicius*: Venafran oil, *garum* from the juices of an Iberian fish, foreign wine five years old, white pepper, vinegar from Methymnian grapes, rocket, bitter elecampane. We might define this sauce as an *oxygarum* – with vinegar – rather than a sweet *oenogarum*.

---

[1] Horace, *Sat.* 2.4.63-9.

Evidence elsewhere for blood *garum* and its use is sketchy and ambiguous. Martial mentions *garum* in his *Satires*: at 11.27 a mistress begs for just half a pint of *garum*, giving the impression that she is actually cheap to ask for so little. Martial's Saturnalia gift of oysters proclaims 'I have just arrived, a shellfish drunk on the waters of lake Lucrine at Baiae. Now I thirst for noble *garum*, extravagant as I am'.[1] The implication here is that the diner or the cook (or slave in attendance) simply poured a little garum on to the oysters before they were eaten. It was clearly common for blood *garum* to be used in high-status contexts in the late first century AD. This poses a question: if blood *garum* rather than fish *liquamen* was used in dishes of the very highest status, what does this say about the recipes in *Apicius*?

These élite sauces from satire have some similarities with the sauces in *Apicius*. In *Apicius*, *liquamen* adds a salt taste to food, providing a flavour-enhancing quality similar to that of monosodium glutamate today. It is present in nearly all the recipes but is most prominent in the compound sauce called *oenogarum*. This was originally a Greek sauce and was probably made with a fish sauce rather then a blood *garum* or a composite sauce. A basic *oenogarum* is a mixture of various kinds of wine (sweetened, reduced and plain) mixed with pepper, occasionally other spices and herbs, and *liquamen*. Oil is very common in these sauces, and a number of the examples resemble modern vinaigrette; some were also thickened with starch. They were used as dipping sauces and to accompany meat or fish as a form of gravy.

Sally Grainger's experiments with these *oenogarum* recipes produce extremely pleasing results, despite an understandable reluctance from many tasters. We use an adjusted modern fish sauce when reproducing these recipes. Similar experiments using the sauces from Horace with quantities taken from the Apician recipes also result in particularly pleasing mixtures. It is possible that the sauces from Horace may be entirely imaginary, or that they contain intentionally inaccurate ingredients designed to show the ignorance of the gourmet. Even so they still reflect the way in which Roman gourmets elevated a basic common sauce found in recipe collections such as *Apicius* into an exclusive and luxurious concoction blended, not with ordinary fish sauce, but with the expensive blood *garum*, sometimes blended at table as some of the evidence suggests, and perhaps blended with a different ratio of wine to *garum* than that found in the Apician recipes.[2]

[1] Martial 13.82.

[2] See also Glossary, *oenogarum*.

The theory that these *oenogarum* sauces could be blended at table by the diner, and that *garum* was also a table condiment, is tentative but compelling for us. We have seen that Manilius seems to give different roles to the various sauces he describes. The 'juice for food' is different from the blood sauce that 'balances taste in the mouth'. Ausonius, quoting from an unknown poem, 'fills his *patinae*' with a blood sauce. The particular wording suggests to us that it is the diner pouring an exclusive fish sauce on his cooked *patina*, rather than the cook making the *patina* with *liquamen*. Martial wants *garum* for his oysters, eaten raw as today. Horace makes the obvious suggestion that his foolish gourmet knows all about these sauces and can entertain his guests with their description. The most interesting evidence for me is the recent work being done with wear patterns on Samian ware. Numerous examples of small double-spear bowls have been found all over the empire, but particularly in Gaul and Italy, which have substantial wear patterns on the bottom of the inside surface clearly made by a tool or spoon. Experiments conducted using various tools, and also attempting to duplicate the pattern by long-term cleaning, have resulted in the conclusion that rapid mixing is the only satisfactory explanation for the marks. Samian ware of this nature is definitely intended for the table, and the numbers of dishes and the consistency in patterning is quite marked. As we have seen, many of the these *oenogarum* sauces are similar to vinaigrette in their nature, needing to be mixed in small quantities, and regularly beaten to achieve a constant emulsion. The inconsistencies in the ratio of fish sauce to oil and wine also suggest that there was no definitive recipe for *oenogarum* and that personal taste dictated the quantity of ingredients. The mixing of *oenogarum* might therefore be undertaken in the dining-room either by the slave or, in more informal meals, by the diner himself.[1]

Thus we can be reasonably confident that *liquamen*, as we have defined it here, was very similar in many respects to modern fish sauces, but that there were crucial differences. First, the length of time that the fish was allowed to dissolve and ferment in ancient varieties of fish sauce was no more than three to four months. Modern production in Thailand involves a fermentation period of up to 18 months. Second, it is clear that the ratio of salt to fish at the manufacturing stage was paramount. The Bithynian sauce from the *Geoponica* has a ratio of 8:1 by volume of fish to salt, which corresponds to 7:1 by weight. We are also

[1] E. Buddulph, 'Samian Ware', *Current Archaeology* 196, pp. 191-3.

told that 2 pints of old wine to 1 pint of fish further dilutes the saltiness. The general ratio of fish to salt, by weight, in modern production of fish sauce in Thailand is three parts fish to one part salt, although it is often closer to one part fish to one part salt. Clearly the salt levels must be adjusted to come closer to an ancient sauce. If we simply dilute the sauce with wine after fermentation to correspond to the Bithynian recipe, we also dilute the cheesy/fishy characteristics that we need. To solve this problem when reconstructing ancient recipes, Sally Grainger uses a reduced wine syrup known as *sapa* boiled down to one-third of its original volume. This ensures the qualities of the fish sauce are retained. There is no fishiness or decay to the product and it is far less unpleasant to taste alone than one might expect. The taste of fish sauce may be identified as the fifth flavour, *umami*, alongside sweet, sour, salt and bitter, and it represents the all-round-the-mouth taste which is found in such things as mushrooms. A recipe that explains the use of *liquamen* perfectly is found at 4.2.25: when a *patella* of fish is finished it is tasted; if it is bland, *liquamen* is added; if it is salty, a little honey is added.

5. CONCORDANCE OF RECIPES WITH EARLIER EDITIONS.

CGSG: this edition; *FR*: Flower and Rosenbaum.

CGSG	FR	MILHAM	ANDRÉ
BOOK I			
1.1	I	I	1
1.2	I.2	II	2
1.3	II	III	3
1.4	III.1	IV.1	4
–	III.2	IV.2	5
1.5	IV	V	6
1.6	V	VI	7
1.7	VI	VII	8
1.8	VII	VIII	9
1.9	VII.2	IX	10
1.10	VIII	X	11
1.11	IX.1	XI	12
1.12	IX.2	XII	13
1.13	X	XIII	14
1.14	XI.1	XIV	15
1.15	XI.2	XV	16
1.16	XI.3	XVI	17
1.17	XII.1	XVII	18
1.18	XII.2	XVIII	19
1.19	XII.3	XIX	20
1.20	XII.4	XX	21
1.21	XII.5	XXI	22
1.22	XII.6	XXII	23
1.23	XII.7	XXIII	24
1.24	XII.8	XXIV.1	25

CGSG	FR	MILHAM	ANDRÉ
–	XII.9	XXIV.2	26
1.25	XII.10	XXV	27
1.26	XII.11	XXVI	28
1.27	XIII	XXVII	29
1.28	XIV	XXVIII	30
1.29	XV.1	XXIX	31
–	XV.2	XXIX.1	32
1.30	XVI.1	XXX.1	33
–	XVI.2	XXX.2	34
1.31	XVII.1	XXXI.1	35
–	XVII.2	XXXI.2	36
1.32	XVIII	XXXII	37
1.33	XIX	XXXIII	38
1.34	XX	XXXIV.1	39
–	XX.2	XXXIV.2	40
1.35	XXI	XXXV	41
BOOK II			
2.1.1	I.1	I.1	42
2.1.2	I.2	I.2	43
2.1.3	I.3	I.3	44
2.1.4	I.4	I.4	45
2.1.5	I.5	I.5	46
2.1.6	I.6	I.6	47
2.1.7	I.7	I.7	48
2.2.1	II.1	II.1	49
2.2.2	II.2	II.2	50
2.2.3	II.3	II.3	51
2.2.4	II.4	II.4	52
2.2.5	II.5	II.5	53
2.2.6	II.6	II.6	54
2.2.7	II.7	II.7	55
2.2.8	II.8	II.8	56
2.2.9	II.9	II.9	57
2.2.10	II.10	II.10	58
2.3.1	III.1	III.1	59

CGSG	FR	MILHAM	ANDRÉ
2.3.2	III.2	III.2	60
2.4	IV	IV	61
2.5.1	V.1	V.1	62
2.5.2	V.2	V.2	63
2.5.3	V.3	V.3	64
2.5.4	V.4	V.4	65

BOOK III

CGSG	FR	MILHAM	ANDRÉ
3.1	I	I	66
3.2.1	II.1	II.1	67
–	II.2	II.2	68
3.2.2	II.3	II.3	69
3.2.3	II.4	II.4	70
3.2.4	II.5	II.5	71
3.3	III	III	72
3.4.1	IV.1	IV.1	73
3.4.2	IV.2	IV.2	74
3.4.3	IV.3	IV.3	75
3.4.4	IV.4	IV.4	76
3.4.5	IV.5	IV.5	77
3.4.6	IV.6	IV.6	78
3.4.7	IV.7	IV.7	79
3.4.8	IV.8	IV.8	80
3.5	V	V	81
3.6.1	VI.1	VI.1	82
3.6.2	VI.2	VI.2	83
3.6.3	VI.3	VI.3	84
3.7	VII	VII	85
3.8	VIII	VIII	86
3.9.1	IX.1	IX.1	87
(3.9.1a)	a	–	–
	b		
	c		
3.9.2	IX.2	IX.2	88
3.9.3	IX.3	IX.3	89
3.9.4	IX.4	IX.4	90

CGSG	FR	MILHAM	ANDRÉ
3.9.4	IX.5	IX.5	91
3.9.6	IX.6	IX.6	92
3.10.1	X.1	X.1	93
3.10.2	X.2	X.2	94
3.10.3	X.3	X.3	95
3.10.4	X.4	X.4	96
3.11.1	XI.1	XI.1	97
3.11.2	XI.2	XI.2	98
3.12	XII	XII	99
3.13.1	XIII.1	XIII.1	100
3.13.2	XIII.2	XIII.2	101
3.14	XIV	XIV	102
3.15.1	XV.1	XV.1	103
3.15.2	XV.2	XV.2	104
3.15.3	XV.3	XV.3	105
3.15.4	–	XV.4	106
3.16	XVI	XVI	107
3.17	XVII	XVII	108
3.18.1	XVIII.1a	XVIII.1	109
–	XVIII.1b	XVIII.2	110
3.18.2	XVIII.2	XVIII.3	111
3.19.1	XIX.1	XIX.1	112
3.19.2	XIX.2	XIX.2	113
3.19.3	XIX.3	XIX.3	114
3.20.1	XX.1	XX.1	115
3.20.2	XX.2	XX.2	116
3.20.3	XX.3	XX.3	117
3.20.4	XX.4	XX.4	118
3.20.5	XX.5	XX.5	119
3.20.6	XX.6	XX.6	120
3.20.7	XX.7	XX.7	121
3.21.1	XXI.1	XXI.1	122
3.21.2	XXI.2	XXI.2	123
3.21.3	XXI.3	XXI.3	124

CGSG	FR	MILHAM	ANDRÉ
BOOK IV			
4.1.1.	I.I	I.I	125
4.1.2	I.2	I.2	126
4.1.3	I.3	I.3	127
4.2.1	II.1	II.1	128
4.2.2	II.2	II.2	129
4.2.3	II.3	II.3	130
4.2.4	II.4	II.4	131
4.2.5	II.5	II.5	132
4.2.6	II.6	II.6	133
4.2.7	II.7	II.7	134
4.2.8	II.8	II.8	135
4.2.9	II.9	II.9	136
4.2.10	II.10	II.10	137
4.2.11	II.11	II.11	138
4.2.12	II.12	II.12	139
4.2.13	II.13	II.13	140
4.2.14	II.14	II.14	141
4.2.15	II.15	II.15	142
4.2.16	II.16	II.16	143
4.2.17	II.17	II.17	144
4.2.18	II.18	II.18	145
4.2.19	II.19	II.19	146
4.2.20	II.20	II.20	147
4.2.21	II.21	II.21	148
4.2.22	II.22	II.22	149
4.2.23	II.23	II.23	150
4.2.24	II.24	II.24	151
4.2.25	II.25	II.25	152
4.2.26	II.26	II.26	153
4.2.27	II.27	II.27	154
4.2.28	II.28	II.28	155
4.2.29	II.29	II.29	156
4.2.30	II.30	II.30	157
4.2.31	II.31	II.31	158

CGSG	FR	MILHAM	ANDRÉ
4.2.32	II.32	II.32	159
4.2.33	II.33	II.33	160
4.2.34	II.34	II.34	161
4.2.35	II.35	II.35	162
4.2.36	II.36	II.36	163
4.2.37	II.37	II.37	164
4.3.1	III.1	II.1	165
4.3.2	III.2	III.2	166
4.3.3	III.3	III.3	167
4.3.4	III.4	III.4	168
4.3.5	III.5	III.5	169
4.3.6	III.6	III.6	170
4.3.7a	III.7a	III.7	171
4.3.7b	III.7b	–	–
4.3.8	III.8	III.8	172
4.4.1	IV.1	IV.1	173
4.4.2	IV.2	IV.2	174
4.5.1	V.1	V.1	175
4.5.2	V.2	V.2	176
4.5.3	V.3	V.3	177
4.5.4	V.4	V.4	178
BOOK V			
5.1.1	I.1	I.1	179
5.1.2	I.2	I.2	180
5.1.3	I.3	I.3	181
5.1.4	I.4	I.4	182
5.2.1	II.1	II.1	183
5.2.2	II.2	II.2	184
5.2.3	II.3	II.3	185
5.3.1	III.1	III.1	186
5.3.2	III.2	III.2	187
5.3.3	III.3	III.3	188
5.3.4	III.4	III.4	189
5.3.5	III.5	III.5	190
5.3.6	III.6	III.6	191

CGSG	FR	MILHAM	ANDRÉ
5.3.7	III.7	III.7	192
5.3.8	III.8	III.8	193
5.3.9	III.9	III.9	194
5.4.1	IV.1	IV.1	195
5.4.2	IV.2	IV.2	196
5.4.3	IV.3	IV.3	197
5.4.4	IV.4	IV.4	198
5.4.5	IV.5	IV.5	199
5.4.6	IV.6	IV.6	200
5.5.1	V.1	V.1	201
5.5.2	V.2	V.2	202
5.6.1	VI.1	VI.1	203
5.6.2	VI.2	VI.2	204
5.6.3	VI.3	VI.3	205
5.6.4	VI.4	VI.4	206
5.7	VII	VII	207
5.8.1	VIII.1	VIII.1	208
5.8.2	VIII.2	VIII.2	209
	a		
	b		
	c		

BOOK VI

6.1.1	I.1	I.1	210
6.1.2	I.2	I.2	211
6.2.1	II.1	II.1	212
6.2.2	II.2	II.2	213
6.2.3	II.3	II.3	214
6.2.4	II.4	II.4	215
6.2.5	II.5	II.5	216
6.2.6	II.6	II.6	217
6.2.7	III.1	III.1	218
6.2.8	III.2	III.2	219
6.2.9	III.3	III.3	220
6.2.10	IV.1	IV.1	221
6.2.11	IV.2	IV.2	222

CGSG	FR	MILHAM	ANDRÉ
6.2.12	IV.3	IV.3	223
6.2.13	IV.4	IV.4	224
6.2.14	V.1	V.1	225
6.2.15	V.2	V.2	226
6.2.16	V.3	V.3	227
6.2.17	V.4	V.4	228
6.2.18	V.5	V.5	229
6.2.19	V.6	V.6	230
6.2.20	V.7	V.7	231
6.2.21	VI.1	VI.1	232
6.2.22	VI.2	VI.2	233
6.2.23	VII	VI.3	234
6.7	VIII	VII	235
6.8.1	IX.1a	VIII.1	236
6.8.2	IX.1b	–	237
6.8.3	IX.2	VIII.2	238
6.8.4	IX.3	VIII.3	239
6.8.5	IX.4	VIII.4	240
6.8.6	IX.5	VIII.5	241
6.8.7	IX.6	VIII.6	242
6.8.8	IX.7	VIII.7	243
6.8.9	IX.8	VIII.8	244
6.8.10	IX.9a	VIII.9	245
–	IX.9b	–	–
–	IX.10	VIII.10	246
6.8.11	IX.11	VIII.11	247
6.8.12	IX.12	VIII.12	248
6.8.13	IX.13	VIII.13	249
6.8.14	IX.14	VIII.14	250
6.8.15	IX.15	VIII.15	251
BOOK VII			
7.1.1	I.1	I.1	252
7.1.2	I.2	I.2	253
7.1.3	I.3	I.3	254
7.1.4	I.4	I.4	255

CGSG	FR	MILHAM	ANDRÉ
7.1.5	I.5	I.5	256
7.1.6	I.6	I.6	257
7.2.1	II.1	II.1	258
7.2.2	II.2	II.2	259
7.3.1	III.1	III.1	260
7.3.2	III.2	III.2	261
7.4.1	IV.1	IV.1	262
7.4.2	IV.2	IV.2	263
7.4.3	IV.3	IV.3	264
7.4.4	IV.4	IV.4	265
7.4.5	IV.5	IV.5	266
7.4.6	IV.6	IV.6	267
7.5.1	V.1	V.1	268
7.5.2	V.2	V.2	269
7.5.3	V.3	V.3	270
7.5.4	V.4	V.4	271
7.5.5	V.5	V.5	272
7.6.1	VI.1	VI.1	273
7.6.2	VI.2	VI.2	274
7.6.3	VI.3	VI.3	275
7.6.4	VI.4	VI.4	276
7.6.5	VI.5	VI.5	277
7.6.6	VI.6	VI.6	278
7.6.7	VI.7	VI.7	279
7.6.8	VI.8	VI.8	280
7.6.9	VI.9	VI.9	281
7.6.10	VI.10	VI.10	282
7.6.11	VI.11	VI.11	283
7.6.12	VI.12	VI.12	284
7.6.13	VI.13	VI.13	285
7.6.14	VI.14	VI.14	286
7.7.1	VII.1	VII.1	287
7.7.2	VII.2	VII.2	288
7.8	VIII	VIII	289
7.9.1	IX.1	IX.1	290

CGSG	FR	MILHAM	ANDRÉ
7.9.2	IX.2	IX.2	291
7.9.3	X	IX.3	292
7.9.4	XI	IX.4	293
7.10.1	XII.1	X.1	294
7.10.2	XII.2	X.2	295
7.11.1	XIII.1	XI.1	296
7.11.2	XIII.2	XI.2	297
7.11.3	XIII.3	XI.3	298
7.11.4	XIII.4	XI.4	299
7.11.5	XIII.5	XI.5	300
7.11.6	XIII.6	XI.6	301
7.11.7	XIII.7	XI.7	302
7.11.8	XIII.8	XI.8	303
7.11.9	XIII.9	XI.9	304
7.12.1	XIV.1	XII.1	305
7.12.2	XIV.2	XII.2	306
7.12.3	XIV.3	XII.3	307
–	–	–	308
7.12.4	XIV.4	XII.4	309
7.13.1	XV.1	XIII.1	310
7.13.2	XV.2	XIII.2	311
7.13.3	XV.3	XIII.3	312
7.13.4	XV.4	XIII.4	313
7.13.5	XV.5	XIII.5	314
7.13.6	XV.6	XIII.6	315
7.14.1	XVI.1	XIV.1	316
7.14.2	XVI.2	XIV.2	317
7.14.3	XVI.3	XIV.3	318
7.14.4	XVI.4	XIV.4	319
7.14.5	XVI.5	XIV.5	320
7.14.6	XVI.6	XIV.6	321
7.15	XVII	XV	322
7.16.1	XVIII.1	XVI.1	323
7.16.2	XVIII.2	XVI.2	324
7.16.3	XVIII.3	XVI.3	325

CGSG	FR	MILHAM	ANDRÉ
7.16.4	XVIII.4	XVI.4	326
7.17.1	XIX.1	XVII.1	327
7.17.2	XIX.2	XVII.2	328
7.17.3	XIX.3	XVII.3	329
BOOK VIII			
8.1.1	I.1	I.1	330
8.1.2	I.2	I.2	331
8.1.3	I.3	I.3	332
8.1.4	I.4	I.4	333
8.1.5	I.5	I.5	334
8.1.6	I.6	I.6	335
8.1.7	I.7	I.7	336
8.1.8	I.8	I.8	337
8.1.9	I.9	I.9	338
8.1.10	I.10	I.10	339
8.2.1	II.1	II.1	340
–	II.2	II.2	–
8.2.2	II.3	II.3	341
8.2.3	II.4	II.4	342
8.2.4	II.5	II.5	343
8.2.5	II.6	II.6	344
8.2.6	II.7	II.7	345
8.2.7	II.8	II.8	346
8.3.1	III.1	III.1	347
8.3.2	III.2	III.2	348
8.3.3	III.3	III.3	349
8.4.1	IV.1	IV.1	350
8.4.2	IV.2	IV.2	351
8.4.3	IV.3	IV.3	352
8.5.1	V.1	V.1	353
8.5.2	V.2	V.2	354
8.5.3	V.3	V.3	355
8.5.4	V.4	V.4	356
8.6.1	VI.1	VI.1	357
8.6.2	VI.2	VI.2	358

CGSG	FR	MILHAM	ANDRÉ
8.6.3	VI.3	VI.3	–
8.6.4	VI.4	VI.4	359
8.6.5	VI.5	VI.5	360
8.6.6	VI.6	VI.6	361
8.6.7	VI.7	VI.7	362
8.6.8	VI.8	VI.8	363
8.6.9	VI.9	VI.9	364
8.6.10	VI.10	VI.10	365
8.6.11	VI.11	VI.11	366
8.7.1	VII.1	VII.1	367
8.7.2	VII.2	VII.2	368
8.7.3	VII.3	VII.3	369
8.7.4	VII.4	VII.4	370
8.7.5	VII.5	VII.5	371
8.7.6	VII.6	VII.6	372
8.7.7	VII.7	VII.7	373
8.7.8	VII.8	VII.8	374
8.7.9	VII.9	VII.9	375
8.7.10	VII.10	VII.10	376
8.7.11	VII.11	VII.11	377
8.7.12	VII.12	VII.12	378
8.7.13	VII.13	VII.13	379
8.7.14	VII.14	VII.14	380
8.7.15	VII.15	VII.15	381
8.7.16	VII.16	VII.16	382
8.7.17	VII.17	VII.17	383
8.8.1	VIII.1	VIII.1	384
8.8.2	VIII.2	VIII.2	385
8.8.3	VIII.3	VIII.3	386
8.8.4	VIII.4	VIII.4	387
8.8.5	VIII.5	VIII.5	388
8.8.6	VIII.6	VIII.6	389
8.8.7	VIII.7	VIII.7	390
8.8.8	VIII.8	VIII.8	391
8.8.9	VIII.9	VIII.9	392

CGSG	FR	MILHAM	ANDRÉ
8.8.10	VIII.10	VIII.10	393
8.8.11	VIII.11	VIII.11	394
8.8.12	VIII.12	VIII.12	395
8.8.13	VIII.13	VIII.13	396
8.9	IX	IX	397
BOOK IX			
9.1.1	I.1	I.1	398
9.1.2	I.2	I.2	399
9.1.3	I.3	I.3	400
9.1.4	I.4	I.4	401
9.1.5	I.5	I.5	402
9.1.6	I.6	I.6	403
9.2.1	II.1	II.1	404
9.2.2	II.2	II.2	405
9.3.1	III.1	III.1	406
9.3.2	III.2	III.2	407
9.4.1	IV.1	IV.1	408
9.4.2	IV.2	IV.2	409
9.4.3	IV.3	IV.3	410
9.4.4	IV.4	IV.4	411
9.5	V	V	412
9.6	VI	VI	413
9.7	VII	VII	414
9.8.1	VIII.1	VIII.1	415
9.8.2	VIII.2	VIII.2	416
9.8.3	VIII.3	VIII.3	417
9.8.4	VIII.4	VIII.4	418
9.8.5	VIII.5	VIII.5	419
9.9	IX	IX	420
9.10.1	X.1	X.1	421
9.10.2	X.2	X.2	422
9.10.3	X.3	X.3	423
9.10.4	X.4	X.4	424
9.10.5	X.5	X.5	425
9.10.6	X.6	X.6	426

CGSG	FR	MILHAM	ANDRÉ
9.10.7	X.7	X.7	427
9.10.8	XI	X.8	428
9.10.9	XII	X.9	429
9.10.10	XIII.1	X.10	430
9.10.11	XIII.2	X.11	431
9.10.12	XIII.3	X.12	432
9.11	XIV	XI	433

BOOK X

CGSG	FR	MILHAM	ANDRÉ
10.1.1	I.1	I.1	434
10.1.2	I.2	I.2	435
10.1.3	I.3	I.3	436
10.1.4	I.4	I.4	437
10.1.5	I.5	I.5	438
10.1.6	I.6	I.6	439
10.1.7	I.7	I.7	440
10.1.8	I.8	I.8	441
10.1.9	I.9	I.9	442
10.1.10	I.10	I.10	443
10.1.11	I.11	I.11	444
10.1.12	I.12	I.12	445
10.1.13	I.13	I.13	446
10.1.14	I.14	I.14	447
10.1.15	I.15	I.15	448
10.2.1	II.1	II.1	449
10.2.2	II.2	II.2	450
10.2.3	II.3	II.3	451
10.2.4	II.4	II.4	452
10.2.5	II.5	II.5	453
10.2.6	II.6	II.6	454
10.2.7	III.1	II.7	455
10.2.8	III.2	II.8	456
10.2.9	III.3	II.9	457
10.2.10	III.4	II.10	458
10.2.11	III.5	II.11	459
10.2.12	III.6	II.12	460

CGSG	FR	MILHAM	ANDRÉ
10.2.13	III.7	II.13	461
10.2.14	III.8	II.14	462
10.2.15	III.9	II.15	463
10.2.16	III.10	II.16	464
10.2.17	III.11	II.17	465
10.2.18	III.12	II.18	466

SELECT BIBLIOGRAPHY

Primary Sources

Anthimus, *De obseruatione ciborum: On the Observance of Foods*, ed. M. Grant (Totnes, 1996).

Archestratos of Gela, ed. S. D. Olson, A. Sens (Oxford, 2000).

Athenaeus, ed. and trans. C. B. Gulick, 7 vols. (*Loeb Classical Library*, Cambridge MA and London, 1959-71).

Apicius

    ed. C. Giarratano, F. Vollmer, *Apicii Librorum X qui dicuntur De Re Coquinaria quae extant* (Teubner, Leipzig, 1922).

    ed. A. Marsili, *Apicius: De Re Coquinaria* (Pisa, Colombo Cursi, 1957).

    ed. and trans. B. Flower, E. Rosenbaum, *The Roman Cookery Book: a Critical Translation of The Art of Cooking by Apicius for use in the Study and the Kitchen* (London, 1958).

    ed. J. André, *Apicius, L'art culinaire* (Paris, 1965; revised ed. 1974).

    ed. M. E. Milham, *Apicii Decem Libri...* (Teubner, Leipzig 1969).

Cato, *De Agricultura*, ed. and trans. W. D. Hooper, rev. H. B. Ash (*Loeb Classical Library*, Cambridge MA and London, 1935); trans. with commentary, A. Dalby (Totnes, 1998).

Columella, ed. and trans. H. B. Ash (*Loeb Classical Library*, vol.1: Cambridge MA and London, 1941); ed. and trans. E.S. Forster, E.H. Heffer (*Loeb Classical Library*, vols. 2 and 3: Cambridge MA and London, 1954-5).

Pliny the Elder, *Historia Naturalis,* ed. and trans. H. Rackham (vols. 1-5, 9); W. H. S. Jones (vols. 6-8); D. E. Eichholz (vol. 10) (*Loeb Classical Library*, Cambridge MA and London, 1938-62).

Secondary Sources, Studies and Translations

J. André, *L'Alimentation et la cuisine à Rome* (Paris, 1961; revised ed. 1981).

M. Bode, *Apicius: Anmerkungen zum römischen Kochbuch* (St. Katharinen, 1999).

E. Brandt, *Untersuchungen zum Römischen Kochbuche. Versuch einer Lösung der Apicius-Frage. Philologus*, Supplementband XIX, Heft III (Leipzig, 1927).

P. P. Bober, *Art, Culture and Cuisine: Ancient and Medieval Gastronomy* (Chicago and London, 1999).

A. Dalby, *Siren Feasts: A History of Food and Gastronomy in Greece* (London and New York, 1996).

——, *Empire of Pleasures: Luxury and indulgence in the Roman World* (London and New York, 2000).

——, *Food in the Ancient World from A to Z* (London and New York, 2003).

——, and S. Grainger *The Classical Cookbook* (London and Los Angeles, 1996; revised paperback ed. 2005).

A. Davidson, *Mediterranean Seafood* (2nd ed., London and Harmondsworth, 1981).

J. Davidson, *Courtesans and Fishcakes: the Consuming Passions of Classical Athens* (London, 1997).

A. A. Del Re, *Marco Gavio Apicio De Re Coquinaria: Libro X, il libro del pesce* (Milan, 1998).

A. Dosi, F. Schnell, *Pasti e vasellame da tavola* (*Vita e costumi dei Romani antichi,* 2: 2nd ed., Rome, 1992).

——, *I Romani in cucina* (*Vita e costumi dei Romani antichi,* 3: 2nd ed., Rome, 1992).

J. Edwards, *The Roman Cookery of Apicius, Translated and Adapted for the Modern Kitchen* (New York, 1984).

P. Faas, *Around the Roman Table* (English ed., Basingstoke and Oxford, 2003).

I. G. Giacosa, *A Taste of Ancient Rome* (trans. A. Herklotz, Chicago and London, 1992).

E. Gowers, *The Loaded Table: Representations of Food in Roman Literature* (Oxford, 1993).

M. Grant, *Dieting for an Emperor: a Translation of Books 1 and 4 of Oribasius'* Medical Compilations *with an Introduction and Commentary* (Leiden, New York, Köln, 1997).

——, *Roman Cookery: Ancient Recipes for Modern Kitchens* (London, 1999).

——, *Galen in Food and Diet* (London and New York, 2000).

M. Grieve, *A Modern Herbal* (ed. and intro. C.F. Leyel, revised ed. London, 1973).

M. E. Milham, 'Toward a Stemma and Fortuna of Apicius', *Italia Medioevale e Umanistica* X (1967), 259-320.

J. Miller, *The Spice Trade of the Roman Empire* (Oxford, 1969).

E. Salza Prina Ricotti, *L'Arte del Convito Nella Roma Antica* (Rome, 1983).

C. Roden, *A New Book of Middle Eastern Food* (revised ed., London, 1985).

J. Svennung, *Untersuchungen zu Palladius und zur lateinischen Fach- und Volkssprache* (Uppsala, 1935).

——, 'De locis nonnullis Apicianis', *Eranos* XXXIV (1936), pp. 14-24.

R. Tannahill, *Food in History* (Harmondsworth, 2nd ed. 1988).

F. Vollmer *Studien zu dem römischen Kochbuche von Apicius*, "Sb. Bayer. A. W.", Abhandlungen 6, (Munich, 1920).

J. Wilkins, *The Boastful Chef: the discourse of food in ancient Greek comedy* (Oxford, 2000).

J. Wilkins, D. Harvey, M. Dobson (eds.), *Food In Antiquity* (Exeter, 1995).

J. D. Vehling, *Apicius: Cookery and Dining in Imperial Rome* (Chicago, 1936; repr. New York, 1977).

INDEX

This is an index to the introduction and appendices, not to the Latin or English texts or their editorial matter.